CASING CRISIS AND RISK COMMUNICATION

Corey J. Liberman
Marymount Manhattan College

Dariela Rodriguez
Ashland University

Theodore A. Avtgis
Medical Communication Specialists

Kendall Hunt
p u b l i s h i n g   c o m p a n y

Cover image © Shutterstock.com

Kendall Hunt
p u b l i s h i n g   c o m p a n y

www.kendallhunt.com
Send all inquiries to:
4050 Westmark Drive
Dubuque, IA 52004-1840

DEDICATION

Corey – To my wife, Sara, and my children, Hailey and Bradley

Dariela – To my partner, Kim, and my family

Theodore – To my son, Aiden, and my partner, Kim

CONTENTS

INTRODUCTION

Unfortunately, both crisis and risk are part and parcel of human behavior. Every time that we tune in to the day's news, we are presented with events that are characteristic of these two terms. We hear about natural disasters. We hear about political scandals. We hear about felonious crimes that took place in geographic regions that we frequent. We hear about global bombings. We hear about organizations who file for bankruptcy. We hear about racial unrest. We hear about terrorist attacks. We hear about product recalls. We hear about oil spills. We hear about individual threats made in cyberspace. We hear about illness outbreaks. This list could go on for quite a while. *Fortunately*, however, we have a well-established body of research that deals with effective crisis and risk communication that explains and describes the process(es) by/through which messages, at different stages of the crisis and risk lifecycles, reach salient stakeholders, enabling them to engage in the behavior(s) deemed appropriate. How do we know that this body of research is well-established? There are many pieces of empirical evidence.

Most importantly, however, is a mere review of the published literature over the past 20 years, which illustrates that this area of communication study is alive and, more importantly, growing and thriving. When the three editors of this text first proposed this project and were seeking contributors, we first reached out to the top publishers of communication textbooks. We realized that well over 25 texts had been published, between the years of 2009 and 2014, including two handbooks. In addition, several academic, peer-reviewed journals have been devoted specifically to the study of crisis and risk communication, including the following: *Journal of Contingencies and Crisis Management, International Journal of Disaster Risk Reduction, Corporate Reputation Review, Risk Analysis, Disaster Prevention and Management, and International Journal of Emergency Management*.

An equally important question that emerges is the extent to which crisis and risk communication seems to matter. In other words, are these areas important enough to educate and train others to become crisis and risk assessors, communicators, and/or managers? There are two markers that these two areas are extremely important. First, universities and colleges have begun to adopt programs devoted, specifically, to the formal study of crisis and risk communication. For example, the graduate program at the University of Kentucky (at which one of this volume's contributors is a faculty member) has a specialization in risk and crisis communication. The graduate program at Ashland University (at which one of this volume's co-editors is department co-chair) offers a degree in health and risk communication. The graduate program at Michigan State University offers a degree in health and risk communication. Chapman University has a graduate program in health risk and crisis communication. This is but a list of a few examples, but such programs now permeate the higher education landscape. Second, in the professional world, job titles such as crisis responder, risk manager, risk assessor, crisis manager, risk counselor, reputation manager, risk strategist, and crisis adviser abound. It is unlikely to find an organization, in today's world, without an individual adopting one of the aforementioned roles.

This is all to say that crisis and risk communication are both well-studied and important to the social fabric of society. Without understanding how to effectively respond to, and potentially avoid, crisis and risk, individuals would find themselves in a state of [potential] eternal entropy. However, because of the abundance of theories, models, and data that have accumulated over the past several decades, the human race is better equipped to deal with the uncertainties and challenges and difficulties and obstacles that accompany a crisis and/or an impending risk.

So…what exactly is crisis and risk communication? There could very well be a book that explores just this question, as it becomes obvious, after reading the literature, that there is little consensus regarding what these terms come to mean and signify. There is more consensus, however, that these terms are semantically different and, as such, need to be parsed out. After having read each of the chapters that follow, and determining what they all had in common, we have decided to adopt the definition of crisis offered by Ulmer, Sellnow, and Seeger (2011), which is "…a specific, unexpected, and nonroutine event or series of events that create high levels of uncertainty and simultaneously present an organization with both opportunities for and threats to its high-priority goals" (p. 7). As you will notice after having read all of the case studies (which deal with crisis communication) to follow, each highlights an organization faced with a particular crisis situation to which it needed to communicatively respond. Since it was unexpected and nonroutine, those affected had high levels of uncertainty and those creating the messages, too, were inundated with certain levels of ambiguity.

Risk, as Fischhoff (2012) cogently makes clear, is an even more difficult term to define, as it differs not only in meaning, but also in magnitude, frequency, and probability. That said, however, we found it fruitful to adopt the definition of risk provided by Morgan, Fishhoff, Bostrom, and Atman (2011), which is "… communication intended to supply laypeople with the information they need to make informed, independent judgments about risks to health, safety, and the environment" (p. 4). The forthcoming chapters that deal with risk communication all argue that the keys to effective message design are (a) providing information to affected, or potentially affected, individuals regarding appropriate actions, (b) providing answers to questions regarding possible risk outcomes, and (c) providing messages in easily-decodable forms.

It should become clear, based on these definitions, that these two words are very closely-related, and it is no wonder that they are so oftentimes discussed in unison. Perhaps Walaski (2011) said it best when she claimed that "…risk communications is most often the process and the messages that occur prior to the occurrence of a hazard…[whereas] crisis communications is the process and messages that are delivered at times of high stress, either because the hazard is already occurring or is imminent" (p. 2). Needless to say, in today's organizational world, both are equally important.

This text provides a series of case studies, all of which deal with the areas of crisis and risk communication, in an effort to cogently bridge the theoretical with the practical. Each chapter focuses on a specific event (or series of events) that transpired, producing some form of ambiguity in the minds of key stakeholders, and describes how communication became the independent variable responsible for sensemaking. All 21 case studies will remind you that although many of the crises and risks that we, as a society, face are unavoidable, they are, by way of effective communication, manageable. It is our hope that, as a result of this text, you will have a deeper understanding of, appreciation for, interest in, and dedication to, two extremely important areas within the field of communication study.

Fischhoff, B. (2012). *Risk analysis and human behavior*. New York, NY: Earthscan.

Morgan, M. G., Fischhoff, B., Bostrom, A., & Atman, C. J. (2011). *Risk communication: A mental models approach*. New York, NY: Cambridge University Press.

Ulmer, R. R., Sellnow, T. L., & Seeger, M. W. (2011). *Effective crisis communication: Moving from crisis to opportunity (2nd Ed)*. Los Angeles, CA: Sage.

Walaski, P. (2011). *Risk and crisis communications: Methods and messages*. Hoboken, NJ: Wiley.

ABOUT THE AUTHORS

Alan Zaremba (Ph.D., University of Buffalo) is the Associate Dean for Undergraduate Programs in the College of Arts, Media and Design at Northeastern University. He is the author of six books, including Organizational *Communication (3rd edition), Speaking Professionally (2nd edition)*, and *Crisis Communication: Theories and Practice.* Dr. Zaremba's 2009 ethnography on sports fandom, *The Madness of March: Bonding and Betting with the Boys in Las Vegas* has been called "an essential read for anyone who wants to get a better window on one of the more interesting gambling and sports subcultures." In 2009 Dr. Zaremba was the Keynote speaker at the Eighth International Conference on Knowledge, Culture, and Change in Organisations held in Cambridge, UK. He has received Northeastern University's Excellence in Teaching Award on two occasions and is also a recipient of the State University of New York Chancellor's Award for Excellence in Teaching. When he was more spry he played basketball for the freshman team at the University at Albany where he earned his BA.

Christopher Caldiero (Ph.D., Rutgers University) is an Associate Professor of Communication Studies at Fairleigh Dickinson University (FDU) in Madison, NJ. His research interests include crisis communication, organizational communication, and rhetorical analysis. His work has appeared in the *Journal of Public Relations Research, American Journal of Communication,* and *Public Relations Review.* Dr. Caldiero has won four "Top Paper" awards from the National Communication Association. He has also recently published book chapters in the *Handbook of Crisis Communication* and *Putting Image Repair to the Test: Quantitative Applications of Image Restoration Theory.* In December 2015, Dr. Caldiero published his first book, *Neo-PR: Public Relations in a Postmodern World* (Peter Lang Press). Dr. Caldiero teaches many of the public relations courses at FDU, including Principles of Public Relations, Public Relations Writing, Public Relations Campaigns, as well as the graduate-level classes Crisis Communication and Stakeholder Relations. He lives in Clifton, NJ.

Cliff Scherer (Ph.D., University of Wisconsin – Madison) is a Professor Emeritus in the Department of Communication at Cornell University. His research focuses on risk, science, environmental, and visual communication in the context of coastal issues most recently including red tide risks and storm surge.

Corey Jay Liberman (Ph.D., Rutgers University) is an Associate Professor in the Department of Communication and Media Arts at Marymount Manhattan College. His research spans the interpersonal communication, group communication, and organizational communication worlds, and he is currently interested in studying the social practices of dissent within organizations, specifically the antecedents, processes, and effects associated with effective employee dissent communication. He is currently working on a book dealing with risk and crisis communication, as well as a case study book focusing on communication theory.

Dariela Rodriguez (Ph.D., University of Oklahoma) is an Associate Professor in the Department of Communication Studies at Ashland University. She has worked with some of the top scholars on interpersonal deception and communication in palliative care. This work has garnered several publications in top peer-reviewed journals and numerous conference papers. Dr. Rodriguez's latest project is a book entitled *Sport Communication: An Interpersonal Perspective,* published by Kendall Hunt Publishing Company. Dr. Rodriguez serves as the coordinator for the sport communication program. She received her doctorate from The University of Oklahoma in 2012 and holds a certificate from the Harvard School of Public Health focusing on case studies and risk and crisis communication.

David Sturges (Ph.D., University of North Texas) is on faculty at the University of Texas Rio Grande Valley (UTRGV) and teaches strategy, organizational behavior, and communication at the graduate and undergraduate levels. He has been teaching for 28 years at the University of Oklahoma, the University of Texas at Dallas, the University of North Texas, and UTRGV. He is published in the *Journal of Management Communication,* the *Journal of International Business Studies, The SAM Advanced Management Journal,* and others. He has specialized in online teaching and has two graduate courses certified by Quality Matters. In addition, he uses Second Life as a virtual class delivery tool for flexplace courses.

Don W. Stacks (Ph.D., University of Florida) is a Professor of Public Relations and Corporate Communication in the School of Communication at the University of Miami. His background is based primarily in corporate/governmental public relations and consulting. He has authored and edited numerous books, book chapters, and articles. His most recent works are in the area of public relations measurement and evaluation and include the *Primer of Public Relations Research* (Guilford Press, now in its third edition) and the *Dictionary of Public Relations Measurement and Research,* which has been translated into several languages. Dr. Stacks is the CEO and executive director of the International Public Relations Research Conference (IPRRC). He also serves on a number of academic and professional review boards, including the Arthur W. Page Society and the Institute for Public Relations.

Gina Eosco (Ph.D., Cornell University) is a Senior Social Scientist and Risk Communication Expert at Eastern Research Group, Inc. Her work focuses on applying risk communication research to the weather, water, and climate community of practice including working with organizations such as the National Weather Service and Environmental Protection Agency.

Heather M. Stassen (Ph.D., Ohio University) is Associate Professor and Program Director of Communication Studies at Cazenovia College in Central New York. Dr. Stassen is a generalist with research, teaching, and consulting experiences in rhetoric, interpersonal communication, and organizational communication.

Henry S. Seeger (B.A., Bowling Green State University) is a graduate student at Illinois State University pursuing a Master's degree in Communication. His primary research interests concern crisis and risk communication, and he is particularly interested in the role of public communication in predicting, responding to, and managing public health crises. Much of his work has focused on issues of food and water safety. Primarily, he has examined the rhetorical construction of post-crisis public communication. In 2014, he was the recipient of the Del Hilyard Book Award from the School of Media and Communication at Bowling Green State University. He has presented his work at the annual conventions of both the National Communication Association and the Central States Communication Association, as well as at the International Crisis and Risk Communication Conference in 2016. Currently, he is working on investigating public communication campaigns aiming to mitigate or reduce risks of water contamination.

Jason S. Wrench (Ed.D., West Virginia University) is an Associate Professor and CHAIR of the Department of Communication at the State University of New York at New Paltz. Dr. Wrench has published ten books: *Stand Up, Speak Out: The Practice and Ethics of Public Speaking* (2nd ed., 2017, Flat World Knowledge), *Quantitative Research Methods for Communication: A Hands-On Approach* (3rd ed., 2016, Oxford University Press), *Organizational Communication: Theory, Research, and Practice* (2015, Flat World Knowledge), *Training & Development: The Intersection of Communication & Talent Development in the Modern Workplace* (2015, Kendall Hunt), *Communication Apprehension, Avoidance, and Effectiveness* (2013, Allyn & Bacon), *The Directory of*

Communication Related Mental Measures (Summer 2010, National Communication Association), *Human Communication in Everyday Life: Explanations and Applications* (2008, Allyn & Bacon), *Principles of Public Speaking* (2003, The College Network), *Intercultural Communication: Power in Context* (2000, Tapestry Press), and *Communication, Affect, and Learning in the Classroom* (2000, Tapestry Press). Dr. Wrench is also the editor of five collections on the subject of organizational communication: *Casing Sport Communication* (2015, Kendall Hunt), *Casing Public Relations*, (2014, Kendall Hunt) *Casing Organizational Communication* (2011, Kendall Hunt), *Workplace Communication for the 21st Century: Tools and Strategies that Impact the Bottom Line: Vol. 1. Internal Workplace Communication*, and *Vol. 2. External Workplace Communication* (2013, both with Praeger). Furthermore, Dr. Wrench has published over 40 articles and book chapters.

Julie L. Taylor (Ph.D., University of Utah) is an Assistant Professor in the Department of Communication Studies at California State University, San Bernardino. Broadly, her research interests are in organizational communication, gender studies, and interdisciplinary studies. Current research questions investigate the organizing of the sex industry. More specifically, asking questions that concern the role of gender in policy construction and implementation, and the consequence of silence as an organizing element of discourse. She has published articles in *Communication Education, Connexions: International Professional Communication Journal, Journal of Business and Technical Communication,* and the *Western Journal of Communication.*

Kathleen Donohue Rennie (Ph.D., Seton Hall University) is an Associate Professor at New Jersey City University, where she teaches integrated marketing communications, crisis communication, executive leadership communication, and media relations in the National Security Studies Department and the University's Business School. She serves as Director of New Jersey City University's doctoral program in Civil Security Leadership, Management and Policy. She also has 20+ years of professional experience through her public relations consulting firm. Kathy holds a Ph.D. in Leadership, Management and Policy and wrote her dissertation on crisis communication.

Kenneth Lachlan (Ph.D., Michigan State University) is an Professor in the Department of Communication at the University of Connecticut, and the Editor-in-Chief of *Communication Studies.* Prior to his arrival at UConn he was the founding chairperson of the Communication Department at the University of Massachusetts – Boston. His current research interests include risk information processing in new media environments, social robotics, and big data applications in emergency response and management.

Kimberly Cowden (Ph.D., North Dakota State University) is currently an Assistant Professor in the Department of Mass Communication and Center for New Media at Colorado State University – Pueblo. She earned her BS in journalism from Minnesota State University Moorhead. She earned her graduate degrees from North Dakota State University. Cowden's research interests include: public relations, crisis communication, health communication, and ethic research collection among American Indian communities. In addition to her scholarship, Cowden has over 20 years of industry experience and operated her own advertising and public relations firm for 15 years. In September of 2015, Cowden was honored with 2015 Scholar of the Year from the Communication, Speech and Theater Association of North Dakota. In February of 2015, she was honored with the Outstanding Faculty Advisor Award from the University of North Dakota. Her research has been featured in the *Journal of Business Communication, Communication, Culture & Critique,* and the *Journal of Indigenous Research.*

Laura Rickard (Ph.D., Cornell University) is an Assistant Professor in the Department of Communication and Journalism at the University of Maine. Her research focuses on the intersection of risk, science, health, and environmental communication in the context of natural resource issues, ranging from climate change impacts to national park safety.

Lisa Chewning (Ph.D., Rutgers University) is an Associate Professor of Corporate Communication at Penn State University – Abington. Her research interests include social networks, crisis communication, public relations, and information and communication technology (ICT). Her research has been published in outlets such as *Management Communication Quarterly, Communication Monographs, Public Relations Review, Journal of Communication, Computers in Human Behavior*, and *Human Communication Research*.

Matthew W. Seeger, (Ph.D., Indiana University) has been a faculty member and administrator at Wayne State University for 34 years. He is currently Dean of the College of Fine, Performing and Communication Arts. Dean Seeger's research concerns crisis and risk communication, health promotion and communication, crisis response and agency coordination, the role of media, including new media, crisis and communication ethics, failure of complex systems, and post-crisis renewal. He has worked with the United States Centers for Disease Control and Prevention for more than a decade. He has worked with the National Center for Food Protection and Defense and with the Food and Drug Administration on issues of food safety and recalls. Seeger also is a member of the World Health Organization Guidelines Development Group for Emergency Risk Communication. He has consulted with several Fortune 500 firms on crisis management planning and response. His work has been supported by the CDC, NCFPD, NSF, NIH, and the State of Michigan with over $5 million in extramural funding. He is currently involved in a multi-year, interdisciplinary project focusing on contamination of the Flint, Michigan water system. His work on crisis, risk, and communication has appeared in more than 100 peer-reviewed articles and book chapters, including the *Handbook of Crisis and Risk Communication, International Encyclopedia of Communication, Journal of Health Communication Research, Health Promotion Practice, Communication Monographs, International Journal of Crisis and Contingency Management, Communication Yearbook, Handbook of Public Relations, Handbook of Applied Communication Research, Communication Monographs, Public Relations Review, Communication Studies, Southern Communication Journal, Journal of Business Ethics, Journal of Business Communication, Management Communication Quarterly, Journal of Applied Communication Research*, and the *Journal of Organizational Change Management*, among several others. Seeger is the author or co-author of eight books, most focusing on crisis and risk communication, including *Communication and Organizational Crisis* (2003), *Crisis Communication and the Public Health* (2008), *Effective Crisis Communication* (2007), *Effective Risk Communication* (2009), *Theorizing Crisis Communication* (2014), *Crisis and Emergency Risk Communication* (Second Edition, 2015), *Narratives of Crisis: Stories of Ruin and Renewal* (2016) and the *International Handbook of Crisis Communication* (2016). He is currently completing *Best Practices in Crisis and Emergency Risk Communication*. He has advised over 40 doctoral dissertations.

Maureen Taylor (Ph.D., Purdue University) is the Director of the School of Advertising and Public Relations at the University of Tennessee. Taylor's public relations research has focused on nation building and civil society, dialogue, and the use of websites and new technologies. In 2010, Taylor was honored with the Pathfinder Award, presented by the Institute for Public Relations in recognition of her "original program of scholarly research that has made a significant contribution to the body of knowledge and practice of public relations." Taylor is a member of the Arthur S. Page Society and serves as an Associate Editor of the *Public Relations Review*.

Michael L. Kent (Ph.D., Purdue University) is a Professor of Public Relations in the School of Advertising and Public Relations, College of Communication and Information, at the University of Tennessee Knoxville. Kent conducts research on new technology, mediated communication, dialogue, international communication, and web communication. Kent has published more than 90 articles, books, book chapters, and other publications, and published in national and international communication and public relations journals, including *Communication Studies, Critical Studies in Media Communications, Journal of Public Relations Research, Gazette, International Journal of Communication, Management Communication Quarterly, Public Relations Quarterly, Public Relations Review,* and others. Kent attended The University of Alaska Fairbanks for his Bachelor's degree, The University of Oregon for his Master's degree, and Purdue University for his Doctoral degree.

Michael J. Liles (Ph.D., Texas A&M University) is a Postdoctoral Researcher at the University of Texas at El Paso and has over a decade's worth of experience working in Central America with local resource users on grassroots biodiversity conservation initiatives, focusing primarily on better understanding the connection between hawksbill turtles and local human communities with whom they share habitat in El Salvador and Nicaragua. After two years in the U.S. Peace Corps collaborating with local farmers to reduce environmental impacts in protected areas of Honduras, Mike moved to El Salvador where he co-founded the Eastern Pacific Hawksbill Initiative (ICAPO). Mike earned a Ph.D. in Wildlife and Fisheries Sciences from Texas A&M University and is a member of the IUCN/SSC Marine Turtle Specialist Group.

Michelle M. Maresh-Fuehrer (Ph.D., University of Nebraska – Lincoln) is Associate Professor of Communication at Texas A&M University-Corpus Christi. She is an award-winning professor who regularly teaches undergraduate and graduate courses in crisis communication, public relations, and research methods. She has co-authored a public relations textbook, titled *Public Relations Principles: Strategies for Professional Success,* and has authored a book on crisis communication, titled *Creating Organizational Crisis Plans.* Her research has appeared in *The Handbook of Crisis Communication, Persuasion in Your Life, Computers in Human Behavior, Communication Teacher,* and numerous other textbooks and journals. She is a member of the i-CERT campus emergency response team on her campus and regularly consults for organizations across a variety of industries. In addition to her teaching and research, Dr. Maresh-Fuehrer enjoys spending time with her family and serving as the Public Image Chair for Rotary International District 5930.

Morgan C. Getchell (Ph.D., University of Kentucky) is an Assistant Professor of Strategic Communication and Convergent Media at Morehead State University in Morehead, Kentucky. Dr. Getchell recently completed her Ph.D. at the University of Kentucky where she focused her scholarship on the areas of risk and crisis communication. Her dissertation, which examined emergent organizations in the 2014 West Virginia water contamination crisis, was funded by a grant from the National Center for Food Protection and Defense, a Department of Homeland Security center of excellence. She has also worked on funded projects through the Centers for Disease Control and Prevention and the United States Department of Agriculture. Her research is published in several refereed journals and has been presented at regional and national conferences.

Nicole Magee (M.A., University of Southern Mississippi) received her Bachelor's and Master's degrees in Communication Studies from the University of Southern Mississippi. Throughout her graduate coursework, her studies primarily revolved around the rhetoric of nonprofit organizations and social movements. She completed her Master's thesis in the spring of 2015, which added to the body of existing literature regarding affect studies and Burke's idea of identification. She was also particularly interested in crisis communication, prompting her to explore companies' public relations responses in times of disaster. With the aid of Dr. Steven Venette, she completed this study on the Carnival Corporation's dilemmas at sea and how such crises affected the organization's relations with the public thereafter. Upon graduation, Ms. Magee chose to pursue a career in higher education. She now works at the University of Southern Mississippi in academic affairs, where she serves as an advisor in the College of Nursing and public speaking instructor.

Robert L. Heath (Ph.D., University of Illinois) is Professor Emeritus at the University of Houston where he conducted research on the petrochemical industry for 20 years and where he created and taught risk communication classes. Heath is author of many articles, chapters, encyclopedias, handbooks, and books on risk communication, crisis communication, public relations, issues management, and strategic communication.

Steven Venette (Ph.D., North Dakota State University) is an Associate Professor in the Department of Communication Studies at the University of Southern Mississippi. He led translational research efforts for the National Center of Food Protection and Defense's risk and crisis communication team. He has completed risk and crisis communication consulting projects for the USDA, DHS, CDC, the National Center for Foreign Animal and Zoonotic Diseases and many other public and private organizations. Much of his study focuses on agriculture generally, and the food system specifically. Topic areas of his research include risk communication, crisis communication, education, persuasion, public relations, organizational communication, terrorism, and argumentation.

Tarla Rai Peterson (Ph.D., Washington State University) is a Professor of Communication at the University of Texas at El Paso and has supervised Ph.D. students conducting research on sustainability in Africa, Asia, Europe, and the Americas. Her research program focuses on how intersections between communication practice, democratic theory, and environmental policy enable/constrain policy options and public life. Her research included topics such as energy system change, land-use planning, and wildlife conservation. Her professional goal is to conduct research that facilitates the emergence and implementation of more sustainable energy and environmental policy, while critiquing the normativity associated with sustainability. She values classroom teaching, and serves as a faculty mentor for graduate teaching assistants. She and her students have developed an active Theory to Practice Program that includes design and evaluation of best practices for facilitating public participation in issues related to energy and environmental policy.

Theodore A. Avtgis (Ph.D., 1999, Kent State University) is Professor of Communication Studies and co-founder of Medical Communication Specialists. He is also an adjunct Associate Professor in the Department of Surgery at West Virginia University. Dr. Avtgis has authored over 60 peer-reviewed articles and book chapters on organizational communication and communication personality, and their impact on healthcare and safety. His work has appeared in journals such as the *Journal of Trauma*, the *Journal of Surgical Education, Communication Education, Management Communication Quarterly*, among others. He is co-author of 10 books and has served as Editor-In-Chief of *Communication Research Reports*. Among several awards, he was recognized as one of the top 12 most productive scholars in the field of Communication Studies (between 1996–2001), recognized as a member of the World Council on Hellenes Abroad, USA Region of American Academics, and, in 2009, was named a Centennial Scholar of Communication by the Eastern Communication Association. He is also the 2011 recipient of the ECA Past President's Award.

W. Timothy Coombs (Ph.D., Purdue University) is a Professor of Communication in Department of Communication at Texas A&M University. He is also an honorary professor in the Department of Business Communication at Aarhus University. Dr. Coombs researches in the area of crisis communication and his works appear in *Management Communication Quarterly, Corporate Communication: An International Journal, Public Relations Review, Business Horizons*, and the *Journal of Communication Management*. He has authored two books on crisis communication, *Ongoing Crisis Communication* and *Code Red in the Boardroom* as well as being co-editor of the Handbook of Crisis Communication and numerous book chapters on the topic. He has received the 2002 recipient of Jackson, Jackson & Wagner Behavioral Science Prize from the Public Relations Society of America and the 2013 Pathfinder Award from the Institute of Public Relations in recognition of his research contributions to the field and to the practice. Dr. Coombs has worked with governments, corporations, and consulting firms in the U.S., Asia, and Europe on ways to improve crisis communication efforts for themselves and their clients. He is also the current editor for *Corporation Communication: An International Journal*.

Timothy L. Sellnow (Ph.D., Wayne State University) is a Professor of Strategic Communication in the Nicholson School of Communication at the University of Central Florida. Dr. Sellnow's research focuses on bioterrorism, pre-crisis planning, and strategic communication for risk management and mitigation in organizational and health settings. He has conducted funded research for the Department of Homeland Security, the United States Department of Agriculture, the Centers for Disease Control and Prevention, the Environmental Protection Agency, and the United States Geological Survey. He has also served in an advisory role for the National Academy of Sciences and the World Health Organization. He has published numerous refereed journal articles on risk and crisis communication and has co-authored five books on risk and crisis communication. Dr. Sellnow's most recent book is entitled, *Theorizing Crisis Communication*. Dr. Sellnow is a recipient of the National Communication Association's Gerald M. Phillips award for Distinguished Applied Communication Research.

Tom Phelan (Ed.D., Syracuse University) earned a doctoral degree from Syracuse University, a University Certificate of Specialist and Master's degree from SUNY Albany, and a graduate certificate from Harvard. He has taught communication courses in colleges, businesses, and humanitarian organizations, specializing in risk and crisis communication, emergency preparedness, public information, and outreach. He authored *Emergency Management and Tactical Response Operations: Bridging the Gap* (2008, Elsevier) in addition to several articles and blog posts related to disasters, public/private partnerships, and higher education. Tom has decades of experience as a teacher and school administrator. He has held positions as a full professor, department chair, consultant, and corporate department manager. His current research is analyzing the gap between literacy levels of critical emergency management messages and the literacy levels of their intended audiences. From 2015 to 2017 he has served as associate faculty at Hamilton College, Royal Roads University, and the Emergency Management Institute/DHS/FEMA.

William L. Benoit (Ph.D., Wayne State University) is a Professor of Communication Studies at the University of Alabama at Birmingham. He has published over 15 books, including a second edition of *Accounts, Excuses, and Apologies*. His most recent book, written with Mark Glantz, examines persuasive attacks on Donald Trump in the 2016 Republican presidential primaries. He has also published over 250 journal articles and book chapters, including numerous case studies of image repair discourse. He enjoys creating art, having been inspired by Piet Mondrian. He had fun swimming with sting rays off of the Grand Cayman Island.

Yi Grace Ji (Ph.D., University of Miami) is an Assistant Professor of Public Relations in the Richard T. Robertson School of Media and Culture at Virginia Commonwealth University. Her research interests center on social-mediated public relations, including stakeholder online engagement, big data application in public relations research, stakeholder decision-making, and relationship management.

Ying Xiong (M.A., University of Oklahoma) joined the University of Tennessee, Knoxville in 2016 as a Ph.D. student in public relations. She received her Master of Arts degree in strategic communication from the University of Oklahoma in the United States and her Master of Arts degree in advertising and public relations from the Huazhong University of Science and Technology in China. She worked as a research assistant in a media psychology research laboratory in the Center for Applied Research at the University of Oklahoma. She also worked for Toyota's public relations campaigns in China. Xiong has presented original research papers at national and international academic conferences. Her research interests are mainly focused on crisis communication, dialogic communication, and cognitive and emotional processing of health communication.

Zifei Fay Chen (Ph.D., University of Miami) is an Assistant Professor of Public Relations and Strategic Communication in the Communication Studies Department at University of San Francisco. Her research interests involve corporate communication, social media, corporate social responsibility, consumer psychology, crisis communication, and relationship management. Chen has previously worked at Ketchum in New York City and at Fiserv in Atlanta, Georgia.

Zongchao "Cathy" Li (Ph.D., University of Miami) is an Assistant Professor of Public Relations in the School of Journalism and Mass Communications at San Jose State University. Her research centers on social media and corporate communication. She investigates how new media have changed the interactions between organizations and users, between technologies and users, and among network users themselves. She is particularly interested in studying the relationships between psychological variables and consumer behavioral outcomes, such as power, online activism, and revenge behaviors.

Chapter 1

Chaos, Informational Voids, and Emergent Organizations: The Case of West Virginia's Water and Freedom Industries

Morgan C. Getchell, Ph.D.
Morehead State University

Timothy L. Sellnow, Ph.D.
University of Central Florida

Introduction

Crises are, by their nature, shocking, disruptive, and often dangerous events. Three characteristics—threat, surprise, and short response time—are indicative of crisis events (Hermann, 1963). Those who are threatened by crises feel a sudden danger that they did not anticipate and they must respond quickly or the danger will escalate. These feelings are most intense when crises pose an immediate health risk. Specifically, if people do not receive adequate warning, they are likely to ingest contaminated food or water, breathe toxic air, or remain in a dangerous location. For example, toxic gas releases create the immediate need for crisis messages, advising nearby residents to evacuate or shelter in place. Chemical spills impacting water supplies create the immediate need for crisis communication messages about avoiding or boiling the drinking water in the area. When food products are contaminated, residents must receive information about how to determine if they have ingested these products or if they have these products in their homes.

Many organizations dealing with toxic chemicals or gases have elaborate warning structures in place, designed to communicate warnings and risk messages to employees and residents in the surrounding area. If, however, these organizations fail to provide adequate warnings and risk messages, the alarm and frustration inherent in crises is intensified. Such was the case in the Charleston, West Virginia metropolitan area. A storage container, owned and operated by Freedom Industries, leaked thousands of gallons of a toxic chemical into the Elk River: the Charleston area's water source for 300,000 residents. The company was slow in responding to the crisis. Residents began to notice a foul odor in their water before a warning was issued. As the crisis continued, residents found the information distributed by state and federal sources to be incomplete or incomprehensible. As a result, the information void was filled by informal, spontaneously forming organizations inspired by individuals.

This chapter examines the West Virginia water crisis through the theoretical framework of Chaos Theory, particularly the concepts of strange attractors and self-organization, in an effort to understand how ad-hoc, or emergent, organizations form and function in crises where information voids appear. First will be a summary regarding the theoretical framework used for analyzing the case. This will be followed by a summary of the Charleston, West Virginia water crisis. The analysis of the case, from the perspective of Chaos Theory, will then be presented, with a discussion about the practical implications of the case concluding the chapter.

Theoretical Framework for Analysis

Crisis communication scholars apply Chaos Theory to understand how meaning is lost, and ultimately reestablished, through emergent self-organization. Chaos Theory provides a guiding set of principles that help one to understand "the interactivity, dynamism, non-linearity and lack of simple predictability associated with complex systems" (Sellnow & Seeger, 2013, p. 108). Crises occur suddenly and create severe disruption and confusion. The fact that a crisis catches one by surprise is due to the complex interaction of seemingly unrelated, or irrelevant, elements within a system. The small variance produced by these interactions in a system can accumulate, producing catastrophic results that overwhelm a system (Sellnow, Seeger, & Ulmer, 2002). Chaos Theory accounts for the complexity of systems and one's inability to see the subtle patterns that lead to crisis. Perhaps more importantly, Chaos Theory also explains how systems change or adapt: not only through formal planning and recovery, but also through spontaneous relationships that develop as individuals seek to comprehend and recover from crises.

Chaos Theory can be divided into four elements: bifurcation, fractals, strange attractors, and self-organization (Freimuth, 2006; Murphy, 1996; Seeger, Sellnow, & Ulmer, 2003; Sellnow, Ulmer, Seeger, & Littlefield, 2009). Bifurcation occurs at the onset of the crisis when danger is high and comprehension is low. This is the point at which the crisis reaches an acute level. For example, a bomb explodes, a tornado touches down in a populated area, or a dangerous flaw is discovered in a widely distributed product.

Fractals are the pieces of information that must be gathered and organized to make sense of the crisis. Once the crisis begins, warning signs, overlooked prior to the crisis, become apparent through post-crisis analysis. The goal with fractals is to identify subtle warning signs before a crisis occurs. Fractals may take the form of subtle failures in a production line, unanticipated levels of toxins in the food or water supply, or an inexplicable rise in injuries or illnesses.

Strange attractors are "values, principles, and social assumptions that draw people together in pursuit of common goals" (Liska, Petrun, Sellnow, & Seeger, 2012, p. 183). Those who spontaneously unite in providing instructions for self-protection are drawn together by strange attractors. For instance, volunteers act on feelings of empathy or sympathy and travel long distances to assist residents of communities whose homes have been damaged or destroyed by hurricanes or earthquakes.

Self-organization occurs as organizations learn from their failures and use this knowledge to "create a new form of order" (Horsley, 2014, p. 298). Wheatley (2007) identifies self-organization as the principal means for "recognizing and managing crises and other unanticipated instigations of change" (p. 33). Ephemeral organizations are a good example of self-organization. Individuals and groups spontaneously align their resources to raise money or provide services for those experiencing or recovering from crises. The case analyzed in this chapter examines several ephemeral organizations that emerged through the self-organization process.

In short, complex interactions within a system produce unanticipated outcomes. These outcomes can create disastrous effects that severely disrupt the system. This disruption is known as bifurcation. The warning signs of crisis often manifest themselves in subtle information known as fractals. Ideally, fractals are noted and appropriate actions are taken in order to avert a crisis. In many cases, however, these fractals, and their meanings, are not comprehended until after a crisis occurs. In response to crises, people are drawn together by their common values and principles. Values, such as the desire to help others in need or to persevere in the wake of tragedy, serve as strange attractors in crises. Finally, the recovery process typically requires some degree of spontaneous self-organization. Ephemeral organizations emerge and existing systems undertake dramatic changes to recover from the crisis and to avoid similar crises in the future.

The Case of West Virginia's Water and Freedom Industries

The surprise, and initial uncertainty, inherent in crises severely interrupt people's perceptions of order, making them feel "shocked, stunned, and dazed" (Blythe, 2002, p. 10). In these moments of chaos and ensuing bewilderment, instructional messages for self-protection are paramount (Coombs, 2009; Sellnow & Sellnow, 2010). These messages function best when they are delivered in comprehensible terms that briefly describe what is happening, who is affected, and what steps should be taken for self-protection (Sellnow & Sellnow, 2014; Wickline & Sellnow, 2013).

If sufficient instructional messages are not provided at the onset of a crisis, an information void is created. For individuals suffering from crisis circumstances, this void is intolerable. In such circumstances, individuals seek information through all available channels (Anthony, Sellnow, & Millner, 2013). Interpersonal communication, traditional media, and new media are all options for information seeking. Through information seeking, individuals achieve a form of "understanding made possible by attending to seemingly disorderly processes" (Dervin, 2003, p. 147). Reticence, or ineffectiveness, by existing organizations at the center of the crisis creates informational voids. Proxy organizations, either established or formed spontaneously, often step forward to provide instructional crisis messages (Millner, Veil, & Sellnow, 2011). Proxy organizations, particularly those that emerge during a crisis, are characterized in Chaos Theory as the manifestation of strange attractors.

Inadequacies in the instructional risk and crisis communication, both at the onset and during the recovery phase of the West Virginia crisis, created an information void. In response, several emergent organizations formed to fill the void. Individuals forming these organizations were inspired by the strange attracting "values, principles, and social assumptions" that residents in the afflicted community needed and should have had access to the best information available to protect themselves (Liska et al., 2012, p. 183). In the following analysis of the case, the crisis communication failures are discussed and examples of spontaneously forming organizations filling the information void are presented.

Freedom Industries is a company that stores chemicals used in the coal mining process. One of the chemicals the company stores is 4-methylcyclohexylmethanol (MCHM), which is used to clean coal. A large storage tank containing MCHM was located at the company's site on the banks of the Elk River in Charleston, West Virginia. This river serves as a major source of water for the residents of Charleston and the surrounding area.

At approximately 10:30 on the morning of January 9, 2014, workers at the Freedom Industries site noticed that a tank containing MCHM was leaking, had exceeded the capacity of the containment dikes, and was leaking into the nearby Elk River. The employees did the best they could to stop the leak and clean up what they could of the spilled chemical, but there was nothing to be done about the 11,000 gallons that had already leaked and contaminated the river. The employees reported the spill to their supervisors, but no effort was made by upper management to report the spill to the proper authorities. Instead, the first complaint was registered with the West Virginia Department of Environmental

Protection (DEP) at approximately 8:15 that morning, when a nearby resident reported what was described as a "funny, licorice-like smell" in the area (Ward & Gutman, 2014). Thus, the tank had been leaking for at least two hours before it was noticed by employees.

The DEP notified the West Virginia American Water Company about the contamination at noon and advised them to monitor the water for signs of contamination. At that time, however, the company was under the impression that its water filtration system would be able to remove any impurities from the water. The company soon realized, however, that this was not the case, and that the chemical was too much for the filtration system to manage. Thus, at 5:45 that afternoon (a full nine-and-a-half hours after the spill was first reported) West Virginia American Water Company issued a "do not use" ban on the water for approximately 300,000 customers. Given the gap in time between when the contamination was noticed and when the ban was issued, residents ingested the contaminated water and bathed in it, leading to 122 hospitalizations and more than 700 calls to the poison control hotline. Symptoms of MCHM exposure include nausea, vomiting, headaches, and skin rashes. Fortunately, there were no fatalities as a result of this water contamination. The other detrimental physical and mental effects were plentiful, though, and little is known about the possible long-term effects of exposure, as the scientific testing of this chemical is limited to lab rats and data from the 1960's.

Those affected by this ban were told they could not drink, cook with, wash with, or bathe in the water. All that residents could do with their water was flush their toilets. The ban lasted approximately two weeks, while the water company struggled to change filters and do everything it could to make the water safe again. During that time, residents had to use bottled water for drinking, cooking, bathing, and washing purposes. Items such as paper plates and plastic cutlery were used in bulk to avoid having to wash dishes after eating and baby wipes were used for personal hygiene. As one could imagine, the stores could not keep bottled water and these items stocked.

On January 13, the first stages of lifting the ban began. On January 18, the ban was completely lifted for all remaining areas. However, the official statement recommended that pregnant women continue to find alternative drinking water sources "out of an abundance of caution." This qualification was problematic because it raised suspicion among residents who felt that, if the water was not safe for everyone to drink, then no one should be allowed, or encouraged, to drink it. This inconsistency was the beginning of a distrust in the water system that continues in that community to this day.

Additionally, affected residents were told that they needed to flush out their piping systems to ensure that all contaminated water was out of the pipes before they resumed normal water use. This prerequisite initiated another source of confusion. Poor instructions were given regarding how to properly flush a home's water system. Residents were told to run their cold water and hot water taps, separately, for approximately 15 minutes. This was problematic because, when the hot water was running, it released a gaseous form of the MCHM into people's homes. Given that the statement was issued in January, during wintry-weather conditions, people did not have their windows or doors open to allow this gas to escape. Thus, many residents unknowingly filled their houses with potentially harmful chemical gases. Another issue was that little, to no, instruction was given about flushing outside taps. Again, the wintry-weather had people less than inclined to stand outside and let cold water run for any amount of time. Perhaps the biggest issue, however, was the fact that even after they flushed their pipes for the recommended amount of time, the residents reported still being able to smell the odd licorice odor and detect the odd taste that was present at the beginning of the contamination. Consequently, many residents continued to question the water's safety and began a "self-imposed ban," continuing to use bottled water for most daily functions.

Freedom Industries, the company at the center of the crisis, has remained largely reticent since the crisis began. The company never issued an apology and did not issue its first official statement, through company President Gary Southern, until the evening of January 10. The company filed for bankruptcy a week later. As of November 2014, a full 10 months after the spill occurred, the community is still struggling to recover fully and there is still a large amount of distrust on the part of the residents when it comes to the safety of their water.

Several emergent organizations formed in the wake of the crisis, each focusing on a different aspect of the event, all formed by unique individuals, and all working to help those affected by the crisis to resolve the issues created by the water contamination. The first emergent organization was a group of scientists studying the effects of the contamination on plumbing systems in the impacted area. Though investigations by government and other agencies are pending, this specific group of individuals was fulfilling an immediate need. Dr. Andrew Whelton, a professor in the Department of Civil Engineering at the University of South Alabama (USA), and several civil and environmental engineering graduate students traveled from Mobile, Alabama to Charleston to research the incident and its impact on the plumbing and water systems in the area. Dr. Whelton and his students undertook this travel and research of their own accord. They were not asked to conduct their investigation, nor did they receive any form of compensation for their time, travel, or trouble. Dr. Whelton, whose research focuses on the materials used in piping and plumbing systems, and its potential effects on drinking water quality and performance following a contamination episode, was interviewed by several media outlets about his team's findings. He also chose to use the West Virginia Water Crisis Blog as an outlet for posting his findings and his recommendations (Bryson, 2014). He was also one of the individuals who provided instruction regarding how to properly flush pipes before resuming normal drinking water practices. A video of him giving these instructions is featured on the West Virginia Water Crisis blog, which is, itself, an emergent organization formed in the wake of this crisis.

The West Virginia Water Crisis Blog was created by PhD candidate, and West Virginian, Krista Bryson. Bryson is a self-described Appalachian Advocate. Not only did the site serve as a place for Whelton and others to provide updates on the situation, but Bryson also encouraged residents affected by the contamination to share their stories, which she posted on the site daily. As of March 14, 2014, the site had nearly 25,000 hits. A post from January 25, entitled "*Your Questions Answered: Flushing Recommendations, Water and Water Systems Safety, and Health Concerns,*" provided readers with a clear set of instructions about how to flush pipes and plumbing systems properly. Bryson also sought to answer residents' questions at a level of satisfaction that was previously lacking (Bryson, 2014). Additionally, a post from February 27 provides readers with a list of "actionable" steps they can take to stand up for themselves and let the powers that be know that a continued series of failures on the part of government and other entities should not be tolerated further. This list includes such items as making donations, sharing information, and lobbying to the state legislature. Bryson continued her work as an Appalachian Advocate by creating a documentary that showcases the stories of affected residents and the relief efforts coordinated by her and other groups.

This blog was not the only example of the community harnessing the power of social media to help disseminate information and band together as a community. The Facebook page *WV Clean Water Hub* was created on January 9, the date the crisis began, and quickly grew to nearly 5,000 likes. Posts on the page focused primarily on providing information about where clean, bottled water would be dropped off, where it was needed, and coordinating efforts to get it from those who were willing to donate water, but could not transport it, and getting water to individuals who, for a variety of reasons, were incapable of getting to the distribution points. Several examples of "good Samaritans," both in and outside West Virginia, are highlighted on the page (WV Clean Water Hub, 2014). Groups from surrounding states, including Kentucky and North Carolina, provided water and other supplies. Additionally, a post dated January 11 gave the contact information of a local couple who were freely giving water from their well (which was not affected by the spill), and encouraged those who needed it to come with as many containers as they could fill.

Another group with a strong presence on Facebook was the *West Virginia Moms for Safe Water*. This group page was created on February 6, 2014. This group was focused mainly on how the contamination was affecting their children, particularly in the public schools. The group used its page to post links to stories about water testing in the affected school districts, as well as information about local town-hall meetings at schools, as well as rallies and marches in the area. Additionally, the page was used as a recruitment tool for a CNN story about the water crisis (West Virginia Moms for Safe Water, 2014). Posts on the site encouraged those with school-aged children who had been exposed to the tainted water and had experienced adverse side effects to share their stories via the national media. The general sentiment expressed on the page by moderators and commenters was that they could not understand why the water had not been declared 100-percent safe before the ban was lifted and why officials began encouraging people to flush their pipes and resume drinking and using their tap water.

These emergent organizations formed quickly and seamlessly as informational needs materialized among residents shortly after the crisis began. It stands to reason that these organizations (the research team from USA, the WV Clean Water Hub, the WV Water Crisis Blog, and the WV Moms for Safe Water) will continue until the community has completely moved beyond the crisis. Given their temporary state, and the fact that they formed in response to a specific crisis, these emergent organizations can be categorized as examples of self-organization.

Discussion and Practical Implications of the Case

The crisis in West Virginia created primary and secondary bifurcation points where danger was high and comprehension was low. Initially, the discovery that the entire water supply was serviceable for nothing but sewage came as a shock, and an acute inconvenience, for residents. Secondarily, once the water ban was lifted, an information or comprehension void developed for residents seeking to purge their homes of the toxic chemical. Ephemeral organizations such as the research team from USA, the WV Clean Water Hub, and the WV Moms for Safe Water brought order to a seemingly chaotic information-seeking process (Dervin, 2003, p. 147). The primary purpose of these organizations was to provide instructional messages for residents seeking to protect themselves, and their loved ones, from further contamination.

The fact that these organizations received considerable traffic on their websites, and at the meetings that they sponsored, suggests that, in addition to providing helpful information, they were trusted by residents. From the perspective of Chaos Theory, self-organization is inspired by strange attractors or the "values, principles, and social assumptions that draw people together in pursuit of common goals" (Liska et al., 2012, p. 183). The emergent organizations in the West Virginia crisis appear to have acted self-lessly. The only apparent motive in their formation was to help the West Virginia residents protect and sustain themselves throughout the crisis. Thus, the same forces that inspired self-organization likely contributed to the trust residents had in the information and advice provided by these emergent organizations.

The West Virginia case revealed a previously unexplored dimension of emergent organizations in crisis situations. Specifically, the emergent organizations relied heavily on new media channels to distribute information to those in need. Although this case provides clear evidence regarding how new media can generate and sustain emergent organizations, this feasibility may be limited by crisis type. For example, when communities are disrupted by natural disasters such as tornadoes, hurricanes, floods, or fires, Internet access may be limited, or absent, for prolonged periods of time. The fact that the West Virginia crisis did not create major damage to the community's infrastructure contributed to the opportunities for social media to serve as a resource. An additional caution about dependence on new media for emergent organizations is the fact that a notable percentage of the population in most communities does not have convenient computer access.

Overall, the bifurcation points in the West Virginia crisis created both confusion and hardship. Residents were uncertain about the purity and safety of their water supply. As the crisis lingered, residents began to rely on ephemeral organizations to interpret fractals, in the form of results produced by ongoing water testing, and to provide instructional information to residents. The ephemeral organizations were created by individuals drawn together by strange attractors that reflected an undaunted determination to help the people of West Virginia. Organizations such as the research team from USA, the WV Clean Water Hub, and the WV Moms for Safe Water are examples of how self-organization functions in the wake of serious crisis. These organizations formed spontaneously and provided a valuable service to the residents.

When an organization fails, remarkably, to provide the information needed by residents for self-protection, strange attractors inspire individuals outside the organization to form emergent organizations. These organizations emerge spontaneously to address the needs of citizens. Their sole purpose is to resolve the crisis by attending to the informational and physical needs of those whose lives are disrupted by the emergency. In the case of the West Virginia water crisis, these needs were primarily informational. Thus, emergent organizations are a valuable asset for both crisis communication and recovery.

DISCUSSION QUESTIONS

1. How has the evolution of social media influenced the way emergent organizations form in response to crises?
2. What are some potential challenges that emergent organizations might face when communicating with various stakeholder groups primarily through social media?
3. What were the primary informational needs of the residents near the spill? To what extent were these needs satisfied and unsatisfied?
4. The article defines strange attractors as the "values, principles, and social assumptions that draw people together in pursuit of common goals" (Liska et al., 2012, p. 183). Explain how the unique circumstances of this crisis created these shared goals that brought people together.

REFERENCES

Anthony, K. E., Sellnow, T. L., & Millner, A. G. (2013). Message convergence as a message-centered approach to analyzing and improving risk communication. *Journal of Applied Communication Research, 41,* 346–364.

Blythe, B. T. (2002). *Blindsided: A manager's guide to catastrophic incidents in the workplace.* New York, NY: Portfolio.

Bryson, K. (2014, January 25). Your questions answered: Flushing recommendations, water and water systems safety, ad health concerns. Retrieved from http://westvirginiawatercrisis.wordpress.com/about/

Dervin, B. (2003). Sense-making's journey from metatheory to methodology to method: An example using information seeking and use as research focus. In B. Dervin & L. Foreman-Wernet (Eds.), *Sense-making methodology reader: Selected writings of Brenda Dervin* (pp. 133–163). Cresskill, NJ: Hampton Press, Inc.

Freimuth, V. S. (2006). Order out of chaos: The self-organization of communication following the anthrax attacks. *Health Communication, 20*(2), 141–148.

Hermann, C. F. (1963). Some consequences of crisis which limit the viability of organizations. *Administration Science Quarterly, 8,* 61–82.

Horsley, S. J. (2014). The method in their madness: Chaos, communication, and the D.C. snipers. *Journal of Communication Management, 18*(3), 295–318. doi: http://dx.doi.org/10.1108/JCOM-01-2010-0003

Liska, C., Petrun, E. L., Sellnow, T. L., & Seeger, M. W. (2012). Chaos Theory, self-organization and industrial accidents: Crisis communication. *Southern Communication Journal, 77*(3), 180–197. doi: 10.1080/1041794X.2011.634479

Millner, A. G., Veil, S. R., & Sellnow, T. L. (2011). Proxy communication in crisis response. *Public Relations Review, 37,* 74–76.

Murphy, P. (1996). Chaos Theory as a model for managing issues and crises. *Public Relations Review, 22,* 95–113.

Seeger, M. W. (2002). Chaos and crisis: Proposition for a general theory of crisis communication. *Public Relations Review, 28,* 329–337.

Seeger, M. W. (2006). Best practices in crisis communication: An expert panel process. *Journal of Applied Communication Research, 34,* 232–244. doi: 10.1080/00909880600769944

Seeger, M. W., Sellnow, T. L., & Ulmer, R. R. (2010). Expanding the parameters of crisis communication: From chaos to renewal. In R. L. Heath (Ed.), *Public relations handbook* (2nd ed.) (pp. 489–500). Thousand Oaks, CA: Sage Publications, Inc.

Sellnow, D., & Sellnow, T. (2014). Risk communication: Instructional principles. In T. Thompson (Ed.), *Encyclopedia of health communication.* (Vol. 17, pp. 1181-1184). Thousand Oaks, CA: SAGE Publications, Inc. doi: http://dx.doi.org/10.4135/9781483346427.n463

Sellnow, T. L., & Sellnow, D. D. (2010). The instructional dynamic of risk and crisis communication: Distinguishing instructional messages from dialogue. *The Review of Communication, 10*(2), 111–125.

Sellnow, T. L., & Seeger, M. W. (2013) *Theorizing crisis communication.* Malden, MA: Wiley-Blackwell.

Sellnow, T. L., Seeger, M. W., & Ulmer, R. R. (2002). Chaos Theory, informational needs, and natural disasters. *The Journal of Applied Communication Research, 30,* 269–292.

Sellnow, T. L., Ulmer, R. R., Seeger, M. W., & Littlefield, R. S. (2009). *Effective risk communication: A message-centered approach.* New York: Springer Science+Business Media, LLC.

WV Clean Water Hub (2014) In *Facebook* [group page] Retrieved July 20, 2015 from https://www.facebook.com/WVCleanWaterHub?fref=ts

West Virginia Moms for Safe Water (2014) In *Facebook* [group page] Retrieved July 20, 2015 from https://www.facebook.com/pages/West-Virgina-Moms-for-Safe-Water/699973913376534?fref=ts

Wheatley, M. J. (2007). *Leadership for an uncertain time.* San Francisco, CA: Barrett-Koehler.

Wickline, M., & Sellnow, T. L. (2013). Expanding the concept of significant choice through consideration of health literacy during crises. *Health Promotion Practice, 14,* 809–815.

Author Note

This chapter was developed with support from the following two grants provided by Department of Homeland Security (DHS) Centers of Excellence: National Center for Risk and Economic Analysis of Terrorism Events, sponsor ID# 132256 35399/ DE-AC05–76RL01830; and the National Center for Food Protection and Defense, Grant Award Number 2007-ST-061–000003. The article has not been formally reviewed by the Department of Homeland Security. The views and conclusions contained in this document are those of the authors and should not be interpreted as necessarily representing the official policies, either expressed or implied, of the U.S. Department of Homeland Security. The Department of Homeland Security does not endorse any products or commercial services mentioned in this publication.

Chapter 2

When Edward Burhardt Spoke, the Crisis Worsened: The Dangers of Crisis Miscommunication

W. Timothy Coombs, Ph.D.
Texas A & M University

Introduction

Lac-Mégantic is a town of approximately 6,000 people that sits on a lake by the same name in the eastern part of Quebec, Canada. Until July of 2013, it was best known as a tourist destination and a producer of forestry products. Just past midnight on July 6, 2013, an unattended train, composed of 72 cars carrying petroleum, began to roll downhill from Nantes to Lac-Mégantic: a distance of just over 6 miles (Bizarre, 2013). There had been a small fire on the train earlier in the evening that was extinguished by local firefighters. When the unattended train hit Lac-Mégantic at 1:15am, it derailed and ignited a fire that would devastate the town. A total of 63 cars derailed in the crash. Approximately 2,000 people (over one third of the town) were evacuated. In the end, 47 people were killed by the derailment and fire. Approximately 150 firefighters fought the blaze that consumed 30 buildings in the downtown. Most of the evacuated residents returned within three days, but over 200 remained outside of the town until the sixth day after the derailment. The investigation of the derailment turned media attention to the Maine, Montreal, and Atlantic Railway (MM&A) and its parent company, Rail World. As with any crisis, people want answers to the question "why?"

Edward Burkhardt was CEO of Rail World at the time of the crash. The 75-year-old CEO became the voice of Rail World during the crisis. Burkhardt demonstrated an amazing ability to communicate the wrong messages during a crisis. His performance demonstrated how crisis communication can make a crisis worse for an organization, ultimately increasing the damage a crisis can inflict on organizational assets, such as reputation. This case study explores Rail World's crisis response using the lens of Situational Crisis Communication Theory (SCCT) and the newly adopted Regenerative Crisis Model. SCCT has been documented to be one of the most influential theories in crisis communication when utilization of the theory in publications is used as a criterion for influence (Avery et al., 2010). Initial development of SCCT began in 1995 with the first published use of the theory's name in 2002. In the nearly two years since SCCT was originated, the landscape of crisis communication has changed. There is now a rather large body of knowledge about crisis communication from the academic side and social media has altered the practice of crisis communication. The changing crisis communication landscape has resulted in revisions to SCCT (Coombs, 2013). The following review considers the new crisis model that guides SCCT and recounts the basic elements of, and recommendations emanating from, the theory.

Revisiting the Crisis Phases

The crisis communication literature recognizes that crises have phases. The crisis phases researchers have identified in various models range, in number, from three to seven (Coombs, 2015). The phases are analytic tools designed to organize one's thinking about crisis communication. In reality, experts realize that it is often difficult to distinguish when a crisis moves from one phase to the next. Originally, SCCT was based on a three-phase view of crises: pre-crisis, response, and post-crisis. The greatest challenge in crisis phases has been differentiating between the response and the post-crisis phases. How does one locate the exact shift between those two phases? It is more realistic to separate crises into two phases: pre-crisis and post-crisis.

The key to the two-phase approach is having a crisis moment that separates the phases. The crisis moment may be a trigger event or recognition that a crisis exists. Many crises have identifiable trigger events, such as an accident, an explosion, a chemical release, or an arrest. Managers know that they are in a crisis when the event occurs. Other crises are more subtle and require managers to recognize/realize that there is a crisis. Reports of product defects, complaints from consumers, and protests from activists can serve as the stimulus for recognizing that a crisis exists. There is no single event for these recognition crises, but, at some point, managers realize the situation should be defined as a crisis. It can take time for managers to realize that there is a problem that warrants it being labeled a "crisis." Hence, the distinction between the pre-crisis and post-crisis phases are not as distinct when the crisis moment is recognition, rather than an event.

Crises are dynamic, rather than static, in nature. New developments can occur that fundamentally alter the crisis situation. For instance, new evidence might reveal that the trigger event was a result of management misconduct, rather than a random accident. Or, stakeholders may force an organization to redefine the situation as a crisis and to take action regarding that crisis. Or, the communicative actions taken by management might spawn a new crisis altogether (Frandsen & Johansen, 2010). The point is that there can be turning points in a crisis that essentially create a new crisis by reframing the situation. This process is referred to as the regenerative view of crises: the turning point causes the crisis to regenerate itself, thereby creating a new crisis. Once a turning point occurs, all previous actions and communication used to address the crisis now become part of the pre-crisis phase, while all subsequent actions become the post-crisis phase. An example will help to illustrate the point.

The Lance Armstrong doping crisis extended over years for the Livestrong Foundation. When Lance Armstrong publicly admitted to doping, that was a turning point. The crisis changed. All of the actions, and crisis communication efforts, prior to the announcement became part of the pre-crisis phase (Vinton, 2012). This would include various denials by Lance Armstrong and his removal from leadership within Livestrong. These actions and messages now form part of the pre-crisis context for the current crisis. A turning point transforms previous post-crisis actions into part of the situation that constitutes the pre-crisis phase. Figure 2.1 illustrates the regenerative view of crises.

Turning points often demand a significant shift in communicative strategies. The Livestrong example illustrates how denial might be removed from the equation by a turning point. Similarly, the findings that an accident was caused by management misconduct would require a shift in communicative strategy as well. Turning points are problematic when they demand a shift in communication strategies. The change in communication strategies creates a sense of inconsistency and reduces the effectiveness of the crisis communication effort (Coombs, 2012). An organization's own words can return to harm them and, thus, early crisis communication efforts become one of the situational factors used to evaluate the current crisis situation. Early crisis communication efforts becoming a problematic part of the crisis situation results in the "double crisis," where the crisis response can create a new crisis for an organization

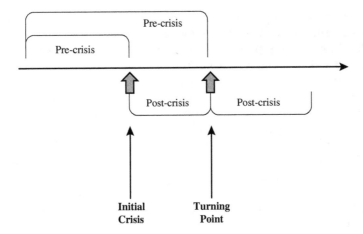

Figure 2.1 Regenerative Crisis Model

(Frandsen & Johansen, 2010). SCCT is based on this dynamic, two-phase conceptualization of a crisis. The model allows SCCT to be applied in crises that have multiple turning points and to extend SCCT into the pre-crisis phase.

Situational Crisis Communication Theory: Application in the Post-Crisis Phase

The train derailment case study explores the post-crisis communication of Rail World. There is a clear event (the derailment) that initiated the crisis. The theory review, above, examines the post-crisis application and does not cover the newly developed application of SCCT to the pre-crisis phase. The initial focus of SCCT was to develop situation-based recommendations for when to utilize various crisis response strategies. The recommendations emphasize reputation protection as the primary outcome for crisis communication. The main components of the theory were the crisis types, intensifiers (contextual factors), crisis response strategies, and reputation (outcomes/goals) (Coombs, 2007). The revision of SCCT involves a reconsideration of all of these main components.

There are two general goals during a crisis: to protect public safety and welfare and to protect organizational assets (i.e., reputations) (Coombs, 2015). SCCT recognizes the importance of public safety and welfare by making *threats to stakeholders* the number one concern in crisis communication. SCCT recommends that any crisis that creates a threat to stakeholders should begin with an ethical base. The ethical base response is composed of Sturges' (1994) instructing and adjusting information. Instructing information tells stakeholders what they can do to protect themselves, physically, from a crisis. Instructing information includes recall information and warnings to shelter-in-place. Recall information warns people about potential harm from a product and what they should do with that product. Shelter-in-place advises people to stay in their homes during a chemical event and to seal off sources of outside air, such as an air conditioner (Coombs, 2015). Adjusting information helps stakeholders to cope, psychologically, with a crisis. Adjusting information can include expression of concern/sympathy, corrective action designed to prevent a repeat of the crisis, and compensation to help stakeholders cope with the situation (Holladay, 2009). The acknowledgement of protecting public safety and welfare was later added to SCCT, but should be a more prominent feature of the theory (Holladay, 2009). Though a vital concern in the initial response, adjusting information remains relevant throughout the post-crisis phase. Memorials (efforts to commemorate the victims of a crisis) can occur well after the initial crisis event and even after a crisis situation is considered back to normal (Coombs, 2015).

Protecting organizational assets is performed after, or simultaneously with, protecting public safety and welfare. SCCT originally focused on reputation as the primary asset, but did add purchase intentions. Moreover, crisis response strategies were found to affect negative word-of-mouth and anger: two factors that can affect reputations and purchase intentions. SCCT now has a set of four outcomes that are relevant to organizational assets. SCCT linked reputation protection to the threat posed by a crisis. The primary driver of the crisis threat is crisis responsibility. Research in public relations and marketing have found that damage from a crisis, including reputational harm, (a) drops purchase intention and (b) increases anger, especially as attributions of crisis responsibility strengthen (Coombs & Holladay, 2007; Jorgensen, 1996). SCCT helps managers to anticipate the crisis responsibility generated by a crisis—to understand the crisis threat.

The crisis threat can be assessed by examining the crisis types and contextual modifiers. Understanding the crisis types and the contextual modifiers allows crisis managers to anticipate the level of crisis responsibility that their crisis in likely to generate. Both factors are refined for the revised model of SCCT.

Crisis types (how a crisis is framed) served as the genesis for SCCT. The crisis type is a frame because it indicates how stakeholders should interpret the crisis event (Coombs, 2007). Obviously, not all stakeholders will share the same frame. Crisis managers must identify the dominant frame and manage that crisis type. The frame is a function of situational factors and how those factors are presented in the legacy and digital media. The initial intent of crisis types was to understand how to respond most effectively to a range of organizational crises. A set of three crisis types was developed for SCCT based upon attributions of crisis responsibility: victim, accidental, and preventable (Coombs, 2007). Victim crises generate very little attributions of crisis responsibility. Organizations can argue that they are victims (have suffered unfairly) in such crises, including hacking, terror attacks, product tampering, natural disasters, and workplace violence. Accidental crises produce minimal attributions of crisis responsibility and include accidents and product-harm crises triggered by technical errors (Coombs, 2007). Preventable crises produce strong attributions of crisis responsibility and include human-error accidents and product-harm and management misconduct.

The initial contextual modifiers were termed "intensifiers" and comprised crisis history and prior reputation. Past crises and negative prior reputations serve to intensify attributions of crisis responsibility, thereby intensifying the crisis threat (Coombs, 2007). Organizations with either, or both, of these intensifiers should expect stronger than anticipated attributions of crisis responsibility—an increased threat from the crisis. However, the contextual factors could moderate, as well as intensify, the crisis threats: hence the shift in terminology to contextual modifier. By assessing the crisis type and contextual modifiers, the crisis managers can estimate the threat posed by the crisis: how strongly stakeholders are likely to attribute crisis responsibility to the organization.

The threat assessment is valuable because it guides the selection of crisis response strategies. The crisis response strategies are what organizations say and do after the crisis occurs (Coombs, 1995). Drawing from the extant literature on crisis accounts and response options, SCCT created a list of the commonly used crisis response strategies. The crisis response strategies were divided into supporting and primary reputation strategies (Coombs, 2015). Supporting strategies were the variations of bolstering which seek to associate some "positives" with the organization. Bolstering is supportive because these strategies would look out-of-place, and be ineffective, as the sole response. At the very least, bolstering would be used in connection with the ethical base response, but can be used with other primary reputation strategies, too. Here are the primary SCCT recommendations for crisis response strategy selection (Coombs, 2015):

1. When there are victims and concern for public safety and welfare, the organization should feature an ethical base response (focus on instructing and adjusting information).
2. When there are strong attributions of crisis responsibility (preventable crisis or accidental crisis with intensifiers), crisis managers should consider adding compensation and/or an apology to the response.
3. Denial should be reserved for situations involving misinformation that links the organization to a crisis (the organization really has no connection with, or responsibility for, the crisis).
4. Bolstering can be used to support any of the three primary crisis response strategies.
5. Crisis managers must be sensitive to significant shifts in the crisis framing and respond appropriately.

The Case Study

Applying SCCT to the Lac-Mégantic train derailment case requires an analysis of the crisis threat that is posed and the actual responses offered by Rail World. The actual reactions can be compared to the recommendations offered by SCCT. The analysis also will consider the regenerative aspect of the Lac-Mégantic train derailment.

The Lac-Mégantic train derailment began as an accident that had created victims. At the start, the cause was unclear, but it is evident that the town had been seriously damaged by fire (over 2,000 people had been evacuated and there were a number of fatalities and injuries). Because the crisis did produce victims, management needed to concentrate on the ethical base response of provided instructing and adjusting information. There also was a need for compensation when victims were suffering from a combination of harm and inconvenience. Bolstering could be added by thanking the first responders who helped to extinguish the fire and to aid the victims (Bizarre, 2013).

Edward Burkhardt's statements included some instructing and adjusting information. There was a general expression of concern for the event and a discussion about helping to repair the damage. For instance, Burkhardt stated, "If I'm a business and it's burned down, I want someone to pay for that loss. It's as simple as that, and that's what we're prepared to do" (Beeston, 2013). Unfortunately, it was 36 hours after the accident before any response was offered by Rail World. Moreover, it was five days before Burkhardt, himself, visited the sight. The symbolic aspect of the response showed little concern for the victims.

Burkhardt undercut the minimal-use adjusting and instructing information by immediately seeking to reduce attributions of crisis responsibility. Burkhardt's initial statements claimed that the company had evidence of tampering. "We have evidence of this," Burkhardt said in reference to the tampering having caused the crisis (Beeston, 2013). He then blamed the firefighters who supressed the initial fire on the train's locomotive for releasing a brake. Burkhardt initially claimed that his employees did nothing wrong and had properly set the brakes on the locomotive (How, 2013). Burkhardt's initial response included efforts to blame others, as well as deny responsibility for the crisis. Burkhardt also made "jokes" about the personal financial loss he would endure as a result of the crisis (a victim strategy). The reputation repair crisis response strategies were very defensive because they ignored victims, while emphasizing the concerns of the organization.

These very defensive crisis response strategies detracted from the limited use of the ethical base response. Media reports were highly critical of Burkhardt's crisis communication:

While Burkhardt did express an 'abject apology,' such words were drowned out by his other comments, as well as the fact that he stayed away from the accident scene for days (How, 2013).

An op-ed piece in a major Canadian newspaper commented:

In many of his statements, he focused on the impact of the derailment…on him, rather than on the citizens of the town. He told us about his 20-hour work days, his net worth having diminished, [and] death threats against him (Bizarre, 2013).

Contrary to SCCT, Burkhardt was focusing the crisis response on his organization and himself: not the victims. Only a minority of the crisis response was about the victims and that message was easily missed due to the self-serving messages about the effects of the crisis on Rail World and Edward Burkhardt.

Within a few days of the crisis, Burkhardt altered his messaging away from denial and toward shifting the blame. Burkhardt blamed one employee for not setting the brakes on the locomotive. This is the individual/group dissociation crisis response strategy: when management claims that a few people are, or one person is, is responsible for the crisis: not the entire organization. People should have felt better about Rail World during the crisis by realizing that only one employee was responsible for the crisis and that the organization was taking action to punish those responsible for the crisis (Hearit, 1994). This is a form of shifting the blame. The problem is that Burkhardt was admitting to a human-error crisis and people are not forgiving when employee mistakes created a crisis. In fact, people tend to still blame the organization for the crisis because the cause is mutable: people can image a situation where the crisis is easily preventable (Coombs & Holladay, 2010). Burkhardt, himself, stated that the accident was avoidable. By blaming an employee, Burkhardt was reinforcing people's perception that Rail World had strong responsibility for the crisis.

It is significant that the crisis moved from an accident with an unknown cause to a human-error accident. The crisis was now firmly placed in the preventable crisis type. Burkhardt needed to consider adding a clear apology and/or specifying the compensation for the victims. Moreover, the initial response's limited concern for victims created an additional need to be accommodative in response to the turning point. Instead, Burkhardt used the potential for lawsuits emanating from the crisis to say very little about it. Burkhardt was engaging in what Fitzpatrick and Rubin (1995) call a traditional legal response. One was given no additional information about compensation efforts beyond Burkhardt's initial promise to help and one was provided with no additional apology. Moreover, there was no elaboration on the limited used of the ethical base response presented at the start of the crisis. When the nature of the crisis type was clarified and the crisis regenerated, the Rail World response did not match the response SCCT would prescribe for the crisis situation. Rail World should have reiterated the ethical base response and, at the very least, highlighted its compensation efforts. The demand for a victim-centered response was intensified by the initial organization-focused response. The initial response was not a contextual factor as part of the pre-crisis phase. Given the pending lawsuits, an apology was unlikely, but compensation and a strong expression of sympathy were still viable communicative options.

CONCLUSION

Edward Burkhardt, CEO of Rail World, illustrated how improper crisis communication can make a situation worse. While providing a limited ethical base response, Burkhardt violated the recommendations of SCCT by emphasizing his personal situation over the concerns of the victims. In his messaging and media coverage of the train derailment, Burkhardt and his disregard for victims became the focus. Lost in the media's negative reaction to Burkhart were the actions that Rail World was taking to address the problems created by their train derailment and fire. Moreover, the case also illustrates how there can be significant shifts in how the crisis is framed, which has ramifications for the organization's crisis response strategies. The accident quickly changed to a human-error crisis, thereby intensifying attributions of crisis responsibility to Rail World. The Rail World response ignored this regeneration of the crisis and continued to marginalize the victims in the crisis response. SCCT can be used to explain why media and crisis experts condemned Edward Burkhardt's crisis communication following the Lac-Mégantic train derailment. Failing to focus on the victims allows crisis communication to make a crisis situation worse, and not better, for the organization in crisis.

DISCUSSION QUESTIONS

1. How does this case illustrate the utility of the regenerative crisis model for explaining crises?
2. What evidence from this case support the claims from SCCT to focus on the physical and psychological well-being of stakeholders during a crisis?
3. What possible explanations could there be for why Burkhardt choose his particular crisis response? How do you think he might justify the response?
4. What does this case reveal about the dangers an ambiguous crisis (one where the cause is not initially known) for crisis managers?
5. What makes victims such a unique stakeholder in a crisis and how might their treatment affect how non-victims perceive the organization?

REFERENCES

Avery, E. J., Lariscy, R. W., Kim, S., & Hocke, T. (2010). A quantitative review of crisis communication research in public relations from 1991 to 2009. *Public Relations Review, 36*(2), 190–192.

Beeston, L. (2013). Lac-Mégantic: Montreal, Maine & Atlantic Railway chairmen certain train that exploded was tampered with. Retrieved from http://www.montrealgazette.com/news/montreal/M%C3%A9gantic+Montreal+Maine+Atlantic+Railway+chairman/8631093/story.html.

Bizarre PR disaster of the Quebec train explosion (2013). Retrieved from http://www.thewire.com/global/2013/07/bizarre-pr-disaster-quebec-train-explosion/67107/.

Coombs, W.T. (1995). Choosing the right words: The development of guidelines for the selection of the "appropriate" crisis response strategies. *Management Communication Quarterly, 8,* 447–476.

Coombs, W.T. (2007). Attribution theory as a guide for post-crisis communication research. *Public Relations Review, 33,* 135–139.

Coombs, W.T. (2013). Evolution Guided by Research: The Revised Situation Crisis Communication Theory (SCCT). Paper presented at *3rd International Conference on Crisis Communication in the 21st Century, Oct. 2013, Erfurt, Germany.*

Coombs, W.T. (2015). *Ongoing crisis communication: Planning, managing, and responding* (4th ed.). Thousand Oaks, CA: Sage Publications.

Coombs, W.T., & Holladay, S. J. (2007). The negative communication dynamic: Exploring the impact of stakeholder affect on behavioral intentions. *Journal of Communication Management, 11,* 300–312.

Coombs, W.T. & Holladay, S.J. (2010). Examining the effects of mutability and framing on perceptions of human-error and technical-error crises: Implications for Situational Crisis Communication Theory. In W.T. Coombs & S. J. Holladay (eds.), *Handbook of Crisis Communication* (pp. 181-204). Malden, MA: Blackwell Publishing.

Fitzpatrick, K. R., & Rubin, M. S. (1995). Public relations vs. legal strategies in organizational crisis decisions. *Public Relations Review, 21*(1), 21–33.

Frandsen, F., & Johansen, W. (2010). Apologizing in a globalizing world: Crisis communication and apologetic ethics. *Corporate Communications: An International Journal, 15*(4), 350–364.

Hearit, K. M. (1994). Apologies and public relations crises at Chrysler, Toshiba, and Volvo. *Public Relations Review, 20*(2), 113–125.

Holladay, S.J. (2009). Crisis communication strategies in the media coverage of chemical accidents. *Journal of Public Relations Research, 21*, 208–215.

How Edward Burkhardt is making the Lac-Mégantic accident even worse. Retrieved from http://www.forbes.com/sites/johnbaldoni/2013/07/15/how-edward-burkhardt-is-making-the-lac-megantic-accident-even-worse/.

Jorgensen, B. K. (1996). Components of consumer reaction to company-related mishaps: A structural equation model approach. *Advances in Consumer Research, 23*, 346–51.

Vinton, N. (2012 Aug. 23). Lance Armstrong stripped of seven Tour de Fance titles, given lifetime ban from Olympic sports as he drops appeal of doping charges, available at: http://www.nydailynews.com/sports/more-sports/lance-armstrong-stripped-tour-de-france-titles-lifetime-ban-olympic-sports-drops-doping-appeal-article-1.1143295#ixzz2TeJJKYj0

Chapter 3

Eric Shinseki's Image Repair for the Veteran's Administration Health Care Scandal

BILL BENOIT, PH.D.
University of Alabama, Birmingham

Introduction

Concerns that veterans were not receiving timely medical care swirled about the Veterans Affairs (VA). In May of 2014, the Inspector General's office issued a report confirming the scandal. Bronstein and Griffin (2014) reported that the VA had kept a secret list of veterans seeking medical care. "The secret list was part of an elaborate scheme designed by Veterans Affairs managers in Phoenix who were trying to hide that 1,400 to 1,600 sick veterans were forced to wait months to see a doctor." Hicks (2014) explained that "The report said 1,700 veterans using a Phoenix VA hospital were kept on unofficial wait lists, adding that 'these veterans were and continue to be at risk of being forgotten or lost in Phoenix HCS (HGS Engineering)'s convoluted scheduling process.'" Hicks also reported that VA documents indicated that 226 patients in a sample waited 24 days for initial appointments, but the actual wait for those patients was 115 days. The VA required timely treatment – or at least the appearance of timely treatment – and administrator bonuses were on the line.

Delays for health care are bad in and of themselves. However, these delays had serious consequences. "At least 40 U.S. veterans died waiting for appointments at the Phoenix Veterans Affairs Health Care system" (Hicks, 2014). Americans have high regard for those who served the United States in the military, making this a very serious scandal. A poll reported by CBS News (2014) found that people believed that General Eric Shinseki, the Secretary of Veterans Affairs, (33%) and the VA (33%) deserved more blame for problems at VA hospitals than local hospitals (28%) or President Obama (17%). On May 30, Eric Shinseki resigned from his position as the seventh U.S. Secretary of Veterans Affairs and apologized for the scandal.

This chapter investigates Shinseki's image repair effort using the theory of image repair discourse (Benoit, 2014). Next will be a description of the method used to analyze Shinseki's May 30th speech, after which will be an evaluation of Shinseki's defense.

Method

Image repair is an area within crisis communication (crisis communication also includes messages designed to respond to natural disasters, as well as human problems). Image Repair Theory argues that a

Table 3.1 Image Restoration Strategies

Strategy	Key Characteristic	Example
Denial		
Simple denial	did not perform act	Reagan did not trade arms for hostages
Shift the blame	another performed act	someone else stole your bike
Evasion of Responsibility		
Provocation	responded to act of another	I broke your phone because I was mad that you didn't pick me up after work
Defeasibility	lack of information or ability	late to meeting: wasn't told new location
Accident	mishap	poor visibility caused my car crash
Good intentions	meant well	I meant to buy you a present, but I forgot
Reducing Offensiveness of Event		
Bolstering	stress good traits	Bush boasted of first term successes
Minimization	act not serious	it is no big deal that I broke your CD; the music was crummy
Differentiation	act less offensive than similar acts	I borrowed your CD player, I didn't steal it
Transcendence	more important values	I stole bread to feed my hungry child
Attack accuser	reduce credibility of accuser	Gingrich accused the liberal media of lying
Compensation	reimburse victim	A waiter offered free dessert after spilling on customer
Corrective Action	plan to solve/prevent recurrence of problem	I will fix the damage I caused to your car
Mortification	apologize	Obama apologized for HealthCare.gov

See Benoit (1995a; 2014)

person's, or organization's, image, face, or reputation is extremely important (Benoit, 1995a, 2014) (for other approaches to image repair, see Coombs, 2012, or Hearit, 2006). Threats to image seem to lurk around every corner, so it is important to understand persuasive messages that can attempt to repair a damaged image. Five general strategies of image repair discourse are available to persuaders who want to respond to image threats, three with specific variants or tactics (see Table 1). Each of these strategies will be discussed in this section.

Denial

Simple denial can take three related forms. Those accused of wrong-doing may deny that the offensive act occurred, deny that they performed the objectionable act, or deny that the act is harmful. Any of these instances of denial, if accepted by the intended audience, have the potential to repair the damaged reputation. Furthermore, a persuader can try to shift the blame. If another person (or group or organization) actually committed the offensive act, the accused should not be held responsible for that offensive act.

Evade Responsibility

This general image repair strategy has four variants. A persuader may allege that the offensive act was just a reasonable response to someone else's offensive act (typically an act performed by the alleged victim) and that the persuader's response was a reasonable reaction to that provocation. Defeasibility claims that the persuader lacked the knowledge or ability to avoid committing the offensive act. A persuader may also argue that the offense occurred by accident. Fourth, the persuader can claim that the act was actually performed with good intentions.

Reduce Offensiveness

There are six different tactics for attempting to reduce the apparent offensiveness of the act. First, a persuader can bolster his or her own image in an attempt to strengthen the audience's positive feelings toward him or her. In this case, it is hoped that these favorable feelings will offset the negative feelings that arose from the offensive act. The tactic of minimization suggests that the act in question is not really as offensive as it seems. Differentiation attempts to distinguish the act in question from other similar, but more offensive, actions. In comparison, the act performed by the persuader may not appear so bad. Transcendence attempts to justify the act by placing it in a more favorable context. A persuader can attempt to attack the accusers, so as to reduce the credibility of the accusations (or suggest that the victim deserved what happened). The tactic of compensation offers to give the victim money, goods, or services to help reduce the negative feelings toward the persuader.

Corrective Action

Corrective action is a commitment to repair the damage from the offensive act. This general strategy of image repair can take two forms. The persuader can promise to restore the state of affairs before the offensive act or the persuader can promise to prevent recurrence of the offensive act.

Mortification

The last strategy, mortification, is to admit committing the offensive act and to ask for forgiveness. It is possible that an apparently sincere apology would help restore the persuader's image with the intended audience. This strategy can take various forms, including admitting guilt, asking for forgiveness, expressing regret or remorse, and apologizing. There is no accepted standard for what constitutes the minimum of "an apology." Ambiguity exists in the statement "I'm sorry." This could represent an expression of guilt and remorse, but it could also be nothing more than an expression of sympathy (short for "I'm sorry for what befell you"). Some persuaders may attempt to exploit this ambiguity, hoping that the audience will accept "I'm sorry" as an apology without actually confessing to any misdeeds.

Benoit (2014) linked Image Repair Theory with Fishbein and Ajzen's (2010) Theory of Reasoned Action. Image repair discourse is best understood by considering the defense in the context of the accusations. Accusations consist of beliefs and values (the components of an attitude), labeled, respectively, blame and offensiveness by Pomerantz (1978). One who seeks to repair an image must identify the relevant audience's attitudes and then attempt to change unfavorable attitudes by changing an unfavorable belief or value or by adding a new and favorable belief or value. For example, denial attempts to change the belief that the accused is to blame. Minimization tries to change a belief so the audience will think the offense is less serious. Transcendence, in contrast, brings another value into play, attempting to justify the act in question (yes, stealing is wrong, but I stole bread to feed my hungry child).

Research has applied Image Repair Theory to discourse in a variety of contexts. Studies have investigated corporate image repair, including rhetorical criticism of defensive messages by Sears (Benoit, 1995b), AT&T (Benoit & Brinson, 1994), USAir (Benoit & Czerwinski, 1997), Firestone (Blaney, Benoit, & Brazeal, 2002), Dow Corning (Brinson & Benoit, 1998), and Texaco (Brinson & Benoit, 1999). Other studies have examined image repair in sports and entertainment, including Hugh Grant (Benoit, 1997), Tiger Woods (Benoit, 2013), Murphy Brown (Benoit & Anderson, 1996), Tonya Harding (Benoit & Hanczor, 1994), Oliver Stone (Benoit & Nill, 1998b), Terrell Owens (Brazeal, 2008), Taiwanese pitcher Chien-Ming Wang (Wen, Yu, & Benoit, 2009), and Floyd Landis (Glantz, 2009). Research has examined international image repair, including the United States and Japan (Drumheller & Benoit, 2004), Saudia Arabia and the United States (Zhang & Benoit, 2009), Queen Elizabeth (Benoit & Brinson, 1999), and China and SARS (Zhang & Benoit, 2009). Political image repair is another topic of interest, with research focusing on President George W. Bush (Benoit, 2006a, 2006b; Benoit & Henson, 2009), President Reagan (Benoit, Gullifor, & Panici, 1991), Clarence Thomas (Benoit & Nill, 1998b), and President Bill Clinton (Blaney & Benoit, 2001) (for a more detailed review of these topics, see Benoit, 2014).

Critical Analysis of Shinseki's Image Repair Discourse

Shinseki (2014) utilized four image repair strategies: bolstering, mortification, corrective action, and shift blame. Each strategy will be discussed and illustrated in this section.

Bolstering

The Secretary spent the first and longest portion of his speech enacting the strategy of bolstering. He observed that:

> The past few weeks have been challenging for everyone at VA—because we take caring for Veterans so seriously. We have done tremendous work together these past five years, and I wanted to acknowledge the hard work and very real accomplishments of all of the good people in this room. (Shinseki, 2014)

He talked about reducing homelessness among veterans, improving outreach for veterans released from prison, and helping reduce prescription drug abuse among veterans. Bolstering gives positive information to try to improve image. These actions are praiseworthy accomplishments and could help with the damage to his image.

Mortification

After working to try to reinforce his (and the VA's) reputation, Shinseki turned to mortification:

> After Wednesday's release of an interim Inspector General report, we now know that VA has a systemic, totally unacceptable lack of integrity within some of our Veterans Health Administration

facilities. That breach of trust involved the tracking of patient wait times for appointments. The initial findings of our ongoing internal review of other large VA healthcare facilities also show that to be true. That breach of integrity is irresponsible, it is indefensible, and unacceptable to me. (Shinseki, 2014)

This is a clear instance of mortification. He explicitly stated that this "breach of integrity" was "irresponsible, indefensible, and unacceptable." He continued in this vein, saying:

Given the facts I now know, I apologize as the senior leader of the Department of Veterans Affairs. I extend that apology to the people whom I care about most deeply—the Veterans of this great country—and to their families and loved ones, whom I have been honored to serve for over five years now—the call of a lifetime. I also offer that apology to Members of Congress who have supported me, to Veterans Service Organizations, and to the American people. All of them deserve better from their VA. (Shinseki, 2014)

Mortification offers an apology and Shinseki explicitly apologized to multiple audiences (Congress, Veterans Service Organizations, the American people).

Shift Blame

However, Shinseki could not simply leave it here. He characterized himself as "too trusting" and described the reports he received as inaccurate:"

I said when this situation began that the problem was limited and isolated because I believed that. I no longer believe it. It is systemic. I was too trusting of some, and I accepted, as accurate, reports that I now know to have been misleading with regard to patient wait times. (Shinseki, 2014)

This statement, if accepted, suggests that true responsibility rests with his subordinates, who are the ones who deserve blame. His only fault is trusting others. Their lack of integrity, on the other hand, is "indefensible." As the Secretary, he said that he "can take responsibility for it, and I do," returning to the strategy of mortification.

Corrective Action

Shinseki also employed the strategy of corrective action, designed to help fix the problem:

"But I know this leadership and integrity problem can and must be fixed—now. So I am taking the following actions. I've initiated the process for the removal of the senior leaders at the Phoenix VA Medical Center. We will use all authority at our disposal to enforce accountability among senior leaders who are found to have instigated or tolerated dishonorable or irresponsible scheduling practices at VA healthcare facilities. I have also directed that no VHA senior executive will receive any type of performance award this year. I've directed that patient wait times be deleted from VHA employees' evaluation reports as a measure of their success. We are contacting each of the 1,700 Veterans in Phoenix waiting for appointments to bring them the care they need and deserve—and we will continue to accelerate access to care for Veterans nationwide who need it, utilizing care both in and outside the VA system." (Shinseki, 2014)

In addition to these changes at the VA intended to improve the problem, Shinseki also proposed other corrective action to be enacted by Congress:

> "I now ask Congress to support Senator Sanders' proposed bill giving VA's Secretary greater authority to remove senior leaders. I ask the support of Congress to fill existing VA leadership positions that are vacant." (Shinseki, 2014)

These are reforms that could help the problem, but they are not changes Shinseki had the authority to implement himself. Accordingly, he suggested that Congress initiate corrective action in addition to the changes he enacted. So, Shinseki ended his tenure with attempts to fix the scandal.

Evaluation

Shinseki did the right thing by resigning, enacting mortification, and ordering corrective action. Of course, after the Inspector General's report, he had little choice. President Harry S. Truman had a sign on his Oval Office desk that said "The Buck Stops Here." Shinseki may not have ordered the scandalous actions, but he was responsible for them. They happened on "his watch" as Secretary of Veterans Affairs. However, doing the right thing does not always improve one's image. Some might wonder if there was more he could have done to prevent and/or correct the problem long before the Inspector General's report was issued.

His use of bolstering and shifting the blame are a human thing to do. People do not like [simply] admitting that they have done the wrong thing. However, these defenses are not likely to have a substantial effect on his damaged image. Doing the right thing (mortification, corrective action) cannot guarantee to restore a damaged image. Perhaps his image will improve over time, but – even though he did the right thing – this scandal was serious and he was the one who was responsible for veterans' health care.

CONCLUSION

Suspicions swirled for years about problematic treatment of American veterans, particularly focusing on long wait times for health care. In May of 2014, concerns were confirmed in a report from the Inspector General's office. Veterans who were waiting for health care were kept on secret waiting lists (secret so statistics on veteran's care would appear better than they were) and 40 died while they were waiting for care. Eric Shinseki, the Secretary of Veterans Affairs, initially denied that there were problems. On May 30, 2014, Shinseki resigned his post. This chapter analyzed his resignation speech and its effect(s) on this scandal. His defense included four strategies: bolstering, mortification, corrective action, and shift blame. He did the right thing in deploying mortification and corrective action. Nevertheless, it will be a very long time before most people forgive him. As the head of Veterans Affairs, he was ultimately responsible for this scandal.

DISCUSSION QUESTIONS

1. Do you think Shinseki's use of mortification was appropriate?
2. Do you think Shinseki's use of corrective action was appropriate?
3. Does it make sense to use bolstering and/or shift blame with mortification? Why or Why not?
4. Do you think Shinseki should have used any of the image repair strategies he chose not to use? Why or why not?

REFERENCES

Benoit, W. L. (1995a). *Accounts, excuses, apologies: A theory of image restoration strategies.* Albany: State University of New York Press.

Benoit, W. L. (1995b). Sears' repair of its auto service image: Image restoration discourse in the corporate sector. *Communication Studies, 46,* 89–105.

Benoit, W. L. (1997). Hugh Grant's image restoration discourse: An actor apologizes. *Communication Quarterly, 45,* 251-267.

Benoit, W. L. (2006a). Image repair in President Bush's April 2004 news conference. *Public Relations Review, 32,* 137-143.

Benoit, W. L. (2006b). President Bush's image repair effort on *Meet the Press:* The complexities of defeasability. *Journal of Applied Communication Research, 34,* 285-306.

Benoit, W. L. (2013). Tiger Woods' image repair: Could he hit one out of the rough? In J. R. Blaney, L. R. Lippert, & J. S. Smith (Eds). *Repairing the athlete's image: Studies in sports image restoration* (pp. 89-96). Lanham, MD: Lexington Books: Rowman & Littlefield.

Benoit, W. L. (2014). *Accounts, excuses, apologies: Image repair theory and research* (2nd ed.). Albany: State University of New York Press.

Benoit, W. L., & Anderson, K. K. (1996). Blending politics and entertainment: Dan Quayle versus Murphy Brown. *Southern Communication Journal, 62,* 73-85.

Benoit, W. L., & Brinson, S. (1994). AT&T: Apologies are not enough. *Communication Quarterly, 42,* 75-88.

Benoit, W. L., & Brinson, S. L. (1999). Queen Elizabeth's image repair discourse: Insensitive royal or compassionate Queen? *Public Relations Review, 25,* 145-156.

Benoit, W. L., & Czerwinski, A. (1997). A critical analysis of USAir's image repair discourse. *Business Communication Quarterly, 60,* 38-57.

Benoit, W. L., Gullifor, P., & Panici, D. (1991). President Reagan's defensive discourse on the Iran-Contra affair. *Communication Studies, 42,* 272-294.

Benoit, W. L., & Hanczor, R. (1994). The Tonya Harding controversy: An analysis of image repair strategies. *Communication Quarterly, 42,* 416-433.

Benoit, W. L., & Henson, J. R. (2009). President Bush's image repair discourse on Hurricane Katrina. *Public Relations Review, 35,* 40-46.

Benoit, W. L., & Nill, D. M. (1998a). A critical analysis of Judge Clarence Thomas's statement before the Senate Judiciary Committee. *Communication Studies, 49,* 179-195.

Benoit, W. L., & Nill, D. M. (1998b). Oliver Stone's defense of *JFK. Communication Quarterly, 46,* 127-143.

Blaney, J. R., & Benoit, W. L. (2001). *The Clinton scandals and the politics of image restoration.* Westport, CT: Praeger.

Blaney, J. R., Benoit, W. L., & Brazeal, L. M. (2002). Blowout! Firestone's image restoration campaign. *Public Relations Research, 28,* 379-392.

Brazeal, L. M. (2008). The image repair strategies of Terrell Owens. *Public Relations Review, 34,* 145-150.

Brinson, S., & Benoit, W. L. (1996). Dow Corning's image repair strategies in the breast implant crisis. *Communication Quarterly, 44,* 29-41.

Brinson, S. L., & Benoit, W. L. (1999). The tarnished star: Restoring Texaco's damaged public image. *Management Communication Quarterly, 12,* 483-510.

Bronstein, S., & Griffin, D. (2014, April 23). A fatal wait: Veterans languish and die on a VA hospital's secret list. *CNN.* Accessed 6/11/14: http://www.cnn.com/2014/04/23/health/veterans-dying-health-care-delays/

CBS News. (2014, May 22). Who do Americans blame for the VA scandal? *CBS News.* Accessed 5/31/14: http://www.cbsnews.com/news/who-do-americans-blame-for-the-va-scandal/.

Coombs, W. T. (2012). *Ongoing crisis communication: Planning, managing, and responding,* 3rd ed. Los Angeles, CA: Sage.

Drumheller, K., & Benoit, W. L. (2004). USS *Greeneville* collides with Japan's *Ehime Maru:* Cultural issues in image repair discourse. *Public Relations Review, 30,* 177-185.

Fishbein, M., & Ajzen, I. (2010). *Predicting and changing behavior: The reasoned action approach.* New York: Psychology Press.

Glantz, M. (2009). The Floyd Landis doping scandal: Implications for image repair discourse. *Public Relations Review, 30,* 157-163.

Hearit, K. M. (2006). *Crisis management by apology: Corporate response to allegations of wrong-doing.* Mahwah, NJ: Lawrence Erlbaum.

Hicks, J. (2014, May 28). Inspector General's report confirms allegations at Phoenix VA hospital. *Washington Post.* Accessed http://www.washingtonpost.com/blogs/federal-eye/wp/2014/05/28/ig-report-confirms-allegations-at-phoenix-va-hospital/

Pomerantz, A. (1978). Attributions of responsibility: Blamings. *Sociology, 12,* 115-121.

Shinseki, E. K. (2014, May 30). Remarks by Secretary Eric K. Shinseki. U.S. Department of Veterans Affairs. Accessed 5/31/14: http://www.va.gov/opa/speeches/2014/05_30_2014.asp

Wen, J., Yu, J., & Benoit, W. L. (2009). Our hero can't be wrong: A case study of collectivist image repair in Taiwan. *Chinese Journal of Communication, 2,* 174-192.

Zhang, J., & Benoit, W. L. (2004). Message strategies of Saudi Arabia's image restoration campaign after 9/11. *Public Relations Review, 30,* 161-167.

Zhang, W., & Benoit, W. L. (2009). Former Minister Zhang's discourse on SARS: Government's image restoration or destruction *Public Relations Review, 35,* 240-246.

Chapter 4

Image Repair in a Chinese Brand Identity Crisis: Will the Real Herbal Tea Company Please Stand Up?

YING XIONG, M.A.
University of Tennessee

MAUREEN TAYLOR, PH.D.
University of Tennessee

MICHAEL L. KENT, PH.D.
University of Tennessee

Introduction

Crises are viewed as a threat to organizational reputation and brand (Coombs, 2007a; Jin & Cameron, 2007) and the consequences of crises can jeopardize a whole corporation (Pearson & Mitroff, 1993). Almost all crises emanate from triggering events and they often occur because organizations fail to engage in issue management (Jordan-Meier, 2011) or they ignore the warning signs of a crisis. For many corporations, crises have the potential to lead to near or actual bankruptcy (Mitroff, Shrivastava & Udwadia, 1987). While many scholars categorize crises as chronic or unexpected, Jordan-Meier (2011) claimed that 75% of all crises could be described as "smoldering," lurking in the background, and ready to ignite if conditions are right.

A smoldering crisis can be lit if crisis managers, the media, publics, or competitors ignite the right (or wrong) issue (Jordan-Meier, 2011, p. 6). Stakeholder respect for an organization is also at risk during a crisis (Coombs & Holladay, 2002). In crisis situations, passions run high and public perceptions of organizational responsibility are often greater than what the reality is. In some crisis cases, the public may attribute more blame to an organization than it deserves. The most vital thing involved in surviving a crisis is not whether an organization should shoulder the responsibility for the crisis, but whether the public thinks the organization is responsible for the crisis (Benoit, 1997).

This chapter explores an international crisis communication situation that took place in China in 2012, through the lens of Benoit's (1995) Image Repair Theory and Coombs' (1995, 2012a) Situational Crisis Communication Theory (SCCT). Image repair and SCCT are related theoretical approaches that identify different response strategies for organizations to use to communicate with publics during a crisis. Image repair (Benoit, 1995) initially identified 14 strategies for organizations to draw from when responding to a crisis. Later, SCCT aggregated Benoit's strategies into four different response options: deny, diminish, rebuild, and reinforce (Coombs, 2012b). The strategies are designed to guide organizational crisis communicators. In crisis situations, organizations select response options, or a combination of options, based on the crisis and situational conditions. Each of Coombs' four options creates different frames to explain crisis communication.

Most of the research on image repair and SCCT has focused on American organizations. There is scant research exploring how people in other nations respond to crises or how culture influences an organization's crisis response. To fill the gaps in the literature, this chapter explores the image repair crisis communication in a Chinese cultural context. The first part of the chapter provides an overview of image theory, crisis communication, and image repair, and the role that culture plays in crisis communication. Because of the international prominence of U.S. business and research, one often sees image repair applied by scholars to Western organizational contexts. However, little research has been conducted to explain how non-western organizations communicate with their audiences or how those audiences interpret and evaluate information about crises (Lee, 2004). The second part of the chapter illustrates image repair through a case study of a famous 2012 lawsuit between two Chinese herbal tea companies (JDB and Guangzhou Pharmaceutical Group) about the ownership of the trademark "Wong Lo Kat." The crisis case study, focused on a brand of tea, provides an opportunity to see how one Chinese organization (a) used image repair to explain its side of the crisis, (b) built its brand, and (c) positioned its new product in a crowded and uncertain marketplace. The third part of the chapter explores the interplay of crisis strategies and cultural background.

Image and Culture in Crisis Communication

Image repair and SCCT come from the same roots. Both theories spring from an article by Ware and Linkugel (1973) from the *Quarterly Journal of Speech* called "They Spoke in Defense of Themselves," an article about "apologia" or how to apologize. Ware and Linkugel were the first to identify apologia strategies and to propose that a genre of rhetoric existed to explain how individuals and organizations might justify their actions in the court of public opinion.

Organizational image and crisis repair have become dominant practices and research areas in the field of public relations because of the frequency with which they are needed/used. Organizations and leaders regularly make mistakes, misbehave, or experience accidents, both within and beyond their control. Image repair and crisis communication strategies give organizations the ability to confront the media and publicly deal with negative reactions from stakeholders and publics over mistakes, accidents, and misdeeds. Often, issue management is necessary for organizational success after a crisis.

Communicating With Publics During a Crisis

When crises happen, there are a variety of ways to deal with them. For example, if an organization experiences an industrial accident, it could attribute the cause to factors outside of its control. If an organization sells a defective product, it might recall the product and take a leadership role in ensuring future safety guidelines. When an organization downsizes, it often reports the decision in its quarterly statement as a way to lower costs and improve profits. Legal crises also create unique public relations needs for organizations. In cases of legal decisions, however, image repair campaigns might be one of the only resources available for organizations after a crisis.

Coombs (2007b) defined a crisis as "a significant threat to operations that might have negative consequences if not handled properly" (p. 1). Crises can be divided into different categories. Coombs claimed that the victim cluster, the accidental cluster, and the preventable cluster are the three distinct clusters of 13 types of crisis (Coombs, 2004). These three types of clusters have different levels of attributions (how people attribute blame) to account for the responsibility of crisis (Coombs, 2007a). Crisis communication refers to "managing the information and meaning in the whole process of crisis management" (Coombs & Holladay, 2012, p. 409). Early crisis communication research was sender-orientated, while lately a receiver/stakeholder perspective has emerged as an important trend in the crisis communication area (Coombs & Holladay, 2010; Coombs & Holladay, 2014). One line of research that has tackled crisis communication is Benoit's Image Repair Theory.

Image Repair

Heath (2006) notes that "crisis response is a narrative" (p. 247). Benoit's (1995) Theory of Image Repair, a comprehensive framework for understanding how organizations explain crises, provides one part of the organizational narrative in crisis. Benoit created Image Restoration Theory based on the work of Aristotle, Burke, Fisher, Goffman, and Ware and Linkugel. The Theory of Image Repair (Benoit's preferred term) is premised on two general assumptions. The first assumption is that communication is goal-oriented. The second assumption is that, as communicators, one central goal is maintaining a positive reputation. In light of these fundamental tenets, Benoit (1995) synthesized much of the previously mentioned scholarship into a typology consisting of five strategies for image restoration—denial, evading responsibility, reducing offensiveness, corrective action, and mortification—which have been broken down into 14 sub-strategies of interest for this study (see Table 4.1).

Table 4.1 Benoit's Image Repair Strategies

Denial (simple denial and shifting the blame)

Evading responsibility (provocation, defeasibility, accidents, and good intentions)

    Provocation occurs when the rhetor claims that the offensive act was performed in response to another wrongful act (and thus, more justifiable).

    Defeasibility can be employed by the rhetor to *plead a lack of information* about the issue at hand.

    Accidents: The third type of evasive strategy is accidents. Here, Benoit (1995) argues that the rhetor can blame *circumstances beyond his/her control.*

    Good Intentions describes a rhetor's attempt to insist that, although responsible, he/she only had the best intentions.

Reducing offensiveness (bolstering, minimization, transcendence, attacking accuser, and compensation.)

    Bolstering occurs when the accused attempts to reduce offensiveness by relating positive attributes he/she possesses, thereby reminding the accuser that the accused has performed positive actions in the past.

    Minimization describes a rhetorical strategy with which the accused can argue that the incident is *"not as bad as it looks,"* thereby minimizing offensiveness.

    Transcendence places the situation against other frames of reference. For example, a government official accused of wanting to raise taxes may defend his/her actions by insisting that the money is needed for elderly care.

    Attacking the accuser, the rhetor can create a number of new situations including a closer examination of the accuser's credibility, the perception that that the accused deserved what happened to him/her, or, at the very least, a deflection of attention away from the accused. Finally, Benoit (1995) defines **compensation** as attempts by the rhetor to remunerate (either financially or in some other way) the accuser in order to lessen the responsibility.

Corrective action to try to restore the situation to a previous state that existed before the incident and/or promise to "self-correct" and *prevent the incident* from ever occurring again.

Mortification describes an *apology* for the act.

Denial, according to Benoit (1995), is the strategy employed when the rhetor decides to deny the action(s) of which he/she is being accused. This strategy can manifest itself in various ways and Benoit (1995) lists two subcategories for denial: simple denial and shifting the blame. The second image restoration strategy proposed by Benoit is *evading responsibility.* Here, Benoit includes four subcategories (provocation, defeasibility, accidents, and good intentions). *Provocation* occurs when a communicator claims that the offensive act was performed in response to another wrongful act (and, thus, is more justifiable). *Defeasibility* can be employed by the rhetor to plead a lack of information about the issue at hand. The third type of evasive strategy is *accidents.* Here, Benoit (1995) argues that the rhetor can blame circumstances beyond his/her control. Finally, *good intentions* describes a rhetor's attempt to insist that, although responsible, he/she only had the best intentions.

The third strategy of *reducing offensiveness* occurs when the rhetor attempts to reduce the degree of offensiveness experienced by the accuser (Benoit, 1995). To this end, Benoit includes six subcategories (bolstering, minimization, differentiation, transcendence, attacking accuser, and compensation). *Bolstering* occurs when the accused attempts to remind the audience of the positive attributes s/he possesses, thereby reminding the accuser that the accused has performed positive actions in the past. *Minimization* describes an argument that the incident is "not as bad as it looks." *Differentiation* describes the rhetor's attempt to place the situation in the context of other, even less desirable, situations, thereby making the current act seem not so bad by comparison. *Transcendence* places the situation against other frames of reference to show how the organization is better than others. In the strategy of *attacking the accuser,* the rhetor calls for a closer examination of the accuser's credibility. Finally, Benoit (1995) defines *compensation* as when the rhetor provides remuneration (either financially or in some other way) to the victims.

The fourth image restoration strategy proposed by Benoit is *corrective action.* The accused can either try to restore the situation to a previous time before the incident and/or promise to "self-correct" and prevent the incident from ever occurring again. Although similar in tone to compensation, Benoit (1995) argues that the 13 corrective action strategies attempt to correct the situation, rather than counterbalance it (p. 79). The final image restoration strategy is *mortification.* Mortification describes an apology for the act. Here, the rhetor admits guilt and asks for forgiveness. Benoit (2006) notes that American politicians (and organizations) "faced with image repair problems offer speeches of *apologia*" (p. 291).

How do organizations experiencing crises communicate these 14 image repair tactics to their stakeholders? They use image repair strategies in official statements and news releases posted on their websites and distributed through wire services, social media, and other communication tools to tell their side of the story in the hopes that the media will use this information in their crisis coverage. During times of crisis, honest and candid responses are the most effective means of regaining the public's trust (Perry, Taylor, & Doerfel, 2003; Seeger, 2006). With regard to organizations and their publics, Benoit (1995, 2006) has noted that the nature of the image restoration response needs to be seen in the context of the nature of the attacks occurring. The next section explores how Coombs and others have built on the image repair strategy research.

Situational Crisis Communication Theory (SSCT)

The theory of Situational Crisis Communication (SCCT) is considered the dominant paradigm in crisis communication research (Avery et al., 2010; Kim, Avery & Lariscy, 2009). SCCT is an effective approach to evaluate the effects of different response strategies for crisis. In this theory, organizations normally have

Table 4.2 SCCT Response Strategies

Deny
     Criticizing accusers (Coombs, 2012b)
     Looking for scapegoats (Coombs, 2012b)
     Ignoring (Liu, 2010)

Diminish
     Excuse (Coombs, 2012b)
     Justification (Coombs, 2012b)
     Separation (Benoit & Brinson, 1999; Hearit, 2006)

Rebuild
     Compensation (Coombs, 2012b)
     Apology (Coombs, 2012b)
     Transcendence (Liu, 2010)

Reinforce
     Bolstering (Coombs, 2012b)
     Ingratiation (Coombs, 2012b)
     Victimization (Coombs, 2012b)
     Endorsement (Liu, 2010)

four different response options: deny, diminish, rebuild, and reinforce (Coombs, 2012b). Coombs' theory goes beyond Benoit's image repair by focusing on the public's perception of the strategies (see Table 4.2).

The *deny* option means that organizations utilize methods such as criticizing accusers, looking for scapegoats (Coombs, 2012), or ignoring the crisis (Liu, 2010) to avoid upsetting the stakeholders. Denial is an image restoration strategy, which either repudiates the censurer or transfers the blame to others (Benoit & Brinson, 1996). The *diminish* option can be further divided into three categories (excuse, justification, and separation) (Benoit & Brinson, 1996; Coombs, 2012b; Hearit, 2006). The response option of *rebuild* consists of measures of compensation, apology (Coombs, 2012b), and transcendence in order to gain an understanding of the public to re-establish the reputation. *Compensation* is an action where organizations use money, compensation, or other methods to compensate the victims (Holladay, 2010). *Apology* is a strategy where the organization acknowledges that they want to accept the full responsibility for the crisis (Holladay, 2010). *Transcendence* is an action in which organizations, in times of crisis, make efforts to lead the public away from the specifics of the crisis to consider larger goals in a broader view. Transcendence also contributes to creation of identification between the organization and its publics when they share the organization's values and larger goals (Coombs, 1995).

The *reinforce* option includes the approaches of bolstering, ingratiation, victimization, and endorsement (Coombs, 2012b; Liu, 2010). *Bolstering* is an approach to counteract negative messages and to enhance the audiences' positive perspective toward an organization in a crisis (Benoit & Brinson, 1994). *Ingratiation* is a way to praise stakeholders (Holladay, 2010). Together, Image Repair Theory and SCCT provide valuable frameworks to explain crisis response.

As noted previously, most of the image repair and SCCT research has focused on American or European organizations' response to crisis. While the U.S. research focus has been useful for gaining insight into crisis communication in general, in today's globalized society, China has become a major economic force, just recently passing the United States in purchasing power. Understanding other cultures and their relationship to the existing crisis literature is a natural next step. This chapter applies the image repair and SCCT frameworks to organizational crisis responses in Mainland China. To understand how image repair can be used in Chinese society, it is first necessary to describe how Chinese culture influences crisis response.

Contexts Influencing Chinese Crisis Responses

As Hofstede (1997) suggested, culture is the "software of the mind." Culture influences the psychological processes and consuming behaviors of publics across the world (Hofstede & Bond, 1984; Matsumoto & Yoo, 2006; Sriramesh, Kim & Takasaki, 1999). In cross-cultural research, scholars have identified several general dimensions of culture variability (e.g., individualism vs. collectivism) and this variability affects everything from interpersonal communication to organizational communication to marketing communication. Culture also influences identification with brands and organizations.

In the Chinese cultural research, four factors influence Chinese values (The Chinese Culture Connection, 1987): integration, Confucian work dynamism, human-heartedness, and moral discipline. The first cultural factor is *integration*. In Chinese culture, integration is regarded as a group-orientation, along with close family ties, and respect for seniority (Liu, 2011). Integration emphasizes 11 values that include harmony with others, non-competitiveness, and trustworthiness. The integration tradition mirrors a kind of traditional Chinese pedagogy notion, emphasizing holistic integration, homeostasis, and collective good, rather than the emphasis on individualism found in the West (Lu, Gilmour, & Kao, 2001).

The second factor, *Confucian work dynamism*, focuses on having a "sense of shame," a "persistence," and reflects Confucian work ethics. Confucius believed that his pragmatic principles of behaviors were the root of social relationships: the basis of stability, peace, and prosperity of the nation, households, and individuals (Chen & Chung, 1994; Yao, 2000, p. 26). The Confucian ethos seeks to form a society that consists of a devoted, motivated, and well-educated population. Responsibility and commitment are also typical features for this Confucian society (Matthews, 2000).

The third factor is *human-heartedness*, which contains values such as patience and courtesy. The positive values focus on benevolence and compassion, whereas the negative values suggest a more severe, legalistic approach. Finally, Chinese culture is influenced by *moral discipline*, which includes "moderation" and "keeping few desires" (The Chinese Culture Connection, 1987, p. 150). Moral discipline refers to modesty, being aloof from pursuing politics and material desires, having fewer desires, adaptability, and deliberateness. The moral discipline dimension is reflected in one's personality and psychological pursuits.

Chinese values are considered to be collectivist-orientated, focusing on sharing, co-operation, and group harmony. These values directly affect and impact Chinese customers' purchasing behaviors (Yau, 1988; Zhang & Neelankavil, 1997). For instance, harmony refers to a person's inner peace balance and the attempts to make balance between individuals and the environment around them to attain social order (Hoare & Butcher, 2008; Pisapia & Lin, 2011). Chinese consumers are more loyal to brands than consumers in Western countries because they value the group's normative standards. They purchase "accepted" products because other members of a group recommend those products (Yau, 1988). In East Asian cultures, cultural values drive people to seek conformity with others. Uniqueness is more favored by European Americans because of their cultural value of individualism (Kim & Markus, 1999).

Another important Chinese value is a sense of *righteousness* (The Chinese Culture Connection, 1987; Wong, 2001; Yuan & Shen, 1998). This value calls on people to make judgments about the righteousness of others, including organizations. Righteousness then leads people to support and uphold righteous organizations and people, and show sympathy for the weak, who are often unfairly treated.

Chinese consumers are in favor of long-established brands rather than new entrants into the marketplace (Melewar, Meadows, Zheng & Rickards, 2004). Indeed, the orientation to the past is a strong Chinese value (Fan, 2000). The Chinese people prefer a brand with a long history. A brand that can tell anecdotal stories about its long-established history is valued above newer brands. There are, of course, many other Chinese cultural values, but integration, Confucian dynamism, human heartedness, moral discipline, righteousness, and preference for long term relationships are useful for understanding crisis communication in China.

Chinese Culture and Crisis Communication

In Chinese culture, conflict is to be avoided. Chinese organizations prefer to resort to non-confrontational communication styles in order to minimize conflicts in crises and, thereby, reduce communication costs. The notion of non-confrontation has its roots in the concept of "harmony" (Chen & Chung, 1994). For the Chinese people, avoiding a fight and keeping a peaceful environment are the preferred approaches to obtaining harmony. Additionally, in Chinese culture, collective goals are put ahead of personal goals and individuals and organizations try to present themselves as positively as possible to others. In a crisis, Chinese organizations seek to save both their "face" and the "face" of other groups, and achieve a harmonious environment in the crisis situation. "Face" is a traditional and often-cited Chinese value. Saving face is the act to protect one's own, or other people's, self-image (Chan, 2006; Goffman, 1955; Hu, 1944; Yu & Wen, 2003). Social "face" means the individual has obtained a position of honor in society (Chan, 2006). Not teasing or embarrassing other people, as is common in U.S. culture, may be regarded as an example of maintaining someone else's face (Ho, 1976). When Chinese organizations experience a crisis, the leaders of organizations normally try to maintain the "face" of both their company and that of their competitors.

Taking the "upper level line" is also a feature of Chinese organizations' approach to crisis communication. The "upper level line" refers to the reliance on government, by organizations, to solve crises and problems (Ye & Pang, 2011). In China, the government is regarded as one of the most important stakeholders of organizations (Taylor & Kent, 1999). Handling the "upper level line" properly will ultimately help Chinese organizations to get a beneficial position in the larger Chinese society, including gaining and maintaining access to powerful government officials.

Individuals in a Chinese society have a strong tendency to respect authority. For example, when experts or opinion leaders appear in advertisements to recommend products, research shows that those advertisements tend to be more effective (Yau, 1988). During a crisis, Chinese consumers often trust the views from individuals or groups with the most prestige. Therefore, some organizations bring in experts or famous external parties to speak on behalf of the organization in times of crisis (Ye & Pang, 2011).

All of these features of Chinese culture and crisis perceptions set the background necessary to examine a recent crisis that happened in China between two herbal tea companies. The remainder of the chapter focuses on the lawsuit between JDB and Guangzhou Pharmaceutical over the trademark "Wong Lo Kat" (pronounced "Wang Laoji" in Chinese). This case study will integrate more details about how modern Chinese corporations deal with crisis and will analyze the crisis using Benoit's (1995) and Coombs's (1995) crisis and image repair frameworks.

The Wong Lo Kat Case Study of Crisis Communication

Wong Lo Kat was chosen for this chapter because the case offers an opportunity to combine both American-based crisis theories and global cultural theories to understand a Chinese crisis context. The lawsuit between the Chinese herbal tea companies, JDB and Guangzhou Pharmaceutical, over ownership of the trademark "Wong Lo Kat" was well-known in China and would be on par with a company like Snapple or Lipton fighting to maintain the right to use its trademark name to sell its products.

Wong Lo Kat herbal tea was founded in the 19th century by Zebang Wang (Qian, 2014). In the early 19th century, a plague spread through his hometown and, in order to avoid the plague, Wang moved his wife and children to a nearby mountain. While on the mountain, Wang met a Taoist priest who gave him an herbal prescription that helped to cure his illness. Later, Zebang left the mountaintop, rejoined his village, and used the prescription he received to make tea. His tea formula helped his neighborhood and the legend says that many people were healed after they drank this special tea (Lan, 2012; Tencent, 2012). Today, the fame of Wong Lo Kat herbal tea is known across China.

The name for the tea came from Wang's nickname, "Lo Kat." Consequently, the villagers called the herbal tea Lo Kat's tea. Over time, Zebang Wang and his son continued to refine the recipe of the tea and eventually created their own herbal tea. In 1828, Zebang's family moved into Guangzhou city (outside of Hong Kong) to start a business selling herbal tea. The shop's name was, after Zebang's nickname, the Wong Lo Kat's herbal teashop. Many people believed that the tea contributed to good health. Additionally, the tea was good-tasting and, thus, became popular in Guangzhou (Qian, 2014).

Over the course of more than 100 years, Wong Lo Kat became a famous trademark in South China. The brand of Wong Lo Kat was developed by Zebang's children and further divided into two branches in the 1950's. One branch was moved to Hong Kong and remained in private ownership. The other one stayed in Mainland China and changed to collective ownership during the "buying-out policy" of the Chinese government in 1956. A buy-out policy occurs when the government purchases the full or partial ownership of a capitalist business to achieve nationalization (state ownership or control). After the shift in ownership, the Wong Lo Kat trademark became operational, with the name of "Wong Lo Kat Pharmaceutical Shop," later changing its name to "Yangcheng Pharmaceutical Shop" in 1982. In 1992, after a joint-stock transformation, "Yangcheng Pharmaceutical Shop" changed its name to Guangzhou Pharmaceutical Group (GPG), a company with little name recognition in China. The government is the dominant stockholder of GPG (Li, 2014). Guangzhou Pharmaceuticals Corporation is a pharmaceutical wholesaling and distribution company headquartered in Guangzhou, China. GPG is a joint venture between Walgreens Boots Alliance (American and Swiss-U.K. companies) and state-owned Guangzhou Pharmaceutical. Today, the Chinese government is a dominant stockholder of GPG (Li, 2014).

In March 1995, GPG leased the Wong Lo Kat name to JDB, a private company. The lease agreement allowed JDB to operate the Wong Lo Kat herbal tea brand in mainland China for 20 years, selling their product in a distinctive red can with yellow packaging. JDB paid approximately $1 million each year to Guangzhou Pharmaceutical in royalties. The situation was even further complicated because Guangzhou Pharmaceutical continued to use the trademark of Wong Lo Kat to produce its own herbal tea, which it sold in green paper box packages. JDB officially gained a patent for their distinctive packing in 1997 (Feng, 2014).

The Wong Lo Kat brand, bolstered by its shiny red can that was easily recognized and widely available, emerged as a national brand in China (and, of course, red and yellow, the colors of the Chinese flag, are as meaningful in China as red, white, and blue are in the United States). The red-can Wong Lo Kat herbal tea (from JDB) was popular with Chinese consumers and its advertising slogan, "Afraid of suffering from excessive internal heat? Take the beverage of Wong Lo Kat," was well known (He, 2009; Li, 2012). In China, excessive internal heat is considered a health risk because it is believed to cause disease. In a society that believes that food and drink can affect health, JDB and the brand flourished. Wong Lo Kat herbal tea developed from a small brand in the South China area to a nationwide brand, and JDB emerged as a well-known and respected organization in China (Feng, 2014; Shi, 2011).

In 2008, the JDB Corporation donated the largest sum of money (16 million U.S. dollars or 100 million RMB) to the National Fundraising Party for disaster relief in China, to help areas destroyed in the Wenchuan earthquake (Shi, 2011). JDB's donation made the herbal tea brand even more famous, as individuals saw the familiar brand take on a philanthropic role that was, at the time, quite new in China (Li, 2013).

In 2011, the market share of the red-can Wong Lo Kat was even higher than that of Coca Cola in China, with sales reaching 16 billion RMB (2.6 billion U.S. dollars) (Zhong & Lin, 2011). The success of the red-can herbal tea led to a great boom of the Wong Lo Kat brand. The JDB red-can popularity also helped to boost the sales and popularity of the green-package teas still made and marketed by GPG. Data from the "China Time-Honored Brand Value Ranking List" ranks the Wong Lo Kat brand fifth in the nation and values the brand at more than 108 billion RMB (17.2 billion U.S. dollars) (Hong, 2011; Li, 2012).

The popularity of the "Wong Lo Kat" brand name prompted government-owned Guangzhou Pharmaceutical Group to announce that they would no longer extend the JDB lease on the trademark (He, 2015). JDB Corporation had only leased the name. However, during the time of the lease, the JDB Corporation had spent 17 years, and millions of dollars, to promote the brand of Wong Lo Kat (Feng, 2014). For JDB, it would not be easy to give up all of their efforts when the lease on the name expired (He, 2009).

Framing the Real "Wong Lo Kat"

In the months leading up to the expiration of the brand lease, each organization made a different argument about their right to the brand name, Wong Lo Kat. Guangzhou Pharmaceutical claimed that they had only *licensed* the name to JDB and that once the lease was over, it was their property again. JDB claimed that they had made the brand more valuable and that their company should be allowed to continue to lease the trademark. The case ended up in court.

On May 9, 2012, the China International Economic and Trade Arbitration Commission (CIETAC) enforced the lease agreement, paving the way for the Guangzhou Pharmaceutical Group to exclusively market their herbal tea product under the popular "Wong Lo Kat" name (Li, 2012). This was a victory for the GPG. It now held the trademark of the biggest herbal tea in China and gained immediate brand recognition and consumer loyalty.

Figure 4.1 Note: after the lawsuit, JDB's can is orange with red letters, and GPG's can retains the distinctive red with yellow letters. [credit line] Courtesy of Maureen Taylor.

After the GPG defeat, JDB's image as the top company in the herbal tea market was taken away. It no longer had a name that was recognized by almost a billion people. JDB quickly began an image repair strategy to explain the situation, build awareness of its brand of tea, and differentiate its products from the famous Wong Lo Kat brand. Although JDB could not use "Wong Lo Kat" as a brand name to sell their herbal tea products, they still owned the red-can brand identity.

Weick (1995) noted that crises are a normal part of organizational life and it is not the crisis that hurts the organization. Rather, it is the crisis response that can hurt the organization. Scholars know that organizations that are viewed as good community partners are often treated more favorably in a crisis by the media and the public. Organizations that have built up goodwill have more people who are aware of their products, policies, and values. But the question remains whether such goodwill would translate in a country like China, which values tradition and stability so highly.

JDB was the better-known company in the trademark dispute. It had spent a large amount of money on Wong Lo Kat brand's marketing and promotion (JDB, 2012). Additionally, JDB had positioned itself as a good corporate citizen in China. JDB had enacted philanthropic activities and donated money for disaster relief efforts. JDB, for example, had helped poor students pay their college expenses (Weng, 2015). As noted, JDB was highly visible in the earthquake relief efforts and their corporate actions helped the organization to obtain substantial media coverage. Conversely, the Guangzhou Pharmaceutical Group was almost unknown to the Chinese public, prior to the 2012 lawsuit. Guangzhou Pharmaceutical had no record of philanthropy, little name recognition, and was part of the Chinese government. The next section examines the crisis and image strategies used by JDB to explain its side of the story.

Organizational Responses to the Brand Crisis

Media coverage prompts many organizations to speak about their crisis. The media, of course, covered the court's decision. Wong Lo Kat was high profile news in a country new to capitalism and legal disputes. After the lawsuit, both JDB and the Guangzhou Pharmaceutical Group sought support from their customers to differentiate their products and rebuild their reputation after the negative publicity of the lawsuit. On May 28, 2012, JDB rolled out their new herbal tea products using the same distinctive red can and yellow text packaging (Fan, 2012). The only difference was the new cans now sported the JDB trademark. JDB's "red-can" sat on the store shelves next to the other Wong Lo Kat cans.

The challenge for JDB was to convince customers that their new brand still contained the same trusted product. After the crisis, JDB engaged in crisis and image repair communication through a variety of channels and tactics, which included efforts to diminish, rebuild, and reinforce. In their official statements after the lawsuit in May 2012, JDB used its official website, news releases, and social media platforms to announce their response to the CIETAC decision. From May to August 2012, JDB published more than 10 statements articulating their opinions and reactions to the chain of events after the legal decision. As Benoit (1995) and Coombs (1995) have noted, organizations often use an assortment of crisis and image repair strategies. In the case of JDB, they had actually done nothing wrong, except being too successful at promoting their products, causing Guangzhou Pharmaceutical to refuse to extend their lease. JDB's crisis was reputational, but not of the variety that has been studied by scholars in the past.

Initially, JDB engaged in *diminishing* strategies. As mentioned previously, Coombs' image repair strategy of diminishing response can be further divided into three categories (excuse, justification, and separation) (Coombs, 20012; Hearit, 2006). Justification is a strategy that explains the attributes of the crisis to its stakeholders and customers, while the separation strategy, on the other hand, seeks to reduce the organization's responsibility for the crisis. JDB explained in one of its earliest official statements released in May that during 17 years of working together, JDB gave money and human resources to Wong Lo Kat and that they would continue to work in the future under the JDB name.

One does see Coombs' strategies at work in the May 16 message. JBD justified its actions (they were forced to change, but will remain loyal to their beliefs) and tried to separate its tea from GPG.

The *rebuilding* strategy involves several possibilities, including (a) compensation, where consumers and stakeholders impacted by an organization's misdeeds are offered a reward or incentive (Coombs, 2012b), (b) an apology, whereby an organization volunteers to accept the full responsibility for a crisis (Holladay, 2010), and (c) transcendence, where an organization in crisis tries to lead the public to consider larger goals and a broader view. Again, as noted above, the JDB crisis was not one of their doing and posed no harm to the public. Thus, the *rebuilding* strategy of JDB did not involve compensation or an apology, but used transcendence to reassure their customers that their products would still be available and that they would work to rebuild their damaged relationships with consumers.

The *reinforcement* strategy includes the approaches of bolstering, ingratiation, victimization, and endorsement (Coombs, 2012b; Liu, 2010). All of the reinforcement strategies have some potential for working to mitigate the crisis. Victimization, for example, which might involve JDB positioning itself as being harmed by the legal decision, and bolstering, an approach to counteract the negative affect and to enhance the audiences' positive perspective toward the corporations in crisis (Benoit & Brinson, 1994), both have the potential to help. Additionally, ingratiation praises stakeholders (Holladay, 2010) and encourages them to continue to provide support to JDB. As noted twice in May, they said that even though their efforts did not prevail, JDB would continue to build a responsible company and they thanked the supporters of their efforts.

In dealing with the crisis, JDB communicated via the mainstream media, advertising opportunities, and social and other free media. Potential crisis responses, and the success of particular crisis responses, are always contingent upon the audience one is communicating with. In China and other "high context" Confucian nations, crises often involve communication to or with government officials (Taylor & Kent, 1999). However, in the case examined here, mitigation of the crisis was actually more of a cultural issue than a political or governmental one. JDB needed to convince consumers that their product was the same, despite the fact that it would carry a new name.

Social Media Allow JDB to Say "I'm Sorry"

Crisis responses, today, involve more than traditional media relations. Social media play an important role and the nature of the channel influences the messages. Part of the JDB strategy involved trying to reach out to consumers directly via social media. At the beginning of 2013, using Weibo, one of the most popular Chinese social media outlets (with 10 million members), JDB employed its "I'm sorry" slogan, a series of messages that included pictures of an infant sobbing and sarcastic message copy with messages like "I am sorry. We are good at selling herbal tea, but bad at engaging in a lawsuit" (Luo, 2013, p. 3; Tu & Liu, 2013, p. 2). Another message pointed to the fact that JDB was not a government company like GPG: "I am sorry. We are from the grass roots and we have the private enterprise gene" (Luo, 2013, p. 4). Other statements pointed to the company's hard work to build the brand: "I am sorry. We are not smart. We used the last seventeen years to make a Chinese herbal tea that has become the only beverage that shares the similar market share as Coca Cola in China" (Hu, 2013, p. 2; Luo, 2013, p. 1; Tu & Liu, 2013, p. 2). These sobbing infant pictures were very striking on social media (Lin, 2014), and more than 170,000 people forwarded the pictures (Zhao, 2013).

One of the strengths of social media is the ability of messages to take on a life of their own, or "go viral" in social media parlance. Immediately following JDB's "I'm sorry" messages, memes (imitations or parodies) started emerging, created by fans of the brand. The meme theme was called "That's all right" and featured a cluster of laughing infant pictures with messages like "That's all right" adding even more humor and sarcasm to the legal decision.

The situation between these two rival companies was tense. In comments via social media, many people expressed sympathy to JDB and pointed out that the focus of this dispute was the fight between a government-owned corporation and a private enterprise. Some netizens argued that the failure of JDB to win the lawsuit might be because it was a private enterprise in a country that still favored state-owned industries (Zhao, 2013).

As is often the case, memes are short-lived, but high impact. "I'm sorry" and "That's all right" became popular phrases in China in early 2013. But they were ultimately short-lived. In terms of its crisis strategies, JDB used ingratiation and victimization as strategies for building identification and support. JDB played a victim's role as a strategy to rebuild its image.

Advertising Responses

Along with the social media messages that went out directly to supporters and bloggers, JDB also employed an assortment of advertising strategies to make consumers aware of their legal issue and, it hoped, retain customers. The advertising messages sought to rebuild and reinforce the brand. Transcendence and bolstering were built into their messages, as well as some image repair strategies like minimization and corrective action.

During the time leading up to the lawsuit, JDB advertised extensively, hoping to show that it was *the* herbal tea company. In the summer of 2012, JDB spent 60-million Yuan (about 9.6 million U.S. dollars) to get title sponsorship of the most popular Chinese TV talent show, *The Voice of China* (Chen, 2012). Their advertising slogan, "Authentic herbal tea, authentic excellent voice," was broadcast across China and the Internet, accompanied by popular singers and compelling melodies. JDB used an assortment of other advertising slogans in their television advertising, including "the red-can herbal tea with top sales volume nationwide has changed its name to JDB" and "Seven of every ten cans of herbal tea sold across China are sold by JDB" (Wang, 2015; Zhu, 2014).

Although JDB's slogans brought immediate public recognition of JDB's new brand, it also led to dissatisfaction from their rival, Guangzhou Pharmaceutical. From Guangzhou Pharmaceutical's perspective, JDB's slogans were deceptive, since they did not own the best-selling brand (they actually had almost no market share yet). Guangzhou Pharmaceutical claimed that the ads were unfair to their company and launched another lawsuit against JDB. Finally, because of unfair competition and misleading propaganda, JDB lost the lawsuit over its advertising slogans and could no longer use the slogans "the red-can herbal tea with top sales" or "seven of every ten cans of herbal tea" (Zheng, 2013; Zhu, 2014).

Discussion

Following the initial lawsuit between the two companies, JDB used multiple image repair and crisis communication strategies to try to persuade their customers to remain loyal to their drink, rather than the brand. What is useful to remember in this crisis case study is that image repair strategies used by JDB took place in a Chinese cultural and political context. The sobbing infant pictures used in social media and the

"I'm sorry" phrase are a reflection of what is acceptable in Chinese youth culture. It is not likely that this campaign would be influential in another culture. Indeed, in the United States, the mention of "I'm sorry" conjures up fear of a lawsuit.

When considering crisis in a cross-cultural context, one can probably assume that the strategies advanced by Benoit (1995) and Coombs (1995) have universal appeal: they describe *potential* rhetorical practices. But how and when they are enacted are, as this case study points out, culturally influenced. For example, one important cultural practice that is strikingly absent from the Wong Lo Kat case is any sense of face maintenance. JDB mocked the Guangzhou Pharmaceutical Group. As noted previously, the use of the legal system to settle corporate disputes has traditionally been a Western phenomenon. Perhaps the use of it here made it impossible for the companies to maintain respect for each other. Or perhaps the amount of money on the line—a billion potential customers and tens of millions of dollars in profits—influenced the communication strategies selected.

Another possibility, of course, it that current image repair and crisis communication theories are simply not equipped to deal with international settings. Any company that allowed a competitor to take its "bread and butter" product, and did nothing to save face, would soon find itself out of the marketplace. Ultimately, some cultural beliefs and practices are likely to be abandoned as organizations increasingly adopt Western business practices. However, how much culture and crisis interact is still unclear. Confucianist values suggest that both companies should have sought to avoid conflict and clash. The owner of the patent could easily have asked for an assortment of concessions, such as a higher royalty payment each year, or simply marketed their own products to match those of JDB's: riding on their coattails, spending no money on advertising themselves, and being able to reap the reward of the brand identity and awareness.

The approach adopted by JDB played to its customers' value of righteousness (The Chinese Culture Connection, 1987; Wong, 2001; Yuan & Shen, 1998), which calls on people to make judgments about the righteousness of others. But the same behavior might be manifested in the West, as support for the underdog. Indeed, the underdog narrative plot goes back centuries, as does righteousness in Chinese culture. The organization's crisis communication strategies, in an effort to activate the sense of righteousness and increase compassion, can easily draw upon rebuilding and reinforcement clusters in Coombs' (1995) SCCT, as well as Benoit's (1995) corrective action and mortification. These strategies may allow the public to believe that JDB has been treated unfairly.

A final issue to consider is how the Chinese preference for tradition and longevity actually impacts buying decisions and brand loyalty. In the case of "Wong Lo Kat" examined here, neither Guangzhou Pharmaceutical, nor JDB, actually possessed a legitimate claim to the elixir developed by Zebang Wang two centuries earlier. The Communist government took over Wong Lo Kat's herbal tea shop and gave the patent to a state-owned company: Guangzhou Pharmaceutical. JDB, a private company made possible by the opening of the Chinese economy in the 1980's, simply leased the name from a corporation that owned it. The agreement can be understood much like renting a culturally relevant domain name from someone on the Internet. Once the lease expired, the name went back to Guangzhou Pharmaceutical, but the essence of the product was never actually theirs, and the cultural baggage associated with the name existed independently of either company. Since Chinese customers are inclined to buy brands with long histories, the reestablishment of JDB's brand faces many obstacles that would be largely insignificant in another nation.

Chinese customers still show more faith in the brand of "Wong Lo Kat" than the manufacturer of the actual product that they purchased. JDB's crisis strategies revolved around reinforcement and rebuilding, and have tried to explain to the public their contributions in promoting herbal tea culture and their long history with this product. But in the end, many will undoubtedly stick with the "brand" rather than the product. The collectivist, group-oriented conformity is an engrained feature of Chinese culture. Once a brand is favored by a large group of people, the popularity becomes self-reinforcing, as customers feel comfortable with popular brands. Hence, JDB's strategy after the trademark crisis, that of reinforcing their place among the collective, reflects a kind of conformity and group psychology (seven out of every ten cans of herbal tea were sold by JDB) in promoting their new brand.

CONCLUSION

The "Wong Lo Kat" case is an interesting one from crisis communication and cultural perspectives. This combination of cultural values sensitivity and crisis and image repair points to an area of research that is still relatively new and is still relatively unexplored: how culture and Western theories of crisis, image repair, issue management, and even public relations interact.

In practice, scholars often accept that theories developed within one culture are universal and applicable within all others, but this chapter raises some red flags about the simplicity of such an assumption. Ultimately, one might argue that strategies and tactics are simply rhetorical and, therefore, universal: that denying, reinforcing, rebuilding, evasion, mortification, and other strategies can be employed anywhere. And, indeed, as the Wong Lo Kat case illustrates, business and legal practices might be more universal than previously considered. But in terms of the "right way" to engage in crisis communication activities, communicators are advised to know the values and intricacies of the culture they are responding to (Taylor, 2000), as well as the universe of potential crisis strategies. This case clearly shows that culture plays a role in crisis messaging. What should also be clear is that U.S. and other Western crisis managers should pay a bit more attention to culture, rhetoric, and persuasion when constructing their own messages. Strategies employed without a consideration of culture and context will have considerably less impact than crisis strategies informed by a holistic situation and audience analysis.

The Wong Lo Kat situation continues to evolve as two cans with identical packaging sit next to each other on shelves all across China. In December 2014, a court in Beijing ordered JDB to pay 150 million yuan (about 23 million U.S. dollars) to the Guangzhou Pharmaceutical Group over their continued use of the name "Wong Lo Kat" and the use of the red can in their marketing efforts. JDB said the decision "showed gross disregard of facts and the fair play principle as well as the integrity of the judicial system" (Jing, 2014, p.3). The fight between the companies will continue and there is no doubt that new image repair strategies will be used as JDB fights for the brand that it brought to widespread fame and favor.

DISCUSSION QUESTIONS

1. Based on what you have learned from this chapter, what are the main strategies in the image repair theory?
2. Based on what you have learned from this chapter, what are the main strategies in situational crisis communication theory for organizations in crises?
3. Explain three cultural factors that impact Chinese values. How are these similar or different than American cultural values?
4. How do Chinese values influence public relations practitioners' plans when crises happen in China?
5. How do you think JDB's "I'm sorry" messages in social media? When you use social media in your daily life, have you seen an organization that applies a similar strategy? Was it effective? Why or why not?
6. If you are hired as a counselor for JDB Corporation, which strategies will you apply to react to the crisis?

REFERENCES

Avery, E. J., Lariscy, R. W., Kim, S., & Hocke, T. (2010). A quantitative review of crisis communication research in public relations from 1991 to 2009. *Public Relations Review, 36*, 190–192.

Benoit, W. L. (1995). *Accounts, excuses, and apologies: A theory of image restoration strategies.* Albany, NY: State University of New York.

Benoit, W. L. (1997). Image repair discourse and crisis communication. *Public Relations Review. 23*, 177–186.

Benoit, W. L. (2006). President Bush's image repair effort on meet the press: The complexities of defeasibility. *Journal of Applied Communication Research, 34*(3), 285–306.

Benoit, W. L., & Brinson, S. L. (1994). AT&T: "Apologies are not enough." *Communication Quarterly, 42*, 75–88.

Brinson, S. L., & Benoit, W. L. (1996). Dow Corning's image repair strategies in the breast implant crisis. *Communication Quarterly, 44*, 29–41.

Chan, K. L. (2006). The Chinese concept of face and violence against women. *International Social Work, 49*, 65–73ff.

Chen, G. M., & Chung, J. (1994). The impact of Confucianism on organizational communication. *Communication Quarterly, 42*, 93–105.

Chen, Q. (2012, November 3). Voice of China's title sponsorship increased more than double; JDB obtained title sponsorship with two hundred million. *The Xinhua Net.* Retrieved from http://news.xinhuanet.com/fortune/2012-11/03/c_113592853.htm

Coombs, W. T. (1995). Choosing the right words: The development of guidelines for the selection of the "Appropriate" crisis-response strategies. *Management Communication Quarterly, 8*, 447–476.

Coombs, W. T. (2004). Impact of past crises on current crisis communication: Insights from Situational Crisis Communication Theory. *Journal of Business Communication, 41*, 265–289.

Coombs, W. T. (2007a). Protecting organization reputations during a crisis: The development and application of situational crisis communication theory. *Corporate Reputation Review, 10*, 163–176.

Coombs, W. T. (2007b, 2011, January 6). Crisis management and communications. *Institute for Public Relations, 10*, 1–17. <www.instituteforpr.org/crisis-management-and-communications>

Coombs, W. T. (2012a), *Ongoing crisis communication: planning, managing, and responding, third edition.* Thousand Oaks, CA: Sage Publications.

Coombs, W. T. (2012b), Protecting organization reputations during a crisis: The development and application of situational crisis communication theory. *Corporate Reputation Review, 10*, 163–176.

Coombs, W. T., & Holladay, S. J. (2002). Helping crisis managers protect reputational assets: Initial tests of the situational crisis communication theory. *Management Communication Quarterly, 16*, 165–186.

Coombs, W. T., & Holladay, S. J. (2010). Amazon.com's Orwellian nightmare: Exploring apology in an online environment. *Journal of Communication Management, 16*, 280–295.

Coombs, W. T., & Holladay, J. S. (2012). The paracrisis: The challenges created by publicly managing crisis prevention. *Public Relations Review, 38*, 408–415.

Fan, C. (2012, September 4). Wong Lo Kat's red can packaging raises another war. *The Legal Daily Online.* Retrieved from http://epaper.legaldaily.com.cn/fzrb/content/20120904/Articel04002GN.htm

Fan, Y. (2000). A classification of Chinese culture. *Cross Cultural Management: An International Journal, 7*, 3–10.

Feng, L. (2014). *Study about commercial packages' legal protection: Case of Wong Lo Kat and JDB's Lawsuit* (Master's thesis). Retrieved from http://d.wanfangdata.com.cn/Thesis/Y2532199

Goffman, E. (1955). On face-work: An analysis of ritual elements in social interaction. *Psychiatry: Interpersonal and Biological Processes, 18*, 213–231.

He, F. (2015). The war between Wong Lo Kat and JDB: Who will be the winner of this lawsuit? *China Economic Weekly*, (26). Retrieved from http://d.wanfangdata.com.cn/Periodical/zgjjzk201526019

He, M. (2009). The development of Wong Lo Kat. *Cases Of Marketing*, 12, 12-24. Retrieved from http://www.cqvip.com/QK/87383X/200912/32506118.html

Hearit, K. M. (2006). *Crisis management by apology: Corporate response to allegations of wrongdoing.* Mahwah, NJ: Erlbaum.

Heath, R. (2006). Best practices in crisis communication: Evolution of practice through research. *Journal of Applied Communication Research, 34*, 245-248.

Ho, D.Y. (1976). On the concept of face. *American journal of sociology, 81*, 867–884.

Hoare, R. J., & Butcher, K. (2008). Do Chinese cultural values affect customer satisfaction/loyalty? *International Journal of Contemporary Hospitality Management, 20,* 156–171.

Hofstede, G. (1997). *Cultures and organizations: Software of the mind, intercultural cooperation and its importance for survival.* London: McGraw Hill.

Hofstede, G., & Bond, M. H. (1984). Hofstede's culture dimensions: An independent validation using Rokeach's Value Survey. *Journal of Cross-cultural Psychology, 15,* 417–433.

Holladay, S. J. (2010). Are they practicing what we are preaching? An investigation of crisis communication strategies in the media coverage of chemical accidents. In W. T. Coombs, & S. J. Holladay (Eds.), *The handbook of crisis communication* (pp. 159–180). New York: Wiley-Blackwell.

Hong, B. (2011). Neither Guangzhou Pharmaceutical Group nor JDB can afford to lose the war. *The Guangzhou Daily Online.* Retrieved from http://gzdaily.dayoo.com/html/2011-12/26/content_1570174.htm

Hu, H. C. (1944). The Chinese concepts of "face." *American anthropologist, 46*(1), 45–64.

Hu, X. (2013, February 6). JDB posted "I am sorry" in Weibo to gain sympathy. *The Beijing Times.* Retrieved from http://epaper.jinghua.cn/html/2013-02/06/content_1967658.htm

Jin, Y., & Cameron, G. T. (2007), The effects of threat type and duration on public relations practitioner's cognitive, affective, and cognitive responses to crisis situations. *Journal of Public Relations Research, 19,* 255–281.

Jing, W. (2014). Herbal tea maker ordered to pay 150 mln yuan over trademark row: Guangdong court tells JDB Group to pay Guangzhou Pharmaceutical Group over dispute involving popular drink in red can. http://english.caixin.com/2014-12-22/100766695.html

JDB. (2012). Official announcement. *The JDB official website.* Retrieved from http://www.jdb.cn/2013/news/news-detail.aspx?newsid=b7432ff4-c873-4b3e-8c27abf81436adac&currentTab=%E5%85%AC%E5%8F%B8%E5%A3%B0%E6%98%8E

Jordan-Meier, J. (2011). *The four stages of highly effective crisis management: How to manage the media in the digital age.* Boca Raton, FL: CRC press.

Kim, H., & Markus, H. R. (1999). Deviance or uniqueness, harmony or conformity? A cultural analysis. *Journal of Personality and Social Psychology, 77*(4), 785–800.

Kim, S., Avery, E. J., & Lariscy, R. W. (2009). Are crisis communicators practicing what we preach? An evaluation of crisis response strategy analyzed in public relations research from 1991 to 2009. *Public Relations Review, 35,* 446–448.

Lan, J. (2012). Brand story of Wong Lo Kat. *Advertiser, 7,* 32. Retrieved from http://d.wanfangdata.com.cn/Periodical/ggzscgc201207017

Lee, B. K. (2004). Audience-oriented approach to crisis communication: A study of Hong Kong consumers' evaluation of an organizational crisis. *Communication Research, 31,* 600–618.

Li, H. (2013). *The study on continuous brand communication strategy of herbal tea: From Wong Lo Kat to JDB* (Master dissertation). Retrieved from http://d.wanfangdata.com.cn/Thesis/D350350

Li, J. (2014). *Wong Lo Kat and JDB's "Chinese style divorce": Research about brand recognition shift* (Master's thesis). Retrieved from http://www.docin.com/p-1049130380.html

Li, S. (2012). First impression effect and brand rebuild: JDB's integrated marketing case. *News World, 10,* 109-110. Retrieved from http://www.cnki.com.cn/Article/CJFDTOTAL-PXWS201210061.htm

Lin, C. (2014, March 22). Can JDB become the Coco-Cola in China? Retrieved from http://finance.sina.com.cn/zl/international/20140322/094518583745.shtml

Liu, B. F. (2010). Effective public relations in racially charged crises: Not black or white. In W. T. Coombs, & S. J. Holladay (Eds.), *Handbook of crisis communication* (pp. 335–358). NY, New York: Wiley-Blackwell.

Liu, S. (2011). Acting Australian and being Chinese: Integration of ethnic Chinese business people. *International Journal of Intercultural Relations, 35*(4), 406–415.

Lu, L., Gilmour, R., & Kao, S. F. (2001). Cultural values and happiness: An East-West dialogue. *The Journal of Social Psychology, 141*(4), 477–493.

Luo, D. (2013, February 5). JDB released "I am sorry" advertising; It is said Wong Lo Kat replied with "that's all right". *The People's Daily Online*. Retrieved from http://ip.people.com.cn/n/2013/0205/c136655-20436832.html

Matsumoto, D., & Yoo, S. H. (2006). Toward a new generation of cross-cultural research. *Perspectives on Psychological Science, 1*(3), 234–250.

Matthews, B. M. (2000). The Chinese value survey: An interpretation of value scales and consideration of some preliminary results. *International Education Journal, 1*(2), 117–126.

Melewar, T. C., Meadows, M., Zheng, W., & Rickards, R. (2004). The influence of culture on brand building in the Chinese market: A brief insight. *The Journal of Brand Management, 11*(6), 449–461.

Mitroff, I. I., Shrivastava, P., & Udwadia, F. E. (1987). Effective crisis management. *The Academy of Management Executive, 1*(4), 283–292.

Pearson, C. M., & Mitroff, I. I. (1993). From crisis prone to crisis prepared: A framework for crisis management. *Academy of Management Executive, 7*(1), 48–59.

Perry, D. C., Taylor, M., & Doerfel, M. L. (2003). Internet–based communication in crisis management. *Management Communication Quarterly, 17*(2), 206–232.

Pisapia, J. R., & Lin, Y. (2011). Values and actions: An exploratory study of school principals in the mainland of China. *Frontiers of Education in China, 6*(3), 361–387.

Qian, C. (2014). Issues about herbal tea brand Wong Lo Kat. *Global Public Relations, 2*, 82-83. Retrieved from http://www.cnki.com.cn/Article/CJFDTotal-GGGJ201402042.htm

Seeger, M. W. (2006). Best practices in crisis communication: An expert panel process. *Journal of Applied Communication Research, 36*, 232-244.

Shi, L. (2011). *Study of Wong Lo Kat's brand development* (Master dissertation). Retrieved from http://d.wanfangdata.com.cn/Thesis/Y1931808

Sriramesh, K., Kim, Y., & Takasaki, M. (1999). Public relations in three Asian cultures: An analysis. *Journal of Public Relations Research, 11*, 271–292.

Taylor, M. (2000). Cultural variance as a challenge to global public relations: A case study of the Coca-Cola scare in Europe. *Public Relations Review, 26*(3), 277–293.

Taylor, M., & Kent, M. L. (1999). Challenging assumptions of international public relations: When government is the most important public. *Public Relations Review, 25*(2), 131–144.

Tencent. (2012, August 6). Wong Lo Kat's long history: How many Wong Lo Kats exist? Retrieved from http://gd.qq.com/a/20120806/000647.htm

The Chinese Culture Connection (1987). Chinese values and the search for culture-free dimensions of culture. *Journal of Cross-cultural Psychology, 18*(2), 143–164.

Tu, R., & Liu, J. (2013, February 6). JDB: I am sorry! Wong Lo Kat: That's all right? *The Guangzhou Daily Online*. Retrieved from http://gzdaily.dayoo.com/html/2013-02/06/content_2148571.htm

Wang, X. (2015, June 2). Wong Lo Kat prosecuted JDB's slogan of "Seven of every ten cans of herbal tea sold across China are sold by JDB". *The Sina Finance*. Retrieved from http://finance.sina.com.cn/chanjing/gsnews/20150602/164122328600.shtml

Ware, B. L., & Linkugel. W. A. (1973). They spoke in defense of themselves: On the generic criticism of apologia. *Quarterly Journal of Speech, 59*(3), 273–283.

Weng, S. (2015, August 4). JDB has been financing impoverished students for fifteen years. *The China Youth Daily*. Retrieved from http://zqb.cyol.com/html/2015-08/04/nw.D110000zgqnb_20150804_2-08.htm

Weick, K. (1995). *Sense making in organizations*. Thousand Oaks, CA: Sage.

Wong, K. C. (2001). Chinese culture and leadership. *International Journal of Leadership in Education, 4*(4), 309–319.

Yao, X. (2000). *An introduction to Confucianism*. Cambridge: Cambridge University Press.

Yau, O. H. (1988). Chinese cultural values: Their dimensions and marketing implications. *European Journal of Marketing, 22*(5), 44–57.

Ye, L., & Pang, A. (2011). Examining the Chinese approach to crisis management: Cover-ups, saving face, and taking the "Upper Level Line." *Journal of Marketing Channels, 18*, 247–278.

Yu, T. H., & Wen, W. C. (2003). Crisis communication in Chinese culture: A case study in Taiwan. *Asian Journal of Communication, 13*, 50–64.

Yuan, B. J., & Shen, J. (1998). Moral values held by early adolescents in Taiwan and Mainland China. *Journal of Moral Education, 27*(2), 191–207.

Zhang, Y., & Neelankavil, J. P. (1997). The influence of culture on advertising effectiveness in China and the USA: A cross-cultural study. *European Journal of Marketing, 31*(2), 134–149.

Zhao, B. (2013). "I am sorry" PK "That's all right," Wong Lo Kat and JDB's fighting in Weibo. *People's Daily Online.* <http://shipin.people.com.cn/n/2013/0207/c85914-20458352.html>.

Zheng, X. (2013, August 7). Slogan of "Seven of every ten cans of herbal tea sold across China are sold by JDB" resulted in disputes. *The Shenzhen Evening News.* Retrieved from http://wb.sznews.com/html/2013-08/07/content_2579752.htm

Zhong, K. & Lin, X. (2012, May 4). JDB may reduce sale goal to 9 billion. The sale volume of last year was 16 billion. *The China Business News.* Retrieved from http://money.163.com/12/0504/01/80KHI6VC00253B0H.html

Zhu, W. (2014, August 7). Slogan of "Seven of every ten cans of herbal tea sold across China are sold by JDB" was abolished. *The Xinhua Daily Telegraph.* Retrieved from http://news.xinhuanet.com/mrdx/2014-08/07/c_133538178.htm

Chapter 5

Informational and Affective Needs: Considering Media Dependency Theory in the Context of Twitter and Natural Disasters

Kenneth A. Lachlan, Ph.D.
University of Connecticut

Introduction

In a relatively short period of time, social media has emerged as a critical resource in the ways in which people make sense of the world around them. Platforms like Twitter and Facebook allow for the production of user-generated content, allowing individuals to broadcast publicly-available comments and observations to follower groups or those searching along particular keywords, and to do so instantaneously. This capacity for "masspersonal" information-sharing has led social media users to both create and consume content and to generate shared understandings of content and observable situations as they unfold (O'Reilly & Battelle, 2009; Westerman, Spence & Van Der Heide, 2012).

While these technologies are rapidly transforming the ways in which we communicate with each other and make sense of the world around us, little is known about the ways in which media dependency processes play out in the social media environment. Media Dependency Theory argues, largely, that people will develop tendencies to use certain media or sources for actionable information under particular circumstances and that these dependencies will grow stronger over time as they prove effective for individual users (Ball-Rokeach, 1985; Ball-Rokeach & DeFleur, 1976).

One circumstance in which media dependencies are especially critical—and especially strong—is in the context of a major crisis or disaster. Some research evidence supports the notion that people may develop especially strong media dependencies under the conditions of uncertainty and fear that are typically associated with impeding crises that pose harm to safety, property, or quality of life. Yet little is known about the manner in which dependencies related to social media evolve under conditions of extreme duress.

The current chapter begins by conceptually introducing Media Dependency Theory. It then goes on to discuss a small number of studies that have examined social media behaviors in the time leading up to natural disasters and connects them to our understanding of dependency processes. It concludes by offering suggestions for future scholarship in the area, including our understanding of repair and restoration efforts, which are, at the moment, largely unknown.

Media Dependency

Crises and disasters present us with a unique set of circumstances, engendering a sense of uncertainty not commonly found alongside other motives for media use. Weick (1993) and others have offered that under these conditions people experience a "cosmology episode," whereby their world is cast into uncertainty and there is a need to restore things to some kind of rational order. This basic compulsion to acquire information, taken in conjunction with the ease and portability of social media platforms, makes it critical to think about the underlying processes inherent in social media use during times of crisis and disaster. Media Dependency Theory (Ball-Rokeach & DeFleur, 1976; Ball-Rokeach, 1985; DeFleur & Ball-Rokeach, 1989) provides a useful theoretical framework for the consideration of these processes.

Media dependency research, as a paradigm, offers that people are dependent on that which they acquire from mediated sources in order to function and to make sense of the world around them. Without unlimited access to information concerning that which they cannot immediately touch or see, mediated information sources become critical in evaluating decisions and best courses of action. As people find a particular source or outlet useful for solving a particular problem, or in making particular sets of decisions, they will then become increasingly dependent on that source and that source will, correspondingly, have more persuasive power over them.

By the same token, there is likely to be a great deal of variability in these dependencies from person to person, place to place, and situation to situation. Certain situations, events, and outcomes are likely to beget differences of dependencies for different people. These dependencies may also be very heavily dependent on personological factors, such as variability in personality, access to available sources, and level of involvement or interest with the concern at hand (DeFleur and Ball-Rokeach, 1989).

Considering the anticipated dependency processes, it is perhaps unsurprising that the media dependency literature has extended toward crises and risks. For the most part, Ball-Rokeach (1973), and others, argue that, when one perceives a loss of control or uncertainty over the most central and important aspects of one's surroundings, this ambiguity will drive affected audiences to becoming even more dependent on mediated information and will turn to sources they consider trustworthy or authoritative. In all likelihood, these dependencies also drive those affected toward using these same sources for affective needs, as a means of reducing anxiety and engaging in coping.

The extant research on information seeking under conditions of crisis and risk makes similar predictions. When risks present themselves that are likely, and that pose legitimate threats to health, property, and well-being, people are likely to seek highly specific information connected to these outcomes (Brashears et al., 2000). Time and time again, research in crisis communication, emergency management, and disaster sociology has offered the same argument: that mass media will emerge as the dominant source of trusted information, likely due to a cultural belief that the news media is inclined to present accurate, timely, and actionable information (Heath, Liao, & Douglas, 1995).

At the same time, this literature is driven by assumptions associated with linear media and with traditional news sources. Social media present us with a myriad of options from which to choose and source credibility may or may not be tied to these cultural associations with traditional media. Indeed, eyewitness accounts and trending posts may be viewed as equally plausible by those who are accustomed to the use of new media. This begs the need for serious inquiry into the dependency processes associated with new media use under the circumstances of crisis and disaster.

It is also the case that under conditions of extreme duress, and given the overwhelming amount of information that is available through social networks, individual users may have to make fast decisions concerning their preferred sources and attributions of their accuracy or utility. In this way, it may be the case that media dependencies associated with social media may develop in an unusually fast manner during crises and disasters. Faced with the need for uncertainty reduction, highly equivocal circumstances, and an abundance of information, quick decisions must be made in separating the wheat from the chaff. It is also likely that first alerts and initial warnings will play a key role in this process, as they will create the lens through which all other information is subsequently evaluated.

Reliance on Media to Reduce Anxiety

Further complicating matters is evidence in the cognitive consistency literature that audiences engage in selective exposure, further threatening the long-held assumptions regarding media dependency and uncertainty reduction (Heider, 1958; Festinger, 1957). This research has long suggested that people are driven to obtain information that already supports standing perceptions or biases. If an impending threat is posing itself to someone who already holds a set of opinions or mental models about the risk, they are likely to systematically seek out only information concerning their pre-existing perceptions of the disaster, those managing the disaster, and the efforts that are likely to be exerted in order to mitigate against harm. Also, some research has argued that a certain degree of negative affect is appropriate for inducing appropriate responses to crises (Sandman, Miller, Johnston, & Weinstein, 1993). Those experiencing insufficient levels of negative affect may not bother to respond to the threats presented by the crisis, while those experiencing too much may choose inaction out of hopelessness or engage in antisocial behavior. Dissonance may encourage people to gravitate toward media that supports their existing mood state, rather than serving as an intervening influence.

In terms of concerns regarding Twitter and media dependency, this presents researchers with two significant concerns. It may be the case that the sudden availability of thousands of information sources through Twitter allows individual users to seek out information that is cognitively consistent with their existing thoughts and beliefs. Second, it may be the case that the positions to which the general public is gravitating may or may not be consistent with those wished for by individuals managing the crisis.

Twitter's Emergence During Crises

These concerns are further magnified by evidence that Twitter is becoming increasingly relied upon during times of crisis and emergency. Decades of research has supported the notion that people will rely heavily on television and interpersonal connections for trusted information during times of crises and that these sources will satisfy the compulsion for information under extremely challenging circumstances (Deutschman & Danielson, 1960; Greenberg, 1964; Spitzer & Spitzer, 1965; Bracken, Jeffres, Neuendorf, Kopfman, & Moulla, 2005). Less is known about Twitter, which has emerged in recent years as a valuable resource, given its capacity for real-time updates and the ability for users to selectively expose themselves to the information they choose (Lachlan, Spence, Lin, & Del Greco, 2014). Of course, this capacity for selective exposure opens up all of the concerns associated with cognitive consistency mentioned above. Further, Twitter, as a medium, blurs the lines between interpersonal and mass media. Thus, many of our assumptions concerning the perceived trustworthiness of mediated information, along with our perceptions of the credibility of individual sources, are called into question.

While it may have been dismissed, at one time, as a novelty medium or a means of purely interpersonal connection, Twitter is becoming increasingly important in providing news and information, and in crisis and disaster scenarios in particular (Armstrong & Gao, 2010; Palser, 2009; Sutton, Palen, & Shklovski, 2008; Westerman et al., 2012; Westerman, Spence, & Van Der Heide, 2014). Several studies suggest that part of the reason for this emergence is that Twitter is widely considered advantageous due to the speed with which information can be updated and that those using Twitter, under the circumstances, respond favorably to its use by emergency management agencies and local responders (Kavanaugh et al., 2011). Further, the public increasingly reports that it will turn to Twitter for information out of a desire for continual updates, as the perception that linear media outlets are not providing updates fast enough has emerged as a major motivating factor in its use (Sutton et al., 2008). Of note, it may be the case that Twitter is used *as a supplement* to mainstream media and that the appeal of Twitter may lie primarily in first alerts and updates, while traditional media are relied upon for more detailed information, complex instructions, and actionable information. (Jin & Liu, 2010; Lachlan, Spence, Lin, & Del Greco, 2014a; Palen et al., 2010; Liu, Jin, & Austin, 2013). If this is the case, it has important ramifications for understanding the media dependencies that may be associated with Twitter under circumstances of crisis and risk. It may be the case that Twitter offers a very specific type of information or meets very specific needs. This is likely to produce powerful dependencies and to produce them quickly.

The capacity for Twitter to provide fast updates is consistent with its formal features. These features allow for linking out to URLs, video feeds, and web resources, and allow Twitter to provide users with more detailed and extensive information than could be provided through the 140-character limitation of the message itself. Shortening services have allowed for the compression of URLs into a tweetable format, further promoting this utility. Numerous studies have suggested that a tweet will stand a greater chance of serial transmission (see below) if it contains some type of URL, indicating that users are able to clearly identify tweeted information that they perceive to be more useful under the circumstances and, thus, worthy of retransmission to others (Suh, Hong, Pirolli, & Chi, 2010). There is also some evidence that tweets transmitted during crises and disasters stand a greater chance of being retransmitted than do those sent under more conventional circumstances (Hughes & Palen, 2009).

Given the drive for information, and the formal features of Twitter that may prove advantageous under the circumstances, it becomes important to consider the utility of Twitter and how it may be used from a media dependency standpoint. However, there are only a small number of studies addressing this issue and most do so from a position not grounded in Media Dependency Theory.

Existing Cases

Only a handful of studies have attempted to examine the motives for Twitter use during these types of highly stressful events. While there are only a small number of studies exploring these processes, they do offer an initial picture of what dependencies may be developing among those using Twitter to make sense of crises and disasters, as well as the human factors at play and the associated implications for emergency responders. First and foremost, these case studies tend to reinforce the notion that individuals may depend on Twitter as a medium for information that they perceive as useful in connecting with other people on some sort of emotional level. Among the first studies to explore this notion was Papacharissi & de Fatima Oliveira's (2012) work on Twitter use during the Arab Spring uprising. In this particular case, Twitter was used less for factual updates about events and more for affective displays and messages concerning bonding and solidarity. Furthermore, these affective messages became more frequent and more intense as the crisis unfolded and moved toward a resolution. Twitter users became increasingly more likely to use the medium as a means of emotional bonding and establishing a sense of connectedness in an otherwise confusing and dangerous political scenario that was fraught with fear and misinformation. The authors concluded that Twitter may be equally, or more, useful for satisfying these affective needs.

This is, oddly, consistent with our understanding of the motivating factors behind information-seeking under the circumstances. Since negative affect is such an important motivating factor in the need for information, it stands to reason that affective content may be available on Twitter that is not otherwise available on more mainstream, linear media. Obtaining this information may help to reduce this initial anxiety and allow the user to proceed in a manner that makes rational sense, as they slowly return to some kind of ordered understanding of the events around them.

As mentioned above, serial retransmission, or retweeting, may be an indication of the perception of information as useful to one's follower list. Sutton and colleagues (2014) conducted a study examining all tweets sent by those responding to the 2012 Waldo Canyon fire in Colorado. The results of this study suggest that retweeting was more likely to occur when the information presented was advisory in nature (as opposed to instructive or vague) and was more likely to be retransmitted when it was phrased in a manner stressing imperativeness and/or was clear in structure. These results seem to indicate that audiences were turning to Twitter for information that was presented in a particular manner, in this case that which was clear, advisory, and indicative of the importance of the fire. Of note, the authors of this particular study claim that, in this case, the most messages sent out by government agencies were reminiscent of those typically sent out through linear media; the responding agencies had an opportunity to provide more nuanced information, perhaps like that which we can expect Twitter users to seek, and failed to do so. Furthermore, the authors point out that those sending the tweets had a chance to engage in direct dialogue with those affected and chose not to.

Other cases have attempted to examine the nature of the content itself in order to establish whether or not this is indicative of what audiences expect from the medium. Given that Twitter is a social medium that involves both consumption and transmission, an evaluation of the content might be indicative of what the users of the medium expect under the circumstance. In other words, it stands to reason that common consumers would broadcast what they want to see. Lachlan and colleagues (2014a) sought to explore the content characteristics of tweets associated with Hurricane Sandy, looking at general Twitter use and the availability of actionable information among the general public. This case specifically examined the information available during the prodromal stage of Sandy (see Fink, 1986), as past evidence suggests that the time immediately leading up to the onslaught of a crisis may be especially compelling in terms of motivating information-seeking behaviors. The authors examined over 27,000 tweets, at specific time intervals, in the three days leading up to the landfall of Sandy in the northeastern part of the United States. The results strongly suggest that information concerning specific behavioral responses was difficult to locate when searching along the hashtag promoted by government agencies managing the crisis (#sandy). Furthermore, as the storm approached landfall, this information actually became more difficult to obtain, as outpourings of affect and fear began to supplant themselves proportionately in the tweets that were available. While it may be the case that those relying on the hashtag were unable to find actionable information, it may also be the case that they don't actually expect it. If we are to assume that user-generated content is consistent with what is expected of the medium by its users, then it may be the case that the dependencies associated with Twitter, under these circumstances, may be more tightly associated with affective needs and solidarity and with recommendations for mitigation (consistent with the findings of Papacharissi and de Fatima Oliveira cited above). Regardless, actionable information was difficult to find alongside the preponderance of humor, expressions of fear and dread, and spam (Spence et al., 2015).

The same research team then attempted to extend this case study by comparing the differences in what can be expected along localized and national-level hashtag strategies. Lachlan and colleagues (2014b) examined a snowstorm that impacted the Boston area, using the hashtags #nemo and #bosnow as search strategies. These tags were selected due to the fact that they were promoted by national-level relief agencies and local media, respectively. The study offers similar findings to the first case, in that the medium was used mostly for affective outpouring and expressions of fear and solidarity. They note, however, that tweets along the localized hashtag seemed to contain more actionable information than did those along the more generalized one. Thus, it may be the case that audiences may not have overarching, affective expectations of Twitter, but that they may form dependencies concerning different types of content that is associated with different search and retrieval strategies, much in the same way that audiences know what channel to turn to in the case of linear media.

It is worth noting that there is some evidence in the behavioral research on the matter that also suggests specific dependencies associated with Twitter. In a different study, Sutton et al. (2008) report that those affected by a wildfire in California were frustrated by "information dearth" from local media and were driven to use mobile technologies because they could not obtain information from more mainstream sources or from government agencies. In this particular study, fewer respondents reported using Twitter for actionable information (consistent, again, with the case studies above). However, those who did report using it primarily for information were more likely to have recently adopted the medium for this purpose. This suggests not only that the crisis scenario spurred technological adoption, but that existing Twitter users were aware of what they could expect to find and that they were more likely to use the medium for motives other than obtaining information.

Underlying Processes

The findings, across all four cases, are consistent with past research exploring patterns of information-seeking through linear media during crises and disasters (Lachlan & Spence, 2007; 2010; Lachlan, Spence & Seeger, 2009; Sandman, Miller, Johnson, & Weinstein, 1993). Media research has long argued that audiences will have very specific cognitive and affective needs during times of crisis and disaster and that appropriate appeals to these concerns may help manage events of this kind. To some degree, this work has argued that people must experience an appropriate level of fear and of risk awareness: enough so that they're motivated to act, but not so fearful that they lack self-efficacy or abandon hope (Sandman, 2003). Perhaps, under these circumstances, individuals have dependencies that are more tightly tied to the affective component of crisis response and are counting on the information they get from Twitter to help allay their fears so that they can seek out detailed information elsewhere and make good decisions. If, as a medium, people turn to Twitter to alleviate fear and establish some sense of connectedness, then those using the medium may be better able to use information effectively when gleaned from elsewhere.

Most central to our current concerns, the findings also offer important lessons in terms of what we might expect from the standpoint of media dependencies. Those affected by an impending crisis will have plenty of places from which they can obtain information. Experienced Twitter users may know what to expect from the medium—perhaps that affective support and first alerts are the most useful function of the medium—and know that they can turn to Twitter for this kind of support. While behavioral research has yet to touch upon this directly, the existing cases in the literature suggest that this may, in fact, be the case. Future research should attempt to measure directly the dependencies people report as they pertain to their use of Twitter and, more specifically, retrieval strategies and specific feeds they turn to when faced with some kind of impending crisis.

CONCLUSIONS AND DIRECTIONS FOR FUTURE RESEARCH

Media Dependency Theory argues that we gravitate toward particular media or sources that we trust and that, over time, these dependencies will become stronger and stronger as we gain faith in their usefulness. Crises and disasters present media users with unique situations that may engender particularly strong dependency responses. While the few cases that have been examined seem to suggest specific affective and behavioral needs that can be satisfied by Twitter, this, in itself, may be completely functional and Twitter users may be becoming more effective in using the medium in accordance with their needs and preferences. Future research should continue to examine the manner in which Twitter users form dependencies that are related to specific types of information under these circumstances so that they may inform first responders regarding the best practices for message placement and design.

DISCUSSION QUESTIONS

1. What do we know so far about the type of Media Dependencies that will drive people toward using Twitter during crises and disasters?
2. What happens to media dependencies over time, especially if they are effective strategies?
3. What have Lachlan and colleagues found out about what is available on Twitter in the time leading up to a crisis?
4. How might the information available on Twitter be different *after* a crisis has taken place? Why? What implications would this have for our understanding of dependencies?
5. How may Twitter be useful in terms of first alerts? Given our understanding of media dependencies and what we can find on Twitter, what might happen then?

REFERENCES

Armstrong, C. L., & Gao, F. (2010). Now tweet this: How news organizations use Twitter. *Electronic News, 4,* 218–235.

Ball-Rokeach, S. J. (1973). From pervasive ambiguity to a definition of the situation. *Sociometry, 38,* 378–389.

Ball-Rokeach, S. J. (1985). The origins of individual media-system dependency. *Communication Research, 12,* 485–510.

Ball-Rokeach, S. J., DeFleur, M. L. (1976). A dependency model of mass-media effects. *Communication Research, 1,* 3–21.

Bracken, C. C., Jeffres, L., Neuendorf, K. A., Kopfman, J., & Moulla, F. (2005). How cosmopolites react to messages: America under attack. *Communication Research Reports, 22,* 47–58.

Brashers, D. E., Neidig, J. L., Haas, S. M., Dobbs, L. K., Cardillo, L. W., & Russell, J. A. (2000). Communication in the management of uncertainty: The case of persons living with HIV or AIDS. *Communication Monographs, 67,* 63–84.

DeFleur, M. L., & Ball-Rokeach, S. (1989). *Theories of mass communication* (5th ed.). White Plains, NY: Longman.

Deutschman, P. J., & Danielson, W. A. (1960). Diffusion of knowledge of a major news story. *Journalism Quarterly, 37,* 345–355.

Festinger, L. (1957). *A theory of cognitive dissonance.* Stanford, CA: Stanford University Press.

Fink, S. (1986). *Crisis management: Planning for the inevitable.* New York: AMACOM.

Greenberg, B. S. (1964). Diffusion of news of the Kennedy assassination. *Public Opinion Quarterly, 28,* 225–231.

Heath, R. L., Liao, S., & Douglas, W. (1995). Effects of perceived economic harms and benefits on issues involvement, use of information sources, and actions: A study in risk communication. *Journal of Public Relations Research, 7,* 89–109.

Heider, F. (1958). *The psychology of interpersonal relations.* New York: John Wiley & Sons.

Hindman, D. B., & Coyle, K. (1999) Audience orientations to local radio coverage of a natural disaster. *Journal of Radio Studies, 6*(1), 8–26.

Hughes, A. L., & Palen, L. (2009). Twitter adoption and use in mass convergence and emergency events. *International Journal of Emergency Management, 6* (3-4), 248–260.

Kavanaugh, A., Fox, E. A., Sheetz, S., Yang, S., Li, L. T., Whalen, T., Shoemaker, D., Natsev, P., & Xie, L. (2011, June). Social media use by government: From the routine to the critical. Proceedings of the 12th Annual International Conference on Digital Government Research, College Park, MD.

Jin, Y., & Liu, B. F. (2010). The blog-mediated crisis communication model: Recommendations for responding to influential external blogs. *Journal of Public Relations Research, 22*(4), 429–455.

Lachlan, K. A., & Spence, P. R. (2010). Communicating risks: Examining hazard and outrage in multiple contexts. *Risk Analysis, 30*, 1872–1886.

Lachlan, K. A., & Spence, P. R. (2007). Hazard and outrage: Developing a psychometric instrument in the aftermath of Katrina. *Journal of Applied Communication Research, 35* (1), 109–123.

Lachlan, K. A., Spence, P. R., Lin, X., & Del Greco, M. (2014a). Screaming into the wind: Examining the volume and content of tweets associated with Hurricane Sandy. *Communication Studies, 65* (5), 500–518.

Lachlan, K. A., Spence, P. R., Lin, X., & Najarian, K., Del Greco, M. (2014b). Twitter use during a weather event: Comparing content associated with localized and non-localized hashtags. *Communication Studies, 65* (5), 519–534.

Lachlan, K. A., Spence, P. R., & Seeger, M. (2009). Terrorist attacks and uncertainty reduction: Media use after September 11th. *Interdisciplinary Research on Terrorism and Political Violence, 1*, 101–110.

Liu, B. F., Jin, Y., & Austin, L. L. (2013). The tendency to tell: Understanding publics' communicative responses to crisis information form and source. *Journal of Public Relations Research, 25*(1), 51–67.

O'Reilly, T., & Battelle, J. (2009). Web squared: Web 2.0 five years on. Retrieved February 1, 2013 from http://assets.en.oreilly.com/1/event/28/web2009_websquared-whitepaper.pdf

Palen, L., Anderson, K. M., Mark, G., Martin, J., Sicker, D., Palmer, M., & Grunwald, D. (2010). A vision for technology-mediated support for public participation and assistance in mass emergencies and disasters. Paper presented at the Proceedings of the 2010 ACM-BCS Visions of Computer Science Conference, Edinburgh, United Kingdom.

Palser, B. (2009). Hitting the tweet spot. *American Journalism Review, 31*, 54.

Papacharissi, Z., & de Fatima Oliveira, M. (2012). Affective news and networked publics: The rhythms of news storytelling on #Egypt. *Journal of Communication, 62*(2), 266–282.

Sandman, P. M. (2003, April). Four kinds of risk communication. *The Synergist*, 26–27.

Sandman, P. M., Miller, P. M., Johnston, B. B., & Weinstein, N. D. (1993). Agency communication, community outrage, and perception of risk: Three simulation experiments. *Risk Analysis, 13*, 585–598.

Spence, P. R., Lachlan, K. A., Lin, X., & Del Greco, M. (2015). Variability in Twitter content across the stages of a natural disaster: Implications for crisis communication. *Communication Quarterly 63*(2), 171–186.

Spitzer, S. P., & Spitzer, N. S. (1965). Diffusion of the news of the Kennedy and Oswald deaths. In B. S. Greenberg & E. B. Parker (Eds.), *The Kennedy assassination and the American public: Social communications in crisis* (pp. 99–111). Stanford, CA: Stanford University Press.

Suh, B., Hong, L., Pirolli, P., & Chi, E. H. (2010). Want to be retweeted? Large scale analytics on factors impacting retweet in Twitter network. Second IEEE International Conference on Social Computing (SocialCom), 2010 August 20–22, Minneapolis, MN. Los Alamitos CA: IEEE Computer Society, 177–184.

Sutton, J., Palen, L., & Shklovski, I. (2008, May). Backchannels on the front lines: Emergent uses of social media in the 2007 Southern California wildfires. Proceedings of the 5th International ISCRAM Conference, Washington, DC.

Sutton, J., Spiro, E. S., Johnson, B., Fitzhugh, S., Gibson, B., & Butts, C. (2014). Warning tweets: Serial transmission of messages during the warning phase of a disaster event. *Information, Communication, & Society, 17*(6), 765–787.

Weick, K. E. (1993). The collapse of sensemaking in organizations: The Mann Gulch disaster. *Administrative Science Quarterly, 38*(4), 628–652.

Westerman, D. W., Spence, P. R., & Van Der Heide, B. (2012). A social network as information: The effect of system generated reports of connectedness on credibility and health care information on Twitter. *Computers in Human Behavior, 28*, 199–206.

Westerman, D., Spence, P. R., & Van Der Heide, B. (2014). Social media as information source: Recency of updates and credibility of information. *Journal of Computer-Mediated Communication, 19* (2), 171–183.

Chapter 6

We All Scream Without Ice Cream: The Blue Bell *Listeria* Crisis

DARIELA RODRIGUEZ, PH.D.
Ashland University

THEODORE AVTGIS, PH.D.
Medical Communication Specialists

Introduction

Housed in the small town of Brenham, Texas is the home of Blue Bell Ice Cream. The town has been linked to "The Little Creamery in Brenham" since Blue Bell ice cream began being produced in the town starting in 1907 (bluebell.com). As Swartz (2015) stated in an article covering the creamery for *Texas Monthly Magazine*, the town and the ice cream makers developed their identity as a small-town, old-time, and safe product, based on the same ideals on which the townspeople prided themselves. One of the best-selling Blue Bell products is their "homemade vanilla" flavor. The people of Brenham rely on Blue Bell to satisfy any number of needs, such as work, charitable donations, infrastructure, and scholarships, just to name a few. When *Listeria monocytogenes* (*Listeria*) was found in the company's products, both the town and the company were sent into a crisis that would impact the safety of the small town and the "little creamery" with which they were all familiar.

Listeria

Listeria is a rod-shaped bacterium which is able to grow either aerobically or anaerobically. Though there are six species of the bacterium, only one, *Listeria monocytogenes*, is able to cause infection or disease in humans. *Listeria* bacteria are able to multiply best in the warmer temperatures that are found naturally in the human body (90–98.6 F) (about-Listeria.com). Though most bacteria thrive in warmer temperatures, one fact that differentiates *Listeria* from other types of bacteria is its ability to survive in freezing conditions and thrive in refrigerated temperatures (about-Listeria.com).

The most common transmission of *Listeria* is by consuming contaminated food. To date, the only human-to-human transmission has been mother-to-fetus. In healthy individuals, ingestion of between 10 million and 100 million colony-forming units is considered mild and the infected person will suffer only gastrointestinal symptoms, such as diarrhea accompanied by fever. However, as was the situation in the Blue Bell health crisis, in individuals with already-compromised immune systems, as few as 1–10 million units can cause serious medical issues, including death (about-Listeria.com).

What Makes Blue Bell Different

For most organizations, a product recall is considered an organizational crisis; in this case, a crisis with the potential to create irreparable damage to brand reputation. Juxtapose this with an agricultural producer recalling lettuce. Such a recall is seen as more of an inconvenience for customers. A relatively minor crisis for the organization with the public perception that such recalls "just happen" sometimes. However, the case of Blue Bell was very different. Part of the situation could have come from the concept of supply and demand. When lettuce recalls happen, there are often other options and vendors from which the consumer can purchase lettuce. Customers do not have to change their meals, their diets, or their plans because of the recall. With Blue Bell, especially in the southern region of the United States and, more specifically, in Texas, Blue Bell represented more than food, and there were no alternatives for ice cream in the minds of the consumers. Because of this, the ice cream recall caused individuals to take notice due to the scarcity of the product(s) in question. This amplified the information being sent to affected publics as the recall grew over the span of several months.

History of Blue Bell Ice Cream

Why is Blue Bell so special to the people in the state of Texas? To understand the love of Blue Bell ice cream, it is important to understand the growth of the company, as well as the relationship it has with its customers. Blue Bell Creameries opened its first location in 1907 in Brenham, Texas, as the Brenham Creamery Company: a factory focused on making butter from the excess cream local framers would bring to the creamery (bluebell.com). Brenham Creamery began making and delivering ice cream in 1911 and helped the farmers to have a sustained income in between harvest seasons. This sustainable income allowed the town of Brenham to grow economically and, though there were many years of financial trouble for the business itself, the creamery was slowly able to grow and find success, ultimately changing its name to Blue Bell Creameries in 1930 (bluebell.com). The new name was taken from the wildflowers that grew in Brenham during the summertime. This connection to the community continues to this day.

As the company continued to grow through increased distribution and advertising, the image that it wanted to continue to portray was that of being a small-town, local company, with strong, local roots. It branded itself as "The Little Creamery in Brenham," which is part of the branding it continues today (bluebell.com). Even though the logo has changed and the company has expanded its markets beyond Texas, increasing its ability to produce a higher volume of product and to increase distribution, the company has kept its identity close to its hometown roots. The trust in the product partially grew from the organic nature of the reputation that grew from this identity of being part of a small town (Swartz, 2015).

The Crisis

Between January 2010 and January 2015, 10 individuals in four different states were infected with several different strains of *Listeria*. Through detailed PulseNet testing, it was found that the bacteria came from Blue Bell ice cream. All 10 individuals were hospitalized and three of these cases were fatal. The 10 ill people were from the states of Kansas (5), Texas (3), Oklahoma (1), and Arizona (1). The three fatal cases were all from Kansas (cdc.gov; Winkler, 2015). Though these cases occurred over the span of five years, information about the illnesses was not released until the deaths in Kansas in 2015. The South Carolina Department of Health and Environmental Control found *Listeria* in Blue Bell products in February 2015, after isolating the bacteria in Great Divide Bars and Chocolate Chip Country Cookie Sandwiches (cdc. gov). Upon further testing, the Texas Department of State Health Services confirmed the findings in the same products that were produced in the Brenham, Texas facility. *Listeria* was also identified in "Scoops" products produced in the Brenham plant (cdc.gov).

In March 2015, the five Kansas victims were identified in a hospital with *Listeria*. All were admitted to the hospital for different reasons, so it was determined that they contracted the illness while they were patients. Four of the five patients' strains were the same as were found in the testing by the South Carolina and Texas health departments. These patients were given milkshakes made with the Blue Bell product ("Scoops") while in the hospital. The fifth patient did not have the same *Listeria* strain as the other four, but did also consume milkshakes made with "Scoops" while a patient. The outbreak of the five patients dated over the span of a year, from January 2014 to January 2015. Blue Bell removed "Scoops" products, as well as others made on the same production line, from shelves and stopped all production on that line in the Brenham plant.

On March 22, 2015, the Kansas Department of Health and Environment identified *Listeria* in Blue Bell's 3oz. chocolate ice cream cups, which were taken from the hospital where the *Listeria* outbreak happened. The same strain of *Listeria* was found in 3oz. ice cream cups sampled from Blue Bell's Oklahoma plant in Broken Arrow (cdc.gov; Winkler, 2015). The next day, Blue Bell announced a recall of the 3oz. cups in several flavors produced in the Broken Arrow facility. More illnesses were identified on April 3, 2015, when investigators used the PulseNet database, which identified six individuals who had the same strain of *Listeria* as was identified in the chocolate ice cream cups from the Oklahoma facility (cdc.gov): four from Texas, one from Oklahoma, and one from Arizona. The individuals from Texas were hospitalized before developing listeriosis (the disease caused by *Listeria* infection) and it was reported that the hospital had received ice cream cups from Broken Arrow and at least one of the patients had consumed the ice cream while in the hospital (cdc. gov). Blue Bell announced that it was suspending operations at the Broken Arrow plant on April 4, 2015.

April 8, 2015 brought three more cases that the CDC was able to link to the Broken Arrow facility's *Listeria* outbreak (cdc.gov). As a result of this news, along with further testing that identified *Listeria* in half gallons of chocolate chip cookie dough ice cream produced in March of 2015, Blue Bell announced, on April 20, that it was voluntarily recalling all of its products on the market, which included ice cream, sherbet, frozen yogurt, and snacks (cdc.gov).

The Fall Out

As the news of the recall started to spread through various media outlets, support for Blue Bell began to ebb and flow. Many were showing signs of support for the "Little Creamery," as they did in Brenham where supporters put yard signs in the front of their homes asking individuals to pray for Blue Bell. Blue Bell took the step of hiring Burson-Marsteller, a global public relations firm, to help with the crisis and image repair. This was the same team that represented Tylenol and Dow Chemical in their respective crises (Swartz, 2015). As the recall was issued, Blue Bell president and CEO Paul Kruse issued a video on the company's website and social media platforms, issuing an apology for the problems that had stemmed from the bacterial outbreak (bluebell.com; Swartz, 2015). As the video spread, so did support for Blue Bell. This support was primarily from the southern region of the United States and the messages that were being sent were focusing on loyal customers who simply wanted their ice cream back.

As news of the recall spread, in terms of crisis communication, Blue Bell tried its best to maintain an open and transparent process. Updates on the company's social media site were positively received. Though the support was strong, Blue Bell was suffering economically as the shutdown of its operations did not seem to have any finite timeline. As of May 2015, Blue Bell announced that 37% of its workforce was going to be laid off: 750 full-time employees and 700 part-time employees (Patsuris, 2015). Many others would have to take pay cuts if they stayed with the company, while others would be furloughed. This step to survive the crisis would be the first time in the history of the organization that they had to lay off workers (Patsuris, 2015).

Though many found fault in Blue Bell for not reacting more thoroughly to the 2010 *Listeria* cases, overall support continued, as the ice cream maker worked to keep its publics aware of the steps it was taking to clean its plants and work to make sure its products were safe for consumption. In July, production was allowed to resume in the Alabama facility, followed by a September re-opening of the Oklahoma facility (Elkind, 2015).

Theory of Independent Mindedness as a Crisis Theory

The Theory of Independent Mindedness (TIM) was developed in direct reaction to the influx of collectivist management theories that made their way through to the United States in the 1980's. This theory, developed by Dominic Infante (1987a), sought to become a concept linked to the idea of cultural congruity. Simply put, any management theory should be based on the concept that any corporate culture should match the larger culture within which it operates. When looking at the culture of the United States and its philosophy concerning work, "American workers have an implicit drive for self-determination, autonomy, and self-expression. Further, the need to conform and give up individual freedom for the good of the group is generally met with resistance, at it is counter to western assumptions of freedom and individualism" (Avtgis & Chory, 2010, p. 292). Infante (1987c) believed that any philosophy which argues that management by consensus is effective in homogeneous cultures is undeniable. However, when applied to a heterogeneous culture (i.e., western culture), where attributes such as deference to authority and seniority become popular, communicating in a respectful and non-confrontational style may not only be inconsistent, but may also be considered inorganic (Avtgis & Chory, 2010).

The TIM is a corporatist theory that is truly communicative in nature. That is, the theory seeks to maximize human productivity in an effort to provide the greatest probability of meeting the organization's goals (Infante, 1987b). One of the components of the TIM is that employees must have the perception that they are an integral part of organizational decision-making. Such a perception is manifested through the relationship (and interactions) between superior and subordinates, in what Gordon and Infante (1987) call the "dialectic exchange" (Rancer, 1995). When an organization integrates these types of interaction patterns, the voice of employees is elevated, with the resulting effect being in direct opposition to the more autocratic strategies, which see such high levels of employee voice as being counterproductive (Avtgis & Rancer, 2007).

The TIM is operationalized through predispositions to express critical thoughts in socially appropriate ways (Avtgis & Chory, 2010; Avtgis & Rancer, 2007). The TIM contends that an organizational communication climate that encourages and fosters high levels of argument does not view such argument as inappropriate, nor as emblematic of the escalation of interpersonal conflict. That is, argument that is absent of verbal aggression results in a form of communication known as *independent-mindedness* (Avtgis & Chory, 2010). In fact, organizations are strongly encouraged to train employees in increasing their ability to form and express arguments in a socially appropriate way (Avtgis & Rancer, 2014).

Looking at the TIM as a crisis communication theory, by providing voice at all levels of the organization, one is providing many layers of observation through which risks can be identified and, in the case of crises, may very well assist in the accelerated mitigation of any given crisis. For example, a prominent plastic surgeon, before performing any surgery, says to everyone in the operating room: "Don't let me do anything stupid." Such an utterance creates a culture where everyone in the room has the authority to speak up. In terms of the Blue Bell case, the messages which were presented to the public from all fronts were exactly the same: Blue Bell and its employees were working hard for the general public to fix the problem and earn back the trust of the customers (bluebell.com). For example, Blue Bell released a commercial featuring employees stating that the issues were being dealt with and that the organization was committed to coming back stronger after the crisis. Though this is an example of a scripted response, the messages that followed all shared the same customer-focused communication. Press releases were the only communication from the creamery outside of the commercials, keeping the messages consistent.

Connection to the Theory of Independent Mindedness

As stated in the explanation of TIM, organizations that do not focus their employees' energy on productive communication can produce negative outcomes during internal conflicts. The same can be said for external conflicts, or crises, involving an organization. If proper employee training and communication styles are not planned for and executed, even a small crisis can grow into a much larger issue. This can include the understanding of an organizational mission, how internal messages should be developed, who is in charge of representing the organization in a public venue, and even how the individuals *are* the organization. This last factor is crucial for employees to understand, as what they say as an individual during a crisis differs from what they say as an individual who works for an organization during a crisis.

The Next Step

After months of media coverage, cleaning of factories and machinery, product testing, and managing the crisis, Blue Bell announced, on November 18, 2015, that it was starting production for distribution out of its Brenham, Texas plant (foodsafetynews.com). The news sent waves of excitement through social media, as fans of the ice cream also found out that distribution of products was planned for December 2015. The successful return of Blue Bell can be attributed to the successful management of communication through the many stages of the recall-to-redistribution timeline.

CONCLUSION

From the initial news of the recall to the widespread news of the deaths attributed to the company's products to the eventual lay-offs that could have devastated the small town of Brenham, the crisis became large in scope. Many companies could have been unable to recover from the many hits that Blue Bell took during this time period. However, through consistent messaging, from upper management to factory employees to the consumer publics, the messages were always those of taking responsibility, focusing on the problem, and working hard to keep trust and keep the customer happy. The organization never put out anticipated return dates that could be broken, as that gives the media an opportunity to speculate as to why the date was missed. Though Blue Bell, itself, may have had dates it sought to meet for strategic planning purposes, the lack of attention to any issue beyond the safety of its products projected an image of a company that was holding true to safety standards, but also the mission of producing the best product for its customers. This made it easy for the public to rally around Blue Bell and for the company to move through the crisis successfully.

DISCUSSION QUESTIONS

1. What ideas and practices set forth in the Blue Bell story helped them find the success needed to keep their company thriving?

2. What lessons could other organizations learn from how Blue Bell dealt with the crisis?

3. What aspects of Blue Bell's strength of brand and operations could another similar organization replicate to help build a stronger brand, which would allow them to weather a crisis situation with a stronger start than other companies may have?

REFERENCES

Avtgis, T. A., & Chory, R. M. (2010). The dark side of organizational life: Aggressive expression in the workplace. In T. Avtgis & A. Rancer (Eds.), *Agruments, aggression, and conflict: New directions in theory and research* (pp. 285–304). New York: Routledge.

Avtgis, T. A., & Rancer, A. S. (2007). The theory of independent mindedness: An organizational theory for individualistic cultures. In M. Hinner (Ed.), The role of communication in business transactions and relationships: *Freiberger beitrage zur interkulturellen und wirtschaftskommunikation: A forum for general and intercultural business communication* (pp. 183–201). Frankfurt, Germany: Peter Lang.

Avtgis, T. A., & Rancer, A. S. (2014). *Argumentative and aggressive communication: Theory, research, and application.* New York: Peter Lang.

Blue Bell Creameries Website. (2015). *Video Press Release: An agonizing decision.* http://bluebell.com/the_little_creamery/press_releases/may-15-update.

Centers for Disease Control and Provention. (2015). *Multistate outbreak of listeriosis linked to Blue Bell Creameries products* [Data file]. Retrieved from www.cdc.gov/Listeria/outbreaks/ice-cream-03-15/.

Elkind, P. (2015, Sept 25). How Ice-Cream maker Blue Bell blew it. *Fortune.* Retrieved from http://fortune.com/2015/09/25/blue-bell-Listeria-recall/.

Gordon, W. I., & Infante, D. A. (1987). Employee-rights: Context argumentativeness, verbal aggressiveness, and career satisfaction. In C. A. Osigweh (Ed.), *Communicating employee responsibilities and rights* (pp. 149–163). Westport, CT: Quorum.

Infante, D. A. (1987a). Aggressiveness. In J. C. McCroskey & J. A. Daly (Eds.), *Personality and interpersonal communication* (pp. 157–192). Newbury Park, CA: Sage.

Infante, D. A. (1987b, July). *Argumentativeness in superior-subordinate communication: An essential condition for organizational productivity.* Paper presented at the American Forensic Summer Conference of the Speech Communication Association, Alta, UT.

Infante, D. A. (1987c, May). *An independent-mindedness model of organizational productivity: Role of communication education.* Paper presented at the annual meeting of the Eastern Communication Association, Syracuse, NY.

Patsuris, P. (2015, May 15). Blue Bell announces first layoffs in 108 years. Retrieved from http://money.cnn.com/2015/05/15/news/companies/blue-bell-layoffs/.

Rancer, A. S. (1995). Aggressive communication in organizational contexts: A synthesis and review. In A. M. Nicotera (Ed.), *Conflict and organizations: Communicative processes* (pp. 151–173). Albany, NY: State University of New York Press.

Siegner, C. (2015, Aug 17). Four months after recall, Blue Bell Ice-Cream is returning to 'select markets' in two weeks. *Food Safety News.* Retrieved from http://www.foodsafetynews.com/2015/08/four-months-after-total-recall-blue-bell-ice-cream-is-returning-to-select-markets-in-two-weeks/#.V3BEuzcoFFI.

Swartz, M. (2015, June). Rocky road. *Texas Monthly.* Retrieved from www.texasmonthly.com/food/rocky-road.

What is *Listeria* and how does it cause food poising? (2016). Retrieved from http://www.about-Listeria.com.

Transmission of and infection with *Listeria*. (2016). Retrieved from http://www.about-Listeria.com.

Whitman, E. (2015). Blue Bell *Listeria* outbreak 2015: Contaminated ice-cream still poses danger, CDC warns after finishing investigation. *International Business Times.* Retrieved from http://www.ibtimes.com/blue-bell-Listeria-outbreak-2015-contaminated-ice-cream-still-poses-danger-cdc-warns-1961738.

Winkler, J. (2015, July 10). Blue Bell is back(ish), but maybe we should remember why it went away in the first place. *Texas Monthly.* Retrieved from http://www.texasmonthly.com/the-daily-post/blue-bell-is-backish-but-maybe-we-should-remember-why-it-went-away-in-the-first-place/.

Chapter 7

Passing Bad Paper

ALAN ZAREMBA, PH.D.
Northeastern University

Sports and Crisis Communication

Followers of sport are regularly made aware of crises that have the potential to damage the integrity of teams and leagues. In the last few years, there have been several high profile cases. Each crisis may have been averted by effective communication. Each required effective communication after the crisis when stakeholders became aware of the incident. Here are but three examples:

- The National Football League and the Baltimore Ravens football team were embarrassed when it became known that a star running back for the Ravens, Ray Rice, had had a physical altercation with his fiancée. The league reviewed the matter and issued a two-week suspension for Rice—a punishment that many deemed insufficient. The league was criticized for what seemed to be nothing more than a slap on the wrist for an outrageous offense. The criticism increased significantly when a video surfaced on YouTube and other media outlets. In the recording, Rice can be seen hitting his fiancée with such force that the woman is knocked to the floor. The NFL and the Ravens then faced a more difficult crisis. They had to address not only the behavior of Rice, but also the apparent indifference and insensitivity of the team and league (Howard, 2014).

- Donald Sterling, the owner of the National Basketball Association's Los Angeles Clippers, made astonishing statements that were captured on a recording. The owner's conversation indicated that he holds attitudes about minorities that are inappropriate, regardless of one's type of work, but incomprehensible for someone in a business in which minorities lead in every area of the enterprise. Sterling's coach, players, other coaches, fans, political groups, and other stakeholders were outraged. The NBA's commissioner, Adam Silver, was new to the job, having taken the place of the previous commissioner who had been in the position for nearly 30 years. Silver needed to respond to the various stakeholders and do so firmly, fairly, and intelligently. The matter transcended the issue of the Clippers and Sterling. How Silver handled the situation would affect perceptions of the league and Silver's fledgling administration (Botehlo, Smith, & Fantz, 2014).

- The Athletic Director at Rutgers University, Julie Hermann, had no sooner taken the job when many of her former athletes accused her of humiliating them when she had been the women's volleyball coach at the University of Tennessee. These athletes claimed that Hermann had unprofessionally, gratuitously, and excessively berated the players. These charges would be difficult for Rutgers in any context, but the situation was aggravated because, months earlier, the university had fired its men's basketball coach for similar behavior with his Rutgers players. This new crisis ignited embers from the previous one. The athletic department had to respond to not only the allegations about Hermann, but to current athletes, coaches, support staff, the general student population, and the fan base, who, tacitly at least, questioned the wisdom of hiring this person to head an athletic department, particularly given recent history (Berman & Shoichet, 2013).

The study of crisis communication in sport contexts is an important area to explore given the exposure of sport and, consequently, the regular surfacing of crisis communication challenges associated with such an enterprise. There are dedicated television networks, talk radio stations, magazines, blogs, and websites, all of which scrutinize the activities of players, coaches, and sport organizations on a 24-hours a day/7-days a week basis. In the Boston area alone, a driver commuting to work can select from three radio stations that are all sports talk all the time. Sports websites, like Bleacher Report (http://bleacherreport.com/press-room), claim to have millions of unique visitors each day.

Sport communication, itself, is an emerging area of study. Researchers examine player-coach interaction, advertising on sport broadcasts, pre-game speeches, post-game press conferences, inter-unit communication within sport organizations, signs and signaling, sport films and books, talk radio, sport broadcasting, promotion and sports information, new media and fantasy sports, and community/charitable outreach (Billings et al., 2015). This list is not exhaustive. One could cite examples of crises within each of these areas which could have been prevented by efficient communication or would require some form of post-crisis response.[1]

Communication researchers examine crises from several theoretical perspectives. In this chapter, several theories that are germane to a specific sports-related crisis that has affected a major university will be reviewed. In brief, the crisis involved student-athletes at the University of North Carolina who were obtaining academic credit for taking bogus classes. Students did not attend a class. They simply submitted a paper at the conclusion of a semester. The papers were often superficial and often leniently graded.

Below is a description of relevant theories that will be employed to analyze this case.

Systems Theory

The basic tenet of Systems Theory is that organizations are composed of interdependent units that should work interdependently, not independently (Zaremba, 2009). For example, in a medical facility, pediatricians will work in one unit, pharmacologists in a second, accountants in a third, maintenance staff in a fourth, human resources in a fifth, and executives in a sixth. Systems theorists argue that each of these units is either directly or indirectly dependent upon one another and no unit can effectively act autonomously. The effect of units acting independently and not interdependently can create crisis situations and limit the effectiveness of organizations when confronted with crises. It is not difficult to imagine how a crisis could surface if pediatricians in a medical facility do not share information with pharmacists or if billing codes for services rendered are not appropriately relayed to the accounting department. In the former case, a patient may be deprived of therapies essential for wellness. In the latter case, the uproar from the resulting confusion could irreparably tarnish the reputation of the facility.

A premise of systems theory is that an organization is composed of systems and subsystems arranged in a hierarchy. Each subsystem is horizontally linked to other subsystems on the same level and vertically linked to systems below it and above it (Zaremba, 2009). The absence of linkages could prove to be

---

[1] Even what may seem like an area not likely to create crises sometimes can. Sixty-five years after New York Giant Bobby Thomson hit a home run to defeat the Brooklyn Dodgers in a playoff series, Dodger loyalists contend that the Giants were stealing signs and were relaying signals telling Thomson what type of pitch was forthcoming.

catastrophic for the organization's customers, staff, and the organization itself. For example, an airline executive who is not connected to her engineering units may make uninformed decisions about equipment that could imperil customers. It is necessary to cultivate, nourish, and exercise upward and horizontal formal communication networks to meaningfully link the subsystems.

While formal, prescribed channels are essential, a reality is that informal networks will also transmit information between subsystems and will function, regardless of organizational intent. The informal networks are not, by definition, prescribed, but they are, nevertheless, typically fast, more accurate than one would think, resilient, and perceived as credible (Davis, 1953). Often, associates in an organization will use the informal networks to gauge the credibility of information they receive from others in the formal network. Messages conveyed within the informal network can, therefore, trump the messages sent within the formal network (Zaremba, 2009). An athletic department may print and distribute a document which claims that every student athlete should pursue a serious academic program. However, if those within the informal network carry the news that it is more important that athletes remain eligible, the result may be that players are encouraged to take easy classes to maintain eligibility.

The existence of prescribed networks is meaningless unless all units/subsystems within an organization have permeable boundaries. If a subsystem has impenetrable boundaries, then information that needs to be shared cannot reach essential receivers who might absolutely need the information. If, for example, there are prescribed networks between trainers and coaches on a baseball team, but coaches do not desire to hear what the trainers wish to tell them, systems theorists would say that the subsystem is not permeable. The organization will eventually suffer. A player may reinjure herself, the school may be criticized on sports talk radio stations for playing a hurt athlete, and prospective athletes may be discouraged from going to the offending institution. If subsystems within organizations are not permeable, the result will be a silo effect. Each subsystem will operate autonomously not knowing or caring about what another related department might be doing. Such ignorance is not benign. Adhering to systems theory principles is essential to preclude crises. Not adhering to these principles—not knowing what is taking place in other parts of the organization—may create crises, as will be seen in the forthcoming case analysis.

Normalization of Deviance

Crises in organizations can occur because inappropriate practices become common and, therefore, accepted. The phrase the *normalization of deviance* has been attributed to sociologist Diane Vaughan. She writes, "…repetition, seemingly small choices, and the banality of daily decisions in organizational life—indeed in most social life—can camouflage from the participants a cumulative directionality that too often is discernible only in hindsight" (Vaughan, 1996, p. 119). The normalization of deviance means what one might think that doing the wrong thing can become normalized. Deviant behavior can become common because a "cumulative directionality" may be camouflaged by repetitive steps in the wrong direction. If, in an organization, it becomes common for people to use sick days for personal days, the "deviant" behavior will become normalized. An associate who might not have considered taking time off and declaring the time "sick time," may decide to do so.

Consider something less benign. Let's assume a physician works for a sports team. Assume that it has become normal to allow players who have suffered concussions to return to the game. It is done. When it comes time for the physician to assess an athlete's ability to immediately return to the game, the doctor only stops those players when they have suffered severe concussions. They do this because allowing players to play with relatively minor head injuries has become normalized, despite what one knows to be the dangers of playing with a concussion of any sort. What the physician knows is wrong no longer seems unconscionable.

In this example, the deviance has become normalized.[2] The result can be a crisis of no small proportion. Players may suffer physical and mental injury. Athletes who have played with concussions may claim that they were unaware of the potential damage to their health and sue the teams and leagues. A team can be tainted by the undesirable reputation of risking the well-being of players for the objective of relatively meaningless victories. In college sports, athletes may choose to attend other schools that have a reputation for greater concern for those who play for the universities. Normalized deviance begets the perpetuation of deviant behavior and—as is apparent in the concussion example above—can lead to organizational crisis.

Richard Feynman's Theory

Richard Feynman, the late physicist, was a member of the Roger's Commission that studied the 1986 Space Ship *Challenger* explosion. During his investigation, he discovered something that was troubling. Apparently, the cause of the explosion was related to a piece of equipment called an O-ring. Under certain temperatures, the O-ring proved not to be sufficiently resilient. What happened on that cold January morning was that outside temperatures dropped to levels that were beyond the tolerances of the O-rings. Feynman conducted a simple, and now famous, experiment in front of all members of the Roger's commission. He placed a piece of the O-ring in a glass of ice water. When he did this he demonstrated that the O-ring was not resilient. The lack of resiliency of the O-ring was *not* what was perplexing to Feynman. What was perplexing was how the rocket scientists could not have known this. Feynman conducted a second experiment. He asked three engineers at the Marshall Space Flight Center to estimate the probability of rocket failure. He also asked a manager to estimate the probability. Instead of telling Feynman what their estimates were, the physicist asked each of the engineers and the manager to write down their estimations. One engineer wrote that the chance of failure was one in 200. Another wrote that the estimate was one in 300. A third engineer wrote that the chances were one in 200. The manager's estimate of one in 100,000 startled not only Feynman, but also the other engineers (Tompkins, 1993).

How could the rocket scientists and the managers have such completely disparate perceptions of reality? To answer his own question, Feynman developed a theory that is applicable to crisis communication. He argued that information that is available at the bottom of an organization often does not rise to the top. He contended that the reason for this is not because there are no existing upward networks, but because the networks that do exist become clogged. Moreover, he argued that the networks are clogged because there is implicit discouragement of messages that would be sent using these networks (Feynman, 1988).

What might occur in a sports organization if decision makers implicitly suppressed information coming from coaches, players, academic advisers, and trainers? What would happen if student-athletes were not students in any real sense and yet those aware of the reality assumed that there was no desire at upper levels to discover what was not taking place in the classroom? When information is implicitly suppressed, people will not know what they need to know. This ignorance can, and has, resulted in crises.

Transmission and Constitutive Theories of Communication

Communication can be understood from both a transmission perspective and a constitutive perspective (Zaremba, 2009). The transmission perspective likens communication to the act of transporting

---

[2] To ensure against this occurring in the NFL, for example, the league has established a protocol that must be followed whenever there is a head injury.

information from one person to another. Person A has a message she wants to convey to person B. She attempts to transport it to B. The extent to which B gets the message as intended determines the degree of success. This perspective is important for all communicators. The transmission and accurate receipt of information can preclude crises.

The constitutive notion of communication provides a different, but complementary, perspective. The constitutive notion suggests that one examine communication not primarily as a transmission phenomenon that occurs within the organization, but rather as behavior that shapes or constitutes the organization. Consider the organization to be some sort of container. The transmission perspective conceives of communication as events that take place within the container—which is the organization—that helps the organization to function. The constitutive perspective suggests that communication does, indeed, take place within a container/organization, but, more significantly, because of the nature of the communication, the size, shape, orientation, and even goals of the organization are affected. In short, the process of communication forms and reforms the container that is the organization (Zaremba, 2009). If, for example, messages are consistently transmitted that imply that student-athletes are incapable of academic success, then the actual structure of athletics at universities will be affected and could become warped. How might academic advisers construct programs for student-athletes if they have heard and digested messages that intimate that athletes cannot succeed in conventional classes?

Crisis communicators need to be aware of both transmission and constitutive notions of communication. To avoid crises, one needs to make sure that messages are transmitted. For example, student-athletes need to be told about policies regarding eligibility so that they do not, inadvertently, commit a violation that would result in forfeited games or suspensions. However, thinking of communication from the constitutive perspective is equally important and this will be illustrated in the analysis of the forthcoming case study: effectively transmitted messages led to the crisis because the residual effects of these communications yielded a flawed constitution.

Legitimacy

Legitimacy is a, if not *the*, key concept in crisis communication theory. It refers to stakeholder perceptions of an organization's behavior. When an organization is perceived as acting appropriately, it is seen as legitimate. When it is perceived as behaving inappropriately, the organization loses legitimacy. An organization does not have legitimacy as much as legitimacy is attributed to it.[3] Image repair theory is based on the premise that effective communication can help repair an organization's legitimacy after a crisis. When an organization is faced with crisis, its ability to *restore* legitimacy is a function of *existing stakeholder perceptions* of legitimacy. For example, if a college coach or a university earns a reputation for violating recruiting policies, and it is faced with another accusation of such an offense, its ability to address the crisis is continuously undermined by stakeholder perceptions that they have been offenders in the past. Crisis communicators identify four Rs when describing the proactive and reactive stages of crisis communication. These four Rs are: (a) the *relationships* the organization has with its stakeholders, (b) the *reputation* the organization has earned, (c) the *responsibility* for any particular crisis, and (d) the *responses* to the various stakeholders. Each of these is affected by organizational legitimacy (Zaremba, 2010).

As will be seen in the case study discussed in the following pages, the University of North Carolina at Chapel Hill may suffer from the depreciation of legitimacy for years to come.

---

[3] Many authors, if not all authors who write about legitimacy, make this claim. For example see (Allen & Callouet, 1994).

Passing Bad Paper: The Case Study

For 18 years, from 1993 to 2011, student-athletes at the University of North Carolina received credit for classes in the Department of African and Afro-American Studies that were, at best, superficial.[4] These classes required no attendance. At the end of a term, a student submitted a paper. During the course of a semester, students in these classes were not mentored by faculty, nor did faculty at the conclusion of the semester grade the papers. An administrator in the department evaluated the papers—very leniently—and submitted final grades. Students might receive an A or B in a course for a paper that lacked any real substance.[5] Some paper submissions consisted of an original introduction and conclusion and then pasted content from other sources in between. Some students were aided in their writings by tutors who wrote sections of the papers. Student-athletes took, and were encouraged to take, these courses to ensure that they maintained their eligibility. Typically, the athletes who took these courses were participants in two revenue-generating sports: basketball and football (Anderson 2014; Smith, 2015; Wainstein, 2014).

Initially, students took these paper classes as Independent Studies. The number of students taking these Independent Studies was staggering: sometimes as many as 300 per academic year. Most departments, at nearly all universities, offer Independent Studies or something similar. With Independent Studies, a student works with an individual instructor on an area of mutual interest. The student and instructor collaboratively map out a study plan and timeline and meet periodically during a semester. The instructor then grades a submission at the end of the term. A very high number of Independent Studies per year in a department might be 20. Three hundred for an academic year is an alarming number.

In 1999, the department began offering "lecture courses" to complement the Independent Study offerings. Despite calling the courses lecture classes, they were essentially the same as the Independent Studies. The lecture courses would be listed as regular classes: students would sign up, or be signed up to be in them, but the classes would never meet. Students would participate as they had, submitting a paper at the conclusion of the term, that would be nominally graded by the student services manager. The advantages of using lecture classes were that they reduced, superficially, the very high number of Independent Studies and also finessed the limit on the number of Independent Study courses any one student could take. As significantly, the lecture classes could count toward new university core curriculum requirements, whereas Independent Study classes could not.

"Bifurcated" classes were a third approach. These were actual classes, but a segment of the registered population did not need to attend. This non-attending segment would, again, simply write a paper and submit the paper for lenient grading by the student services manager. A similar, fourth, approach was to add students to a traditional class roster, assign paper topics to these students, and provide grades for the students without the instructor, allegedly, being aware that these students had been added to the rolls.

---

[4] At the beginning of the period, the Department of African and Afro-American Studies had a slightly different name. It was referred to as the African and Afro-American Studies Curriculum.

[5] An egregious example was submitted as evidence by a whistleblower in this case. The "paper" was less than two hundred words long, was clearly superficial, and contained several spelling errors. It read as follows: *On the evening of December Rosa Parks decided that she was going to sit in the white people section on the bus in Montgomery, Alabama. During this time blacks had to give up there seats to whites when more whites got on the bus. Rosa parks refused to give up her seat. Her and the bus driver began to talk and the conversation went like this. "Let me have those front seats" said the driver. She didn't get up and told the driver that she was tired of giving her seat to white people. "I'm going to have you arrested," said the driver. "You may do that," Rosa Parks responded. Two white policemen came in and Rosa Parks asked them "why do you all push us around?" The police officer replied and said "I don't know, but the law is the law and you're under arrest."*

In sum, student athletes received credit for classes that were, at best, superficial. They were either Independent Study courses, bogus lecture classes, classes that were composed of students taking the course conventionally and student-athletes who had only to submit a paper, and courses where students, who had only written a paper, were added on to a conventional roster at the end of the term. Taking these ersatz classes allowed student-athletes to maintain their academic eligibility.

Two people have been identified as central to the operation of the activity: the student services manager, who will be referred to as Wilson in this chapter, and the Chairperson of the Department of African and Afro-American Studies, who will be called Jones (the real names of these persons are available to anyone who reads the reports from the case).

Wilson initiated the paper class system. She registered the students, graded the papers, and submitted the grades. She was motivated by her sense of compassion for student-athletes, who she felt needed and deserved assistance, and her passion for University of North Carolina athletic teams. Jones was a hands-off chairperson who, tacitly at least, condoned the paper class activity, allowing Wilson to act autonomously. Others were aware of the paper classes, particularly academic advisers who encouraged student-athletes to take the courses, and, in some cases, discussed with Wilson the grades that were necessary in order for a student-athlete to maintain eligibility. When Wilson announced in 2008 that she would be retiring, there was anxiety among these student-athlete advisers who had relied on Wilson to help keep athletes eligible (Wainstein, Jay, and Kukowski, 2014).

In 2011, two stunning news items surfaced. Taken together, these suggested academic fraud involving student athletes and spurred an investigation. The first, in July 2011, involved a student-athlete named Michael McAdoo, a football player, who had been suspended from the team for academic violations. McAdoo sought to be reinstated. He acknowledged that he had, indeed, submitted a plagiarized paper, but also claimed that not only were plagiarized papers normal for students enrolled in the class, but, astonishingly, there really was no actual class. He had, he claimed, been enrolled in a class that wasn't real and only had to submit a paper to get academic credit. The second revelation came in August of 2011. The *Raleigh News & Observer* ran a story about a student-athlete named Marvin Austin. Austin's high school record was such that he would not have been eligible to play football in the fall of 2007. One academic deficiency was related to his writing skills and he, therefore, needed to take a remedial writing course and would do so later in his time at UNC. However, it was made clear, in the newspaper story, that Austin, who needed to take remedial writing, was somehow capable of enrolling in a 400-level course in Swahili during the summer of 2007 and, remarkably, had earned a B+ in the course. The credit and grade made him eligible to play football (Smith and Willingham, 2015).

The McAdoo and Austin stories suggested that perhaps there was something problematic going on at UNC. The university began to explore these and related irregularities.

Permeability and Communication Networks

An independent agency conducted an exhaustive investigation of what transpired with these paper classes. In October 2014, the committee issued a report of its findings. Two excerpts from the executive summary to that report read as follows:

> "Despite the fact that these classes involved thousands of students and coordination between [Wilson] and numerous University employees, the Chapel Hill administration never scrutinized AFAM's [Department of African and Afro-American Studies] operations or the academic integrity of their course offerings. It was only when media reports raised questions about AFAM classes in

2011 that administration officials took a hard look at the AFAM Department. They were shocked with what they found" (Wainstein, Jay, & Kukowski, 2014).

"We found no evidence that the higher levels of the University tried in any way to obscure the facts or the magnitude of this situation. To the extent there were times of delay or equivocation in their response to this controversy, we largely attribute that to insufficient appreciation of the scale of the problem, an understandable lack of experience with this sort of institutional crisis and some lingering disbelief that such misconduct could have occurred at Chapel Hill" (Wainstein, Jay, & Kukowski, 2014).

As discussed previously, systems theorists contend that units within an organization are inherently interdependent and must be linked by navigable and horizontal communication networks. In addition, the walls to all subsystems within an organization must be permeable in order for information travelling within these networks to get through to appropriate audiences. If we are to accept, at face value, the excerpts from the Wainstein report cited above, there could not have been viable communication networks that linked subsystems at UNC. When the head basketball coach was confronted with the information about the paper classes, his response was that he was "dumbfounded." If his statement was sincere, and the committee's conclusions accurate, the walls of the subsystems at UNC could not have been permeable. The networks were either not there, not used, or illusory. If communication channels had existed, as systems theorists contend, then the head coach would not have been dumbfounded. He would have received information about the fraudulent classes.

Normalization of Deviance

The activity that took place seems outrageous to anyone who has ever worked in, or attended, a university. Yet, the practice continued for nearly two decades. At some point, participants accepted the deviance as not improper: not because it was proper, but because it had become normal. The anomalies had no longer become anomalous. An advantage of adopting principles of Systems Theory is that connectivity between units allows for relatively dispassionate individuals to observe as foul an activity that may no longer have a scent to those who are immersed in it daily. Crisis communication is not solely about reactive messages; it involves proactive communication that will preclude crises (Zaremba, 2010). What may become normal within an organizational silo would be discovered as abnormal and improper if the information is shared beyond the silo. If a university-wide curriculum committee, for example, had seen the extraordinarily high numbers of Independent Studies taught by a single faculty member, it is likely that the practice would not have been allowed to continue and certainly not for 20 years. The seeds of the crisis were planted and nourished because the deviant behavior had become normalized within a subsystem and the subsystems did not share information as prescribed by systems theorists.

Richard Feynman's Theory

Feynman contended that upward networks become clogged because leaders may implicitly, if not actively, suppress information that they do not want to hear. One could reasonably make the assumption that this might have been happening at UNC—perhaps without the leaders even being aware that they were, in fact, suppressing information. One must consider that even if information had no formal networks through which to travel, the informal networks did carry related information within them. There was an awareness that bogus, easy lecture classes existed. At one point there were more non-student-athletes enrolled in the so-called lecture courses than those student-athletes who had been encouraged to take them to maintain eligibility. Wilson was concerned that information about the easy classes had gotten to "the frat circuit" (Wainstein, 2014). If the information had found its way to "the frat circuit," is it possible that it did not, at some point, seep elsewhere? Feynman's theory could account for any seepage not reaching administrative levels. What could have happened is that coaches who wanted their players to remain eligible had subtly suppressed information that would otherwise have compelled the coaches to suspend a student athlete.

Transmission vs. Constitutive Conceptualizations

The lack of permeability and the absence of genuine networks are sources for organizational crisis. Without networks, information cannot be transmitted. Yet, a factor that seeded this crisis was efficiently transmitted communication. The distillate of these efficiently transmitted, if erroneous, messages fueled the enterprise. A desire, even a well-meaning, genuine desire, to provide assistance to student-athletes can be used to rationalize behavior that could eventually launch a paper-class-type malignancy. Having worked with student-athletes for more than 30 years in the classroom, and having been a student-athlete myself, I realize that the notion that student-athletes require paper courses to succeed academically is inaccurate and irrational. Moreover, it is insulting and invidious. Eighteen years of implicit and explicit messaging that suggested that student-athletes could not succeed without sham courses were the bricks and mortar for what became a flawed and warped container. The crisis evolved because the transmitted message that "the athletes cannot succeed without these courses" created a foundation for unethical, illegal behaviors that will haunt the university for years.

Legitimacy

An organization does not "have legitimacy." Stakeholders attribute legitimacy to the organization. Stakeholders in athletic departments include alumni, prospective students, media representatives, community members, fans, conference associates, faculty, and donors. It will take some time before researchers can assess the long-term effects on perceptions of culpability and UNC's legitimacy. Thus far, the image repair strategies employed have been "corrective action" and "displacement."

Corrective action is an image repair strategy that refers to taking—and communicating that the organization will take—actions in order to either (a) eliminate the chances that such a crisis can occur in the future or (b) mitigate the effects of the crisis (Zaremba, 2010). A review of the UNC website about the incident indicates a list of several comprehensive reforms that have been implemented to preclude similar crises (Frequently Asked Questions, Issues Related to the Academic Irregularities, 2014).

The UNC displacement strategy, however, has left many with raised eyebrows. Displacement approaches attempt to rid the organization of blame by blaming someone else. In other words, displacing the onus of responsibility. Much of the blame in this case has been placed squarely on Wilson and Jones. Wilson is portrayed as a kind-hearted person who misguidedly, and nearly unilaterally, orchestrated the sham. Jones is depicted as a weak leader and venal: someone who may have been good-hearted like Wilson, but abdicated his responsibilities.

The narrative that these two could have perpetrated, and perpetuated, the crisis by themselves can reasonably make stakeholders wonder. And some have. The headline of one online editorial reflects a typical reaction: "'[Wilson] did it' leaves a lot unexplained at UNC" (Barnett, 2014). Another headline reflects the perception that UNC was culpable: "Woeful lack of oversight at UNC enabled [Wilson's] deception." Reader comments on that article are revealing: "If they knew, it's criminal. If they didn't it's inept." "This is a complete white wash job. This investigation was set up to place all the blame on [Wilson]. How could no one in upper management in 18 years of this going on not know anything about it, not possible" (Stancill, 2014).

There will be stakeholders who latch onto the Wilson-and-Jones-did-it scenario to avoid the dissonance of wanting to be loyal to UNC, while concurrently supporting moral behavior. But, for others, it is reasonable to assume that the four *Rs* of crisis communication will be tested. *Relationships* will be frayed; *Reputation* sullied; *Responsibility* attributed to others besides Wilson and Jones; and penitential *Responses* sought. Pseudonyms have been used in this chapter because the weight of responsibility on these two may yet need to be reconsidered. Writers should be careful not to provide traction to a narrative that may not, in fact, be comprehensive.

SUMMARY

Sport organizations, because of the media attention they, for the most part, enjoy, are susceptible to lingering crisis-related damage. Administrators, managers, and all organizational women and men can avert crises by (a) creating linkages between units that reflect an understanding of Systems Theory, (b) discrediting flawed messages that are transmitted as truths (e.g., student-athletes require bogus classes to remain eligible), (c) fostering upward communication channels to preclude problems related to Feynman's theory, and (d) vigilantly identifying deviant behaviors that have become normalized by dint of their regular occurrence. In this case study, such activity might have precluded the ongoing troubles that have stained the reputation of an otherwise excellent university.

DISCUSSION QUESTIONS

1. Several theories could be used as an appropriate lens to examine this case. How would you apply systems theory to the events? Cultural theory?
2. Ethics and ethical decision-making are factors for communicators. Was the crisis described in this chapter a result of unethical behavior or poor communication? How does the "normalization of deviance" apply to this case?
3. Leaders can make decisions that preemptively eliminate crises. What could leaders at UNC have done to reduce the chances that this crisis would have evolved?
4. Crisis communication often involves minimizing the effects of crises after the events have unfolded. What steps would you have taken, after the crisis was exposed, to minimize the damage to the institution?

REFERENCES

Allen, M.W., & Callouet, R. H. (1994). Legitimation endeavors: Impression management strategies used by an organization in crisis. *Communication Monographs, 61*(1), 44–62.

Anderson, R. J. (2014). *Tarnished heels: How unethical actions and deliberate deceit at the University of North Carolina ended the Carolina way.* Strategic Media Books.

Barnett, N. (2014, October 25). *'Crowder did it' leaves a lot unexplained at UNC.* Retrieved from The News & Observer: http://www.newsobserver.com/opinion/opn-columns-blogs/ned-barnett/article10107629.html

Berman, J., & Shoichet, C. E. (2013, May 28). *Fresh abuse claims rock Rutgers; new athletic director denies accusations.* Retrieved from CNN: http://www.cnn.com/2013/05/27/sport/rutgers-ad-controversy/

Billings, A., Butterfield, M., & Turman, P. (2015). *Communication and sport: Surveying the field,* Second Edition. Thousand Oaks, CA: Sage.

Botehlo, G., Smith, M., & Fantz, A. (2014, April 29). *NBA commissioner bans Clippers owner Sterling, pushes to 'force a sale' of team.* Retrieved from CNN: http://www.cnn.com/2014/04/29/us/clippers-sterling-scandal/

Davis, K. (1953, September–October). Management communication and the grapevine. *Harvard Business Review,* 43–49.

Feynman, R. (1988, February 2). An outsider's inside view of the Challenger inquiry. *Physics Today, 41*(2), 26–37.

Frequently Asked Questions—Issues Related to the Academic Irregularities. (2014). Retrieved from University of North Carolina at Chapel Hill: Our Commitment: http://carolinacommitment.unc.edu/faqs/#faq8

Howard, A. (2014, 9 8). *NFL suspends Ray Rice after new footage of domestic abuse surfaces.* Retrieved from MSNBC: http://www.msnbc.com/msnbc/shocking-footage-ray-rice-domestic-abuse-revealed-tmz

Smith, J. M., & Willingham, M. (2015). *Cheated: The UNC scandal, the education of athletes, and the future of big-time college sports.* Washington, DC: Potomac Books.

Stancill, J. (2014, October 24). *Woeful lack of oversight at UNC enabled Professor Debby's deception.* Retrieved from *The News & Observer*: http://www.newsobserver.com/news/local/education/unc-scandal/article10107065.html

Tompkins, P. K. (1993). *Organizational communication imperatives: Lessons of the space program.* Oxford, UK: Oxford University Press.

Tompkins, P. K. (2004). *Apollo, Challenger, Columbia: The decline of the space program: a study in organizational communication.* Oxford, UK: Oxford University Press.

Vaughan, D. (1996). *The Challenger launch decision: Risky technology, culture, and deviance at NASA.* Chicago: University of Chicago Press.

Wainstein, K. L., Jay, A. J., & Kukowski, C. D. (2014, October 16). Investigation of Irregular Classes in the Department of African and Afro-American Studies at the University of North Carolina at Chapel Hill. 2, 6, 19. Retrieved from http://media2.newsobserver.com/smedia/2014/10/22/13/42/1rQra6.So.156.pdf#storylink=relast

Zaremba, A. J. (2009). *Organization communication* (3rd ed.). Oxford, UK: Oxford University Press.

Zaremba, A. J. (2010). *Crisis communication: Theory and practice.* New York: Routledge.

Chapter 8

Social Media Crisis in the Global Age: Lessons From the Siemens "Refrigerator Gate" in China

ZIFEI CHEN, PH.D.
University of San Francisco

YI JI, PH.D.
Virginia Commonwealth University

ZONGCHAO LI, PH.D.
San Jose State University

DON W. STACKS, PH.D.
University of Miami

Background

In September 2011, a Chinese blogger, Luo Yonghao, posted a complaint on Weibo (China's equivalent of Twitter) about a Siemens refrigerator door being difficult to close. Siemens underestimated the groundswell a single "tweet" could generate and failed to respond. This quickly evolved into a reputational nightmare for Siemens, a crisis later known as the Siemens "Refrigerator Gate" in China. The problem seemed to be small at first, as it was one customer and one microblog post. However, Siemens' failure to properly address the problem turned this seemingly small problem into a large crisis across the nation.

Globally, social media have flipped the power balance between organizations and consumers. With online social networks, users can exert influence to virally affect organizational decisions (Li & Stacks, 2014). Social media users are highly aware of their influence over others online and the collective power that they may exert over companies. With quicker access to information, unconstrained communication, and global connectivity, the networked population is building stronger rapport and taking collective actions to demand social change (Li, 2016). This empowered action by a few can easily (and rapidly) spread to the larger population, thus triggering crisis situations.

Crisis Communication

All crises come with suddenness, uncertainty, and time compression. Nevertheless, not every troublesome occurrence can be defined as a crisis, unless it is beyond the expectations of a specific organization.

Three features distinguish crises from other unpleasant incidents: surprise, threat, and short response time (Hermann, 1963). A troubling event will not reach the level of crisis unless it occurs as a surprise beyond the expectations and causes severe threats that need to be responded to within a short timeframe (Ulmer, Sellnow, & Seeger, 2011). For example, when the hoax video was uploaded to YouTube by two Domino's Pizza employees, showing how they contaminated the ingredients, it soon went viral, urging Domino's to provide its response to the paradoxical challenge within an extremely short span of time (Veil, Sellnow, & Petrun, 2012). Crisis is not only a matter of non-expectancy, but also threat. The threat of a crisis will affect an organization in every facet, including financial security, customer relations, community safety, and, most importantly, organizational reputation (Coombs, 2014). As demonstrated on September 11, with a terrorist attack in the United States in 2001 and the Wenchuan earthquake in China in 2008, crises always develop a contingency that if one earlier incidence is not taken care of, it will trigger even more severe aftermaths as a domino effect (Hopkins, 1986). Therefore, organizations should have a well-designed crisis plan handy that allows them to respond to the public in an extremely short time span.

A crisis can be viewed from the perception of stakeholders. Coombs (2014) defined a crisis as "the perception of an unpredictable event that threatens important expectations of stakeholders and can seriously impact an organization's performance and generate negative outcomes" (p. 3). When negative stakeholder perceptions are created within corporate confines, and are crisis-initiated, the crisis could destroy a company's reputation. With increasing challenges and opportunities brought by globalization and social media, how to prevent and manage crisis has become one of the most important tasks for companies.

Crisis Management and Organizational Reputation

Crisis communication theorists have pointed out that the central focus of crisis management is reputation repair (Benoit, 1995). There is a strong association between crisis communication and corporate reputation management. Although there is no universal definition of corporate reputation, the existing literature suggests that collectivity and cognitive perceptions are its most salient traits (Fombrun & Van Riel, 2003). These two attributes are closely related to strategic stakeholders. Under the impact of relationship management strategies, stakeholders' cognitive perceptions aggregate, accumulate, and are influenced by their peers. Through this process, an organization is being continuously evaluated by different strategic publics, such as employees, customers, and regulators. For instance, employees may evaluate their relationships with an organization based on leadership style and symmetrical internal communication (Men, 2014). Likewise, consumers may evaluate a company based on perceived corporate ability and corporate social responsibility (Kim, 2011). However, organizational reputation, which is perceived as a valuable asset, accumulated over a long time span, can be severely damaged by a single crisis. Therefore, organizations are putting great effort into crisis management: especially reputation repair.

Crisis Response Strategies

A series of studies have systematically witnessed the development of theories in crisis response strategies and their applications in restoring organizational reputation. Among them, and the first to be investigated, is known as *apologia*. Apologia was adopted, in general, as a defense by an organization. Researchers asserted that organizations would need to utilize apologia to protect themselves from attacks in a crisis, defending themselves in front of stakeholders (Coombs, 2014). Although the construct *accounts* was added to apologia, it was not versatile enough for organizations to cope with, given the various crisis situations.

Based on the foundation of apologia, Benoit (1995, 1997) introduced an extended theory of message strategies—*image restoration strategies*. In order to understand the image repair strategies, it is first important to understand the nature of attacks or complaints which may cause a corporate crisis (Benoit, 1997). Compared to other theories (apology, accounts), image restoration strategies are more exhaustive, with 10 crisis communication message strategies classified into five broad categories (Benoit, 1995).

Similar to Benoit (1995, 1997), Coombs' Situational Crisis Communication Theory (SCCT) originated from Apology Theory as a refinement of Benoit's image restoration strategies and created ways of corresponding the crisis types based on the internal/external and intentional/ unintentional matrix using attribution theory. The SCCT treats corporate reputation as a primary outcome to examine how crisis response strategies could be adopted to protect, or even restore, a company's reputation in a time of crisis (Coombs, 2013). SCCT highlights that crisis strategies are employed based on crisis type, crisis history, and prior reputation. Crisis type may vary based on the level of responsibility, such as a natural disaster (little responsibility), a technical-error accident (low responsibility), and an organizational misdeed (high responsibility) (Coombs, 2014). Crisis history shows that if an organization has experienced similar crises before, the current crisis will bring higher reputational threat. Prior reputation impacts stakeholders' perception because the reservoir of goodwill may bring the organization the benefit of the doubt in early stages of a crisis. In addition, SCCT is also formulated on the attribution approach that stakeholders attribute an event to different factors, looking for actual causes of a crisis. Studies show that if stakeholders hold an organization accountable for a crisis, they will evaluate this organization's reputation more negatively (e.g., Coombs & Holladay, 2004; Lee, 2004; Schwarz, 2012). However, crisis situations could also be viewed as opportunities that can positively influence an organization's reputation, if the appropriate response strategies are adopted (Coombs, 1995).

To have a closer look at why crisis management plays a critical role in organizational reputation management, an analysis of the Siemens "Refrigerator Gate" crisis case in China is applicable. This case study features the most salient characteristics of crisis management in a globalized and social-mediated world. Implications are discussed regarding how multinational corporations should protect organizational reputations in a social media crisis.

The Siemens "Refrigerator Gate" in China

Siemens AG is a German, multinational company, specialized in the fields of electrification, automation, digitalization, and health care, with approximately 362,000 employees across almost 200 countries (Siemens website, n.d.). The conglomerate has been operating in China for more than 140 years, with nearly 32,000 employees, 20 research and development hubs, and 76 operating companies across the country (Siemens website, n.d.). In China, Siemens produces and markets its home appliances through its local joint venture, BSH Electrical Appliances.

Luo Yonghao is an influential Chinese blogger. As a high school dropout, Luo held many occupations in his career and became famous for his witty and liberal views when he taught English at the New Oriental School: a private, Chinese educational institution. In 2006, Luo opened his own blog "Bullog. cn" (later Bullogger.com), which later became one of China's most popular and influential blogs. Eventually, it was shut down due to censorship issues. Nevertheless, Luo continued his status as an opinion leader. At the time of the crisis, Luo had three million (now over nine million) followers on Weibo (a micro-blogging site and one of the most popular social media platforms in China).

The social media landscape in China is different from the rest of the world (Luo & Jiang, 2012). Due to media censorship, people in China cannot get access to the major social media platforms such as Facebook, Twitter, and YouTube. Instead, they turn to domestic sites such as Kaixin, Weibo, and Youku. In China, social media has drastically changed the breadth and nature of communication. In particular, Sina Weibo, a micro-blogging site, considered to be the Chinese equivalent of Twitter, has become one of the most popular social media platforms in China and a major source of information for Chinese netizens. Although each Weibo post allows only 140 characters, it can deliver much more information as compared with 140 characters in English, due to language differences. In addition, Weibo also includes features such as threaded comments, rich media, micro topics, and a medal reward system, which encourage more active participation on the social networking site (Falcon, 2011). To better engage with Chinese stakeholders, many multinational companies, including Siemens, have official Weibo accounts.

The "Refrigerator Gate" crisis occurred in September 2011. In one of his Weibo posts on September 29, 2011, Luo complained that the door of a Siemens refrigerator he bought was difficult to close and the company was not responding to his complaint about this quality issue. Luo's post was echoed by many Chinese consumers and was reposted more than 3,000 times. Nearly 500 netizens also messaged Luo on Weibo saying that they encountered the same problem with their Siemens refrigerators.

On October 15, 2011, Siemens finally responded to the complaints on its official Weibo account, with a statement saying that they had been in contact with consumers who had problems closing the refrigerator door. Meanwhile, Siemens also contacted Luo, directly, through its public relations firm, BlueFocus Communication Group. Privately, the firm promised to fulfill Luo's request to acknowledge the quality problem, to publicize the serial numbers of the defective refrigerators, and to set up an agenda to fix the problem. Luo recorded and posted the conversation to his Weibo account, threatening to smash the refrigerators in front of Siemens' Chinese headquarters in Beijing if the company failed to keep its promise (Capozzi & Rucci, 2013).

Siemens failed to meet Luo's request and more consumers complained about the problematic doors on their Siemens refrigerators. To protest, Luo did what he promised on Weibo. On November 20, 2011, Luo smashed three Siemens refrigerators in front of the Siemens Chinese headquarters in Beijing. One of the refrigerators belonged to Luo and the other two belonged to famous Chinese entertainers: musician Zuo Xiao Zuzhou and writer Feng Tang.

In response to Luo's protest, Siemens released a statement on its official Weibo account in a very official tone. In the statement, Siemens made two major points. First, Siemens respected the act from those protesting consumers, but suggested that they take rational and legal actions to protect their rights. Second, BSH Home Appliances took responsibility for the production, sale, and services of those refrigerators and Siemens encouraged BSH to communicate with customers and solve the problem (Siemens, n.d.).

Siemens' statement was soon criticized by Chinese netizens. Some pointed out that the refrigerator was labeled "Siemens" and customers were encouraged to call the "Siemens hotline" when they had problems. Some satirized the situation on Weibo, saying that Siemens was happy to market the refrigerators with its own brand and logo, but, when problems occurred, those refrigerators were changed into "BSH fridges" instead (Gao, 2011).

Following the "fridge smashing" event, BSH/Siemens held several media conferences in major cities in China. In media interviews, the BSH vice president, Wang Weiqing, denied crisis responsibility by stating that the refrigerators *did not* have quality issues and it was the consumers, who improperly closed the door the wrong way, who caused the problem.

Despite Siemens' threat from its public relations firm, to major traditional media in China, about not advertising with those who published stories about Luo smashing the refrigerators, news coverage on this issue kept rolling. On December 4, 2011, Roland Gerke, President and CEO of Siemens Home

Appliances in China, finally stepped forward and released a video message. In the video, Gerke apologized to those who were not satisfied with the refrigerators and promised to solve the problem. In the message, Gerke promised that Siemens would (a) set up a Weibo account to follow up with the issue, (b) provide free, on-site inspection, and (c) add a door-closer-device where it was technically possible (Siemens, n.d.). Yet, Luo was not easily satisfied. He challenged Gerke's video release with three additional questions: which refrigerators were affected? Under what conditions would Siemens add the door-closer devices? How would Siemens help those who were not Weibo users (*China Daily*, 2011)?

Because Siemens failed to answer Luo's three questions, another protest occurred. On December 20, 2011, Luo held a one-hour lecture in Beijing regarding this issue and smashed another 10 Siemens refrigerators. Luo's protest against Siemens continued for more than a year, during which he posted numerous blogs regarding complaints and negative issues against the company. The "Refrigerator Gate" crisis has badly hurt Siemens' reputation and credibility among its Chinese customers and significantly decreased its market share of refrigerators in China (Jerri, 2011).

Post-Crisis Reflection and Implications

Siemens made several mistakes that escalated the problem to a crisis. First, Siemens was not able to respond to the complaint in a timely manner. Crisis communication requires a timely response, especially in the age of social media. Siemens failed to realize the power of social media, not to mention that Luo was an opinion leader among Chinese netizens. Luo made his complaint on Weibo on September 29, 2011, yet Siemens did not issue an official response until two weeks later. At that time, Luo's complaint had been reposted more than 3,000 times. When Siemens responded, publicity had already (and drastically) increased, putting Siemens at a disadvantage from the start.

Second, Siemens did not choose the right strategies to communicate with Luo and its angry customers. In its first official statement on Weibo, Siemens neither acknowledged the problem, nor did it deliver a sincere gesture to its unsatisfied customers. Later, when Luo and other angry customers smashed the refrigerators, and when the issue was reported by media outlets across the nation, Siemens employed defensive strategies by *attacking the accuser* (saying Luo should take rational and legal actions and blaming the door problem on the consumers) and *denial* (shifting blame to BSH and refusing to acknowledge the quality issue) (Coombs & Holladay, 2002). It was not until more than two months after Luo's initial complaint that Siemens finally adopted a more accommodative strategy, in which the CEO delivered an apology and promised corrective action*s* (setting up a Weibo account to address the issue and adding door-closer devices) (Coombs & Holladay, 2002). However, the remedy was too late for Luo and the angry customers in China, and its contradictory messages further hurt Siemens' credibility among Chinese consumers.

Moreover, Siemens did not communicate transparently on the issue and tried to control the exposure and news coverage that it actually had no control over. Instead of issuing a response to Luo's complaint in public, Siemens tried to resolve the problem with Luo privately, ignoring the complaints of other, "less influential" customers. Its public relations firm also tried to "kill" the story by threatening not to advertise with media outlets that reported the issue. Siemens' decision not to communicate transparently was neither ethical nor effective in resolving the crisis.

Finally, as a multinational corporation, Siemens failed to act consistently across the globe. Internationally, Siemens is committed to the core values of being "responsible," "excellent," and "innovative" (Siemens, n.d.). When it comes to international operations and marketing, the quality of the products should be consistent and adhere to the same core values. In fact, Siemens' failure was not only a communication issue, but also an issue of failed management. For multinational corporations to prevent similar crises from occurring, value and quality need to be delivered globally, while adapting to the local culture. The communication team should always have a voice when making management decisions.

In order to prevent crises from happening, organizations need to monitor their environments, be aware of potential risks, and be proactively prepared for contingencies. In addition to learning from its management failures and ineffective crisis responses, there are several implications one can derive from Siemens' "Refrigerator Gate" crisis, as discussed below.

A popular saying in China goes "When one's Weibo fans exceed 100,000, the influence is equal to that of a big city daily; if the number reaches one million, it is comparable to a national newspaper; once the number goes beyond 10 million, it's the equivalent of a TV station; and if the number of fans soars to 100 million, it is equal to the reach of China Central Television station" (*China Daily*, 2011). Although Weibo is considered the Chinese equivalent of Twitter, 140 characters in Chinese, Weibo's unique features encourage more participation. As research indicates, individuals living in China tend to have significantly more negative online crisis reactions as compared with those living in the United States (Chen & Reber, in press). For multinational companies, the risk of such negative online crisis reactions cannot be ignored. In this regard, companies need to actively communicate with the Chinese public on Weibo and build mutually beneficial relationships before any crisis can occur.

Another factor that became salient during the Siemens crisis case is social media. In contemporary public relations models, promotional communication (i.e., marketing, advertising) outcomes are divided into financial indicators and nonfinancial indicators (see Figure 8.1). In this model, nonfinancial indicators, such as credibility, trust, reputation, relationships, and confidence, are those that have demonstrated the value and impact of public relations efforts. These are perceptual variables that indicate the "soft" power, which, together with the "hard" financial indicators, affect stakeholders and stockholders' return on expectations (ROE) and ROE, in turn, influences the return on investment (ROI). On social media, the nonfinancial indicators become highly visible. The direct interactions and communications between the organization and the users make these relationship-based indicators highly critical in evaluating organizational performance.

Multinational companies need to adapt to the local culture, while maintaining their global values and quality, when operating internationally. When Siemens signed its contract with BSH for the production, marketing, and servicing of its refrigerators in China, it already exposed itself to risks. Would BSH adhere to the quality standards of Siemens? Would it provide the services that Siemens promised to provide?

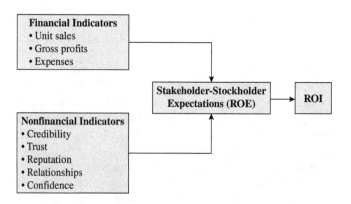

Figure 8.1 Relationship of Financial and Nonfinancial Indicators to ROI (Stacks, 2011)

Those were two important issues to consider when making management decisions, further suggesting that risk and crisis communication should be considered at the highest decision-making levels. The communication team leader should be part of the "dominant coalition" in order to be involved in the corporate-level decision-making process.

DISCUSSION QUESTIONS

1. What was the tripwire of the crisis?
2. What response strategies did Siemens adopt? How effective were they?
3. Would Siemens' "Refrigerator Gate" crisis unfold differently without Weibo?
4. What was the role of social media in Siemens' crisis evolvement?
5. How did the "Refrigerator Gate" crisis in China impact Siemens as a multinational corporation?

REFERENCES

About Siemens. (n.d.). Retrieved from http://www.siemens.com/about/en/.

Benoit, W. L. (1995). *Accounts, excuses, and apologies: A theory of image restoration strategies* (p. 69). Albany: State University of New York Press.

Benoit, W. L. (1997). Image repair discourse and crisis communication. *Public Relations Review, 23*(2), 177–186.

Capozzi, L., & Rucci, S. R. (2013). *Crisis management in the age of social media.* New York: Business Expert Press.

Chen, Z., & Reber, B. H. (in press). Examining public responses to social media crisis communication strategies in the United States and China. In L. Austin & Y. Jin (Eds.), *Social media and crisis communication.* New York: Routledge.

Coombs, W. T. (1995). Choosing the right words: The development of guidelines for the selection of the "appropriate" crisis-response strategies. *Management Communication Quarterly, 8*(4), 447–476.

Coombs, W. T. (2014). *Ongoing crisis communication: Planning, managing, and responding* (4th Ed.). Thousand Oaks, CA: Sage.

Coombs, W. T. (2013). Situation of crisis: Situational Crisis Communication Theory and corporate reputation. In Carroll, C. (Ed.), *The handbook of communication and corporate reputation.* Oxford, UK: Wiley-Blackwell Publishers.

Coombs, W. T., & Holladay, S. J. (2002). Helping crisis managers protect reputational assets: Initial tests of the situational crisis communication theory. *Management Communication Quarterly, 16*, 165–186.

Coombs, W. T., & Holladay, S. J. (2004). Reasoned action in crisis communication: An attribution theory-based approach to crisis management. In D. P. Millar & R. Heath (Eds.), *Responding to crisis. A Rhetorical approach to crisis.* Mahwah, NJ: Lawrence Erlbaum Associates.

Falcon, A. (2011). Twitter vs. Weibo: 8 things Twitter can learn from the latter. Retrieved from http://www.hongkiat. com/blog/things-twitter-can-learn-from-sina-weibo/.

Fombrun, C. J., & Van Riel, C. B. M. (2003). *Fame & fortune: How successful companies build winning reputations.* Upper Saddle River, NJ: Prentice Hall.

Gao, C. (2011, November 21). Siemens sparks refrigerator rage. *The Economic Observer.* Retrieved from http://www. eeo.com.cn/ens/2011/1124/216405.shtml.

Hermann, C. F. (1963). Some consequences of crisis which limit the viability of organizations. *Administrative Science Quarterly, 8*, 61–82.

Hopkins, W. E. (1986). A timeless organizational question: Crisis management or contingency planning? *American Business Review, 3*(2), 46.

Jerri, L. (2011, December 9). Siemens fridge show strategic defeat. *Open Articles.* Retrieved from http://www.open-articles.com/article.php?title=Siemens-Fridge-Show-Strategic-Defeat-By-Jerri-Lily&article=105224.

Kim, S. (2011). Transferring effects of CSR strategy on consumer responses: The synergistic model of corporate communication strategy. *Journal of Public Relations Research, 23*(2), 218–241.

Lee, B. K. (2004). Audience-oriented approach to crisis communication: A study of Hong Kong consumers' evaluation of an organizational crisis. *Communication Research, 31*(5), 600–618.

Li, Z. (2016). Psychological empowerment on social media: Who are the empowered users? *Public Relations Review, 42*(1), 49–59.

Li, Z., & Stacks, D. W. (2014). A great leap: Bridging a new media era of organization-public relationships. In Vaidya, K. (Eds.), *Public Relations and Social Media for the Curious: Why Study Public Relations and Social Media* The Curious Academic Publishing. Available from: http://eprints.uwe.ac.uk/26108. (ISBN 978-1-925128-20-8).

Luo, Y., & Jiang, H. (2012). A dialogue with social media experts: Measurement and challenges of social media use in Chinese public relations practice. *Global Media Journal—Canadian Edition, 5*(2), 57–74.

Men, L. R. (2014). Why leadership matters to internal communication: Linking transformational leadership, symmetrical communication, and employee outcomes. *Journal of Public Relations Research, 26*(3), 256–279.

Schwarz, A. (2012). Stakeholder attributions in crises: The effects of covariation information and attributional inferences on organizational reputation. *International Journal of Strategic Communication, 6*(2), 174–195.

Siemens faces more fridge bashing. (2011, December 21). *China Daily.* Retrieved from http://www.chinadaily.com.cn/china/2011-12/21/content_14300990.htm.

Siemens in China. (n.d.). Retrieved from http://w1.siemens.com.cn/en/about_us/profile.asp.

Siemens values and vision. (n.d.). Retrieved from http://www.siemens.com/jobs/en/ataglance/values_vision.htm.

Siemens. (n.d.). Roland Gerke's video message to Siemens refrigerators customers (transcript). Retrieved from http://w1.siemens.com.cn/news_en/news_articles_en/1902.aspx.

Stacks, D. W. (2011). *Primer of public relations research* (2nd ed.). New York, NY: Guilford Press.

Statement from Siemens. Retrieved from http://upload.eeo.com.cn/2011/1124/1322118911488.jpg.

Ulmer, R. R., Sellnow, T. L., & Seeger, M. W. (2011). *Effective crisis communication.* Thousand Oaks, CA: Sage.

Veil, S. R., Sellnow, T. L., & Petrun, E. L. (2012). Hoaxes and the paradoxical challenges of restoring legitimacy: Dominos' response to its YouTube crisis. *Management Communication Quarterly, 26*(2), 322–345.

Year-ender: Call it a year of Weibo. (2011, December 8). *China Daily.* Retrieved from http://www.china.org.cn/china/2011-12/08/content_24101840.htm.

Chapter 9

Using the Social-Mediated Crisis Communication (SMCC) Model to Examine Post-Crisis Rhetoric: A Case Study of *Deflategate*

COREY J. LIBERMAN, PH.D.
Marymount Manhattan College

HEATHER M. STASSEN, PH.D.
Cazenovia College

KATHLEEN D. RENNIE, PH.D.
New Jersey City University

Deflategate: An Introduction to the Crisis

During the 2015 American Football Conference (AFC) championship game, which saw the New England Patriots playing host to the rival Indianapolis Colts, fans cheered as their home-team became victorious: a win that provided them a ticket to the Super Bowl. However, the headlines surrounding the game focused more on scandal than it did on victory, as the events surrounding what some media analysts and sports critics have called the most infamous team misconduct to ever manifest itself unfolded. With just over nine minutes remaining in the second quarter of the game, and the Patriots leading 14-0, Indianapolis Colts' D'Qwell Jackson, an inside linebacker, intercepted a ball thrown by Tom Brady, the quarterback of the opposing team. Given that this was such an important game, Jackson decided to keep the intercepted ball as a souvenir, so, once back on his team's sideline, he gave the ball to a member of the equipment staff and asked him to safeguard it for him. This moment began the genesis of what has become infamously known as the *Deflategate* crisis.

After noticing that the intercepted ball seemed to be under-deflated, the equipment staff member let Head Coach Chuck Pagano know, which then began a chain of communication: from Pagano to Ryan Grigson (the General Manager of the Colts) to Mike Kensil (Director of Operations for the National Football League, or NFL) to the on-field referees during halftime of the game. During halftime, Kensil asked that two of the referees for the game, Clete Blakeman and Dyrol Prioleau, measure the amount of air, in PSI (pounds per square inch), in the hometeam's footballs. According to the NFL's rules and regulations, the minimum PSI for a football to be used for play is 12.5. There are, according to players, analysts, and scientists, two major advantages of an offensive team playing with under-inflated footballs: they are easier to throw (for the quarterback) and easier to catch (for the receiver). After halftime testing of 12 New England Patriots footballs, it was found that 11 of them were under-inflated. Interestingly, however, the PSI numbers calculated by Blakeman and Prioleau were inconsistent with one another, as evidenced by the 2015 Ted Wells report (i.e., the same football measured as having an 11.35 PSI reading by Prioleau had a 10.90 PSI reading by Blakeman), which clearly perturbed hometown fans and increased the complexity of the scandal/crisis. For purposes of clarity, Ted Wells is the name of the attorney who investigated the controversy. Before both teams returned to the field for the second half, all under-inflated footballs were replaced by footballs which met the league's regulatory PSI levels, the game resumed, and the Patriots won by a final score of 45-7.

Following the victory, however, it was not the team's forthcoming trip to the Super Bowl which permeated social media outlets. Rather, it was public responses on behalf of players, team staff, fans, and media spokespeople that created, fostered, and, in a sense, resolved the crisis communication that surrounded what became known as *Deflategate*. On May 11, 2015, after more than four months of investigative work, the New England Patriots franchise was found guilty of football tampering and was issued several punishments, including (a) a four-game suspension of their quarterback, (b) a fine of $1 million, and (c) the loss of two future draft pick selections.

The purpose of this chapter is to shed light on the use of social media during times of organizational crisis and how such mediated communication formats provide both opportunities and challenges for message producers and consumers. To follow is a brief overview of some of the recent scholarship dealing with social media and their use during the crisis communication process. Next will be a discussion of Jin and Liu's (2010) Social-Mediated Crisis Communication (SMCC) Model, which attempts to shed light on the effective use of social media during times of organizational crisis. This will be followed by a look at the myriad of ways that those connected, both directly and indirectly, to the *Deflategate* scandal communicated to and with various constituents using social media platforms, and the goals that they had in so doing. Finally, the chapter concludes with a discussion that links these crisis communication strategies to Jin and Liu's (2010) SMCC Model. In the end, the goal of this chapter is not to determine whether and to what extent communication following the scandal had occurred. It certainly did. The more important question, from a crisis communication perspective, is the extent to which it could be deemed ***effective***. That is the goal of this chapter.

The Use of Social Media During Times of Organizational Crisis

As Austin, Liu, and Jin (2012) make clear, "…while social media such as Facebook and Twitter receive more attention, social media include a range of types relevant to the study of applied communication, such as blogs, micro-blogs, forums, photo and video sharing, Wikis, social bookmarking, and social networking" (p. 190). At the macro level, Schroeder, Pennington-Gray, Donohoe, and Kiousis (2013) perhaps said it best when they claim that "…social media has undoubtedly influenced the landscape of crisis communications" (p. 133). First and foremost, individuals have increased (and expedited) access to information as compared to media outlets of yesteryear. They have information about what happened. They have information about what is being done to remedy the crisis in question. They have information about key players in the crisis process. They have information about what to do as the crisis is being resolved. More importantly, they have access to this information almost immediately. From a public-relations perspective, this independent variable of immediacy producing an effective crisis response in the mind of message consumers is hugely salient for the process of crisis communication (Taylor & Perry, 2005). Using the verbiage of Heath (2004), social media provide an important vehicle for both the production and the consumption of the "crisis narrative" through, among other things, the dissemination of information.

In addition to the divulgence of data, social media also provide crisis communicators with the opportunity to engage in mediated conversation with, and to hear the testimonial reactions of, affected stakeholders. As Kent and Taylor (2002) highlight, an important role of the effective public relations practitioner is to open two-way, dialogic communication exchange between an organization and its key publics. Social media have provided both organizations and key publics with a means to become intimately involved in the organizational communication process, and the unfolding of a crisis is a prime example of this dialogic process in action. As such, if those affected by the crisis have a particular communicative need (e.g., need for information, need for clarification, need for help), there are now mediated strategies for interacting with organizational representatives. Interestingly, as Stephens and Malone (2009) found, not only do social media provide stakeholders with the opportunity to communicate with organizations during times of crisis, when the need for social support arises, but they also provide the opportunity for stakeholder-to-stakeholder communication: something [largely] unavailable prior to social mediated technologies. As Veil, Buehner, and Palenchar (2011) claim, "…social media makes the community part of the actual crisis communication response" (p. 110).

Finally, and which is made poignantly clear by Jin, Liu, and Austin (2014), having access to social media during times of crisis allows those affected to become more involved in the crisis communication process, both as active participants, as noted elsewhere (i.e., Brown & Billings, 2013), and, perhaps, as passive consumers. These authors claim that "…organizations no longer have a choice about whether to integrate social media into crisis management…the only choice is how to do so" (Jin, Liu, & Austin, 2014, p. 76). In an interesting study dealing with the role of social media in the post-crisis stage of the crisis communication process, Van der meer and Verhoeven (2013) found that users of Twitter are able to effectively influence the way that others frame a crisis, through what the authors called "*mass self-communication*." From a crisis communication perspective, however, what becomes important here is ***how*** the organization in question can try its best to manage these tweets and not allow the public stakeholders to incorrectly or improperly frame the crisis: which social media have provided the unfortunate opportunity of doing. Similarly, Pang, Hassan, and Chong (2014) provide examples of social media users not only informing others about, but also creating the formal frames for, both national and international crises (e.g., the Boston bombings of 2013 and Iran's Twitter Revolution of 2009). In short, these scholars argue that social media platforms provide the opportunity for users to become journalists and shape both the course and outcome of crises.

In the end, with access to social media, users are going to use them during times of crisis. With these three overarching characteristics associated with social media and their relationship to crisis communication (providing increased access to information, providing increased likelihood of dialogic exchange between and among the organization and stakeholders, and the sheer likelihood of social media use), it is no wonder that so much recent attention has been paid to their role in the crisis communication process. However, merely knowing that the use of social media for crisis communication is ubiquitous is only part of the battle. Understanding how to use social media effectively for crisis communication is the more important goal.

The Social-Mediated Crisis Communication (SMCC) Model

The Social-Mediated Crisis Communication (SMCC) Model, originally called the Blog-Mediated Crisis Communication (BMCC) Model, developed by Jin and Liu (2010), which was later adapted and reconfigured to account for social media outlets that extend beyond the blog, analyzes the effect of crisis communication as a product of the information public and the goal(s) of the information consumer. First, the model assumes that the organization in question has encountered a crisis and has subsequently communicated this crisis using a combination of traditional media (e.g., television, radio, newspaper) and social media (e.g., websites, blogs, Twitter, Facebook). Austin, Liu, and Jin (2012), the authors and developers of the model, argue that three salient publics, or stakeholders, become involved in the dialogic process of crisis communication. First are the *influential social media creators*, which are best defined as those who are using social media outlets in order to create the crisis information to which other publics or stakeholders are gaining access and reading. It would be apt to call these the authors or the sources or the producers or the initiators or the generators.

Second are the *social media followers*, which are best defined as those who, through their access to social media platforms, are the recipients of the information provided by the creators. Although not explicitly stated in the original configuration of the model, it seems as though the only two prerequisites necessary to become a social media follower during a time of crisis are (a) information about an entity's existence and (b) the financial wealth to be able to become a participant of a particular social media platform (perhaps an extension of Tichenor, Donohue, and Oilen's (1970) Knowledge-Gap Hypothesis).

Third are the *social media inactives*, which are best defined as those who do not use social media for one reason or another, yet receive crisis-related information from the followers. As one can see from the model itself (Figure 9.1), there are bidirectional arrows connecting each public to all other publics; each public to the organization; each public to both forms of media (traditional and social); and both forms of media (traditional and social) to the organization. The lines connecting these arrows indicate the flow (or distribution) of information from one entity to the next and a solid line indicates that such a flow is direct, while a dotted line indicates that such flow is indirect. For example, the distribution of

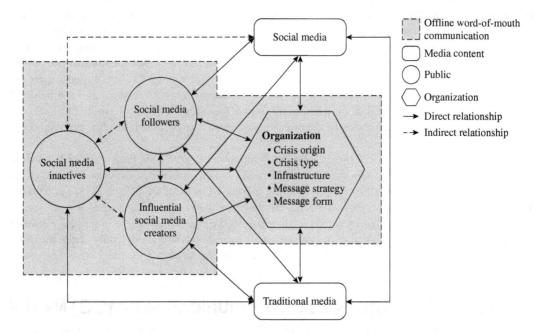

Figure 9.1 Social-Mediated Crisis Communication (SMCC) Model [credit line] *From Journal of Applied Communication Research,* Vol. 40, No. 2, May 2012 by Lucinda Austin, Brooke Fisher Liu and Yan Jin.

information from the organization to the social media inactive is direct (this individual does not use social media for accessing information, but does, in fact, use traditional forms of media), whereas the distribution of information from the influential social media creator to the social media inactive is indirect (this individual receives the information from word-of-mouth communication, likely from a social media follower, emblematic of the two-step flow model).

Finally, the model has, at its core, the idea that adopting one of the information public's roles (influential social media creator, social media follower, or social media inactive) is predicated on the goal of this public as a consumer of organizational-level, crisis-based information. As Austin, Liu, and Jin (2012) explain, for example, one is going to adopt a different information public role if he/she has a goal of ascertaining information versus self-expressing versus creating affiliation with others.

In short, the SMCC argues that when a crisis emerges, there exist two predominant forms of media (traditional and social) and three interrelated types of information publics (creators, followers, and inactives). Although it is the organization that will be the original source of crisis communication (without knowledge of the crisis, even the influential social media creator would have no content to create), each information public, then, plays an important role in the dissemination of information and the overall framing of the crisis event. Although Gonzalez-Herrero and Smith (2008) asked whether or not the Internet has provided a social outlet for the creation or resolution of an organizational crisis, what they call the "trigger or facilitator effect," it becomes clear that the SMCC helps explain the role of social media as a communicative platform for resolution, not conception.

Social Media Use During Deflategate: The Case Study

In sum, the intensity of the mediated conversation surrounding the football-tampering crisis was linked primarily to the social commentary of fans, sports reporters, and commentators regarding statements from the New England Patriots organization and the NFL at critical junctures during the controversy. [Note: For this analysis, social spikes were tracked in a number of different ways. The advanced search feature on Twitter was utilized to search "*Deflategate*" from January 1, 2015 to November 30, 2016. Twitter's "Top Search" function, which maps high engagement, was also analyzed. In addition, a media audit of articles reporting on the social media conversation around *Deflategate* was conducted to confirm spikes]. The Patriots, themselves, did not specifically address the controversy on their official social media accounts (e.g., Twitter, Facebook, Instagram, Snapchat, YouTube) until May 6, 2015, when the team finally tweeted a link to Robert Kraft's (the team's owner) statement on the Wells Report that was posted on the team's website (New England Patriots, 2015). The Wells Report was a 243-page investigative report that found that Tom Brady had a "more probable than not" involvement in the *Deflategate* scandal. This tweet was followed by a May 7th tweet about Brady's reaction to the Wells Report (New England Patriots, 2015) and a May 14th tweet that provides a link to a WordPress blog called the "Wells Report in Context" (https://wellsreportcontext.com) (New England Patriots, 2015). The Patriots organization, and their entire counsel, created the blog site to address concerns with the Wells Report. Throughout the remainder of the controversy, the Patriots' social messaging focused only on responding through the "Wells Report in Context" blog site, with the occasional, indirect (or what some might call passive aggressive) posts, in conjunction with major announcements associated with the case. For example, on May 12, 2015, one day after Tom Brady was penalized for his involvement in the crisis, the Patriots changed all of their social media avatars to a photo of his jersey and posted the photo to their Instagram account (Traina, 2015). The team, again, changed all of their social media avatars to Brady's jersey the day of the NFL draft in April of 2016 (Curtis, 2016).

More specifically, the mediated response to *Deflategate* can be tracked by examining five major spikes in social commentary regarding the crisis, including the following: (a) in January of 2015, when initial allegations surfaced regarding the team tampering with footballs and following the team's subsequent news conference; (b) in May of 2015, when the NFL released its investigative report and suspended Tom Brady for four games; (c) in July of 2015, when Roger Goodell (the Commissioner of the NFL) upheld the suspension in an internal appeal of Tom Brady's suspension; (d) in September of 2015, when Richard Berman, the Federal Judge of the Southern District of New York, overturned the suspension of Tom Brady; and (e) in July of 2016, when Tom Brady announced that he would accept the suspension. While the social conversation made its way to Instagram, Facebook, YouTube, and Vine, the vast majority of the social commentary transpired on Twitter. As such, the great majority of the analysis that follows will focus on communication via this social media platform. In fact, social data from Synthesio, a social intelligence and listening platform that was given the top global rank by Forrester, a market research firm providing information about the impact of different technology outlets, in multiple independent reports, shows that, among the aforementioned social media platforms, the conversation breakdown regarding *Deflategate* (from January 1, 2015 to June 30, 2016) was as follows (see Figure 9.2 for a breakdown of Twitter use by month):

- Twitter (69.02%)
- Facebook (5.10%)

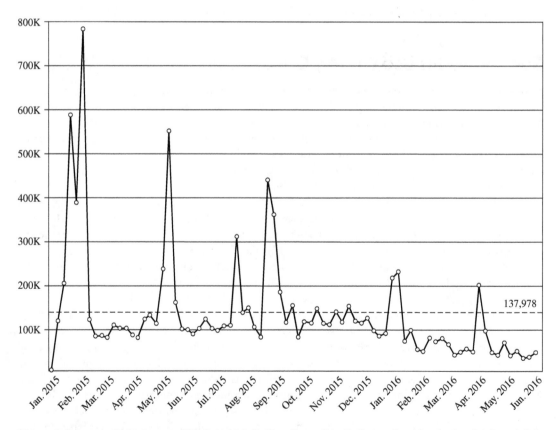

Figure 9.2 January 2015–January 2016 Social Media Data Regarding *Deflategate* from Synthesio, a leading global social intelligence platform. Reprinted with permission from Synthesio, December 2016.

- Instagram (1.37%)
- YouTube (<1.00%)
- Vine (<1.00%)

According to the Wells Report, the first suggestion of wrongdoing came in at 12:55 am (EST) on January 19, 2015. Bob Kravitz, a sports reporter for WTHR, an NBC-affiliated television station in Indianapolis, Indiana, lit up the twittersphere with his tweet: Breaking…a league source tells me the NFL is investigating the possibility the Patriots deflated footballs Sunday night…more to come (Kravitz, 2015). Hours later, Kravitz tweeted again: Just heard from an NFL spokesman…the league is in fact investigating the matter (Kravitz, 2015). Other news outlets and fans quickly jumped on board and primarily used Twitter as a communicative outlet to respond to the potential crisis. While some news outlets, such as *The Boston Globe* (The Boston Globe, 2015) and ESPN (ESPN, 2015), created content for which the outlets shared links; other outlets, like *Sports Illustrated* (SI Now, 2015), Fox Sports Radio (Fox Sports Radio, 2015), and *Newsday Sports* (Newsday, 2015), as well as sports radio personalities and fans, began to speculate, inquire, and debate about *Deflategate*. As an example, on January 24, 2015, Bob Glauber, long-time football columnist for *Newsday Sports*, wondered if Spygate, a scandal/crisis that haunts the Patriots organization from back in 2007, could taint the evidence in the *Deflategate* case and ultimately tarnish, once and for all, the legacies of coach Bill Belichick and quarterback Tom Brady. Deflategate1 tweeted, on January 20, 2015, questioning the validity of the victory – raising the ultimate question regarding whether the Patriots had cheated. He then posted a link to an article published by *The Bleacher Report*, which explained why the New England Patriots were being investigated. Compare this to the tweet posted by Deflategate2, who, on that same day, posted that (s)he believed that the Patriots had won because they were the better team overall. Finally, Deflategate3 tweeted on January 21, 2015 that the Patriots were cheaters (now and in the past).

Fans also took to Twitter with memes that poked fun at the crisis. As a prime example, a tweet from Deflategate4, on January 20, 2015, referenced the Patriots as "Cheatriots" and called for sanctions against the team. The only New England Patriot who commented on *Deflategate* during the initial phase of the crisis was Rob Gronkowski, the team's tight end. On the evening of January 19, 2015, Gronkowski tweeted a meme that read: Warning…Gronking may cause deflation…whoops…lol (Breech, 2015).

Interestingly, some non-football brands leapt into the social conversation, taking the opportunity to promote their own messaging, including Krispy Kreme Doughnuts. On January 21, 2015, the company tweeted a photo of a donut, shaped like a football, with the following headline: Ours are fully loaded… #Deflategate (KrispyKreme, 2015). Other examples of this include eBay, which tweeted a photo of a football with the caption "fully inflated…guaranteed…#Deflategate" (eBay, 2015); the Staten Island Yankees, who tweeted a photo of baseballs with the caption "never deflated…always 5–5¼ ounces… #Deflategate" (StatenIslandYankees, 2015); and even *Amazon*, which tweeted a link to an air pump, recommending consumers purchase one "…in case you ever need to pump deflated footballs" (Amazon, 2015).

On January 22, 2015, Bill Belichick and Tom Brady held a news conference. The coach noted that he was shocked about the deflated football allegations. He highlighted the fact that his star quarterback worked to focus on his love of the game and adherence to league rules. He also indicated that he was unfamiliar with the game-ball selection process and promised that the team would be more cautious in the future:

When I came in Monday morning I was shocked. I had no knowledge of the various steps involved in the game balls and process that [they] went through. We will certainly inflate footballs above that low level [indicated by the rules] to account for any possible changes during the game. We have cooperated fully, quickly, and completely with every request that they have made. I have no explanation for what happened. We will turn all our attention and focus to the Seattle Seahawks (in the Super Bowl)…a very well-coached, tough, competitive football team. (Sessler, 2015, Video Transcript)

Tom Brady responded to reporters' questions later that day and his sentiments seemed to echo those of Belichick: "I didn't alter the ball in any way…I would never do anything to break the rules…I was as surprised as anyone…[the Super Bowl] is where the importance is as far as I'm concerned" (Full Tom Brady, 2015). On Twitter, verified accounts of reporters and sports commentators were flush with tweets regarding the press conference, but the team and Brady did not post any comments in response to the initial allegations. Football fans reacted on social media and their sentiments were decidedly split. Patriots fans defended their beloved quarterback and their team, continuing to celebrate a big win, while other NFL fans were skeptical and criticized the Patriots organization. For example, there is Deflategate5, who, after hearing Bill Belichick's explanation of the series of events, tweeted, on January 24, 2015, that Bill Belichick was lying and made a comment mocking Belichick by calling him "Pinocchio." Deflategate6, on January 24, 2015, tweeted in support of Belichick's leadership throughout the crisis. Deflategate7 communicated a similar sentiment, moments earlier, that same day, noting his favor for Belichick's coaching and leadership. Finally, Deflategate8 tweeted, on January 24, 2015, that he believed Belichick was lying and hoped the Patriots would lose in the upcoming contest.

On May 6, 2015, the 243-page report, which followed a four-month investigation led by Theodore V. Wells, Jr., was released. The report found that Tom Brady was very likely involved in the scandal. Statements to the media regarding the Wells Report followed from Roger Goodell, Robert Kraft, and Don Yee (Tom Brady's agent). As reported by the *New York Times* (Pennington, 2015), Goodell noted that he supported the punishment issued by Troy Vincent, the league's executive vice president for football operations, for "…conduct detrimental to the integrity of the NFL." Kraft's statement gave the organization's "unconditional support" to Brady and further noted that "…despite our conviction that there was no tampering with footballs, it was our intention to accept any discipline levied by the league." He continued by saying that "…today's punishment, however, far exceeded any reasonable expectation. It was based completely on circumstantial, rather than hard or conclusive, evidence" (Pennington, 2015). Don Yee said that his client, Tom Brady, would appeal. The Patriots then tweeted a link to Kraft's statement regarding the Wells Report on May 6 (New England Patriots, 2015). This tweet was followed by the team's May 7th tweet about Brady's reaction to the Wells Report (New England Patriots, 2015).

While news outlets and individual reporters tweeted portions of the Wells Report and statements from Goodell, Kraft, and Yee, football fans jumped to social media after the Wells Report, significantly intensifying their "cheating" rhetoric and blasting the team and its quarterback. For example, Deflategate9 tweeted, on May 6, 2015, that Tom Brady was a cheater and lamented that the incident appeared profitable for Brady and the Patriots. Responding to the Wells Report, Deflategate10, that same day, tweeted his enthusiastic support for the findings. Finally, Deflategate11 tweeted his belief that Brady does not respect the game or its rules. It soon became clear that such anti-Brady, anti-Patriots verbiage inspired the Patriots. On May 12, 2015, one day after Brady was penalized for *Deflategate*, the Patriots organization changed all of its social media avatars to a photo of Brady's football jersey and posted the photo to their Instagram account (Traina, 2015). On May 14, 2015, the Patriots issued a very specific and detailed response to the Wells Report via a dedicated WordPress blog site (www.wellsreportcontext/com). The site's introductory statement reads "…the conclusions of the Wells Report are, at best, incomplete, incorrect, and lack context." The site featured YouTube videos of individuals "debunking *Deflategate*," the Patriots' cooperation memo, the team's correspondence, and a section labeled "critical articles." When the Patriots tweeted the link to the site, it received nearly 1,770 retweets and nearly 1,725 likes.

Another spike in the social conversation around the *Deflategate* crisis came on July 28, 2015, after Roger Goodell upheld Tom Brady's four-game suspension. Don Yee issued a statement that got much play on social media from ESPN, *The Washington Post*, and other sports news outlets. The statement claimed that "…the appeal process was a sham, resulting in the Commissioner rubber-stamping his own decision" (Reiss, 2015). Many reporters and fans took to Twitter to publicly criticize Yee's description of the process as a "sham." For example, Deflategate12, in a tweet on July 28, 2015, referred to Brady as a cheater, crybaby, and sham. Deflategate13 tweeted, on July 28, 2015, after hearing Yee's description of the appeal process, that Yee only believed the process was a sham because he did not get his desired outcome. On that same afternoon, Deflategate14 explicitly called Don Yee a "sham." While Tom Brady does not have a personal Twitter account, he used his Facebook account on July 29, 2015 to issue a statement that expressed his disappointment with "…the NFL's decision to uphold the four-game suspension," disagreeing "…with the narrative surrounding his cellphone." Brady further noted that he was "…overwhelmed and humbled by the support of family, friends, and fans" who supported him "…since the false accusations were made after the AFC conference game" (Brady, 2015).

On September 3, 2015, Richard M. Berman, the Federal Judge of the Southern District of New York, overturned the suspension of Tom Brady, nullifying his four-game suspension and making him eligible to play for the Patriots during their Week-1 matchup against the Arizona Cardinals. Robert Kraft issued a statement praising the process and praising Tom Brady. Links to the full statement were tweeted out by many reporters, including ESPN's Adam Schefter (from NFL Insider). Several players from the Patriots franchise also took to Twitter to celebrate the news that their quarterback would be able to play in the first game of the season. For example, Rob Gronkowski tweeted the following on September 3, 2015: Let's go…this season to be one heck of another ride (Schilken, 2015). That same day, Jamie Collins, a linebacker for the Patriots, tweeted the following: #freeBrady#tb12 (MacDougall, 2015). LeGarrette Blount, a Patriots running back, tweeted the following the same day: Let's goooo TB12…this is gonna be a fun season…1st win of the year for PatsNation (Schilken, 2015). On September 9, 2015, the Patriots tweeted an invitation to win a signed Tom Brady football jersey. The invitation featured three pictures of the quarterback (one holding the Super Bowl trophy, one displaying his four Super Bowl rings, and one in uniform). While no mention was made of *Deflategate* or the suspension nullification, the image(s) clearly celebrated Brady. The Patriots' Facebook page was updated to feature a photo of Brady holding the Super Bowl trophy and celebrating as confetti rained down upon him. The team's Instagram featured a game-day photo of Brady celebrating a play with his fist raised in the air. Rather than join the celebration, the league issued a statement from Goodell noting disagreement with the decision and the intention to appeal "…the ruling in order to uphold the collectively-bargained responsibility to protect the integrity of the game" (ESPN, 2015). Networks, major newspapers, and sports reporters tweeted the news of the nullified suspension, as did fans, including Donald J. Trump: Congratulations to Tom Brady on yet another great victory…Tom is a friend and a total winner (Campbell, 2015). Brands also came back into the conversation, as they had at the start of the controversy, including Michelin USA: Despite today's ruling we want to remind everyone that proper inflation does matter…#Deflategate (Petrella, 2015).

On July 15, 2016, Tom Brady announced that he would accept the suspension via Facebook. The post, which received 108,000 likes, 13,000 comments, and 23,000 shares, read as follows:

> I'm very grateful for the overwhelming support I've received…it has been a challenging 18 months and I have made the difficult decision to no longer proceed with the legal process. (Brady, 2016)

As can be expected, messages permeated the social media world. Those who were pro-Brady and pro-Patriots took to Twitter and publicly communicated their sentiments. For example, Deflategate15 tweeted, on July 15, 2016, that Tom Brady handled the situation with dignity and respect for the process, despite being innocent of the accusations. Deflategate16 tweeted, that same day, that Tom Brady is the most accomplished quarterback in NFL history. Deflategate17 posted, just a few hours later, arguing that Tom Brady will mute naysayers by having a successful season in 2016–2017. Those who were anti-Brady and anti-Patriots took to Twitter as well. Deflategate18 tweeted, on July 15, 2016, that Brady was a cheater and ought to accept the punishment. Deflategate19 tweeted, that same day, support and perceived joy that Brady's punishment was upheld.

DISCUSSION AND CONCLUSION

The crisis reviewed throughout this case study was, indeed, a specific type of crisis: one that would, in all likelihood, be labeled, according to Seeger (2006), an intentional event. As Seeger (2006) explains, "… distinguishing between various crises and disasters is important because the type of event influences the requirements for effective communication" (p. 235). The *Deflategate* crisis did not, according to Coombs's (2010) parameters for crisis communication, necessarily fit the perfect process mold, insofar as there was no pre-crisis phase of which to speak. There was no inherent risk to imagine. There were no potentially affected stakeholders to contact. There were no imminent warning signs. This was the type of crisis that began and emerged at the crisis response phase: the point at which organizational constituents communicate to affected publics about the crisis itself. However, even a cursory review of the crisis communication literature provides the information necessary to deduce that *Deflategate* was, indeed, a crisis. In his article dealing with best practices concerning the process of crisis communication, Sandman (2006) focuses heavily on the role of emotion in the production of messages. That is, when determining how organizations develop, and when organizations disseminate, their crisis messages, what role do emotions, such as fear, anxiety, sadness, and nervousness, play in the decision-making process? As Sandman (2006) makes quite clear, emotional communication is an independent variable necessary for effective crisis communication, but this emotional communication needs to mirror the needs, wants, and desires of the target(s). According to this case study, what were the emotional communication needs, wants, and desires of the target(s)? Who were the targets? Who were the sources?

When crisis communication takes to social media, the entire landscape has changed, solidifying Heath's (2006) claim that "…the Internet gives everyone the power to be a reporter [because] any fool can get media attention" (p. 246). Closely related is Heath's (2006) argument that "…crises have a way of giving voice to many people" (p. 246). This, in short, is what the Social-Mediated Crisis Communication (SMCC) Model provides for crisis communication scholars and practitioners: a way of understanding the myriad of stakeholder voices, likely with differing goals and, thus, different emotional needs, that come to shape an organizational crisis as it unfolds.

As mentioned earlier, and according to the Wells Report, the first social media disclosure of information related to the crisis occurred when a sports reporter tweeted some incipient news about a potential issue facing the New England Patriots organization. However, even though Bob Kravitz was the first to potentially "break the story" on social media, he heard the information, from a "league source," through traditional media. Going back to the visual depiction of the SMCC (Figure 9.1), there are three important pieces of the model here: Bob Kravitz (the Influential Social Media Creator), Traditional Media (the communicative modality through which Bob Kravitz originally found out about the crisis), and Social Media (Twitter, which was the first social media platform that Bob Kravitz used to communicate the possible, forthcoming crisis). This one post, and the post that followed (see the preceding section), opened up a breeding ground for dialogic exchange among a myriad of different stakeholders: fans of the Patriots, anti-Patriot fans, sportscasters, the general public, and the like. Some stakeholders were trying to make sense of the situation by seeking information and, as such, their communication was rife with the emotions of surprise or determination or astonishment. Some stakeholders were trying to provide sensemaking of the situation by issuing information and, as such, their communication was infused with trust and kindness. Still other stakeholders were, regardless of the truth, ready to blame Tom Brady and the Patriots franchise for wrongdoing and, as such, their communication was rife with anger, hatred, and indignation. Finally, there were those fans who would stick by the Patriots organization regardless of what the forthcoming crisis had in store and, as such, their communication was filled with courage, love, and joy. As Seeger (2002) explains, even at this early stage of the *Deflategate* crisis, "…disorder [was] necessary to order" (p. 331). Again using the SMCC model, the social media followers about whom Austin, Liu, and Ji (2012) speak became influential social media creators and, in all likelihood, vice versa. The idea, however, is that the crisis communication process began with a source receiving a message via traditional media and then this source communicating his message through a social media platform. This message was then received by social media followers who, in turn, became influential social media creators themselves.

This process seemed, at least according to the review of social media posts in this chapter, to follow this basic, communicative structure at all five major commentary spikes, where comments made by fellow fans would spark responses by others; comments made by media reporters or media analysts would spark responses by others; and comments made by the New England Patriots organization would spark responses by others (see Figure 9.2). The only stakeholder that could not be assessed in this case study, according to the SMCC Model, was the social media inactive, as one's existence in this category necessarily precludes him/her from online participation.

The question begged at the introduction to this chapter was not whether crisis communication had occurred, but whether or not it was effective. As such, it is now time to finally return to this question. According to Ulmer, Seeger, and Sellnow (2007), "…organizations interact with individuals to rhetorically construct and maintain perceptions of reality" (p. 131). As can be seen from this case study, although rhetorical constructions emerged, which could be an objective measure of crisis communication effectiveness, different perceptions of reality were created at different points throughout the historical trajectory of the crisis by different stakeholders. As Hiltz, Diaz, and Mark (2011) contend, however, this is merely a reflection of responding to crisis within a mediated, interoperable world, where many different stakeholders need to operate within one given system. According to these scholars, "…there are many social and cognitive aspects [of interoperability] that must be taken into account if users of systems from different organizations are to be able to use the information for joint sensemaking and coordination of actions" (Hilts, Diaz, and Mark, 2011, p. 3). The system spoken about in this chapter is composed of such stakeholders as the Patriots team, the Patriots administrative offices, fans of the team, opponents of the team, sports writers, and sports critics. Collectively, this is interoperability in action. Perhaps the fact that each stakeholder was given the opportunity to both receive and produce, or what the SMCC Model terms follow and create, a crisis reality, or explanation of the *Deflategate* crisis, is evidence enough that the communication that surfaced via social media could be deemed effective.

In the end, if Brown and Billings (2013) are correct, and "…fans become an extension of a [team's] crisis response strategies – via social networking websites" (p. 75), then there is further validation for the use of the SMCC Model to understand the role of social media for responding to organizational crises. As this analysis illustrated, and it is important to bear in mind that this case study neither systematically, nor holistically, content analyzed social media content, individuals utilize online communication platforms often to both receive and create crisis-related communication, producing, as Veil, Buehner, and Palenchar (2011) say, "…a community part of the actual crisis communication response" (p. 110). Although it may well be, upon further review, that social media provide more of what Schultz, Utz, and Goritz (2011) call "secondary crisis communication" vehicles (p. 26), there is no denying that social media play a large, and salient, role in the post-crisis phase of the crisis communication process: with numerous (and important) stakeholders dialogically involved.

DISCUSSION QUESTIONS

1. Explain the role of social media when an organization encounters a crisis. What are the opportunities that media provide? What are the potential problems that media present during the post-crisis phase of the crisis communication process?

2. What is meant by the crisis narrative and how does this come to shape how stakeholders come to view the crisis (both its genesis and outcome)? Do social media help or hinder this narrative process?

3. What does the Social-Mediated Crisis Communication (SMCC) Model argue about the crisis communication process and what are the strengths and weaknesses of this model? What variables could potentially be added to it in order to strengthen its validity?

4. How does the SMCC Model explain social media "coverage" of the *Deflategate* crisis? Who, in the end, became the most important source(s) in the message dissemination process?

REFERENCES

Austin, L., Liu, B. F., & Jin, Y. (2012). How audiences seek out crisis information: Exploring the social-mediated crisis communication model. *Journal of Applied Communication Research, 40*, 188–207.

Amazon [amazon]. (2015, January 19). In case you ever need to pump deflated footballs. [Tweet]. Retrieved from https://twitter.com/amazon/status/557343161702301697?ref_src=twsrc%5Etfw

Brady, T. (2015, July 29). I am very disappointed by the NFL's decision… [Facebook Post]. Retrieved from https://www.facebook.com/TomBrady/posts/956989441008873

Brady, T. (2016, July 15). I'm very grateful for the overwhelming support… [Facebook Post]. Retrieved from https://www.facebook.com/TomBrady/posts/1188349551206193

Breech, J. (2015, January 20). LOOK: Rob Gronkowski explains in tweet why Patriots balls were deflated. CBS Sports. Retrieved from http://www.cbssports.com/nfl/news/look-rob-gronkowski-explains-in-tweet-why-patriots-balls-were-deflated/

Brown, N. A., & Billings, A. C. (2013). Sports fans as crisis communicators on social media websites. *Public Relations Review, 39*, 74–81.

Campbell, C. (2015, September 3). Donald Trump: I just spoke with Tom Brady "he is so thrilled and happy." *Business Insider.* Retrieved from http://www.businessinsider.com/donald-trump-tom-brady-suspension-deflategate-2015-9

Coombs, W. T. (2010). Parameters for crisis communication. In W. T. Coombs & S. J. Holladay (Eds.), *The Handbook of Crisis Communication (pp. 17–53).* Hoboken, NJ: Wiley-Blackwell.

Curtis, C. (2016, April 29). The Patriots paid tribute to Tom Brady on social media during the NFL draft. For the Win USA Today Sports. Retrieved from http://www.foxsports.com/buzzer/story/new-england-patriots-tom-brady-deflategate-avatars-051215

eBay [eBay]. (2015, January 20). Fully inflated. Guaranteed. #Deflategate ebay.to/1C5L0nM [Tweet]. Retrieved from https://twitter.com/eBay/status/557749705678290947/photo/1

ESPN [ESPN]. (2015, January 19). Tom Brady's thoughts on the NFL investigating whether the Pats used intentionally deflated footballs? Laughter: http://es.pn/1zrSnWT [Tweet]. Retrieved from https://twitter.com/espn/status/557236567673430016

ESPN [ESPNNFL]. (2015, September 3). BREAKING: Tom Brady wins Deflategate appeal against NFL, judge nullifies 4-game suspension http://es.pn/1PNt6dW [Tweet]. Retrieved from https://twitter.com/espn/status/639443919261057025

FOX Sports Radio [FoxSportsRadio]. (2015, January 19). JOIN US- @SGSFOX has a special #MLKDay show for you. #Deflategate, #TigerWoods loses a tooth, #Broncos get a coach & more on #GormanSports! [Tweet]. Retrieved from https://twitter.com/FoxSportsRadio/status/557311563351470080

Gonzalez-Herrero, A., & Smith, S. (2008). Crisis communications management on the web: How Internet-based technologies are changing the way public relations professionals handle business crises. *Journal of Contingencies and Crisis Management, 16*, 143–153.

Heath, R. L. (2004). Telling a story: A narrative approach to communication during crisis. In D. P. Millar and Robert L. Heath (Eds.), *Responding to crisis: A rhetorical approach to crisis communication (pp. 167–188)*. Mahwah, NJ: Erlbaum.

Heath, R. L. (2006). Best practices in crisis communication: Evolution of practice through research. *Journal of Applied Communication Research, 34*, 245–248.

Hiltz, S. R., Diaz, P., & Mark, G. (2011). Introduction: Social media and collaborative systems of crisis management. *Transactions on Computer-Human Interaction, 18*, 1-6.

Jin, Y., Liu, B. F., & Austin, L. L. (2014). Examining the role of social media in effective crisis management: The effects of crisis origin, information form, and source on publics' crisis responses. *Communication Research, 41*, 74–94.

Kent, M. L., & Taylor, M. Toward a dialogic theory of public relations. *Public Relations Review, 28*, 21–37.

Kravitz, B. [bkravitz]. (2015, January 19). Breaking: a league source tell me the NFL is investigating the possibility the Patriots deflated footballs Sunday night. More to come. [Tweet]. Retrieved from https://twitter.com/bkravitz/status/557053826415755265

Kravitz, B. [bkravitz]. (2015, January 19b). Just heard from an nfl spokesman the league is in fact investigating the matter. [Tweet]. Retrieved from https://twitter.com/bkravitz/status/557159360733126656

Krispy Kreme [krispykreme]. (2015, January 21). Fully filled #Deflategate[Tweet]. Retrieved from https://twitter.com/krispykreme/status/557920121532870656?ref_src=twsrc%5Etfw

MacDougall, A. (2015, September 3). Patriots teammates take to Twitter to celebrate. *The Boston Globe*. Retrieved from https://www.bostonglobe.com/sports/2015/09/03/patsreact/sD5zF5V31wDtucxa1eT81M/story.html

New England Patriots [Patriots]. (2015, May 6). Statement from Robert Kraft on the Wells Report: Link to Patriots.com [Tweet]. Retrieved from https://twitter.com/Patriots/status/595997757099225090

New England Patriots [Patriots]. (2015, May 7). Brady responds to a question about his reaction to the Wells Reports at the Salem State Speakers Series event: (cont) tl.gd/n_1sm3osc [Tweet]. Retrieved from https://twitter.com/Patriots/status/596471253998956544

New England Patriots [Patriots]. (2015, May 14). Patriots counsel provides detailed context: Link to wellsreportcontext.com. [Tweet]. Retrieved from https://twitter.com/Patriots/status/598867540215861248

Newsday [Newsday]. (2015, January 21). #Deflategate update: @Colts told @NFL about @Patriots' deflated footballs after Nov. 16 game [Tweet]. Retrieved from https://twitter.com/Newsday/status/558060412546318336

Pang, A., Hassan, N. B., & Chong, A. C. (2014). Negotiating crisis in the social media environment: Evolution of crises offline, gaining credibility online. *Corporate Communications: An International Journal, 19*, 96–118.

Pennington, B. (May 11, 2015). Patriots' Brady suspended for four games in deflation case. *New York Times*.

Petrella, S. (2015, September 3). Patriots, Boston thrilled by decisions; Everyone still hate Roger Goodell. *Sporting News*. Retrieved from http://www.sportingnews.com/nfl/news/tom-brady-suspension-deflategate-overturned-null-roger-goodell-court-judge/1och8yshdjlr31jgpdw72lodww

Reiss, A. (July 29, 2015). Tom Brady's agent, Don Yee, rips NFL in strongly worded statement. Retrieved from www.espn.com/blog/boston/new-englandJuly 29

Sandman, P. M. (2006). Crisis communication best practices: Some quibbles and additions. *Journal of Applied Communication Research, 34*, 257–262.

Schilken, C. (2015, September 10). Tom Brady decision receives generally positive reaction around the league. *Los Angeles Times*. Retrieved from http://www.latimes.com/sports/sportsnow/la-sp-sn-tom-brady-reax-20150903-htmlstory.html

Schroeder, A., Pennington-Gray, L., Donohoe, H., & Kiousis, S. (2013). Using social media in times of crisis. *Journal of Travel and Tourism Marketing, 30*, 126–143.

Schultz, F., Utz, S., & Goritz, A. (2011). Is the medium the message: Perceptions of, and reactions to, crisis communication via Twitter, blogs, and traditional media. *Public Relations Review, 37*, 20–27.

Seeger, M. W. (2002). Chaos and crisis: Propositions for a general theory of crisis communication. *Public Relations Review, 28*, 329–337.

Seeger, M. W. (2006). Best practices in crisis communication: An expert panel process. *Journal of Applied Communication Research, 34,* 232–244.

Sessler, M. (2015, January 22). Bill Belichick 'shocked' to learn of football controversy. *National Football League.* Retrieved from http://www.nfl.com/news/story/0ap3000000461956/article/bill-belichick-shocked-to-learn-of-football-controversy

SI Now [SInowLIVE]. (2015, January 15). Watch: @GregBishopSI explain if there is any substance to Patriots latest deflate-gate on.si.com/14ZjHy1 [Tweet]. Retrieved from https://twitter.com/SInowLIVE/status/557311653969006593

Staten Island Yankees [SIYanks]. (2015, January 21). Never deflated. Always 5-5 1/4 ounces. #Deflategate[Tweet]. Retrieved from https://twitter.com/SIYanks/status/557923194955632642?ref_src=twsrc%5Etfw

Stephens, K. K., & Malone, P. C. (2009). If the organizations won't give us information: The use of multiple new media for crisis technical translation and dialogue. *Journal of Public Relations Research, 21,* 229–239.

Synthesio (December 2016). DeflategateSocial Tracking. Reprinted with Permission.

Taylor, M., & Perry, D. C. (2005). Diffusion of traditional and new media tactics in crisis communication. *Public Relations Review, 31,* 209–217.

The Boston Globe [Boston Globe]. (2015, January 20). #NFL says #Deflategateinvestigation will be completed in 'two or three days' ow.ly/HFfGf [Tweet]. Retrieved from https://twitter.com/BostonGlobe/status/557684513133043713

Tichenor, P. A., Donohue, G. A., & Oilen, C. N. (1970). Mass media flow and differential growth in knowledge. *Public Opinion Quarterly, 34,* 159–170.

Traina, J. (2015, May 12). The Patriots change all social media avatars to Tom Brady photo. Fox Sport @theBuzzer. Retrieved from http://www.foxsports.com/buzzer/story/new-england-patriots-tom-brady-deflategate-avatars-051215

Ulmer, R. R., Seeger, M. W., & Sellnow, T. L. (2007). Post-crisis communication and renewal: Expanding the parameters of post-crisis discourse. *Public Relations Review, 33,* 130–134.

Van der meer, T. G., & Verhoeven, P. (2013). Public framing organizational crisis situations: Social media versus news media. *Public Relations Review, 39,* 229–231.

Veil, S. R., Buehner, & Palenchar, M. J. (2011). A work-in-progress literature review: Incorporating social media in risk and crisis communication. *Journal of Contingencies and Crisis Management, 19,* 110–122.

Chapter 10

Carnival's Response to the Costa *Concordia* Crisis: A Test of Situational Crisis Communication Theory

NICOLE MAGEE, M.A.
University of Southern Mississippi

STEVEN VENETTE, PH.D.
University of Southern Mississippi

Carnival's Trouble on the Seas

According to 2016 data, nearly 23 million people worldwide will embark on a cruise (Cruise Market Watch, 2016), and approximately 10 million of those individuals will board a Carnival vessel to reach their desired location (Carnival Corporation & PLC, 2006a). Succulent dishes, live entertainment, exotic destinations, and a "guaranteed" great time are just a few of the benefits customers are assured when booking a Carnival cruise (Carnival Cruise Line, 2014). Yet, as of late, the "world's most popular cruise line" has been the target of one maritime disaster after another (Arthur Page Society, 2012). Several unfortunate incidents occurred in early 2013, including an engine room fire aboard the Carnival *Triumph*, a malfunction in the Carnival *Dream*'s diesel generator, and a stalled sailing speed that affected the Carnival *Legend* (Davies, 2013). These mishaps provided passengers with uncomfortable conditions, rerouted destinations, and canceled excursions. However, the lives of the travelers were not threatened in any of these setbacks. Passengers aboard one recent nautical expedition were not as fortunate. Individuals who embarked upon the Costa *Concordia* cruise ship experienced an accident so horrific that it has been likened to that of the *Titanic* (Lush, 2012). This vessel incident, deemed "the worst cruise-line accident in years" (p. 3), also belonged to none other than the Carnival Corporation (Esterl & Lublin, 2012).

At the time of the tragedy, the industry was largely controlled by two well-known cruise lines: the Carnival Corporation and Royal Caribbean International (Arthur Page Society, 2012). Still, Carnival, which ranked as the world's largest provider of vacations at sea, more than doubled the size of its closest competitors at Royal Caribbean (Esterl & Lublin, 2012). The company owned 10 different cruise ship brands, including AIDA Cruises in Germany, the Cunard Line and P&O Cruises in the United Kingdom, Iberocruceros of Spain, P&O Cruises of Australia, Costa Cruises of Italy, as well as several in the United States: Carnival Cruise Lines, the Holland America Line, the Seabourn Cruise Line, and Princess Cruises (Carnival Corporation & PLC, 2006a). Carnival's acquisition of the Italian line Costa Crociere occurred in September of 2000, after it purchased the rights of an English-owned line, Airtours. This expansion into the European market increased Carnival's fleet by 13 ships and provided them the opportunity to sail the Italian waterways (*CNN Money*, 2000).

With $16 billion worth of annual revenue (Esterl & Lublin, 2012) and its recent extensions, the Carnival Corporation proved to be thriving in the cruise industry, priding itself on its reputation for the security of its ships and well-being of its passengers. That is, until January 13, 2012, when the Costa *Concordia*, Italy's largest cruise liner, ran aground off the coast of Giglio, Italy (Dake, 2012). At approximately 9:45 pm, just hours after leaving port in Civitavecchia, the vessel, holding 3,206 passengers and 1,023 crew members, sailed too close to the rocky Italian coastline, tearing a hole in the left-side hull of the boat. The *Concordia*, measured to be longer than the length of three football fields, began to take on water, completely flooding the engine rooms and causing the ship to lose power (*BBC News*, 2013). The situation that was initially reported to passengers and the Coast Guard as a "blackout" quickly escalated into a life-threatening emergency as the ship began to tilt and sink deeper into the coastal waters. Just before 11:00 pm Captain Francesco Schettino ordered an evacuation of the cruise liner. Passengers were evacuated using lifeboats with the aid of the Italian Coast Guard (*National Post*, 2012). Shortly after announcing the evacuation, Captain Schettino departed *Concordia*, leaving his second in command to handle the situation. Yet, the second master also fled the ship minutes later to save his own life. With over 300 people still onboard, the sinking boat had no leader to direct the stranded individuals (*BBC News*, 2013). Even when the Coast Guard demanded Captain Schettino re-board the vessel to ensure the safety of his passengers, he denied the command and went ashore (Arthur Page Society, 2012). The marooned travelers were left to the mercy of the Coast Guard who helped people abandon the ship via helicopters. Still, others who were panicked took matters into their own hands by jumping from the bow of the ship into the dark waters below in a desperate attempt to save their lives (Dake, 2012).

Although there was an apparent lack of leadership to direct the evacuation, this process might have been more effective if all the travelers had participated in an emergency drill prior to the disaster. But, this was not the case, as over 600 passengers boarded the ship in nearby Rome. Since the accident took place shortly after they boarded the vessel, these individuals were unaware of the proper emergency protocol (Arthur Page Society, 2012). This misfortune, along with the inability to use some of the lifeboats because of the unexpected tilting of the ship, is a likely cause of the 32 deaths reported (Burrough, 2012).

In the wake of the disaster, much controversy existed regarding what exactly took place that night on the water and who should be held responsible for the crisis. Rather than the Carnival Corporation taking responsibility for the wreck, it let its Italian subsidiary, Costa Crociere, be held accountable for the incident. Still, there is an apparent disconnect between the level of responsibility Carnival willingly accepted for the event and the amount of liability the public believed the company should assume. Thus, the reaction Carnival provided to the general public was deemed inadequate and potentially could have damaged the reputation of the company (Dunham-Potter, 2012).

Recognizing an organization's reputation as a valuable resource (Coombs & Holladay, 2002), Coombs (2007b) argues that post-crisis communication can be used to restore the stakeholders' evaluations of the organization. This study will analyze Carnival's responses to the *Concordia* disaster through the lens of Coombs' (2007b) Situational Crisis Communication Theory (SCCT), which states that an organization's level of response to a crisis must match its level of responsibility for the event (Coombs, 2006). While previously conducted studies have used the SCCT as a means to investigate various crises, this research seeks to extend this perspective by arguing that responsibility is not best explained by intentionality, or whether an organization meant to deliberately cause harm. But, in Carnival's case, its level of obligation was dependent upon the organization's liability, or the level of legal responsibility for the *Concordia* crash it should assume based on the company's actions and omissions (Jennings, 2012).

Situational Crisis Communication Theory

The public's perception of an organization, known as its reputation (Coombs & Holladay, 2002), is a vital resource that warrants defense when a crisis occurs (Coombs, 2007b). The company's post-crisis response to the dilemma is critical to its future relationships with stakeholders and must be used appropriately in order to minimize damage (Sisco, Collins, & Zoch, 2010). Crisis scholars suggest organizational crises can be managed using the Situational Crisis Communication Theory (SCCT), which evaluates the public's reactions to the crisis to determine how the company should respond, while seeking to diminish reputational harm (Howell & Miller, 2009). Coombs (2007b) created this "evidence-based" theoretical structure that promotes post-crisis communication in order to restore a positive organizational reputation. Through implementing the SSCT, organizations must analyze both the crisis situation and the crisis response strategy before developing a system to match these two elements accordingly (Coombs, 2006). This investigation should also help determine the company's personal control over the occurrence of the event, as well as its accountability for the crisis, or how worthy the organization is of accepting blame (Coombs & Holladay, 2002).

When using the SSCT, companies must first estimate the organizational threat, or how much harm the event could have on its reputation if no corrective action is taken to solve the issue (Coombs, 2007a). Crisis managers begin this process by evaluating the company's initial crisis responsibility. Sisco (2012b) argues that the organization must not only assess who is actually at fault for the crisis, but, more importantly, how much the public believes the company itself is to blame for the occurrence of the event. Based upon how the crisis in framed, noting that similar events can be handled in the same way (Coombs & Holladay, 2002), the organization can react using the appropriate level of responsibility.

The three frameworks that crises may be a part of are known as victim, accident, and preventable clusters (Howell & Miller, 2009). The type of crises that falls into the victim category claims that the organization was damaged by the event, in addition to the general public (Coombs, 2007b). Because harm was inflicted upon both the company and its stakeholders, crisis managers are forced to take very little responsibility for the situation (Sisco et al., 2010). Coombs (2006) points to rumors, natural disasters, workplace violence, and product tampering as examples of this form of crisis. Events included in the accident category are said to be unintentional or uncontrollable by the organization (Coombs, 2007b). Thus, the company's actions preceding the situation were not intentionally dangerous to stakeholders, but, nonetheless, resulted from the organization's involvement in the matter (Coombs & Holladay, 2002). Mega damage, technical breakdown accidents or recalls, and challenges are each attributed to accidental crisis events (Coombs, 2006), which require more moderate levels of accountability to be assumed by the company (Sisco et al., 2010). Finally, the preventable cluster, previously known as the intentional category (Coombs, 2007a), involves crises when the organization knowingly placed stakeholders in harm's way, either through taking incorrect actions or the violation of a regulation (Coombs, 2007b). These acts are considered purposeful because preventative measures were not taken to avert the incident (Coombs & Holladay, 2002). Human breakdown accidents or recalls, organizational misdeeds, and misconduct are each instances which were preventable by the company; thus, these events call for much greater levels of organizational responsibility (Sisco et al., 2010).

Upon assessing the company's initial crisis responsibility, crisis managers must consider two additional factors that may also shape organizational threat, including the crisis history and prior relational reputation (Coombs, 2007b). Coombs (2006) explains that organizations that have previously experienced similar crises will likely experience additional damage to their reputation because of those prior mishaps. High consistency in the company's negative relationship history with its stakeholders will, in turn, increase its organizational threat (Jeong, 2009). Moreover, the ways in which the company has treated its patrons in recent years will also play a role in the organization's credibility. Low distinctiveness, or poor preceding relations with the public in other contexts, will intensify the organizational risk as well (Coombs, 2007a). An evaluation of these three components provides companies with the necessary information to make an informed choice regarding which crisis response strategy to employ that is congruent with its level of responsibility for the incident (Coombs & Holladay, 2002).

Selecting the proper crisis response strategy is the second measure a company must take after encountering a crisis, monitoring its words and actions (Coombs, 2006). Sisco (2012a) claims these reactions must shape the way the public views the situation, alter the perceptions of the organization's role in the dilemma, and lessen the negative influence caused by the crisis. To fulfill these objectives, companies may implement either a deny, a diminish, or a rebuild response as an acceptable organizational reaction, depending on the specific situation (Sisco et al., 2010).

A deny response is an appropriate tactic to use when seeking to eliminate any affiliation between the company and the crisis (Coombs, 2007b). This type of reply either indicates no "real" crisis exists or that the organization itself holds no responsibility for the crisis that has taken place. Denial may involve attacking the accuser, clarification, or scapegoating, which shifts the blame from the company to another party involved (Coombs, 2006). Sisco (2012a) argues that negation of organizational responsibility is suitable when the crisis is part of the victim cluster, indicating that because the company was also harmed by the event, they should not be held responsible for the damage that was done.

The diminish strategy can be relied upon when the organization desires to reduce the public's negative attitudes of the crisis by expressing that the event is not as bad as people think. Furthermore, if the company can convey it has no connection to a situation (Coombs, 2007b), then it can demonstrate its lack of organizational control in the occurrence through making excuses or justifications of its actions (Sisco, 2012b). Accident cluster crises would benefit from using this type of response in times of turmoil (Sisco et al., 2010) through a company's illustration of its unintentional contribution to the crisis, and, thus, its defense of taking less responsibility for the event.

The final reaction strategy, known as the rebuild response, involves taking action to compensate for the crisis through offering material aid to victims or a personal apology (Coombs, 2007b). Expressing compassion and regret for what happened helps meet public expectations (Coombs & Holladay, 2002) and is the appropriate corrective action to use in preventable crisis instances (Sisco et al., 2010). This response, in addition to the previously mentioned types of reactions, allows an organization to protect its reputation from potential harm by accommodating those affected by the unfortunate event. In doing this, the company publicly holds itself accountable for its participation, or lack thereof, in the occurrence, thereby reducing reputational threat and the public's negative judgments (Coombs, 2007a).

Carnival's Response

Upon being informed of the cruise disaster, Carnival first acknowledged the event through a post on Facebook and Twitter, expressing their concern on January 13, which read: "Our thoughts are with the guests and crew of the Costa *Concordia*. We are keeping them in our hearts in the wake of this very sad event" (McNaughton, 2012, p. 1). But, there was no mention of Carnival's involvement in the accident or what future actions the company planned to take to support the victims.

The following day Carnival uploaded an additional message online that stated: "Our hearts go out to everyone affected by the grounding of the Costa *Concordia* and especially the loved ones of those who lost their lives. They will remain in our thoughts and prayers in the wake of this tragic event. We wish to recognize and thank the Italian Coast Guard and everyone in Italy who has provided such extraordinary assistance" (Carnival Cruise Lines, n.d.). While condolences were expressed for what happened, no official apology was issued from the company on behalf of itself or its subsidiary, Costa, for their participation in the event.

Later the same day, a defective link to the official statement from the Carnival Corporation was posted on their social media accounts, causing users to complain that they could not access the report (Dunham-Potter, 2012). Facebook comments below this post also revealed that the contact numbers to Costa Cruises listed on the official press release were incorrect. Thus, friends and family of the *Concordia* passengers were unable to reach their office to receive information about the accident and the whereabouts of their loved ones (Carnival Cruise Lines, n.d.). The Carnival Corporation never responded to these complaints, whether through its social media accounts or press releases, in an effort to resolve the public's concerns regarding the misinformation.

The press release, which was also published on Carnival's website, recapped what happened during the crisis, before expressing sympathy for the traumatic experiences this caused for the victims and their families (Arthur Page Society, 2012). The company claimed it was using all of its available resources to help those affected by the disaster and thanked the Italian Coast Guard for the tremendous amount of aid it provided during the relief efforts. To conclude, Carnival remarked that it was investigating exactly what occurred (Carnival Corporation & PLC, 2006b), which indicated it still lacked a detailed account of the events that had transpired.

Throughout the succeeding days, Carnival released several additional posts to its social media accounts, reiterating the safety precautions it enforces on its cruise lines. Statements echoing that the passengers and crew are the company's first priority, its ships are safe to sail on, and its navigation systems are accurate were conveyed on its Twitter and Facebook sites, along with a safety video which is shown to passengers onboard its ships (McNaughton, 2012). From these messages, Carnival hoped to reinforce the public's perception that its cruise liners were secure for passengers to sail.

The final post which referenced the crisis appeared on January 19, less than a week after the crisis occurred, to notify the public that Carnival was stepping away from its social media accounts in order to devote more time to focus on the disaster. The message read as follows:

> "Hi, everyone. Out of respect for all those affected by the recent events surrounding our sister line, Costa cruises, we are going to take a bit of a break from posting on our social channels. We will still be actively listening and answering any questions you have about your past or upcoming cruises, but for now, the majority of our time will be spent focusing on all those affected by this event. We thank you again for all your support" (Engler, 2012).

After providing this farewell response, a message that was met with much public criticism (Egler, 2012), Carnival did not resume posting on its social media channels until January 24, when it released its "we're ready to re-engage" post (McNaughton, 2012). All messages after this date were irrelevant to the crisis situation, resuming Carnival's attempts to advertise and connect with its followers.

Micky Arison's Response

The Carnival Corporation was not the only party that commented on the *Concordia* crisis; its CEO, Micky Arison, also made remarks pertaining to the disaster after it occurred. Although there are no Facebook posts on his personal profile since January 11, 2012 (Micky Arison, n.d.), he actively used Twitter as his primary means of communication with the public following the wreck (Schaal, 2012). Arison, who ranked as the 75th richest American in a recent Forbes report (Walker, 2012), expressed his heartfelt sorrow from the comfort of his luxurious 200-foot yacht in Miami, the location of Carnival's headquarters, until several days after the instance (Gallo, 2012). He first tweeted "Tonight our thoughts and prayers are with the passengers and crew of the Costa *Concordia*" on January 13 (Arthur Page Society, 2012).

After a few days of silence, Arison again addressed the public via Twitter on January 17, in two separate posts, stating "Since Friday night, I've been focused on the response to this tragedy. I want to thank you for all for your support this week," and "I am deeply saddened by reports of more deaths following the grounding of #Concordia." Later that day, he posted a link to his condolence statement, also released on Carnival's website (Booton, 2012), in which he, again, expressed his sorrow for the event. Arison claimed he and his team were in contact with Costa to provide them with additional support and thanked *Concordia*'s crew and the Italian Coast Guard for their efforts (Carnival Corporation & PLC, 2006b). While his statements acknowledged the occurrence of the unfortunate event and conveyed his condolences, Arison never claimed to be affiliated with the crisis in any way.

On January 18, he tweeted a link to his personal assurance statement on the Carnival website, which reaffirmed that the company would take care of all passengers who experienced the wreck and their families (Carnival Corporation & PLC, 2006). He informed audiences that lodging and transportation to return home would be offered to the victims, as well as counseling services as needed. The company would also account for personal possessions lost on board and planned to refund passengers both the cruise fare and costs they incurred while onboard the ship (Bhasin, 2012).

The next day, Arison posted the link to the safety and emergency response message, which can be found across all cruise lines, on his Twitter account (Arthur Page Society, 2012). This document confirmed that the Carnival Corporation did own the Costa line. But, whereas Carnival had a great reputation for safety, this wreck had questioned its ability to protect its passengers. As a result, the company wanted to make certain that this type of crisis did not recur during future excursions (Micky Arison [MickyArison], n.d.). Later on January 19, when the Carnival Corporation announced their "break" from social media, Arison also commented "I won't be as active on Twitter for the next while. Helping our @costacruises team manage this crisis is my priority right now. Thnx." (Engler, 2012). Much like the public's response to Carnival's Facebook post, many people remarked that, as the voice of Carnival, the CEO should not have been invisible when the spotlight was on him (Esterl & Lublin, 2012).

Finally, on January 24 Arison re-entered the social media scene providing a link that clarified "inaccurate" media reports (Micky Arison [MickyArison], n.d.). In this document, he supported the company's refutation of rumors that it had offered *Concordia* passengers 30% off their next cruise (Bennett, 2012) rather than refunding the victims the $14,500 fare and cost of travel they each had to pay (Booton, 2012). Upon posting this message, Arison no longer addressed the crisis situation from his personal Twitter account.

Though reports reveal his attendance at a Miami Heat game on January 27, the *Concordia* wreck did not appear to warrant a public appearance from Arison until March 10, 2012, nearly two months after the incident, when he was interviewed about the disaster for the first time (Arthur Page Society, 2012). His response to the tragedy included sympathy for the "accident," support of Carnival's high safety regulations, and reassurance that Pier Luigi Foschi, the then-CEO of Costa Crociere, and his team would work their way through the misfortune (Rivkind, 2012). This reaction left the public with a sour attitude towards the CEO and his failure to admit his faults in the situation.

DISCUSSION

Upon analyzing the findings of this case, Carnival underestimated the organizational threat the Costa *Concordia* crisis would have for the company. Initially, Carnival correctly referenced its nearly flawless previous record of providing safe cruises and honoring its customers as its top priority (Micky Arison

[MickyArison], n.d.). This reliance on its positive crisis history and relational reputation with consumers slightly alleviated the organizational threat. But, the organization's shortcomings appear to be a direct result of its misinterpretation of the initial crisis responsibility standards the public expected it to uphold.

After the shipwreck, Carnival partially placed itself in the "victim" cluster, acting as if the company itself, as well as *Concordia*'s passengers, had fallen prey to Costa's wrongdoings. While both the organization and its CEO expressed their concerns for the victims and their families (Arthur Page Society, 2012), they never held themselves accountable for the mistake. Instead, Carnival issued statements in support of Costa's relief efforts (Carnival Corporation & PLC, 2006b), indicating that its subsidiary line was resolving the issue, and Arison reassured audiences that he was confident in the Costa team's ability to get through the difficult situation (Rivkind, 2012). These acts of scapegoating were Carnival's attempts to employ a denial response strategy that would weaken the connection between the company and the cruise ship disaster. However, upon reading these messages, the public's reaction was that of frustration and disgust. Consumers disapproved of Carnival's attempt to remove itself from the limelight by framing the situation as their "sister" line's dilemma (Booton, 2012).

Carnival also partly placed itself in the "accident" cluster, suggesting that the events that ensued were out of the company's control and victims were unintentionally harmed as a result. In fact, in Arison's personal interview, he publicly declared the crisis as an accident on Costa's part (Arthur Page Society, 2012). Still, through using the diminish strategy to make excuses that the disaster was part of its sister line's technical breakdown, the company and its CEO failed to accept responsibility for Carnival's role in the wreck.

Carnival associated itself with the victim and accident forms of crises, but failed to acknowledge the *Concordia* disaster as a preventable situation. Because the wreck was not intentional, meaning Carnival had no desire to deliberately bring harm to the ship's passengers, the company did not classify the situation as being able to be avoided. However, Coombs and Holladay (2002) would categorize the *Concordia* crisis as an "industrial accident caused by human error," known as a human breakdown accident. This form of crisis, located in the preventable category, requires greater levels of responsibility to be assumed by the organization (Sisco et al., 2010).

Using the rebuild response strategy would have been Carnival's most effective reply pertaining to the shipwreck (Sisco, 2012). This approach argues that compensating all material items, offering a full apology, and providing a plan for future organizational actions is the proper way for companies to reduce their reputational threat and the public's negative judgments (Coombs, 2007a). While partial compensation was offered, though the specific amount has been disputed (Bennett, 2012), Carnival should have taken greater measures to clearly convey that it would reimburse passengers for any and all expenses associated with their cruise, as well as additional costs they have incurred as a result of the traumatic experience. Yet, Arison clarified that only the cruise fare and costs incurred while on the *Concordia* would be reimbursed to passengers (Bhasin, 2012). A full apology, publicly accepting responsibility for the situation and seeking the consumers' forgiveness (Coombs & Holladay, 2002), was also lacking in both the Carnival Corporation and Arison's responses. Instead, Carnival failed to take ownership of the mistake, blaming Costa for the wreck, in hopes that the public would not hold the company liable (Burrough, 2012). Future actions were also not addressed by the company to convey what measures it would take to solve the problem. Instead, both Carnival and Arison's social media posts vaguely stated that they were focusing on those affected by the event as a justification for their absence online (Engler, 2012). However, neither defined what their efforts consisted of, leaving the public to wonder whether or not they were involved in the resolution process.

From these results, one can conclude that Carnival did not provide the proper response to the Costa *Concordia* disaster because the company did not classify the situation appropriately. Rather than categorizing the shipwreck as a preventable instance, Carnival and its leaders sought to portray themselves as the victims of Costa's accident. However, the disaster can clearly be defined as an avoidable event since it was a human breakdown accident. Thus, intentionality, which is a typical determinant of preventable crises, in this case, does not equate to purposeful actions taken by the company; but, in actuality, the factor is dependent upon the liability of the organization for its actions. The public held Carnival to the highest standard of accountability in this case because of its legal responsibility to act on behalf of its customers in order to protect them from harm. However, the Carnival Corporation responded by taking as little responsibility as possible for the disaster. Thus, this case suggests that if the company had deemed itself liable for Costa Crociere's actions, it could have taken full responsibility for the shipwreck by responding with a full apology. Offering this type of reaction would have acted as an acceptance of guilt and been congruent with the public's expectations of Carnival's accountability.

In conclusion, the Carnival Corporation will likely continue to thrive in the cruise industry, guaranteeing potential passengers a great time while onboard its vessels. Indeed, the *Concordia* crisis may not have ruined the company's reputation among the public. However, enough negative attention was attracted that should cause Carnival to reevaluate its responses to future maritime dilemmas. With misfortunes at sea becoming the new norm, Carnival must seek to correctly estimate its initial crisis responsibility for upcoming events and provide reactions which will reduce the overall organizational threat.

DISCUSSION QUESTIONS

1. From the evidence presented in this case study, which of the frameworks or "clusters" should the Carnival Corporation have associated itself with? Should either Micky Arison or Costa Crociere be coupled within the same cluster? Why or why not?

2. Should the Carnival Corporation's level of accountability have been contingent upon its legal responsibility for the disaster? Explain why or why not.

3. Based on Situational Crisis Communication Theory (SCCT), which of the proposed response strategies would lessen the negative influence caused by the crisis? How does that single strategy or combination of strategies shape the ways in which the public views the situation?

4. Provide further suggestions the Carnival Corporation could implement to improve its response to crises in future disasters based on Situational Crisis Communication Theory (SCCT) or other post-crisis communication theories.

REFERENCES

Arthur Page Society. (2012). Carnival corporation: The Costa *Concordia* Crisis. Retrieved from http://www.awpagesociety.com/wp-content/uploads/2013/03/Carnival-Corporation-Case-A-and-B.pdf

BBC News. (2013). Costa *Concordia*: What happened. Retrieved from http://www.bbc.com/news/world-europe-16563562

Bennett, C. (2012). Deadly shipwreck line offers victims 30% off their next voyage. Retrieved from http://nypost.com/2012/01/23/deadly-shipwreck-line-offers-victims-30-off-their-next-voyage/

Bhasin, K. (2012). Carnival is failing spectacularly in the handling of its Costa *Concordia* crisis. Retrieved from http://www.businessinsider.com/carnival-is-failing-spectacularly-in-its-handling-of-the-costa-Concordia-crisis-2012-1

Booton, J. (2012). Carnival fails Crisis 101 in Costa response. Retrieved from http://www.foxbusiness.com/travel/2012/01/26/experts-say-carnival-should-have-learned-from-wendys-fedex-post-crisis/

Burrough, B. (2012). Another night to remember. Retrieved from http://www.vanityfair.com/culture/2012/05/costa-Concordia-sinking-scandal-italy

Carnival Corporation & PLC. (2006a). Corporate information. Retrieved from http://phx.corporate-ir.net/phoenix.zhtml?c=200767&p=irol-prlanding

Carnival Corporation & PLC. (2006b). Press releases. Retrieved from http://phx.corporate-ir.net/phoenix.zhtml?c=200767&p=irol-newsArticle&ID=1648204

Carnival Cruise Lines. (2014). Why Carnival? Retrieved from http://www.carnival.com/cruising.aspx

Carnival Cruise Lines. (n.d.) Timeline [Facebook page]. Retrieved March 15, 2014 from https://www.facebook.com/Carnival?ref=br_rs&fref=nf

CNN Money. (2000). Carnival takes Costa's helms. Retrieved from http://money.cnn.com/2000/08/28/deals/carnival/index.htm

Coombs, W. T., & Holladay, S. J. (2002). Helping crisis managers protect reputational assets: Initial tests of the Situational Crisis Communication Theory. *Management Communication Quarterly, 16*(2), 165-186.

Coombs, W. T. (2006). The protective powers of crisis response strategies: Managing reputational assets during a crisis. *Journal of Promotion Management, 12*(3–4), 241–260.

Coombs, W. T. (2007a). Attribution Theory as a guide for post-crisis communication research. *Public Relations Review, 33*(2), 135–139.

Coombs, W. T. (2007b). Protecting organization reputations during a crisis: The development and application of Situational Crisis Communication Theory. *Corporate Reputation Review, 10*(3), 163–176.

Cruise Market Watch. (2016). Growth of the cruise line industry. Retrieved from http://www.cruisemarketwatch.com/growth/

Dake, S. (2012). A short history of the Costa *Concordia*. Retrieved from http://maritimematters.com/2012/01/a-short-history-of-the-costa-Concordia/

Davies, A. (2013). A photo history of Carnival cruise ship disasters. Retrieved from http://www.businessinsider.com/carnival-disaster-timeline-in-photos-2013-3?op=1

Dunham-Potter, A. (2012). Carnival Corporation issues statement regarding Costa *Concordia*. Retrieved from http://travel.usatoday.com/alliance/cruises/expertcruiser/post/2012/01/Carnival-Corporation-issues-statement-regarding-Costa-Concordia/603389/1

Egler, G. (2012). Retreat from social media backfires on Carnival after Italy ship disaster. Retrieved from http://adage.com/article/digitalnext/post-disaster-retreat-social-media-backfires-carnival/232723/

Esterl, M., & Lublin, J. S. (2012). Carnival CEO lies low after wreck. Retrieved from online.wsj.com/news/articles/SB10001424052970204624204577177131752006116

Gallo, C. (2012). 3 things Carnival must do now to manage the Costa crisis. Retrieved from http://www.forbes.com/sites/carminegallo/2012/01/18/3-things-carnival-must-do-now-to-manage-the-costa-crisis/

Howell, G. V. J., & Miller, R. (2009). Organizational response to crisis: A case study of Maple Leaf Foods. *The Northwest Journal of Communication, 39(1)*, 91–108.

Jennings, M. M. (2012). *Business: Its legal, ethical and global environment*. Mason, OH: Cengage Learning.

Jeong, S. H. (2009). Public's responses to an oil spill accident: A test of the Attribution Theory and Situational Crisis Communication Theory. *Public Relations Review, 35*(3), 307–309.

Lush, T. (2012). Many make *Concordia, Titanic* comparisons. Retrieved from http://www.dispatch.com//content/stories/national_world/2012/01/16/many-make-Concordia-titanic-comparisons.html

McNaughton, M. (2012). Crisis communication: Will Carnival maintain social media silence about the Costa *Allegra*, too? Retrieved from http://therealtimereport.com/2012/02/27/crisis-communications-will-carnival-maintain-social-media-silence-about-the-costa-allegra-too/

Merriam, S. B. (2009). *Qualitative research: A guide to design and implementation*. New York: John Wiley & Sons.

Micky Arison. (n.d.). Timeline [Facebook page]. Retrieved March 15, 2014 from https://www.facebook.com/MickyArison

Micky Arison [MickyArison]. (n.d.). Tweets [Twitter page]. Retrieved March 15, 2014 from https://twitter.com/mickyarison

National Post. (2012). The Costa *Concordia*'s final moments. Retrieved from http://news.nationalpost.com/2012/01/20/graphic-the-final-moments-of-the-costa-Concordia/

Rivkind, B. (2012). Carnival Corporation's Micky Arison expresses sorrow about Costa *Concordia* disaster. Retrieved from http://www.maritimeinjuryattorneyblog.com/2012/03/carnival-corporations-micky-ar.html

Schaal, D. (2012). After Costa *Concordia*, Carnival reduces marketing and expects no long-term impact. Retrieved from http://www.tnooz.com/article/after-costa-Concordia-carnival-reduces-marketing-and-expects-no-long-term-impact/

Sisco, H. F., Collins, E. L., & Zoch, L. M. (2010). Through the looking glass: A decade of Red Cross crisis response and Situational Crisis Communication Theory. *Public Relations Review, 36*(1), 21–27.

Sisco, H. F. (2012a). The ACORN story: An analysis of crisis response strategies in a nonprofit organization. *Public Relations Review, 38*(1), 89–96.

Sisco, H. F. (2012b). Nonprofit in crisis: An examination of the applicability of Situational Crisis Communication Theory. *Journal of Public Relations Research, 24*(1), 1–17.

Walker, J. (2012). Costa cruise disaster: Spotlight shifts to Carnival – Where's Micky? Retrieved from http://www.cruiselawnews.com/2012/01/articles/social-media-1/costa-cruise-disaster-spotlight-shifts-to-carnival-wheres-micky/

Chapter 11

Organizational Sensemaking in a Mixed-Media Environment: The Case of Paula Deen

Lisa Chewning, Ph.D.
Pennsylvania State University – Abington

Introduction

The rise of online media has changed not only the way organizations communicate with external stakeholders, but also the way that organizational crises are created, perpetuated, and managed (Sweetser & Metzgar, 2007; Choi & Lin, 2009). The 24/7 news cycle, combined with the "every-person editorial" capabilities of blogs and other social media, has enabled the creation of an environment in which organizational missteps get uncovered, editorialized, and rehashed across media platforms. Crisis communication is more than a two-way street; it is an intersection where competing interests and voices all get a say. The result is an environment that amplifies both the opportunities and the dangers inherent in crisis communication, as external stakeholders can comment on crisis in real time, lending both support and criticism to the organization's crisis narrative (Chewning, 2015; Chewning, in press; Choi & Lin, 2009).

The mediated environment has changed the nature of several types of crisis, including the *faux pas*. A *faux pas* is "an unintentional act that an external agent tries to turn into a crisis" (Coombs, 1995, p. 455). An example of a *faux pas* is when a highly visible organizational agent, such as CEO or spokesperson, says or does something that violates social values, causing backlash among publics. While CEOs and others have historically been taken to task for criminal or other transgressions, a *faux pas* can be a crisis in which something personal that a CEO or other organizational figurehead says or does gets inextricably intertwined with the brand, causing damage to the organization's reputation. Sometimes, as was the case with Barilla and Chik-Fil-A CEOs' statements about gay marriage, CEOs are asked their personal opinion about an issue, and, in giving their opinion, inadvertently make a social statement. Other times, the organizational figurehead or CEO says something that he or she thinks is non-inflammatory, but which ignites anger in the public, as was the case with Abercrombie & Fitch's CEO's statements about whom *he* thought should shop at A&F stores. Or, something that is said in private can become public, causing backlash against the brand, as was the case with Paula Deen's racially charged comments. This type of crisis is receiving more attention than ever before, perpetuated by the new state of media, in that (a) the public has a more personal view of CEOs than ever before, as they become more transparent and accessible via media and (b) a story that would not have been a mainstay on the news circuit before the 24/7 media cycle gets continually rehashed on several platforms.

This chapter examines the fall, and possible resurrection, of the Paula Deen brand in terms of organizational sensemaking, paying particular attention to the role of online media in conveying organizational messages, garnering support for the brand, and taking action. It will begin with an examination of the communicative elements of a *faux pas* crisis and the potential ramifications of such a crisis. Following this is an examination of organizational sensemaking in crisis and how conflicting messages in social and traditional media can complicate the sensemaking process. Finally, the implications of organizational sensemaking in a mixed-media environment will be applied to the case of Paula Deen.

The Faux Pas

The *faux pas* is part of Coombs' (1995) crisis typology rooted in Attribution Theory. Coombs (1995) names and categorizes four types of crises (terrorism, *faux pas*, accident, and transgression) in terms of where each falls within the classification of internal/external, intentional/unintentional, veracity of evidence, performance history, and damage. Where a crisis falls within these dimensions can impact how stakeholders attribute blame and, therefore, can affect subsequent actions by both stakeholders and organizations.

The internal/external dimension focuses on locus of control (i.e., was it something done by the organization or caused by an agent or force outside of the organization). Intentional crises are those in which the triggering event was committed purposefully, while unintentional crises are not committed purposefully. Intentionality also relates to control, in that something intentional is more controllable than something unintentional (Coombs, 1995). The locus of control, and controllability, of a crisis can often affect both organizational action and stakeholder response, as stakeholders are less likely to blame an organization for a crisis that was either out of its control or uncontrollable (Coombs, 1995). Veracity of evidence focuses on the amount of evidence that supports the idea that a crisis exists. Evidence can be true, false, or ambiguous. (Coombs, 1995). Performance history is whether or not the organization has been involved in a similar crisis in the past and is directly related to credibility in the present crisis. Finally, damage involves the consequences of the crisis. For example, death or environmental harm. Damage is also related to locus of control, in that the more extreme the damage, the more blame is attributed to the offending organization (Coombs, 1995).

As an example of the above, terrorism involves a malicious act against an organization by an outsider. Such a crisis is external, and likely difficult to control. In such cases, stakeholders generally sympathize with the organization. An accident, on the other hand, is something that the organization does (therefore internal), but that wasn't done with malicious intent and is often uncontrollable or unstable. However, depending on performance history and damage, stakeholders will attribute more or less anger to the organization. A transgression is both internal and intentional, usually involving some type of deception. Such a crisis will likely evoke anger and mistrust from stakeholders, which can be amplified by poor performance history or severe damage.

The *faux pas*, which is the focus of this chapter, is classified as an unintentional crisis with an external locus of control. While an organization may commit an offensive act, it is not purposeful or illegal. The crisis occurs in the external *perception* that the act was offensive. The offended party then challenges the organization (e.g., in the form of protests or boycotts), thus bringing attention to the organizational action and framing it in a negative way. While there is a degree of internal control, as the organization did perform the offense, Coombs (1995) asserts that "ambiguity is a facet of *faux pas*. The publics involved must decide which definition of the organization's action to accept" (p. 455). Arguably, subjectivity is another facet, in that what is offensive to some will not be offensive to others. Thus, stakeholders are left to decide if the action is an offense, according to their own and the organization's definition, and, therefore, the veracity of evidence can vary among stakeholder groups. With a *faux pas*, an organization can be caught off-guard with little defense, as the incident taken as a *faux pas* was not only unintentional, but often a true reflection of the values of the organizational figurehead, who may not perceive that any wrongdoing has, in fact, occurred.

Although seemingly more benign than other types of crises that involve intentional deception on behalf of the organization, the *faux pas* can be especially dangerous because of the ambiguity and subjectivity involved. While not all crises directly affect reputation (e.g., there is little subjectivity involved with natural disasters and terrorism), a *faux pas* does threaten reputation because it is closely aligned with values. That is, stakeholders must tap into their value systems to assign the perception of crisis to a given act. Constituent expectations are built on a combination of factors, including organizational identity, stakeholder values, and societal values. When organizations act in accordance with these values, and maintain a similarly aligned identity, they generally develop a positive relationship with stakeholders, which leads to a positive reputation (Coombs & Holladay, 2010). By extension, in order for an organization to resonate with stakeholders, it must reflect stakeholder values. Therefore, a crisis that causes stakeholders to question the way their values align with the organization is especially dangerous, in that it implies that the relationship that the stakeholder has built with the organization is false. This, in turn, negatively affects reputation.

A mixed media environment amplifies the discussion of values and ethics, as organizations become more accessible, and even humanized, though social media. Stakeholders come to expect more of them, in terms of behavior, even on issues that don't pertain specifically to the organization. Additionally, stakeholders expect to have a say in the issue, either defending or interrogating the offending organization in a very public forum. These expectations have the capability to change the trajectory of the crisis, as stakeholders can insert themselves into the crisis narrative by using both the organization's own, and alternative, media (Chewning, 2015; Choi & Lin, 2009). Sometimes this results in support for the organization, as stakeholders vigorously support a brand, while other times, this can lead to stakeholders publicly maligning the brand and bringing new facts to light (Chewning, 2015; Chewning, in press; Choi & Lin, 2009). While traditional crisis communication strategies focus on the message strategy prescribed, in part, by the crisis type (e.g., recommended strategies for organizations committing a *faux pas* are distance and nonexistence), crisis communication in a mixed media environment integrates organizational, media, and stakeholder voices (Chewning, 2015). The resulting cacophony complicates organizational response, as well as highlights the fact that there are many other factors that come into play as organizations respond to crisis, such as organizational history and damage. All of these factors contribute to how organizations make sense of the crisis and decide how to move forward.

Organizational Sensemaking

Crisis is time of "high consequence, low probability, ambiguity, and decision-making time pressure" (Runyan, 2006, p. 13) that "represents a fundamental threat to the very stability of a system, a questioning of core assumptions and beliefs, and risk to high priority goals" (Seeger & Ulmer, 2002, p. 126). Thus, standard understanding, goals, and actions are often inadequate to deal with the crisis environment. Actors are left with a need to adapt, and quickly. As such, "We often do not know if we are responding effectively to a crisis until we see the consequences of our initial response" (Sellnow & Seeger, 2013, p. 76). Organizational sensemaking (Weick, 1988) explores the need to act in order to understand by positing that action creates understanding, while at the same time affects future events. So, actors simultaneously act, understand, and create change, which leads to further understanding. Essentially, "situations, organizations, and environment are talked into existence" as a way to reduce uncertainty and ambiguity, guide actions during crisis, and answer the question, "what's the story?" (Weick, Sutcliffe, & Obstfeld,

2005, pp. 409–410). Coombs (1999) refers to crisis response as a symbolic resource that can be used for the preservation of reputation. Through narrative, organizations seek to regain control over the crisis and move toward resolution. Thus, how organizations make sense of, and then communicate, the crisis holds implications for maintenance and restoration of organizational reputation.

This process of learning and adaptation is set off by a triggering event that leads to a cosmology episode, or the feeling that the world in which the organization exists is no longer a "rational, orderly system" (Weick, 1993, p. 633). This forces the organization to take action in order to make sense of the system, which is accomplished through enactment, selection, and retention. Enactment is the idea that through action, actors produce structures that both enable and constrain them in ways that were not present before they took action (Weick, 1988). Essentially, enactment creates new opportunities (or limits future opportunities) for action. This creates an enacted environment in which actors engage in an "if-then" process of observing their behavior, drawing feedback, and taking further action. However, Weick (1988) points out that our actions are always further along than our understanding, which means that an actor can make things worse before realizing what is being done (p. 308). For better or worse, enactment sets the trajectory of the crisis (Weick, 1988, p. 309). For example, whether an organization discloses or hides evidence of a misdeed sets the stage for what the organization can or cannot do in its next steps. It creates the action environment in which the organization must act within the parameters of the story it started or risk losing "control" of the narrative.

Enactment involves the principles of commitment, capacity, and expectations (Weick, 1988). Each of these elements can occur at any point in the sensemaking process, creating detours and road-blocks to navigating out of the crisis. Commitment is the act of persistently adhering to a justification of the event, to the extent that it structures all future communication. The more public the explanation, the more committed an actor becomes, often leading to blind spots that flaw future sensemaking (Weick, 1988; Maitlis & Sonenshein, 2010). Capacity directs what actors will pay attention to, in that they are more likely to attend to factors that they feel they can effectively attend to. The more areas in which an agent feels like he or she has capacity to enact change, the more he or she will perceive in a crisis situation, thus broadening the scope of possible responses. Likewise, expectations act as beliefs that set courses of action. Weick (1993) uses the example of the Bhopal Union Carbide chemical leak to demonstrate these principles of enactment. Because of the organization's commitment to keep the danger of the production process secret in order to reduce public fear, this secrecy was a consideration when the crisis was detected, leading the organization to choose a delayed and intermittent sounding of the public warning siren, as opposed to a direct and immediate call for evacuation. High turnover and understaffing, leading to little institutional knowledge, resulted in fewer people feeling that they had the capacity to handle the crisis and, therefore, less intervention. Finally, management's expectation that their plant was unimportant, and therefore putting fewer resources toward maintaining it, served as a self-fulfilling prophecy that resulted in an environment that was conducive to the actions that caused the Bhopal crisis.

During the selection process, actors "interpret what they have done, define what they have learned, [and] solve the problem of what they should do next" (Weick, 2001, p. 214). Essentially, they apply meaning to what they have learned through enactment. Actors consider the information within the entirety of the environment. Retention involves keeping and filing away selected interpretations as part of "organizational history" (Weick, 2001, p. 304). The story becomes more substantial because "it is related to past experience, connected to specific identities, and used as a source of guidance for further action and interpretation" (Weick, Sutcliffe, & Obstefeld, 2005, p. 414), subsequently laying the groundwork for future sensemaking.

A mixed-media environment can both help and hinder sensemaking during crisis. Added to the multiple other voices in the system, such as traditional media and business partners, newer media, such as social media and blogs, exponentially increase the sources of feedback that any organization receives, adding both more and more discordant voices to the mix. That is, when individuals are able to voice their opinions via social media platforms, such as Facebook and Twitter, there are endless variations of responses to the situation at hand. Such noise can either clarify or confuse sensemaking. While these voices might provide more avenues of action for the organization, they might also cause miscues that misrepresent the full extent of the crisis environment. Weick says that "the less adequate the sensemaking process directed at crisis, the more likely it is that the crisis will get out of control" (1988, p. 305). Arguably, such was the case when Paula Deen came under fire for using racist language, leading to a series of actions that altered the course of the Paula Deen brand.

Case Study

In May 2013, food entrepreneur Paula Deen gave a deposition in a racial discrimination lawsuit filed against her and her brother by a former manager at their restaurant, *Uncle Bubba's Oyster House*. In this deposition, she admitted to using the N-word and, at one time, wanting to plan a plantation-themed wedding in which black waiters would dress up and play the role of slaves. One month later, details of the deposition, including a full transcript, leaked, and in addition to the tales of Deen's racist comments, other unsavory details of business operations at Deen's restaurant became public. The result was an immediate backlash against Deen, which, over the course of eight days, led to her firing from the Food Network, the cancellation of her upcoming cookbook, and her being dropped from six sponsorships. Although the case was dismissed from court on August 12, 2013, freeing her from any legal responsibility, the "Queen of Southern Cuisine" had arguably been dethroned. While the crisis had started as a legal problem, it ended as an issue of reputation, which played out in the court of public opinion.

Defining this incident as a *faux pas* implies that Deen's actions, while questionable, were not a crisis until external parties (such as the media) sounded the alarm and framed them as such. Although the trigger to the crisis was Deen's racially charged language and owning an organization that allegedly cultivated a racist and sexist environment (Wilson, 2013), the cosmology episode occurred much later (between June 19 and 20, 2013) when the deposition was leaked. At that time, her environment shifted in a way that likely left her feeling "I've never been here before. I have no idea where I am, and I have no idea who can help me" (Weick, 1993, pp. 633–634). Although she was not a stranger to crisis, given the moderate backlash that she received over her announcement of being a Type-2 diabetic, in tandem with announcing a deal with diabetes medication Novo Nordisk. However, this was different, in that she did not reveal the information herself and her personal statements were being portrayed negatively. This led to an enactment environment where Deen, her sponsors, and her fans all had to make sense of the ambiguity and uncertainty associated with the *faux pas*.

Enactment

As action is "a means to get feedback, learn, and build an understanding of known environments, then a reluctance to act could be associated with less understanding and more errors" (Weick, 1988, p. 306). Although Deen did communicate early on, her initial attempts at enactment were ambiguous, leaving room open for others to take charge of the emerging narrative. The first two statements were not given by Deen, but rather were given by her attorney and a representative. In the time between the leak of excerpts and the publishing of the full transcript of the deposition, Deen's attorney, Bill Franklin, issued a statement saying "Contrary to media reports, Ms. Deen does not condone or find the use of racial epithets acceptable. She is looking forward to her day in court" (Tepper, 2013). However, as the full transcript became public, Franklin's statement did not make sense in light of the printed document. On June 20, Deen's company issued a statement admitting that Deen had used the language, but in a "quite different time" in American history, saying "She was born 60 years ago when America's South had schools that were segregated, different bathrooms, different restaurants and Americans rode in different parts of the bus. This is not today" (Duke, 2013). Deen went from denial to justification, attempting to create a reality via retroactive sensemaking of the changes to the environment as new facts emerged.

Deen's next act of communication contributed to the ambiguity, as she cancelled a scheduled appearance on the *Today Show*, citing exhaustion. Later the same day, Deen took to her own social media issuing a brief apology to the *Today Show* and also to "those I have hurt" (Deen, YouTube, 2013). She released three videos, in all, on YouTube and linked to the first one from her Twitter account. The first issued an apology, but contained three obvious edits, indicating that it took several takes for her to get through the apology. It was taken down and a second video featured Deen alternately apologizing "to those I have hurt" and characterizing herself as having "spent the best of 24 years to help myself and others" (Deen, 2013). A third addendum video, only 36 seconds long, apologizes directly to Matt Lauer for the cancellation, citing how hard the last 48 hours had been and that even though she is usually a strong woman, she wasn't that day. In these videos, she both apologizes and bolsters, portraying herself as both perpetrator and victim. Additionally, the focus on apologizing to Matt Lauer, alongside apologizing for using racist language (which she never directly addresses: she only says that she is sorry for those she has hurt), muddles the apology further.

Inconsistent with the idea of commitment in enactment, Deen was unable to put together a tenacious justification and move the story forward. Each time she publicly committed, she was, at best, reactive, and, at worst, backpedaled and changed her story. This left her without a consistent or believable story upon which she could effectively enact crisis response. Consistent with the *faux pas*, a crisis in which action is taken that the organization (or figurehead, in this case) did not perceive as incorrect, Deen seemingly didn't have the ability to adjust her capacity to understand the situation (i.e., why the crisis was, in fact, a crisis) or her expectation that (a) her behavior was appropriate and that (b) her fans and established business contacts would support her (as they had in the previous Novo-Nordisk crisis). Therefore, her ambiguity created an enactment environment in which others could take control of the narrative and, therefore, influence the trajectory of the crisis. From a public relations perspective, this potentially left her lacking credibility and vulnerable. However, as will be seen, many of her supporters filled in this gap with their own versions of the story, lending credibility and strength to Deen's brand.

Environmental Feedback

In the first three days of the crisis Deen received feedback from multiple sources, including traditional media, stakeholders via social media, and sponsors. A LexisNexis search for "Paula Deen" between the dates of June 19 and June 21, 2013 delivers 187 results, an average of 62.33 articles per day in U.S. newspapers, blogs, newswires, trade publications, and magazines. They ranged from scornful to speculative to neutral. Her cancellation of a scheduled appearance on the *Today Show* was met with skepticism and admonishment by the show's hosts, with Al Roker portraying her as "a friend of this show," who "needs to address this [situation]" (Labrecque, 2013). Roker is, at once, offering help and calling into question Deen's actions thus far in the enactment environment. Lauer and Roker made similar comments regarding the situation on their Twitter feeds. No doubt this influenced her initial apology videos, two of which directly apologize to Lauer.

Stories citing more examples of pervasive racism at Deen's restaurant surfaced, while social media simultaneously displayed overwhelming support, sarcasm, and disbelief aimed at Deen (Jeffries & Washington, 2013). The hashtag Paula'sBestDishes was created, highlighting potential Deen meals such as "White's Only Rice" (@ParallelRhymes) and KKKesadillas (@santagati) and earning a number-one spot on Twitter's trending topics (Huffington Post, 2013). On Facebook, "We Support Paula Deen" and "Bring

Back Paula Deen" pages generated more than 128,000 likes and 1,200 likes, respectively. Additionally, fans took to Food Network's Facebook page, threatening boycott of the network. #Paula'sBestDishes continued to trend on Twitter and she was mocked on Comedy Central's fake news program, *The Daily Show*, all the while personal appearances on Paula Deen cruises continued to book. Also on social media, responses to Deen's recut apology video were split 50/50, with 10,517 viewers giving it a thumbs up and 10,943 viewers giving it a thumbs down. Sponsors began to "evaluate their relationship" and subsequently drop Deen over the next few days. Food Network, then Smithfield Farms, severed their partnerships with Deen altogether, while QVC maintained that they were monitoring the situation.

It is in this highly polarized environment that Deen enacted sensemaking. "Official sources," such as her sponsors and mainstream media, harshly criticized her. However, support from her fans was more positive. Such conflicting feedback likely complicated Deen's decision-making. Before social media, narrative creation in crisis communication consisted of a primary narrative created by the media and a secondary, metanarrative created by the organization (Venette, Sellnow, & Lang, 2003; Hay, 1996). Stakeholders outside of the media played a passive communicative role and were not positioned as part of the narrative, except through extreme action, such as boycotting. Even then, mainstream media was responsible for publicly portraying the boycotts. However, as seen in this case, social media has the potential to change both the roles in, and the order of, narrative creation during crisis. Such a cacophony arguably amplified the feeling of disorientation that comes with a cosmology episode, thus leaving Deen struggling to find an appropriate response to the crisis.

Selection

It was in the context of this multi-media environment that Deen took to Facebook and spoke out for the first time since June 21. On June 24, in addition to announcing her rescheduled appearance on the *Today Show*, she wrote: "Hi, it's me Paula. I just had to stop long enough to send love and thanks for the kind words you have all shared with me and my family, and all the support you have shown me over the past week. Please keep me in your thoughts and prayers. Love, Paula" (Deen, Facebook, 2013). Her Twitter feed was more active, twice announcing her upcoming appearance on the *Today Show*, once thanking Al Sharpton for his support, and twice thanking "ya'll" for their support, all between June 24 and June 27.

Responses to these posts were overwhelming, particularly on Facebook. Her post about the *Today Show* received 25,958 comments and 210,258 likes, and her post asking for prayers got 95,041 responses, with 651,131 likes. Of the top 1,000 responses to her support post, 90% were positive, with defending, supporting, and overtly forgiving Deen (Chewning, in press). Unlike media and sponsor responses, these posts were (a) in response to something she had said and (b) directed to her, possibly giving them different weight to Deen. Feedback directly from stakeholders, even electronically, can be useful in crisis situations, as it can let organizations know that stakeholders are "ready and waiting" (Chewning, Lai, & Doerfel, 2012). It is with this feedback that she went to the *Today Show* two days later.

In her interview on the *Today Show*, Deen emotionally shifted tactics, alternately portraying herself as a victim in the situation, evading responsibility for her actions by placing them in another time and place, shifting the blame, and even attacking those who attacked her by implying that they have no right to judge her (for a description of these strategies in crisis response, see Benoit, 1997, and Blaney, Benoit, & Brazeal, 2002). In doing so, she defended her character, saying that she is not a racist and made those comments worlds ago. When prompted for her views on the use of the N-word, she expressed her confusion over the situation, shifting blame to "young people" who work in her kitchen and use the word freely. Literally incorporating a phrase that was repeated frequently by her supporters on her social media platforms, she said "anyone out there who has never said something they wish they could take back, pick up that stone…" In a final act of sensemaking, she asserts her identity, saying: "I is who I is."

This serves as her final word on the situation and becomes her tenacious justification (Weick, 1988). Based on the fact that she expresses gratitude for the several partners (sponsors) who have not parted ways with her, it seems that she is interpreting the positive feedback she has received from stakeholders and the lack of action on the part of some sponsors to mean that she is moving forward in the right direction. Her decision to internally adopt this persona and publicly make this stand establishes the future trajectory of the Paula Deen brand.

Had Deen only been exposed to the feedback from official media and her sponsors, she may have chosen an entirely different course of action. Or, it is possible that her capacity, as defined in the enactment stage, limited her ability to see herself as anyone but "who she is," therefore leading her to take the only course of action she could effectively stand behind. Indeed, sensemaking "is not about truth and getting it right…it is about continued drafting and redrafting of an emerging story so that it becomes more comprehensive, incorporates more of the observed data, and is more resilient in the face of criticism" (Weick, et al., 2005, p. 415). While the noise of the mixed media environment originally confused her sensemaking, causing her to take several contradictory actions during enactment, the feedback from those actions, combined with the vocal support of her fans, provided her with a plausible story that resonated with her sense of identity. Bolstered by the narrative her fans were creating, coupled with her own capacity to perceive her role in the situation, Deen selected a course that built on what made her popular with her stakeholders in the first place.

Retention

Other than one more post on Twitter on June 27, in which she refers to her dropped partnership with Novo Nordisk as a mutual decision, Deen's social media returns to normal, indicating that she has, at least publicly, reasserted her identity given her sensemaking of events. Arguably, her sense of events does not match that of her sponsors, as she continued to lose all of her sponsors over the next two days. However, it does resonate with fans, who continue to support her on social media and visit her at interpersonal appearances.

Essentially, during the retention stage, Deen lived out her statement "I is who I is" by returning all public communication to "normal" by no longer acknowledging the crisis publicly, as well as resuming her "down-home" persona as if it had never been called into question. From a public relations perspective, she was declaring the crisis over. While crisis response has many goals, including integration of lessons learned (Ulmer, Sellnow, & Seeger, 2011), one of the main objectives of post-crisis communication is to maintain the public perception of the organization (Coombs, 1995). With the backing of her fans, it is possible that Deen felt that she had accomplished this goal to the greatest extent possible, despite the loss of her sponsorships.

CONCLUSION

A theory of sensemaking in crisis implies that there are no absolutes. Accordingly, there are no absolute takeaways from the case of Paula Deen. That is, just as there was more at play than sensemaking in the unfolding of the crisis, there can be more than one interpretation of what went wrong, or right, in this case. Indeed, it raises more questions than it answers. Among those questions:

1. *Whose opinion matters most? When traditional media take one route and social media the other, what happens?* Deen's empire did not die. Although her organizational structure was depleted as sponsors and partners cancelled her contracts, and her reputation suffered in the mainstream media as she found a semi-permanent place on the 24/7 news cycle, she experienced a surge of support via her

online media platforms. With this support, she was able to continue to operate, although without any tangible products or deals other than personal appearances, until she was ready to launch a new endeavor. In traditional crisis communication models, the media are the gatekeepers between the organization and stakeholders. However, in this crisis, fans took to social media and shared their support, helping Deen to construct a narrative in which she was alternately perpetrator and falsely persecuted victim. Constructing this narrative helped Deen to reaffirm her identity and move forward, even in the face of losing her sponsors.

2. *If an organization loses its formal backing, and consequently organizational structure, but still has supportive stake-holders, can it recover?* Yes and maybe. As previously stated, despite the lack of any formal endorsement deals, Paula Deen has been able to perpetuate her brand via social media, with fresh content being posted daily. She also still runs her magazine, which was nominated for an *AdWeek's* Hot List Readers' Choice Award in Fall 2014. By 2015, she had opened a new restaurant, was running an online empire, and even appeared as a contestant on *Dancing with the Stars*. While it is unclear if her reach will ever be what it was, it is clear that the support she has received from fans has enabled her to maintain her brand.

3. *Does message strategy matter and, if so, can one strategy ever be successful?* Much crisis communication literature focuses on the role of message strategy in reputational repair (Benoit, 1995, Coombs & Holladay, 2002). However, Deen enacted several different strategies in an attempt to make sense of the crisis, each responding to, and causing different interpretations of, the environment (and it is unlikely that she consciously employed strategies: rather, she simply communicated in ways that fit existing typologies). This implies that while message strategy matters, it is not as straightforward as crisis literature would suggest and that context and feedback might be better indicators of an appropriate message strategy than crisis type.

4. *What is successful crisis communication?* Although Deen did not successfully "manage" her crisis communication by any stretch of existing definitions, she did use communication to make sense of her environment, which helped her to bracket the feedback she was receiving via social media to reassert her identity and maintain her fan base. Although she was unsuccessful in keeping sponsorships and suffered public ridicule, she was successful in keeping her brand. In an era where organizations arguably create lifestyles over products, a brand provides something for stakeholders to identify with, attach to, and return to. Therefore, she might have emerged with the asset that matters the most.

Deen's case, it seems, is awash in contradiction. While organizational sensemaking is supposed to generate retrospective organizational learning to be employed in future crises (Sellnow & Seeger, 2013), it seems to have reified Deen's sense of self, allowing her to successfully move forward, despite the fact that she has not outwardly changed in terms of identity and communication. However, at the end of the day, she listened to her fans and it has brought her this far. Only time will tell whether or not that was supposed to be the lesson learned.

DISCUSSION QUESTIONS

1. Which stage (enactment, selection, retention) is most crucial to organizational sense making? Do you think this varies by case, or is always the same?

2. What are factors that can negatively affect organizational sensemaking in a crisis situation?

3. Do you agree with Deen's decision to stay firm in her identity? How would you have advised her given the enactment environment in which she was operating?

4. What are some of the ways by which organizations can effectively interpret the quantity and range of voices in a mixed media environment for organizational sensemaking?

REFERENCES

Benoit, W. L. (1995). *Accounts, excuses, and apologies: A theory of image restoration strategies.* Albany, NY: State University of New York Press.

Benoit, W. L. (1997). Image repair discourse and crisis communication. *Public Relations Review, 23*(2), 177–186.

Blaney, J. R., Benoit, W. L., & Brazeal, L. M. (2002). Blowout! Firestone's image restoration campaign. *Public Relations Review, 28*(2), 279–392.

Chewning, L.V., Lai, C.-H., Doerfel, M. (2012). Organizational resilience following disaster: A longitudinal view of information and communication technologies use to rebuild communication structure. *Management Communication Quarterly, 27*(2), 237–263.

Chewning, L.V. (2015). Multiple voices and multiple media: Co-constructing BP's crisis response. *Public Relations Review, 41*(1), 72–79.

Chewning, L.V. (in press). Measuring the enactment of IRT via Social Media: What are organizations and stakeholders saying during crisis? In J. Blaney (Ed.), *Putting Image Repair to the test: Applications of image restoration* (133–156). Lanham, MD: Lexington Books.

Choi, Y., & Lin, Y. (2009). Consumer responses to Mattel product recalls posted on online bulletin boards: Exploring two types of emotion. *Journal of Public Relations Research, 21*(2), 198–207.

Coombs, T.W. (1995). Choosing the right words: The development of guidelines for the selection of the "appropriate" crisis response strategies. *Management Communication Quarterly, 8*, 447–476.

Coombs, T.W. & Holladay, S.J. (2002). Helping crisis managers protect reputational assets: Initial tests of the situational crisis communication theory. *Management Communication Quarterly, 16*, 165–186.

Deen, P. (21 June 2013). YouTube apology video. https://www.youtube.com/watch?v=jkwbyNKC9Kg

Duke, A. (2013/7/7). *Celeb chef Paula Deen admits to using the 'N word.' CNN.*Retrieved from: http://www.cnn.com/2013/06/19/showbiz/paula-deen-racial-slur/.

Jeffries & Washington. (2013/6/23). Puala Deen scandal continues as employees tell Rainbow/PUSH of alleged discrimination. *The Huffington Post.* http://www.huffingtonpost.com/2013/06/23/paula-deen-scandal-continues-employees-tell-rainbow-push-alleged-discrimination_n_3484607.html?utm_hp_ref=@food123

Labrecque, J. (21 June, 2013). Paula Deen cancels *Today* interview, citing exhaustion. *Entertainment Weekly.* Retrieved from: http://insidetv.ew.com/2013/06/21/paula-deen-cancels-today-interview/

Matilis, S., & Sonenshein, S. (2010). Sensemaking in crisis and change: Inspiration and insights from Weick (1988). *Journal of Management Studies, 47*, 551–577.

n.a. (2013/6/19) Paula's best dishes: Twitter hashtag pokes fun at Paula Deen's unsavory side as allegations of racism surface. *Huffington Post.* Retrieved from: http://www.huffingtonpost.com/2013/06/19/paulas-best-dishes-twitter-reactions-allegations-of-racism_n_3467877.html

Runyan, R. C. (2006). Small businesses in the face of crisis: Identifying barriers to recovery from a natural disaster. *Journal of Contingencies and Crisis Management, 14*(1), 12–26.

Seeger, M.W., & Ulmer, R.R. (2002). A post-disaster discourse or renewal: The cases of Marden Mills and Cole Hardwoods. *Journal of Applied Communication Research, 30*(2), 126–142.

Sweetser, K., & Metzgar, E. (2007) Communicating during crisis: Use of blogs as a relationship management tool. *Public Relations Review, 33*(3), 340–342.

Sellnow, T. L., & Seeger, M.W. (2013). *Theorizing crisis communication.* Malden, MA: Wiley-Blackwell.

Tepper, R. (2013). Paula Deen racist comments, use of n-word allegedly caught on video. *Huffington Post.*

Weick, K. E. (1988). Enacted sensemaking in crisis situations. *Journal of Management Studies, 25*, 305–317.

Weick, K. E. (1993). The collapse of sensemaking in organizations: The Mann Gulch disaster. *Administrative Science Quarterly, 38*, 628–652.

Weick, K. E., Sutcliffe, K., & Obstefeld, D. (2005). Organizing and the process of sensemaking. *Organizational Science. 16* ,401–421.

Wilson, M. (2013/6/24). Amid racist allegations, Paula Deen booted from Food Network. *PR News Daily.* Retrieved from: http://www.prdaily.com/crisiscommunications/Articles/14713.aspx.

Chapter 12

Susan G. Komen Foundation and Planned Parenthood: An Application of Neo-PR

CHRISTOPHER CALDIERO, PH.D.
Fairleigh Dickinson University

Introduction

All organizations deal with risk and therefore it is safe to assume that almost all organizations face crises. Two questions arise: What specific risks does an individual organization face and how can those risks manifest into crises? These are important queries and ones that have garnered countless analyses in public relations and crisis communication scholarship (Heath, 2002; Jordan-Meier, 2011; Kent, 2010). However, one type of organization largely ignored in these analyses has been the non-profit organization. Indeed, it is likely often assumed that non-profit organizations, by their very nature, are immune to risk (other than the risk of lack of financial support) and therefore immune to crisis. In truth, non-profit organizations are as susceptible to risk and crisis as any other type of organization. Further, in today's practice of public relations, it is worth examining this type of organizational crisis in the context of new thinking about how crisis communication is, and can be, done. Specifically, Caldiero's (2010) concept of "Neo-PR" can shed light on postmodern crisis communication practices and implications. This chapter examines the Susan G. Komen/Planned Parenthood crisis in the context of Neo-PR.

In 2011, the American public was made aware of a crisis facing Susan G. Komen, a non-profit organization dedicated to breast cancer research and support. In short, the Komen organization chose to "defund" the Planned Parenthood Federation of America (commonly called "Planned Parenthood" [referred to here as PP]), after Komen learned that PP was under "Congressional investigation into whether her group had illegally used federal funds for abortions" (www.washingtonpost.com). The story was widely reported in the media in November and December 2011, and continued to receive attention as Komen first defended its decision and then reversed course and reinstated funding to PP. Other elements of the story (that further fueled its media attention) included resignations from Komen leadership and changes in Komen policy regarding conditions for funding. By early February of 2012, the crisis had largely "blown over" and Komen began the process of attempting to restore its damaged reputation.

The circumstances of the crisis aside for a moment, the Komen/PP story highlighted an important implication for current and future understandings of crisis communication. As stated by Kent (2010) in his attempt to filter through the multiple (and sometimes less useful) definitions of what a crisis actually is, writes, "True crises often define the future actions of organizations, how organizations relate to their external environments, and they have long-lasting implications for organizational climate and profitability" (p. 709). Kent argues that scholars must refocus their attentions, away from definitional issues and towards concerns of cyclical processes of issues and crisis and, "how crises are often used strategically (ethically and unethically) to advance organizational goals" (p. 709). This is especially true for those crises involving damaged reputation.

Neo-PR

"Neo-PR" is a term appropriated in part from Eco's (1997) concept of Neo-TV. Eco saw television as so absorbed in itself that it had virtually turned its back on the external world. Eco argued that, while this was not always the case with television, certain trends indicated that television was (and continues to be) so "closed" that there had to be a new way to consider television's impact and meaning. This new way was termed "Neo-TV."

Eco (1984) argued that the fascination (and underlying meaning) of what we often see on television is not due to the *reference* of the subject itself, but rather to the fact that what we are seeing is *on television*. By extension, this fascination is not just experienced by the audience, but by television itself, which has become very adept at congratulating itself on its own productions, its own operation, and its own ability to "make history."

French philosopher Jean Baudrillard has gone even farther. Baudrillard has examined many forms and functions of media, sometimes with controversial results. One of his most lasting contributions is his discussion of "simulation." On its simplest level, simulation refers to the replacement of objective reality with imagery. Baudrillard argued that society's obsession with images has fundamentally altered our world (1988). Representations of reality have saturated our lives to such an extent that we can only experience the world within the bounds of these representations. In other words, the line between reality and representation is all but erased. Everything we experience and everything we are subjected to we see through a filter of preconceptions and expectations that imagery, usually delivered through the media, has already delivered to us. Baudrillard saw this simulation (he referred to it as "simulacrum") as affecting almost every aspect of our daily lives.

Taken together, Eco's "Neo-TV" and Baudrillard's ideas of simulation come together to inform what Caldiero (2010) calls Neo-PR. In short, Neo-PR describes recent trends in public relations practice whereby the *acts* (or, in some cases, the lack of action) of public relations and the *representations* formed by these acts have become more of a "reality" than any transgression, new product, crisis, etc. that initiates the public relations effort. Focus by the media on the public relations response (or lack thereof) becomes more of the story than what may have initiated any public relations communication in the first place. As such, public perceptions of the initial story are irreparably re-formed and, perhaps more dramatically, *replaced* by the media and public relations communication. Instead of becoming a copy or representation of the real, public relations efforts and the resulting perceptions *become* the real, or as Baudrillard called it in reference to media, the *hyperreal* (1988).

Thus, according to Caldiero (2010), the principles of Neo-PR are as follows:

1. Public relations is not just an organizational function. Public relations helps co-create meaning in an increasingly diverse world.

2. Public relations does not, nor should it, seek a singular, objective truth.

3. Public relations rejects three specific metanarratives:

    a. Linearity of communication

    b. Publics as audiences

    c. ymmetry as definitive

In our postmodern world, the impact of technology and social media on organizational communication seems to increase exponentially with each passing month and year. For some time, particularly in the early 2000's, it was unclear to what extent new communication tools, such as Twitter and Facebook, would affect such established, modernistic phenomena as public relations. Although some noted the Internet's increased use as a news-information tool (and the notable decrease in more traditional forms such as newspapers, magazines, and television) (Brody, 2004), most scholars, and certainly most organizations and PR practitioners, did not and could not foresee the many different ways social media would impact communication.

Today, it is likely a foolish endeavor to argue that social media has little or no impact on how, when, and why organizations communicate with their publics. Indeed, the reverse has become equally true and impactful. Social media has, perhaps unlike any other tool before, allowed and encouraged publics to help shape the realities of organizational situations. Publics have never before had the meaning-making impact they are now capable of through dialogic, social-media driven communication. Additionally, the empowerment of publics through the use of social media falls right in line with the principles of Neo-PR, particularly those addressing multiple truths and a rejection of linear communication. Lastly, as Holtzhausen (2000) has wisely argued, in a postmodern world, the PR practitioner must become an activist. A public relations activist is one who makes ethical, professional choices based on his/her conscience, in the context of what is best for both the organization *and* its publics. This is all very clear in the instance of the 2011–2012 case of the Susan G. Komen Foundation and Planned Parenthood.

Susan G. Komen and Planned Parenthood

Beginning in early 2011, and continuing through that year, the Susan G. Komen Foundation took a number of actions that led, ultimately, to a decision to "defund" their monetary contributions to Planned Parenthood. The resulting fallout from this decision and the role that social media played in the story were both noteworthy. Komen was funding Planned Parenthood in the neighborhood of $700,000 and, while this is a large amount of money, it is miniscule in light of the dollars each organization regularly deals with. Komen raised more than $400 million in 2010; Planned Parenthood's total revenue that year was over $1 billion (Rovner, 2012). So, when Komen's board voted unanimously in November 2011 to bar funding to Planned Parenthood (see Appendix A for a more detailed timeline of events), the amount of money was a very small fraction of the overall funds that both organizations were used to dealing with. Nonetheless, Komen's decision set off a firestorm of reaction, with the story making the national news.

The politics behind the closed-door decisions are uncertain, of course. However, some have speculated that there was a very clear set of circumstances and choices that indicate Komen's move to defund Planned Parenthood was largely the work of one woman, Karen Handel. Handel, who had earlier run for governor of the state of Georgia on a platform including a strong anti-abortion stance, was hired by the Komen organization in January 2011 as a consultant (Rovner, 2012).

Later in 2011, while internal discussions at Komen were brewing with regard to Komen's continuing grant funding of Planned Parenthood, Komen staff members decided to meet formally to debate, discuss, and recommend a course of action. Among these staff members was John Hammarley who, according to *Atlantic Magazine*, had served as "Komen's senior communications adviser and who was charged with managing the public-relations aspects of Komen's Planned Parenthood grant" (Goldberg, 2012). Here is what Hammarley said regarding the months leading up to Komen's Board's decision to cut off funding to Planned Parenthood:

> About a year ago, a small group of people got together inside the organization to talk about…the options…what would be the ramifications of staying the course…of telling our affiliates they can't fund Planned Parenthood, or something in between. As we looked at the ramifications of ceasing

all funding, we felt it would be worse…from a public-relations standpoint…and from a mission standpoint. The mission standpoint is, 'how could we abandon our commitment to the screening work done by Planned Parenthood?' (Goldberg, 2012)

Ultimately, as Hammarley indicates, a subcommittee of staff members recommended continuing funding to Planned Parenthood. However, this recommendation was ignored by Komen's Board of Directors and, on November 29, 2011, the Board voted unanimously to bar funding. The very next day, Mollie Williams (named in various accounts as Komen's "senior official in charge of community grants ["Timeline of key events," February 2, 2012] and as Komen's "top public health official" [Goldberg, 2012]) resigned from the organization. Hammarley opined, "Mollie is one of the most highly respected and ethical people inside the organization, and she felt she couldn't continue under these conditions" (Goldberg, 2012). Hammarley, himself, was laid off by Komen in 2011 as part of what was referred to as a reorganization of the group's media division.

Once the decision to bar funding was complete, the story and circumstances moved very quickly (as they are wont to do in a postmodern world), and, within eight days from the story breaking in the news (January 31, 2012), the Komen organization changed their story twice, reversed course, renewed funding, and saw the resignation of Karen Handel (February 7, 2012). How can Neo-PR inform our understandings of this situation and what elements were in play for Komen and Planned Parenthood?

Neo-PR Applied to the Komen/PP Case

Let us consider the principles of Neo-PR in the context of this public relations scenario. The first principle tells us that public relations is not just an organizational function. Public relations helps co-create meaning in an increasingly diverse world. Here, we see the impact and effects of social media most apparently. Traditional, modernistic public relations practice dictates that the organization is responsible for, and most impactful in terms of, shaping the meaning of the situation. Traditional tools (news releases, press conferences, media kits) are used to shape the message and create the meaning for an organization's publics. This model no longer works, certainly not as efficiently and effectively as perhaps it once did. Social media has played a large role in this paradigm shift. An individual's ability to comment, share, and effectively take part in shaping meaning for both an organization and publics is directly correlated with the postmodern tenet of pluralism; many voices and potentially many meanings.

On January 31, 2012, the Associated Press broke the story that Komen had decided to defund Planned Parenthood due to (in Komen's words) the congressional investigation that Planned Parenthood was under. This congressional investigation, led by conservative Republican and anti-abortion Congressman Cliff Stearns of Florida, intended to discover whether or not Planned Parenthood was using federal funds to help pay for abortions. Social media reaction to the AP story was swift and voracious. Tens of thousands of people posted comments to both Planned Parenthood's and Komen's Facebook and Twitter pages. Facebook "likes" increased dramatically in hours. In the case of Planned Parenthood, the increase was 10,000 and, notably, $3 million was donated in the just three days (Lynch, 2012). At last check (October 2014), Planned Parenthood had 115,000+ likes on Facebook and 117,000+ followers on Twitter. Komen's numbers are 800,000+ likes and 93,000+ followers.

Planned Parenthood President Celine Richards credited social media outlets, and specifically Facebook and Twitter, for helping shed light on the specifics of Komen's decisions (Rothschild, 2012). In effect, social media turned what might have lain dormant into a full-blown controversy that ultimately shaped the meaning and outcome of events. Not only did the use of social media greatly impact meaning, but it helped shape the actual financial bottom line of both organizations. Richards said, "It's been incredible.

We're…shifting through the numbers. I absolutely believe the exposure on Facebook and Twitter really drove a lot of the coverage by the mainstream media." (Lynch, 2012). Indeed, Richards went on to suggest that even new relationships for Planned Parenthood had become possible due to the social media coverage, including those with other high profile non-profit organizations, such as Livestrong (Lance Armstrong's non-profit organization, itself a case study of crisis due to Armstrong's admitted use of performance-enhancing drugs).

In response to the social media reactions, and the resulting news media coverage, Komen attempted to shape its own meaning of the situation. Indeed, Komen tried this twice. First, on February 2, 2012, and two days after the story hit the mainstream media, Komen insisted that the reasoning behind their decision was rooted in Planned Parenthood's mammogram policy. Komen founder and CEO Nancy Brinker commented that, "she wants to support groups that directly provide breast health services, such as mammograms. She noted that Planned Parenthood was providing only mammogram referrals" (Sun, et al., 2012). Apparently, this explanation did not sit well with many people and, on the following day, February 3 (four days before Handel's resignation), Brinker released a statement which included the following passage:

> We want to apologize to the American public for recent decisions that cast doubt upon our commitment to our mission of saving women's lives. The events of this week have been deeply unsettling for our supporters, partners and friends and all of us at Susan G. Komen. We have been distressed at the presumption that the changes made to our funding criteria were done for political reasons or to specifically penalize Planned Parenthood. They were not. Our original desire was to fulfill our fiduciary duty to our donors by not funding grant applications made by organizations under investigation. We will amend the criteria to make clear that disqualifying investigations must be criminal and conclusive in nature and not political. That is what is right and fair. (www.komen.org)

So, in the course of approximately three days, Komen's story (and attempts at meaning creation) changed three times. The reasoning for the defunding decision had gone from a decision not to support Planned Parenthood because it was under congressional (non-criminal) investigation, to Planned Parenthood's mammogram policies, and, finally, to a decision to "re-fund" Planned Parenthood and amend policy to defund (disqualify) only those organizations undergoing "criminal and conclusive" investigations. This was quite a remarkable turnaround, and one largely driven by an unexpected and impactful social media response.

The first principle of Neo-PR does not suggest that meaning creation should be fluid, inconsistent, and subject to the whims of an organization or public(s) (Caldiero, 2010). Instead, what it does tell us is that organizations no longer (and perhaps forevermore) wield the exclusive power of creating meaning. To some degree, publics (e.g., customers, investors, media, members) have always had some ability to inject whatever meaning into an organization's circumstances and communication they saw fit. However, technology, such as social media, and the increasing diversity of an organization's constituents reinforce the postmodern idea that plurality of meaning is the standard for today's public relations practice.

Kent and Taylor's (2002) important work in dialogic communication (itself a "precursor" to co-creating meaning) lends itself to this discussion. Largely by default, organizations (in their attempts to open up new forms of dialogue with publics [chat boxes, customer service avatars, Twitter feeds]) have opened the door to meaning being created by multiple entities, and the existence of more than one meaning. In essence, the demands of today's publics, specifically with regard to expectations of technology and rapid responses from organizations given new technologies, force organizations to find and employ new ways of communicating with publics. By doing so, they lose some control of the ability to define the meanings of the public relations scenarios they experience.

The second principle of Neo-PR dictates that there is no longer a singular, objective truth and that public relations practitioners should not waste their time seeking it. What does this mean in this context and how might Komen have better handled what turned out to be a public relations and communication debacle/crisis? First, we should be clear that plurality of "truth" does not imply or certainly encourage deceit on the part of the organization. Rather, this principle recognizes (and related actions based on this principle account for) the very real conditions of multiple truths for multiple organizations and publics.

Indeed, organizations are increasingly getting "caught" when they try to communicate their version of the truth and it is discovered to be anything but. This was certainly the case with Komen. Should they have released a statement boldly proclaiming that their new, high-level consultant was a former anti-abortion, anti-Planned Parenthood gubernatorial candidate and, of course, as a result they would be seriously considering (and ultimately deciding) to defund Komen's grants to Planned Parenthood? No. However, when an organization assumes that its publics are too dimwitted to see the truth behind the veil, it sets itself up for a fall.

The "truth" here is that Komen has always tried to present itself as an apolitical entity dedicated to women's health issues, and nothing more. Nonetheless, when Komen hired Karen Handel, they immediately opened the door to potential backlash for any and all future funding decisions, given Handel's political leanings. As such, for Komen to suggest that their decision to defund Planned Parenthood was not "done for political reasons or to specifically penalize Planned Parenthood" (komen.org), was disingenuous. As Culler (1982) surmised, truth consists of propositions that can be justified according to currently accepted modes of justification. Komen's excuse that funding was to be terminated because of a congressional investigation seemed, on the surface, justifiable; at least by what Culler called an accepted code of justification. In this case, that code was a type of [potential] wrongdoing or malfeasance. This was Komen's "truth," constructed and intended to be acceptable to the organization's publics.

Komen's public relations team (including the aforementioned John Hammarley) should have begun with the proposition that the decision to defund Planned Parenthood (if that indeed was to be the ultimate decision—a debate on whether they should have even entertained the thought notwithstanding) would be viewed from a multiplicity of contexts by multiple publics. As such, communication about the reasoning for the decision should have incorporated voices of Komen's constituents. Indeed, as Holtzhausen (2000) implores, practitioners must shoulder more of the burden of activism within their organizations. Postmodern thinking in public relations allows for "the opportunity to further explore (the) political role of PR practitioners and highlights their complicity in maintaining ideology…" (Holtzhausen, 2000, p. 101). Komen's PR team erred by not actively fighting for the publics that Komen's own mission states that it represents. Modernistic and traditional power structures that propagate the tenet of truth by organizational mandate no longer stand on solid footing, nor reflect the realities of today's organization/public relationships.

The third principle of Neo-PR involves the rejection of some specific metanarratives that have helped define public relations over the last 100 or so years. Each of these will be discussed, in due course, with respect to the Komen/Planned Parenthood case. The first metanarrative that postmodern public relations thinking must reject is "linearity of communication" (Caldiero, 2010). Since the early days of public relations practice (and indeed the early days of "formal" communication theory study), communication was seen as existing and needing to exist in a linear mode. First-year communication studies students are taught about the sender-message-receiver paradigm that has existed since Aristotle's days. The 20th century saw not only the birth of modern public relations, but the birth of modern communication study, and it is no surprise that the theoretical frameworks for both match up in many ways. From Aristotle to Lasswell to Shannon and Weaver, and on and on, we have been instructed as to the linear form of communication. Of course, other alternative models and theories have been presented, including not only those that discuss feedback, fields of experience, and cyclical communication, but entirely alternative frameworks such as semiotics (meaning-making, especially in the context of signs), hermeneutics (text interpretation), and social constructionism (meaning as a socially constructed phenomenon).

These alternative models and frameworks are all useful in their own ways, but we must not deceive ourselves; from a public relations perspective, the modernistic communication paradigm in place for most of the 20th century was linearity. Organizations needed to communicate about something, be it a product, a service, personnel, finances, logistics, or crisis, and the way to do it was to "speak" to its publics. This has been the model of public relations. In today's postmodern world, that linearity is a very wide, fuzzy "line" at best. It is true that organizations might begin the communication process (although a semiotician might tell you that there is no beginning), but once the organization communicates something, linearity is lost to the wind and all bets are off with regard to the "directions" communication may go.

The week of January 30-February 3, 2012 was the turning point in the Komen/Planned Parenthood case. On Tuesday, January 31, the Associated Press reported on the defunding of Planned Parenthood. That very evening, social media sites erupted with communication about the Komen decision. By one account, over 100,000 tweets were sent or "retweeted" that night alone (Rothschild, 2012). Rothschild goes on to report that of the 28 top hashtags, 24 of those were "pro-Komen," three were "pro-Planned Parenthood," and one was "ambiguous. Some of the names of the top tweeters were #stopthinkingpink (Komen's color), #Raceforthecrazy (a play on Komen's slogan of "race for the cure"), and #shameonkomen. Interestingly (and tellingly), Rothschild refers to these top tweeters as "influencers." The linearity of communication all but disappeared within hours of the breaking story. Whatever attempt Komen might have made at that point to create a starting point for a line of communication vanished in the miasma of social media. Again, we see plurality playing a major role in the new realities of public relations. Linearity implies singularity, and that simply will not do in our postmodern world.

The second metanarrative that Neo-PR rejects is "publics as audiences." In the most basic sense, we understand an audience to be a receiver of a specific message. An organization may have many different target markets and, within those markets, many different target audiences; the difference being that the audiences are to receive specific messages that are intended to elicit a positive response for an organization. As that description implies, audiences are often considered in the contexts of marketing and advertising. However, there has always been an inherent connection (rightly or wrongly) with public relations communication and the "audiences" that communication is intended for.

Something else is at play here as well. There is, in various circles, a tendency to relegate audiences to simple and passive receivers of information and to elevate publics to actively engaged groups that play a role in shaping the realities of a situation. This simply will not do for today's public relations practitioners. Any organization that believes that its external communication is being received by a passive audience is destined to learn a hard lesson. Yet modernistic public relations constructed this dynamic from its earliest beginnings. How did Komen communicate and what did it believe its communication would achieve? On February 1, 2012, before Komen reversed its decision to defund Planned Parenthood, Komen released the following statement:

We are dismayed and extremely disappointed that actions we have taken to strengthen our granting process have been widely mischaracterized. It is necessary to set the record straight. Throughout our 30-year history, our priority has always been and will continue to be the women we serve. As we move forward, we are working to ensure that there is no interruption or gaps in services for the women who need our support most in the fight against breast cancer. (www.komen.org)

Beyond the obvious attempt at shaping the meaning of the situation, there are some clues in the statement that make it clear that Komen was attempting to communicate to an audience, and not a "public." Consider the references to wide "mischaracterizations," "setting the record straight," some arguing standards that are "too stringent," and an ambiguous "they" who have given Komen "their trust." Who exactly are they communicating to in this statement? There seems to be little concern or attempt at inviting Komen's specific publics (i.e., donors, recipients of funds, breast cancer patients) to join the conversation. Instead, the statement reads (as most modernistic press releases might read) as a missive intended for press distribution to an abstruse mass receiver...and audience.

The third metanarrative that Neo-PR rejects is "symmetry as definitive." Of course, symmetry in the context of public relations is most notably reflected in the work of Grunig and Hunt's (1984) four models of public relations (itself, a newer metanarrative of public relations thought). Indeed, we know that the four models, in many ways, mirror the historical progression of the public relations field, from press agentry to (attempts at) symmetry. While Grunig and Hunt's description of symmetry as being most "excellent" and the most ethical way to practice PR (Grunig, 1989) and many have praised symmetry (and Grunig and Hunt) for setting a new plateau for ideal public relations practice, symmetry has not been without its critics (see Stoker & Tusinski, 2006, for a deeper discussion of this criticism).

Relevant to the Komen/Planned Parenthood case, one can further examine the problems with symmetry as the end all and be all for effective ethical public relations practice. First, symmetrical communication can actually empower organizations. Stoker and Tusinski (2006) argue, "Instead of promoting the open communication valued by public relations, dialogue emphasizes limited participation in the process and heightened control over the interchange" (p. 161). A note: dialogue here (as is the case with many who analyze symmetry) is seen as an example of symmetrical, two-way practice. This is an interesting paradox. Attempts at opening up dialogue by organizations with their publics can have an antithetical effect; organizations gain more control (or power, in a true "Foucauldian" sense) over the communication than without the dynamic dialogue.

In this context, one can consider Planned Parenthood's public relations strategies as the story quickly unfolded. According to Stanek (2012), moments after the Associated Press reported the news, Planned Parenthood:

> ...blasted news releases via e-mail and Twitter and posted the information on Planned Parenthood's Facebook wall. More than 2,000 supporters shared that post with their own friends on the social network. On Twitter, Planned Parenthood wrote "ALERT: Susan G. Komen caves under anti-choice pressure, ends funding for breast cancer screenings at PP health centers." More than 500 Twitter users reposted that message.

Recall, Planned Parenthood was made aware of the pending defunding some six weeks before the story broke. Stanek (2006) contends that it was Planned Parenthood that eventually leaked the story to the AP and, therefore, strategically planned its moves before doing so. Even if that is not entirely true (Stanek, after all, was writing for a pro-life "news" organization), and the AP broke the story through its own investigations, there can be little doubt that Planned Parenthood used its considerable social media resources to drive the "dialogue" in those first hours and days of the story. From politico.com:

> Twitter users sent more than 1.3 million Tweets referencing Planned Parenthood, the Susan G. Komen Foundation and related terms and hashtags. Planned Parenthood helped spur the conversation by using a "promoted tweet." (Hagey, 2012)

Social media must surely be seen as part (a large part) of today's dialogic communication. As such, when an organization, such as Planned Parenthood, helps to "spur the conversation," it, in effect, assumes some level of control over the dialogue. One must remember that we are walking a fine line here. The suggestion is not to abandon dialogue as it is merely a façade for organizational power over its publics. Indeed, true dialogue between organizations and their publics and opportunities for publics to contribute to the communication are real. Rather, the call in our postmodern world is to do two things. First, public relations practitioners must not assume that symmetry, as a driving metanarrative for ethical and effective practice, is always appropriate, ethical, or effective. Second, practitioners should not lose sight of the fact that a lack of dialogue and/or symmetry (i.e., two-way communication) does not mean a lack of co-creation of meaning. In this way, the three guiding principles of Neo-PR do not contradict one another. Peters (1999) presents it succinctly and wonderfully:

> Clearly there is nothing ethically deficient about broadcasting as a one-way flow. Nor are the gaps between sender and receiver always chasms to be bridged; they are sometimes vistas to be appreciated or distances to be respected. The impossibility of connection, so lamented of late, may be a central and salutary feature of the human lot. The dream of communication has too little respect for personal inaccessibility. (p. 59)

Implications of the Komen/Planned Parenthood Case

As a doctoral student primarily researching and writing about crisis communication, I often lamented about the "effectiveness" of it all. I thought, what is the point of effective (or ineffective, for that matter) crisis communication if the organizations at the heart of the matter emerged largely unscathed from it all. That thinking sprang to mind again as I considered and analyzed this case. Regardless of the initial blowback for or against Komen and Planned Parenthood, what did it ultimately matter? Did either Komen or Planned Parenthood wither on the vine and die as a result of either bad policy or poor communication? No.

There were consequences to be sure. In November 2012, some eight months after that tumultuous week in February, the *New York Times* reported that Komen suffered a 21% drop in "brand health" and that "the organization's signature Race for the Cure attracted 19 percent fewer participants through October than in the same period last year. Several Komen affiliates have reported that preliminary fundraising figures from recent races were down from last year" (Wallis, 2012). The article went on to cite a crisis communication specialist who speculated it would take four years for Komen to "depoliticize" itself. Nonetheless, a viable argument can be made that, beyond the very real resignations of key Komen employees, the organization itself will ultimately (if it hasn't already) emerge and exist as it once did.

As disheartening as it can sometimes be not to see what we think are viable and substantial consequences for organizations we deem to have done wrong, we must soldier on and find the useful lessons taught by every public relations scenario we choose to examine. In this case, the ways that both Komen and Planned Parenthood communicatively engaged with their publics shed valuable insight into both our postmodern condition and the ways that organizations can and should practice public relations.

Given the importance and impact of social media, Komen was caught off guard. This is somewhat surprising given the otherwise savvy acumen of Komen's leadership. Watt (2012), in her post-feminist analysis of the case, writes, "Pink marketing has become so ubiquitous that it has largely overwhelmed voices of dissent within the larger breast cancer and women's health movements and has raised billions of dollars for breast cancer research" (p. 68). And yet, even given Watt's description of Komen founder Nancy Brinkman as a pioneer of cause-related marketing, and the ubiquitous Komen pink ribbon as being synonymous with breast cancer, the organization appeared clueless and completely unprepared for the social media backlash.

Naïveté aside, it can be argued that Komen's lack of preparation and awareness reflected an old-fashioned, modernistic perspective on its public relations strategy; disseminate information, try to frame the narrative, assume acceptance of said narrative, and do not seek out your publics' input. Watt (2012), again, said:

> Rather than engage the personal testimonies, Brinker attempted to transcend the controversy and account for concerns about women's empowerment by emphasizing Komen's image as a prominent fundraiser. Her rhetorical strategy distanced the organization from the women's health movement and instead employed a postfeminist rhetoric which focused on consumption-based fundraising… (p. 75)

Non-profit organizations, such as Komen, must consider and develop strategies that reflect postmodernistic thinking. The principles of Neo-PR can help organizations better apply what sometimes flies in the face of traditional, modernistic public relations practices. If Komen had been prepared to acknowledge the multiple truths at play in this delicate scenario, understood the co-creation of meaning inherent in today's organization/publics relationships, and rejected the dominant metanarratives of modernistic PR, the organization may have fared much better than it did.

DISCUSSION QUESTIONS

1. According to the concept of "Neo-PR," it can be the case in today's public relations practice that, "the *acts*…and the *representations* formed by these acts (can) become more of a 'reality' than any transgression, new product, crisis, etc., that initiates the public relations effort." Can you think of any specific examples of this phenomenon?

2. Can it ever be the case that "politics" and subjectivity are removed from the decisions made by non-profit organizations?

3. How are the concepts of "dialogic" communication and "Neo-PR" related?

4. Why does the author argue that "publics as audiences" is a concept that simply does not work in today's public relations practice?

5. What are your thoughts on crisis communication "effectiveness?" Does it matter how an organization communicates about a crisis if, over time, the organization does not seem to suffer any long-term effects?

REFERENCES

Baudrillard, J. (1988). Simulacra and simulations. In Mark Poster (ed.), *Selected works* (pp. 166–184). Stanford, CA: Stanford University Press.

Brody, E. W. (2004). What's really going on in the media world? *Public Relations Quarterly, 49*(1), 9–10.

Caldiero, C. (2010). *A postmodern perspective on public relations: Neo-PR, metanarratives…and Tiger Woods.* Paper presented at the 2010 National Communication Association Conference, San Francisco, CA.

Culler, J. (1982). *On Deconstruction: Theory and criticism after structionalism.* Cornell University Press, NY.

Eco, U. (1997). A guide to the neo-television of the 1980s. (Zyg Baranski, Trans.). In P. Brooker & W. Brooker (Eds.), *Postmodern after-images: A reader in film, television and video* (pp. 154–161). London: Arnold.

Goldberg, J. (2012). Top Susan G. Komen official resigned over Planned Parenthood cave-in. Retrieved September 9, 2013, from http://www.theatlantic.com/health/archive/2012/02/top-susan-g-komen-official-resigned-over-planned-parenthood-cave-in/252405/#.Tyq3j4YVZ48.twitter

Grunig, J. E. (1989). Symmetrical presuppositions as a framework for public relations theory. In C. Botan, & Hazelton, V. (Ed.), *Public relations theory* (pp. 17–44). Hillsdale, NJ: Lawrence Erlbaum Associates, Inc.

Grunig, J. E., & Hunt, T. (1984). *Managing public relations.* New York: Holt, Rinehart & Winston.

Hagey, K. (2012). Susan G. Komen flap spurred on by social media. Retrieved September 24, 2013, from http://www.politico.com/news/stories/0212/72442.html

Heath, R. L. (2002). Issue management: Its past, present, and future. *Journal of Public Affairs, 2,* 209–214.

Holtzhausen, D. (2000). Postmodern values in public relations. *Journal of Public Relations Research, 12,* 93–114.

Holtzhausen, D., & Voto, R. (2002). Resistance from the margins: The postmodern public relations practitioner as organizational activist. *Journal of Public Relations Research, 14,* 57–84.

Jordan-Meier, J. (2011). *The four stages of highly effective crisis management: How to manage the media in the digital age.* Boca Raton, FL: Taylor & Francis.

Kent, M. (2010). What is a public relations "crisis"? Refocusing crisis research. In Coombs, W. & Holladay, S. (Eds). *The Handbook of Crisis Communication,* (pp. 705–712). Chichester, UK: Wiley & Sons.

Kent, M., & Taylor, M. (1998). Building dialogic relationships through the world wide web. *Public Relations Review, 24*(3), 321–334.

Kent, M., & Taylor, M. (2002). Toward a dialogic theory of public relations. *Public Relations Review, 28,* 21–37.

Lynch, R. (2012). Komen learns power of social media: Facebook, Twitter fueled fury. Retrieved September 9, 2013, from http://latimesblogs.latimes.com/nationnow/2012/02/facebook-twitter-fueled-fury-against-in-susan-g-komen-for-the-cure-.html#sthash.9CQjX5t7.dpuf

Lyotard, J.–F. (1992). Answering the question: What is postmodernism? In C. Jencks (Ed.), *The postmodern reader.* London: Academy Editions.

Peters, J. D. (2000). *Speaking into the air: A history of the idea of communication.* Chicago, IL: University of Chicago Press.

Rothschild, D. (2012). The Twitter users who drove the furor over Komen and Planned Parenthood. Retrieved September 23, 2013, from http://news.yahoo.com/blogs/signal/twitter-users-drove-furor-over-komen-planned-parenthood-160326208.html#d6kD399

Rovner, J. (2012). Planned Parenthood vs. Komen: Women's health giants face off over abortion. Retrieved September 5, 2013, from http://www.npr.org/blogs/health/2012/02/01/146242621/planned-parenthood-vs-komen-womens-health-giants-face-off-over-abortion

Stanek, J. (2012). Planned Parenthood used social media to Crush Komen. Retrieved September 24, 2013, from http://www.lifenews.com/2012/02/07/planned-parenthood-used-social-media-to-crush-komen/

Stoker, K.L., & Kusinski, K.A. (2006). Reconsidering public relations' infatuation with dialogue: Why engagement and reconciliation can be more ethical than symmetry and reciprocity. *Journal of Mass Media Ethics, 21*(2&3), 156–176.

Sun, L.H., Kliff, S., & Aizenman, N.C. (2012). Komen gives new explanation for cutting funds to Planned Parenthood. Retrieved September 12, 2013, from http://articles.washingtonpost.com/2012-02-02/national/35442163_1_komen-decision-komen-executives-komen-founder-nancy-brinker

Wallis, D. (2012). Komen Foundation struggles to regain wide support. Retrieved September 25, 2013, from http://www.nytimes.com/2012/11/09/giving/komen-foundation-works-to-regain-support-after-planned-parenthood-controversy.html?pagewanted=all&_r=0

Watt, S. S. (2012). A postfeminist apologia: Susan G. Komen for the Cure's evolving response to the Planned Parenthood controversy. *Journal of Contemporary Rhetoric, 2*(3/4), 65–79.

Appendix A

Key Moments in the Susan G. Komen/Planned Parenthood Timeline

(Excerpted from http://articles.washingtonpost.com/2012-02-07/national/35444734_1_karen-handel-mollie-williams-founder-nancy-brinker)

January 2011

After an unsuccessful run for Georgia governor, Karen Handel joins the Susan G. Komen Foundation as a consultant. She was then hired as a senior vice president for public policy. During the Georgia primary, Handel's platform included advocating for Planned Parenthood's defunding.

Spring 2011
The Komen board forms a three-member subcommittee to look into Planned Parenthood funding. Komen staff also begin meeting on the issue. Both the staff review and board subcommittee conclude that funding for Planned Parenthood should continue.

Sept. 29, 2011
Rep. Cliff Stearns (R–Fla.) sends a letter to Planned Parenthood president Cecile Richards, notifying her of a congressional investigation into whether her group has illegally used federal funds for abortions.

Nov. 29, 2011
The Komen board votes unanimously to take action that would bar funding Planned Parenthood.

Nov. 30, 2011
Mollie Williams, a senior official in charge of Komen's community grants, resigns.

Dec. 16, 2011
Komen President Elizabeth Thompson calls Planned Parenthood President Cecile Richards to inform her of the foundation's decision.

Jan. 31, 2012
The Associated Press breaks the news that Komen has adopted new grant policies that bar Planned Parenthood from receiving funding. A Komen spokesperson says the new policy bars funding to groups under government investigation, citing Rep. Stearn's probe in Congress.

Feb. 3, 2012
The Komen Foundation reverses course to say that only those under "criminal" investigation will be barred. Planned Parenthood is once again eligible to apply.

Feb. 7, 2012
Handel sends Komen CEO and Founder Nancy Brinker a letter of resignation, effective immediately.

Chapter 13

Apple's "Bendgate" Crisis and the Technology-Image Expectancy Gap

MICHELLE M. MARESH-FUEHRER, PH.D.
Texas A & M – Corpus Christi

Introduction

Our society has been fascinated by technology for decades. In 1985, *Back to the Future*—the first install-ment of a movie trilogy franchise about time travel—was released and grossed more than $385 million (*Back to the Future*, n.d.). Throughout the trilogy, many predictions were made about the technological advances that would be present in the future (October 2015). Although we are not all driving flying cars to work and class, many of the advances predicted in the franchise have made their way into our everyday lives. Technological advances, such as being able to watch multiple television channels simultaneously, receiving messages on video billboards, controlling video games without hand-held controllers, and video conferencing, have all contributed to the American public's expectation that such technological developments will have an overall positive impact on society (Smith, 2014).

The results of a national survey by the Pew Research Center and *Smithsonian Magazine* indicated that 59% of the American public is optimistic that upcoming technological advances will make life in the future better (Smith, 2014). The results of this survey also serve as an example of the lofty expectations that the public has for future technological innovations. Eighty-one percent of those surveyed, for example, "expect that within the next 50 years people needing new organs will have them custom grown in a lab," and 51% "expect that computers will be able to create art that is indistinguishable from that produced by humans" (Smith, 2014).

Given all of our technological advancements, coupled with the public's expectations for the abilities of technology, it is no wonder that many organizations are being criticized for their inability to meet these expectations. Examples such as the failure of the HealthCare.gov website, and the data breaches of both Target and Home Depot, illustrate the false sense of security that the public receives from technol-ogy, as well as organizations' vulnerability to crises caused by a violation of the publics' expectations for its technology. In the following case study, this topic will be explored further, as will the role of Technology-Image Expectancy Gap Theory in understanding Apple's Bendgate crisis.

Technology-Image Expectancy Gap Theory

Just as people have expectations of each other in interpersonal communication settings, publics have a variety of expectations for their experiences with organizations and their services. Technology-Image

Expectancy Gap Theory is a public relations theory that was created to understand how "the marketing of technology, coupled with media coverage of technological advances, creates unrealistic expectations as to the ability of organizations to meet the needs of their stakeholders" (Kazoleas & Teigen, 2006).

The propositions of Technology-Image Expectancy Gap Theory are rooted in Expectancy Theory, which posits that individuals behave a certain way because they are motivated by the desirability of the expected result of that behavior (Vroom, 1964). Although Vroom related expectations to job-related performance, viewing Expectancy Theory under the lens of consumer behavior allows us to understand how our satisfaction with a product or service is based on the discrepancy between our expectations for that product/service and the actual performance of the product/service. As a result, satisfaction only occurs when our expectations for that product/service have been met. Unfortunately, if our expectations for a product/service are too high, it may be nearly impossible for an organization to satisfy us. Consequently, the notion of a technology-image expectancy gap suggests, "stakeholders have unrealistic beliefs regarding the ability of the related organization to perform, to produce, or to meet their needs" (Kazoleas & Teigen, 2006, p. 419).

Several researchers have discussed the connection between technology and unrealistic expectations. Fidler (1997) coined "technomyopia" as a term to describe what happens when the public overestimates the short-term impacts of new technology because of an inability to distinguish between hype and reality. Additionally, West (1996) devised "technological utopianism" as a term to describe the process that occurs when technology developers make promises about the impact that their products will have on society and that technology fails to live up to its expected potential. These expectations, and their consequences, are exacerbated by the fact that organizations are now being forced to compete with other organizations—even small "mom and pop" companies—by promising better, faster, and more reliable performance in a smaller package. According to Kazoleas & Teigen (2006), "to meet these expectations, and to succeed in the new arena of competing agendas and messages on-line in a technology-saturated environment, companies are forced to market their technological abilities to establish brand placement and brand differentiation" (pp. 423–424).

At the heart of Technology-Image Expectancy Gap Theory is the argument that an expectancy cycle begins that creates expectations regarding the capabilities of organizations, such that:

> Society, the media, and individuals come to expect that companies can create products that are 100% reliable, are never defective, and are always safe, and that if individuals need to communicate, organizations will provide the means to do so effectively 24/7. (Kazoleas & Teigen, 2006, p. 426)

As a result, two sets of false expectations are created: we expect more, as a whole, from technology, and we begin to have specific expectations for organizations. These assertions form the basis for the theory's six propositions (Kazoleas & Teiger, 2006):

- *Proposition 1:* As technological advancements become more of a focus in a society, so will the generalized expectations that individuals will have regarding the uses of that technology.
- *Proposition 2:* As technological advancements become more of a focus in a society, the media through the agenda-setting process will devote more coverage and discussion to technology and technology-based issues.
- *Proposition 3:* As the media increase their coverage of technological innovations, the number of unrealistic expectations will also increase. This may be manifested by unrealistic expectations about the quality of products and services in general, and perhaps in the underassessment of risks in traditionally risk-laden activities.

- *Proposition 4:* As the media focus on technology increases, organizations (particularly those that are publicly traded) will increase their emphasis on technology in their image-building, image-enhancing, and reputation-management strategies.
- *Proposition 5:* As organizations increase their emphasis on technology as part of their image, the specific expectations regarding the quality of goods, products, services, and behavior will also increase.
- *Proposition 6:* Organizations can moderate the expectancy gap by monitoring relevant publics' perceptions and expectancies, and by creating message strategies that are targeted at creating more realistic expectations of organizational abilities.

Apple's Bendgate Crisis

On September 9, 2014, Apple announced its new iPhone 6 and iPhone 6 Plus phones, boasting their release as "the biggest advancements in iPhone history" (Apple, 2014). Among the many features listed in the news release are "a dramatically thin and seamless design," "stunning 4.7-inch and 5.5-inch Retina HD displays," "blazing fast performance and power efficiency," "ultrafast wireless technologies," and the inclusion of iOS8, "the latest version of the world's most advanced mobile operating system, featuring a simpler, faster and more intuitive user experience" (Apple, 2014). Apple CEO, Tim Cook, was also quoted as saying, "Only Apple can combine the best hardware, software and services at this unprecedented level and we think customers are going to love it" (Apple, 2014).

Approximately one week later, on September 17, Apple also announced the "biggest iOS release ever" for iOS8, the operating system that is used to run the iPhone (Apple.com, 2014). The new iOS version was touted as having "big updates to apps," "exciting new connections between apps and between devices" for everyone to enjoy, as well as new tools for developers to create new apps, "with capabilities that were never possible before" (Apple.com, 2014). Just three days after the September 19 launch of iPhone 6 and iOS8, Apple announced record sales of iPhones: over 10 million across 10 countries (Yarow, 2014).

Although Apple seemed to be on top following their new release and the resulting excitement over sales, their customers began posting negative comments about iOS8 to social media websites, such as Twitter. Individuals who updated their devices to iOS8 complained about issues with keyboards, glitches with iMessage and multitasking gestures, frequent crashes of the "Settings" app, issues with the Notification Center, lagging notifications, intermittent Wi-Fi, issues with audio, and phone crashes (Yarow, 2014). Twitter CEO, Dick Costolo, during their 2014 fourth-quarter-earnings call with investors, also blamed iOS8 for a loss of four million users due to "an 'unforeseen bug' in the release of iOS8 as it related to Twitter" (dela Paz, 2015).

Although the problems with iOS8 were plentiful, they seemed minimal when compared to the crisis that occurred on the next day due to a barrage of social media reports of users who claimed that they bent their phones by simply placing them in the front pockets of their pants. The reports first surfaced on the Mac Rumors forum and then quickly spread to social media, culminating in a series of videos of people purposely bending their iPhone 6 Plus phones and the start of several humorous Twitter hashtags (#Bendgate and #Bendghazi) to share their experiences. One particular video that was posted to YouTube as a "bend test" of the new iPhone went viral and features a close-shot of someone holding the new iPhone 6 in their hands and pressing down on both sides at the same time with varying levels of force. The phone does eventually bend toward the top of the phone near the volume buttons as the male on the screen confirms that the phone does bend "quite significantly" because of its aluminum exterior. Furthermore, social media became a source for creating and sharing unofficial Apple advertisements flaunting the iPhone 6 Plus' new "feature." In response to this crisis, Apple emphasized that they "perform rigorous tests throughout the entire development cycle, including 3-point bending, pressure point cycling, sit, torsion, and user studies" and that, with normal use, a bend is extremely rare and that only nine customers had contacted them about a bent iPhone 6 Plus during the first six days of sales (Tibken, 2014).

As a result of Apple's statement, claiming that only nine customers had complained about bent iPhones, a website called "One of the Nine," and its accompanying Twitter account (@one_of_the_nine), went live. This website included a compilation of over 180 Twitter and Instagram users' complaints, along with an open letter to Apple demanding an explanation (Sparkes, 2014). One user, listed as number 150, wrote,

> I've had my iPhone 6 for about a month, and I have been extremely careful with it. I had it in my front pocket for a short time on Saturday and the top 1/5 is bent. I called Apple to find out about a replacement since I heard on the news that this is a problem. The employee acted like it was just an internet hoax. I can assure you, it is not a hoax. (One of the Nine, 2014, n.p.)

The onset of Apple's Bendgate crisis may be best understood through an analysis of the propositions of Technology-Image Expectancy Gap Theory. As previously discussed in this chapter, the first proposition assumes that the public's general expectations for technology increase as technological advancements become a focal point in society. Apple is clearly aware of these expectations, as they purposefully used their September 9 launch news release to highlight features that the public would logically expect in a new version of the iPhone, given the technological advances that have occurred sequentially in previous iPhone versions. Users have come to expect thinner phones, larger, high-definition displays, and faster operating systems. Furthermore, the second proposition argues that the media will devote more coverage and discussion to technology and technology-based issues. The launch of the iPhone 6, iPhone 6 Plus, and iOS8 received a generous share of media coverage. On September 9, Apple held an exclusive event to unveil the new products to members of the media, Apple employees, invited guests, and celebrities, including Rupert Murdoch, *Vogue's* Anna Wintour, Dr. Oz, and many more (Golson, 2014). The media coverage dedicated to this new technology was not limited to traditional media, however. Apple made an effort to make the event social, with an official hashtag (#AppleLive) and a social hub with photos, behind the scenes commentary, attendee reactions, and live streaming (Mashable Team, 2014). The helicopters that were seen flying over the arena, in hopes of catching a glimpse of what Apple was planning to unveil, may be the best indicator of the media's interest in Apple's newest technology.

The third proposition of Technology-Image Expectancy Gap Theory suggests that as media increase their coverage of technological innovations, the number of unrealistic expectations will increase. Herein lies the cause of the crisis for Apple. Given the extensive media coverage that their new operating system and phones received, a record number of sales were made of their product. These sales imply that customers liked what they had heard about the product's new features and had expectations for the product to meet the expectations that they had for those new features. Apple's emphasis on the new technology features in the image-building strategies that they used in their advertising is partially to blame for these expectations (proposition four). The language that they used to describe their products in the launch release—dramatically thin, seamless design, blazing fast performance, ultrafast wireless technologies, simpler, faster, more intuitive—and the promise that the CEO made in the news release about the company being the only one that "can combine the best hardware, software and services at this unprecedented level" and his assumption that "customers are going to love it" all contributed to an image of Apple as being an infallible leader in technology. The consequences of this perception may lead to an image crisis if consumer expectations are not met. As Kidman (2014) explains:

>The problem with infallible images is that you have to live up to them, and there's little doubt that Apple, like anyone, can stumble. When you do that and you're the world's biggest technology company, people are bound to notice. (n.p.)

The fifth proposition contends that public expectations regarding the quality of goods, products, services, and behavior increase along with organizations' increasing emphasis on technology as part of their image. As the hype for the technological specifications of the seemingly "perfect" iPhone 6/iPhone 6 Plus increased, so, too, did consumers' expectations for this particular product. The retail price of an iPhone 6 ranges from $199 with a data plan from AT&T, Sprint, or Verizon to $649 for a contract-free purchase through T-Mobile. This price, and the technological innovations of the newer, faster, slimmer iPhone model, lead to customers expecting a perfect product. Unfortunately, the major flaw of the phone—that its aluminum exterior could bend due to excessive pressure—resulted in the Bendgate crisis, making Apple the target of public criticism. Apple's main competitor, Samsung, also used the Bendgate image crisis to sell their Galaxy Note 4, which it claims is immune to bending (Mlot, 2014).

Implications

The Bendgate crisis is not the first time that Apple has had a "scandal" surrounding the launch of a new device. The previous three versions of the iPhone all received a great deal of media attention and public scrutiny surrounding a violation of the publics' expectations for the product. From an unwanted U2 album showing up as a gift on iPhone users' phones drawing criticism for violating users' privacy (Sherman, 2014) to the "Antenna-Gate" scandal caused by the iPhone 4 dropping calls when it was held a certain way ending in a class-action legal settlement (Oliver, 2013) to Apple Maps' inaccurate directions costing former Senior Vice President of iOS, Scott Forstall, his job (Yglesias, 2012), it is clear that Apple has violated stakeholders' perceptions on more than one occasion. Although these crises may not have caused much of a financial dent in the pocketbook of Apple's executives, they have created an image crisis for a company that relies on consumer support in a marketplace where other technologies, such as Google Maps and Samsung's Galaxy phones, are gaining consumer interest.

Apple's Bendgate crisis, viewed through the lens of Technology-Image Expectancy Gap Theory, provides crisis managers with four key implications, which further advance the theory's six propositions:

1. Given organizations' emphasis on promoting products based on technological innovation, organizations are more vulnerable to crisis due to a violation of the public's expectations.
2. Although the public falls victim to unrealistic expectations, they tend to purposely seek flaws that expose an organization's inability to meet their expectations.
3. Competitors (like Samsung) who attempt to capitalize on an organization's failed expectations (such as the advertisement for the Galaxy Note 4 that mocks Bendgate) further perpetuate the Technology-Image Expectancy Gap by making customers believe that such expectations are attainable.
4. Users, through social media, also engage in agenda-setting by generating hype about a product or service, giving attention to product successes and failures.

Given these implications, it is important for crisis managers to consider Technology-Image Expectancy Gap Theory as they conduct risk and vulnerability assessments for their respective organizations. Considering the promises made during the promotion of a product or service, and monitoring the publics' perceptions and expectations of a product can help mitigate a crisis caused by violated expectations. As such, all organizations should consider the messages, or promises, that they are sending to the public regarding their products and services. Although large companies like Apple may escape this type of crisis with little more than short-term reputational damage, smaller companies, or those with a poor reputation prior to the crisis, may not be able to recover fully from such a violation of expectations.

DISCUSSION QUESTIONS

1. Think about the technology that you use on a daily basis (e.g., cars, phones, computers, video game consoles, etc.). What are your expectations for this technology? Has this technology ever failed to meet your expectations?

2. Using the Internet, do a search of current product recalls (recalls.gov is a great resource) – select one recall and discuss how the public's expectations for this product may have been violated. Do you feel this is an unrealistic expectation, why or why not?

3. Do you believe that Apple could have anticipated the crisis discussed in this chapter before it occurred? Why or why not?

4. Put yourself in the shoes of Apple's public relations team. What would you have done differently in responding to the "Bendgate" crisis?

5. If you were on Apple's public relations team, how might you change your promotion of future iPhones based on what you have learned about the "Bendgate" crisis?

REFERENCES

Apple (2014, September 9). Apple announces iPhone 6 & iPhone 6 Plus—The biggest advancements in iPhone history. *Apple Press Info.* Retrieved from http://www.apple.com/pr/library/2014/09/09Apple-Announces-iPhone-6-iPhone-6-Plus-The-Biggest-Advancements-in-iPhone-History.html

Apple.com (2014). iOS8. Retrieved from https://www.apple.com/ios/

Back to the Future (n.d.). *The Numbers.* Retrieved from http://www.the-numbers.com/movie/Back-to-the-Future#tab=summary

dela Paz, S. (2015, February 6). Twitter blames Apple iOS8 for its lost 4 million users. *Yibada.* Retrieved from http://en.yibada.com/articles/12223/20150206/twitter-blames-apple-ios-8-lost-4-million-users.htm

Fidler, R. (1997). *Mediamorphosis: Understanding new media.* Thousand Oaks, CA: Pine Forge Press.

Golson, J. (2014). Live coverage of Apple's September 2014 iPhone and iWatch event. *MacRumors.* Retrieved from http://www.macrumors.com/2014/09/09/iphone-6-iwatch-event-live/

Kazoleas, D., & Teigen, L. G. (2006). The technology-image expectancy gap: A new theory of public relations. In C. H. Botan & V. Hazleton (Eds.). *Public relations theory II* (pp. 415–433). Mahwah, NJ: Lawrence Erlbaum Associates, Inc.

Kidman, A. (2014). Bendgate has Apple feeling the pressure. *The Drum.* Retrieved from http://www.abc.net.au/news/2014-09-26/kidman-bendgate-has-apple-feeling-the-pressure/5770954

Mashable Team (2014). Apple debuts two new iPhones and a watch. *Mashable.* Retrieved from http://mashable.com/2014/09/08/apple-unveils-its-future-follow-along-in-our-live-blog/

Mlot, S. (2014, October 3). Samsung mocks Apple 'bendgate' in Galaxy Note 4 ad. *PC Magazine.* Retrieved from http://www.pcmag.com/article2/0,2817,2469720,00.asp

Oliver, S. (2013, April 23). Apple's $15 settlement checks for iPhone 4 'antennagate' begin arriving. *Apple Insider.* Retrieved from http://appleinsider.com/articles/13/04/23/apples-15-settlement-checks-for-iphone-4-antennagate-begin-arriving

One of the Nine (2014). *Are you one of the nine?* Retrieved from http://www.oneofthenine.com

Sherman, E. (2014, September 16). Apple's $100 million U2 debacle. *CBS Moneywatch*. Retrieved from http://www.cbsnews.com/news/apples-100-million-u2-debacle/

Smith, A. (2014, April 17). U.S. views of technology and the future: Science in the next 50 years. *Pew Research Internet Project*. Retrieved from http://www.pewinternet.org/2014/04/17/us-views-of-technology-and-the-future/

Sparkes, M. (2014, October 24). iPhone 6 owners demand answers on 'bendgate.' *The Telegraph*. Retrieved from http://www.telegraph.co.uk/technology/apple/11184851/iPhone-6-owners-demand-answers-on-bendgate.html

Tibken, S. (2014, September 25). Apple: Only 9 customers have complained about 'Bendgate.' *CNET*. Retrieved from http://www.cnet.com/news/apple-says-only-9-customers-have-complained-about-bendgate/

Vroom, V. H. (1964). *Work and motivation*. San Francisco: Jossey-Bass.

West, J. (1996). Utopianism and national competitiveness in technology rhetoric: The case of Japan's technology infrastructure. *The Information Society, 12,* 257–272.

Yarow, J. (2014, September 22). Apple announces opening weekend iPhone 6 sales were over 10 million. *Business Insider*. Retrieved from http://www.businessinsider.com/apples-opening-weekend-iphone-6-sales-2014-9

Yglesias, M. (2012). Why I'm bearish on Apple. *Slate*. Retrieved from http://www.slate.com/articles/technology/technology/2012/11/scott_forstall_fired_from_apple_the_company_struggles_to_keep_an_all_star.html

Chapter 14

Crisis Communication Node: The Case of UT-Rio Grande Valley Start Up

DAVID L. STURGES, PH.D.
University of Texas Rio Grande Valley

Introduction

In 1994, a concept was introduced that suggested that crisis management theories and applications were limited in their focus on the communication objectives that should be addressed during a crisis's lifetime (Sturges, 1994). It pointed out that most crisis management publications focused on managerial actions in response to a crisis perceived to be a catastrophic negative outcome (Barton, 1993; Dutton, 1986). This paper introduced, and supported, the idea that any action of extraordinary level that predicts positive or negative impact on an organizational entity is a crisis (Dutton, 1986; Mitchel 1986). Very little light was shed on the communication needs during a crisis (Barton, 1993; Newsom & Carrell, 1986).

In 1986, Steven Fink defined the activities of a crisis in terms of a life cycle (see Figure 14.1). He defined the steps of a crisis as four sequential types of activity. First was the prodromal period, or build-up stage, during which symptoms of the impending crisis emerge and became more open and indicative of the major action. Second was the break-out stage, where the actual crisis occurs and has its most intense effect on people and things. The third stage, or abatement, was the period in which continued response to the crisis is initiated by the affected organization in response to long-term crisis effects. The last stage

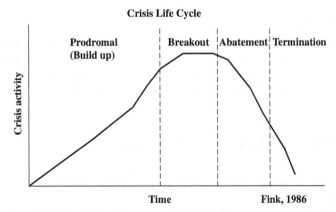

Figure 14.1 Life Cycle of Crisis [credit line] Courtesy of David Sturges

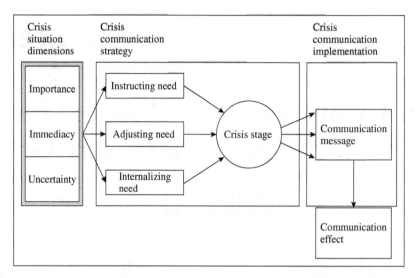

Figure 14.2 Crisis Communication Management Content Strategy [credit line] Courtesy of David Sturges

was termination, when the optimum responses are made and the general condition of organizational operation returns to a roughly pre-crisis stand (Fink, 1989).

The 1994 discussion introduced the idea that communication issues during the life cycle of a crisis formed a public opinion node representing the magnitude of positive or negative opinion toward the crisis entity during the passage of time (Sturges, 1994). The analysis suggested that communication content at each stage of the crisis life cycle focused on three main categories of information (see Figure 14.2 illustrating these components of the crisis life cycle).

This model in Figure 14.2 suggests that each segment of the crisis life cycle may require varying combinations of each information category, as needed, to maximize the impact on the target audience (Sturges, 1994). The possible variations are illustrated in Figure 14.3.

Early in the crisis life cycle, during the "internalizing content" stage, information that focuses on images of the object entity is the primary content of messages sent to the stakeholders influenced by the crisis outcome (Sturges, 1994). During the "break-out" stage, when the crisis reaches its apex, internalizing is least effective in influencing the opinion of stakeholders and instruction about how to react to the crisis becomes the primary content of the messages (Sturges, 1994). During the "abatement" phase, information designed to help the stakeholders psychologically cope with the magnitude and outcome of the crisis eruption becomes the most significant message content (Sturges, 1994). It is only after the crisis has cycled through its life to reach the termination phase that internalizing information again has any influence on the opinions among the stakeholders (Sturges, 1994).

A New University as a Case Study

During a recent establishment of a new university from two previously existing universities, communication of events was widely disseminated to a number of potential audiences. The circumstances of the university's processes of creating the new entity meant that the university faced crisis in relationship to more than one audience.

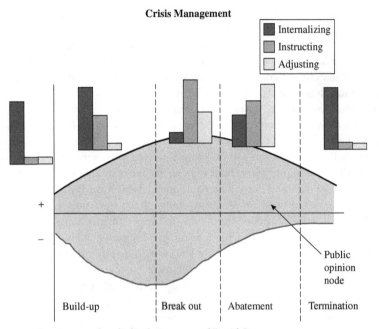

Figure 14.3 Communication Strategy [credit line] Courtesy of David Sturges

One of the universities in the new entity has been in existence since 1927 and has evolved through several redefinitions of its higher education mission. Founded as a community college, the first major redefinition elevated it to university status. It then evolved to offer graduate level programs. Finally, in 1998, it was incorporated into the University of Texas (UT) System as a four-year institution, with doctorate-granting graduate programs.

In 2012, the Chancellor of the University of Texas System, Dr. Cigarroa, announced that a new initiative was to be put into place to alter the higher education structure in the Rio Grande Valley of Texas (University of Texas System, Dec 4, 2102). For decades, activists have charged that this part of Texas has been underdeveloped for higher education opportunities. In fact, such charges resulted in a lawsuit in 1987, when the Mexican American Legal Defense Fund (MALDEF), sued the State of Texas for perceived discrimination against the population of South Texas in higher education opportunities (i.e. LULAC et al. v. Richards et al.). Although special funding was the result of the suit, a technicality in classification of higher education institutions made the University of Texas-Pan American (UTPA) and the University of Texas at Brownsville (UTB) ineligible for the Texas Permanent University Fund (PUF)[1] that provides funding for campus development at UT System schools.

Chancellor Cigarroa and the UT System administration initiated the concept of closing UT Brownsville and UT Pan American schools and opening a new university to stand in their places. This new university would be created with the goal of classifying it as an Emerging Research1, Carnegie institution. The criteria

---

[1] This is an endowment fund set up by the State of Texas based on the ownership of public lands in west Texas to support the cost of educational institutions in Texas. After the Permanent Endowment Fund was set up, oil deposits were found on the public lands that now have created a huge amount of funding available for higher education support; however, the support categories are limited in the expenses that can be paid for from the fund.

for such status include awarding more than 20 doctoral degrees in a minimum of three different disciplines each year, with more than $100 million in research grants (Carnegie Classification of Higher Education, 2015). This status would make the new entity eligible for the Texas Permanent University Funds to support physical plant development in South Texas. In addition, the new university would contain a medical school: the first in South Texas. The presence of a medical school in South Texas has been one of the main points of criticism of the state legislature for decades (LULAC et al. v. Richards et al.).

The new university's public announcement comprises the beginning of a crisis. It is not the typical crisis, in that it does not automatically portend a major negative outcome event like a plant explosion or a tanker running aground. It does meet the Crisis Communication Strategy criteria of (1) being perceived as important, (2) being perceived as immediate, and (3) being perceived as uncertain in outcome (Sturges, 1994).

Initial assessment of communication about the establishment of the new university suggested that the crisis began its life cycle with first communication on the subject on December 4, 2012. The predicted "break-out" stage was determined to be the opening of the new university on September 1, 2015. Applying the life cycle stage concepts, the "build-up" stage (or prodromal stage) would extend from December 4, 2012 to just before the school opening on approximately August 1, 2015. This period includes a time when communication to stakeholders is intended to influence public opinion, preferably in the direction of positive opinion about the new entity.

Between December 4, 2012 and December 20, 2014, the University of Texas System had issued 54 press releases, 12 newsletters, 10 videos, held four campus meetings, and held several public meetings, local governmental meetings, and civic group meetings to communicate to stakeholders about the new university and aspects of its ongoing development.

The primary surrogate in this review for public opinion is the "Question and Answer" resource placed on the UT System's website for anyone to post questions for response from the development group. The questions were reviewed for content analysis criteria that defined them as "Very Hostile," "Hostile," "Positive," and "Very Positive." A middle area of "No Feeling" was eliminated and the analysis forced a placement into one of the four categories. The result was that a few of the questions that were neutral were generally forced into the "Positive" category.

In addition, surrogates for public opinion included content of published articles placed in the *McAllen Monitor*, the *Brownsville Herald*, and other print and electronic media. Some reviews were conducted using video and audio from local television and radio stations.

As the review progressed, trends began to reveal themselves: that subordinate crises were beginning to shape as time progressed. For example, the first sub-crisis that emerged was the naming of the new university president. After this crisis cycled through, the second sub-crisis was the transition of faculty from existing schools to the new university.

In all, five major sub-crises were identified (Figure 14.4 shows an illustration of the relationship between the mother crisis, the opening of the university, and the five sub-crises).

Mother Crisis: Opening the New University

The initial defined crisis was the opening of the new university. Its life cycle is suggested to have begun on December 4, 2012, with the first press release announcing the plan to create the new institution, the University of Texas Rio Grande Valley (UTRGV) from the remains of two existing universities in the Rio Grande Valley. After the initial announcement, press releases are dated approximately a week apart. In general, they are classified as "Internalizing Information," as they focused on high-order, abstract concepts of the vision for the new university. As time progressed, and the sub-crises began to emerge, the frequency of

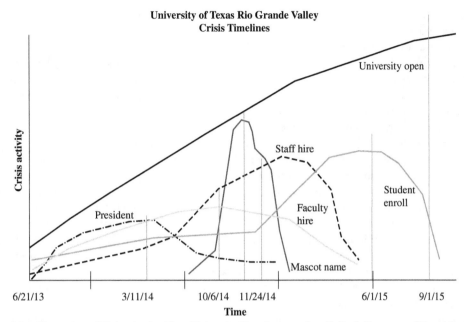

Figure 14.4 Illustration of Crises in the New University Development [credit line] Courtesy of David Sturges

press releases increased, especially around the dates for the regular Board of Trustees meetings: especially those where some action was required regarding the development of the new university. As the press releases emerged, they began to focus on the specifics of the sub-crises. Overall, the total increase of press releases, in general, led to an overall increase in primary crisis activity, as illustrated in Figure 14.4.

The Five Sub-Crises

The first sub-crisis, naming the new president, had its beginning in the crisis life cycle at about the same time as the other five sub-crises began to evolve. In the illustration timeline, the president crisis reached its break-out stage on about March 11, 2014, with the naming of Dr. Guy Bailey as the new UTRGV president. A total of six press releases communicated this issue, with the majority during the two weeks prior to the announcement. At the "break-out" phase, no instructing information entered the press releases to provide better assistance to the stakeholders in reacting to the announcement.

Following the "break-out," which passed quickly, a series of press releases, during what was a very short abatement phase, were distributed to provide information about the fate of the two current presidents. These included information about what the presidents were going to do after the administrative transition and instructions to the stakeholders about what they could do in response to the announcement. Principally, this was instruction about attending ceremonies to honor the presidents' contributions and to wish them "best of luck" in the future. In spite of attempts to make the presidents' fates pleasing to the stakeholders, a general negative opinion was prevalent in response to the news relating to the president of UT-Pan American, who had become a highly respected administrator and perceived "friend" in the office. The opinions expressed in the Q&A, Op Ed pages of newspapers, and stories in news were tantamount to obituaries and caused a perception of the beloved president being severely mistreated in the process. The UTPA president announced his resignation from the post. He disappeared from public view and a bitter feeling remains among students, faculty, and public stakeholders as a result of the perceived sorry treatment he received.

The president of UT Brownsville announced her departure. However, she was designated to be the director of a new center located on the campus of UT Brownsville. Her situation had a positive resolution, it is speculated, because her career evolution took a step forward in the crisis situation, as her stakeholders received sufficient coping information about her career continuation to ease the minds of supporters.

The second sub-crisis to emerge was the hiring of faculty. Press releases and administrative newsletters began addressing the issue shortly after the announcement of the primary crisis: the opening of the university. The early press releases focused on internalizing information based on the vision of the new university. But almost immediately, concerns were expressed in the Q&A about the concept that UT Brownsville and UT Pan American would be closed, ending all faculty contracts, and that UTRGV would be opened, requiring new contracts for all faculty, including tenured faculty. This concept caused considerable concern, especially among UT Brownsville faculty, who had recently undergone a period of uncertainty and confusion, as UTB was separated from Texas Southmost College. The result of that action led to faculty layoffs associated with changing organizational structure. The specter of the transition to the new university opened old wounds. None of the press releases, newsletters, or answers to posted questions in the Q&A alleviated the concerns. In fact, in the Q&A, it became clear that the carefully crafted answers by UT System personnel made the uncertainty and concern escalate.

In this sub-crisis growth phase, communication through newsletters addressed the issue. The closer the process got to the break-out date, the more instructing information was included. This advised faculty how to prepare effective application materials and, eventually, how to submit them. Except for a minor glitch in the online application submission technique, the fulfillment of the instructions worked well and the break-out date of October 6 was met with letters sent to all accepted faculty on that date. Upon passage of the transition hiring, the rising issue became "what about faculty who did not receive offers?" During the abatement phase of this sub-crisis, newsletters were published to address the concern, including a Phase 2 hiring for faculty positions not filled in the Phase 1 transition and an accounting of what the numbers were in the final Phase 1 transition, announcing that only 25 of the applying faculty were not offered employment letters in Phase 1.

In all, this sub-crisis evolved through its life cycle successfully. Although some issues still are active, involving the faculty who did not receive offers in Phase 1, the general demeanor among faculty is satisfaction with the outcome.

The most difficult of the sub-crises was the rebranding effort for the new university. The announcement that the new university was starting from scratch with the elimination of reference to the mascots from the two existing universities arose quickly in the timeline. It increased in crisis-related actions considerably in a short amount of time and had a break-out stage that continued through time. The sub-crisis was introduced in late September as one of the steps to the process of initiating the new university. A previous announcement and early information about the establishment of the university indicated that the new school would have NCAA Division 1 status. UTPA had had Division 1 status for years and competed in all Division 1 sports except for football. UTB had been a Division 3 school since its inception and competed in most sports at that level, except for football, which it does not participate in at all. This relationship led to the coaching faculty at UTPA being transferred directly to UTRGV, since they already had considerable experience with NCAA Division 1 sports. This decision led to significant negative feedback, especially from UTB supporters, in the school and the community.

UTB had recently completed a comprehensive branding and mascot change as the first edition of the school, an upper division/graduate school, separated from Texas Southmost College, a community college with which UTB had been partnered since the early 1990s. The negative feeling may be attributed to the belief that UTB faculty, staff, and administration were to be treated like a "stepchild" in the final decision process regarding aspects of the new school.

The initial announcement of university branding, and the new mascot of UTRGV, resulted in factions immediately developing among the university audiences, from faculty to students to alumni. Various levels of resistance magnitude developed in the audiences associated with both schools, as well as community resources in both geographic areas associated with the universities. The new mascot selected was "The Vaqueros." Vaqueros were Mexican cowboys who were the original cattle ranch workers during the growth of the cattle business as a South Texas primary economic element. The naming of The Vaqueros resulted in much positive response, ranging from letters to the editor to major newspapers in the Rio Grande Valley to press releases and newsletter reports from the president's office of athletic and civic support expressed to the president. The negative view resulted in letters to the editor in the same newspapers, articles in the student newspaper, and a protest demonstration held on the UTPA campus, with approximately 2,000 people participating. The primary argument expressed in these communication tools was that the mascot would be "cartoonized" and ridiculed during athletic competitions and other public appearances of a created character representation of a Vaquero. The argument was that this was no different from the current opposition to the Washington, DC professional football team and fans for the way they ridicule the "Redskin."

The conflict culminated with an article in the *McAllen Monitor* newspaper, and picked up by others, announcing the results of a survey that had been used by the mascot selection committee that reported the options for selection to the UTRGV president. It reported that the results were: The Vaqueros receiving 12 percent of the positive response, the Phoenix receiving 21 percent of the positive response, and none of the above receiving 41 percent of the positive response. This supported the negative position considerably (*The Monitor*, 2014).

As time passed (abatement phase), negative reactions to the mascot began to decline, while the president continued to reaffirm the selection of the mascot in a vote of the University of Texas Board of Regents. The general tenor of the communication on this topic seemed to be that, since the vote by the Board of Regents, there was nothing that could be done to change the recommendation. A final note to this very poorly handled sub-crisis occurred on December 11, 2014, when an email group, perceived to be faculty and staff of UT-Pan American, received an email asking the reader to vote in a survey for selecting a mascot. It was the same email sent months earlier when an actual survey was taken to get the public's feelings. It was followed the next day by an email asking the reader to ignore the email as a mistake. This error caused reinforcement to many people in their opinions that the president did not represent the faculty and students of the UTRGV on this issue.

Sub-crisis three does not conform to the model for communication strategy in any way. The model suggests that communication content has, as its goal, to achieve positive opinion in targeted audiences. The analysis of communication to the audiences relevant to sub-crisis three reveals little attempt to include content with better probability of meeting the needs of the audience in the crisis stages. This result is that this sub-crisis remains a point of distrust and negative opinions among a majority of constituents.

Although the faculty hiring and transition to UTRGV, sub-crisis two, was handled well, with positive public opinion outcomes, sub-crisis four, the hiring of staff for UTRGV, was a disaster.

This sub-crisis began with the announcement of the new university and the plans for shutting down the two existing schools and initiating a new school. The actions and public opinion on this sub-crisis were slow to grow in the "build-up" stage. Early communication on this issue indicated that staff transition would not begin until after completion of faculty transition. But following the completion of Phase 1 faculty transition, the concern of staff on the transition issue began to skyrocket.

Until this time, communication (press releases, meetings, and, most influential of all, presidential news-letters) focused on high-order abstractions in the internalizing information category. Much was made of the plan to create a "university of the 21st century" and "a leading university in global education." No specifics of organization or processes to create the organization were suggested, except for vague references that staff transition would be finalized by Thanksgiving (UT Rio Grande Valley Newsletter, 2014). However, as the fall months passed, no additional instructive information regarding the process was circulated. The university system administration did attempt one effort for appropriate instructive information distribution by securing a personnel-consulting firm to institute training and support for staff to better prepare them for the hiring process: whenever it was to occur.

The communication related to this effort ended up creating increasingly (and serious) negative opinions among audiences. Staff members were herded into auditoriums for training sessions on preparing résumés and reviewing interview techniques. Along with these efforts, the press releases, newsletters, and meetings focused on a concept that, regardless of length of service at either university, all staff applications would be pooled in central personnel availability with assignment of a staff post based on "best fit" of a person's skills-to-position availability. This led to very negative interpretations of actions. For example, a staff person was told that she would not be guaranteed the staff position she had occupied for 35 years and that she would most likely find herself in a different position that could be anywhere in the five physical locations of UTRGV offices over an 80-mile span. This led to severe negative opinions because of the failure to include outcomes in the instructions that could have helped staff be more confortable about the process they were facing (Message from UTRGV: Update in Hiring, 2014).

The letters and questions regarding this issue were met with carefully crafted wording to make no commitment, promise, or clear instruction. This cannot be determined as purposeful or incidental in design. It may be that the responding personnel were trying their best to provide some reassurance, while meeting legal suggestions to ensure no expectations were created. If the latter is the case, then this is a good example of the legal need overshadowing the communication content to protect perceived legal ramifications, while resulting in major negative public opinions that could contribute to chaos for years to come.

Thanksgiving had come and gone and this sub-crisis was only a little closer to resolution than it was when it erupted. The day before Thanksgiving saw a newsletter sent from the president's office that focused on the hiring transitions that had been completed, apparently in an attempt to communicate that the transition process was proceeding at a good pace. This report included physical plant, safety offices, and other "non-competitive" staff personnel (Message from UTRGV: Update of Hiring, 2014).

As for clerical staff, the only instructive information they received in the form of an update to the situation was a newsletter on December 18 that merely suggested that the transition hiring was placed on "hold" until after the new year. No additional instructive information was included to help ease the minds of this group (Message from UTRGV: Update Hiring Process, 2014).

The fifth and final sub-crisis, student recruitment, began almost the day of the announcement of the new institution, with a webpage posted as a link from the university websites leading to a discussion of how students would be treated in the transition process. This ranged from information about continuing students to issues of concern for potential students applying to UTRGV itself. This sub-crisis was suggested to have its break-out stage in the summer of 2015, as final student acceptance into the UTRGV was expected to reach its zenith. Communication for this sub-crisis was slow to develop because the crisis date in the summer of 2015 is far enough away that it may not be perceived as critical (speculation only). In November of 2014, a new website was introduced for UTRGV, which was targeted to multiple publics, but particularly to students. It included the inventory of programs that were to be offered at the new university, as well as application procedures for new students. The result was a fairly complete set of instructive communication messages to be used by prospective students and high school support personnel to help students in decision processes.

This sub-crisis increased its activities and opinion development in the spring semester, as the crisis break-out in summer of 2015 approached. The biggest potential problem that loomed in the sub-crisis information need was a schedule of courses for Fall 2015. Since the new UTRGV had classes spread across five physical locations, and online, the need to have schedules completed in time for student registration seemed unlikely to be met. This element was influenced by communication that began in January to cover instructions for students about how to react to the lack of schedule information.

The results of this crisis sub-set was confusion and administrative difficulty during enrollment periods from spring 2015 through summer 2015. Schedules used by students had differentiation about what physical campus courses would be assigned to, but students had trouble identifying this information. Early fall 2015 was filled with students processing course changes to change classroom locations for more convenience.

CONCLUSION

This chapter provides a case analysis of how communication during a crisis is measured against the recommendations for organizational success in communication to stakeholders. Success focuses on achieving better public opinion among stakeholder groups than existed in the groups prior to the beginning of crisis-related activities. The review of this case was on the University of Texas System offices, University of Texas Rio Grande Valley, University of Texas-Pan American, and University of Texas at Brownsville. It included communication messages from a number of constituents and the resulting expressions of public opinion exhibited in and through multiple public media.

The crisis identified first was the announced opening of a new university and the closing of two existing campuses. This crisis was the original target of this review. As the actions of crisis management became more active, five sub-crises were identified, each exhibiting its own "life cycle." Each sub-crisis was viewed to determine the success, or lack of success, in management of public opinion, given expectations of the communication content recommendations for the primary model. Only one of the five sub-crises was found to exhibit information conforming to the suggested strategy for public opinion influence. The faculty hiring and transition sub-crisis resulted in demonstrated positive opinion in the primary stakeholder group. Overall, this sub-crisis confirms the information content strategy for opinion outcome. Of the remaining sub-crises, the information distributed did not conform to the content model and the result was negative opinion outcome for three of the sub-crises and "too early to determine" for a fourth sub-crisis (though this fourth sub-crisis will continue to be observed through its "break-out" stage).

The mother crisis, the opening of the university, continues to suffer the negative opinions resulting from the sub-crises' outcomes. As such, the opening of the university has some opinions among stakeholders that portend serious negative support for implementation of the main crisis break-out during the summer of 2015. Continued monitoring of communication and opinion outcomes will continue in order to measure outcomes.

DISCUSSION QUESTIONS

1. The framework of crisis communication suggests three types of information are significant. What are the three types and what is their impact on a firm's target audiences?
2. The Model of Crisis Management suggest that different types of information have greatest impact at different times during a crisis lifecycle. Explain the difference of communication content though the stages of the lifecycle.

3. The main crisis associated with the opening of the new university was found to have sub crises in application. What were the sub crises audiences? Were they positive or negative crises in outcome?

4. Of the sub crises, which appears to have been the most problematic for positive outcome? Why do you think this?

5. What recommendations would you make to the university's public information department if you were a communication consultant guiding its actions?

REFERENCES

A message from President Bailey (Justification for Vaqueros name selection). UTRGV Newsletter. Nov. 10, 2014.

Ann RICHARDS, Governor of the State of Texas, et al., Appellants, v. LEAGUE OF UNITED LATIN AMERICAN CITIZENS (LULAC), et al., Appellees. 868 S.W.2d 306 Legal™. http://leagle.com/decision/1 9931174868SW2d306_11158.xml/RICHARDS%20v.%20LULAC(1993).

Barton, L. (1993). *Crisis in organizations: Managing and communicating in the heat of chaos.* Cincinnati, OH: South-Western.

Carnegie classification for institutions of higher education. (2015). Basic Classification Methodology. The Trustees of Indiana University. http://carnegieclassifications.iu.edu/methodology/basic.php

Decision on UTRGV colors and team nickname to happen next week. UTRGV Press Release, Oct. 31, 2014.

Dutton, J. E. (1986). The processing of crisis and non-crisis issues. *Journal of Management Studies, 35*(5), 3501–3517.

Fink, S. (1986). *Crisis management: Planning for the inevitable.* New York: AMACOM.

Message from the UT Rio Grande Valley: Hiring Process Update. UTRGV Newsletter, Dec. 18, 2014.

Message from the UT Rio Grande Valley: Hiring Update. UTRGV Newsletter, Oct. 20, 2014.

Message from UT Rio Grande Valley: Help UTRGV Plan for the Future. UTRGV Newsletter, Oct. 29, 2014.

Message from UT Rio Grande Valley: New Applicant Portal. UTRGV Newsletter, Oct. 22, 2014.

Message from UTRGV: Appointment of Athletics Director. UT Rio Grade Valley Newsletter, Nov. 6, 2014.

Mitchell, T. H. (1986). Coping with corporate crisis. *Canadian Business Review, 13,* 17–20.

Newsom, D., & Carrell, B. J. (1986). *Public relations writing: Form and style.* Belmont, CA: Wadsworth.

Sturges, D. L. (1994). Communicating through a crisis: A strategy for organizational survival. *Management Communication Quarterly,* 7, 297–316.

Palomo Acosta, T. (2014). Mexican American Legal Defense and Educational Fund, *Handbook of Texas Online* (http://www.tshaonline.org/handbook/online/articles/jom01), accessed December 26, 2014. Uploaded on June 15, 2010. Published by the Texas State Historical Association.

The Monitor. Fight against Vaquero not over for UTPA students. Nov. 11, 2014.

"UT System announces groundbreaking, transformational plan for advancing excellence in education and health in South Texas." University of Texas System. Press Release, Dec. 4, 2012.

UT System Board of Regents approves "Vaqueros" as athletic nickname for new university. UTRGV Press Release, Nov. 6, 2014.

UTRGV President recommends "Vaquero" as athletic nickname for new university. UTRGV Press Release, Nov. 5, 2014.

Chapter 15

A Tender Song For Tough Times: When Crisis Communication Goes Viral

Kimberly Cowden, Ph.D.
Colorado State University Pueblo

Introduction

In early December 2011, McNeil PCC, a Canadian pharmaceutical subsidiary of U.S. corporate giant Johnson and Johnson (J&J), responded to Internet consumer outrage at the disappearance of the ultra-absorbent o.b. tampon. Comments on Internet sites such as *Jezebel*, *ipetitions*, and *Write the Company* featured loyal o.b. tampons users responding in disbelief and outrage to the shortage. In response to the Internet criticism, J&J sent an email notice to users inviting them to the o.b. tampons website to view a video apology that ultimately garnered 27 million unique views (Lowe & Partners, 2012) and awards for the advertising agency that developed the campaign.

As one of the first examples of corporate apology to go viral, this case provides a context in which to study social media operating idiosyncrasies. This chapter contributes to our current understanding of social media use to mitigate outrage and restore organizational personae, and the use of crisis communication as a marketing opportunity.

Social Media and Viral Marketing

It is estimated that 85% of American adults routinely share content with friends through email, with 63% reporting doing so once a week and 25% reporting sharing once a day (Ellison, 2006). These forwards can be photos, website links, videos, and other areas of web interest. Organizations today are working to harness the power of peer networks for communication in the form of viral marketing. There are several current definitions of viral marketing (Ellison, 2006; Phelps, Lewis, Mobilio, Perry, & Raman, 2004; Scott, 2011; Subramani & Rajagopan, 2003), yet Scott (2010) provides a formula to define viral communication as having "some great Web content that is groundbreaking or amazing or hilarious or involves a celebrity, plus a network of people to light the fire, and all with links that make it very easy to share" (p. 94). Some of the advantages of viral marketing for organizations are low product costs and instant communication connections. However, viral marketing does come with confounding variables as well.

Viral communication is still an emerging marketing channel with risks to organizations. Scott noted, "The web is hyperefficient at collective investigative reporting and smoking out trickery, so these campaigns rarely succeed and may even cause great harm to reputation" (p. 94). The confounding variables associated with this approach include the difficulty in accurately measuring reach, frequency and diffusion rates, as well as the risk that the viral message will be poorly received by publics.

Some of the first documented examples of organizational viral marketing include hotmail.com and Chevrolet. Hotmail.com grew its email subscriber list from zero in 1996 to 30 million by February 1999, using links at the bottom of every email sent (Ellison, 2006). Hotmail.com is an obvious success story, yet viral marketing can also backfire on the organization because of the lack of organizational control in the viral process. For Chevrolet's marketing department, a creative attempt to engage audiences in 2006 by having users create their own Tahoe commercials and upload them to an online site turned into an organizational crisis. The endeavor backfired when environmentalists used the tools to enlighten publics on the sport utility vehicles' large green, rather than carbon, footprint. Internet comments criticized the tactic, citing the fuel and emissions expenditures of SUV, versus smaller, vehicle makes and models. Chevrolet needed to shift the conversation from branding the Tahoe to bolstering corporate initiatives using ethanol and alternative fuels. Organizations using online or viral tactics risk losing control over a message, as users interpret and interact with a company's framed message in different ways.

Scholars have studied the viral marketing phenomenon from conception of the viral messaging (creative) to seeding strategies to evoke peer-to-peer diffusion (dissemination) to evaluation of viral marketing initiatives. Some advocate the use of evocative positive emotional content (see Berger & Milman, 2012; Doblele, Toleman & Beverland, 2005; Eckler & Bolls, 2011), the use of celebrities (Southgate, 2010), and personalization that increases the interactivity and novelty of the message (Phelps, Lewis, Mobilio, Perry & Raman, 2004). Creatively designed message content is supported in the literature, as is the strategic dissemination (Hinz, Skiera, Barrot & Becker, 2011), or seeding, of viral marketing (Doblele, Toleman & Beverland, 2005). Because this chapter examines crisis communication acting as viral marketing, it is imperative to examine the intersections of current knowledge about social media and crisis communication.

Social Media and Crisis Communication

Organizational crisis is inevitable (Fink, 1986). Sellnow, Seeger, and Ulmer (1999) define crisis as "specific, unexpected, and non-routine events or series of events that [create] high levels of uncertainty and threat or perceived threat to an organization's high priority goals"(p. 228). The o.b. tampons case represents a crisis because the shortage of tampon inventory, and the subsequent removal of the super absorbent line, caused unanticipated consumer response among social media outlets, specifically among bloggers and Facebook users. Organizational response was necessary to address social media commentaries, as well as squelch rumors that could have damaged J&J's organizational persona.

In 2009, Domino's Pizza was one of the first organizations to experience a viral social media crisis, when Domino's Pizza employees uploaded a video to YouTube featuring the food handlers sneezing on an order and using cheese that was first inserted into a worker's nostril. The contaminated food was never delivered to consumers, but the video was viewed by more than one million people (Clifford, 2009). In other words, it went viral. Domino's responded to the crisis via statements uploaded to YouTube and by creating a Twitter account to directly address issues. Veil, Sellnow & Petrun (2011) analyzed the case to argue that "responding to a hoax through the same medium by which it was distributed is imperative to counter the hoax message for the same audience that received it" (p. 344). Responding to Internet outrage with online or Internet channels is an advocated approach to crisis response.

Organizations should scan and monitor their environments to identify salient stakeholder issues in order to identify and mitigate the risk of crises (Heath, 1999). Additionally, organizations should pre-plan for crisis by establishing and updating crisis communication protocols (Coombs, 1999). Seeger (2006) identifies 10 best practices in risk and crisis communication: processing approaches and policy development; pre-event planning; forming partnerships with the public; listening to the public's concerns and understanding the audience; being honest and open; collaborating and coordinating with credible sources; meeting the needs of the media and remaining accessible; communicating with compassion, concern, and empathy; accepting uncertainty; and delivering messages of self-efficacy. These best practices represent pre-event planning, crisis mitigation strategies, and response development. Yet, the burgeoning world of social media adds a new dimension to crisis planning. Where once organizations monitored media accounts, shareholder perceptions, and activist initiatives, they must now consider the myriad of postings available on the Internet through blogs, social forums, and applications, such as YouTube, Facebook, and Twitter. Social media adds new dimensions to traditional issue management and reputation management strategies.

Veil, Buehner, and Palenchar (2011) revisited the best practices in risk and crisis communication to contextualize social media into the risk and crisis best practices. They developed 11 recommendations for incorporating social media in risk and crisis communication: determining social media engagement as part of the risk and crisis management policies and approaches; incorporating social media tools in environmental scanning to listen to risk and crisis bearer concerns; engaging social media in daily communication activities; joining the conversation, including rumor management, and determining best channels to reach segmented publics; checking all information for accuracy and responding honestly to questions; following and sharing messages with credible sources; recognizing that the media are already using social media; remembering that social media is interpersonal communication; using social media as the primary tool for updates; asking for help and providing direction; and remembering web 2.0 is not a panacea (pp. 118–119). Essentially, Veil et al. (2011) reinforce traditional media applications to risk and crisis best practices and caution that Internet response is another communication tool and not *the* new tool for crisis communicators. Seeger (2006) and Veil et al. (2011) provide best practices in risk and crisis communication, incorporating social media, but there remain questions of implementation. In what ways can we craft risk and crisis messaging for Internet audiences that will bolster organizational personae?

Scholars have identified response strategies. Coombs (2007) offered a master list of nine reputation repair strategies: attack the accuser, denial, scapegoat, excuse (provocation, defeasibility, accidental, good intentions), justification, reminder, ingratiation, compensation, and apology (these are reviewed elsewhere). In applying these strategies, an organization can respond by criticizing the accuser, by denying that the organization was involved, by accusing someone else, by pleading that the organization was provoked or did not know about events, by minimizing the seriousness of the event, by focusing on the good works of the organization, by praising constituents, by offering something in return for the event, or by accepting responsibility using an apology. These approaches are compelling and similar to other strategies, yet even Coombs states that Benoit "has done the most to identify the reputation repair strategies" (Coombs, 2007b, para 25).

Benoit (1995) identifies five main organizational image restoration strategies: denial (simple denial or shifting the blame), evading of responsibility (provocation, defeasibility, accident, or good intentions), reducing the offensiveness of the event (bolstering, minimization, differentiation, transcendence, attack accuser, and compensation), corrective action, and mortification. In terms of application, using denial, an organization can deny that an event happened or can respond by focusing the blame on another organization or factor crisis. An organization can evade responsibility by communicating that it was forced to take an action because of outside forces (provocation), because the organization lacked information (defeasibility), because the event was simply an accident (accident), or because the organization was attempting to do something beneficial for a stakeholder (good intentions). Organizations can employ the strategy of reducing the offensiveness of an event by communicating the good works of the organization (bolstering), attempting to reduce the significance of the event (minimization), shifting focus from the event to a macro-discussion (transcendence), attacking the publics that are attacking the organization (attack accuser), or by offering monetary or other stipends to affected parties (compensation).

Finally, there are corrective action and mortification, which do not have sub-strategies. An organization that communicates corrective action is one that offers an analysis of the crisis event and, in addition, offers solutions to avoid similar events in the future. An organization using a mortification strategy takes responsibility for the event and offers an apology. While crisis scholars advocate being open and honest in crisis discourse (Seeger, 2006), the reality mandates that public relations professionals and legal professionals are often at odds during crisis events about what information to disclose because of the litigiousness of crises. Admitting fault and acceptance of responsibility for a crisis event is often believed to place organizations at risk for lawsuits.

Benoit's strategies work alone, or in conjunction, to help organizations issue rhetoric to restore organizational legitimacy in the aftermath of criticism. While, historically, this theory has been used, descriptively, to conduct post-crisis or incident analysis, the theory is beginning to be used prescriptively to proactively prepare organizational rhetoric for times of crisis (Dardis & Haigh, 2009).

Benoit's Image Repair Strategies (IRS) (1995) have been used to study health crises (Brinson & Benoit, 1996), political rhetoric (speeches), organizational labor relations (Cowden & Sellnow, 2002; King, 2006), and, most recently, the study of the BP's responses to the Gulf of Mexico oil spill (Harlow, 2011; Muralidharan, Dillistone, & Shin, 2011; Rogers, 2012). Studies in image repair strategies have been useful in understanding how specific tactics are beneficial or ineffective in organizational rhetoric, but there remains a void in the application of Benoit's work extending IRS tactics themselves. Some argue that understanding their utility is problematic because of the predominant application of IRS tactics to a case study methodology (Ferguson, Wallace & Chandler, 2012). Additionally, there are arguments about the misinterpretation of corporate discourse using IRS because organizations are typically multi-layered and non-linear. Thus, interpretations of such discourse can lead to fragmented analyses (Burn & Bruner, 2000). With these criticisms in mind, IRS theory serves as a launching pad to understand organizational discourse used in a social media context. Specifically, there is little work that addresses how the impact of the immediacy of social media channels affects dissemination of organizational image repair.

Case Study

In September of 2010, reports on online blogs, such as *Jezebel* and *Write the Company*, disseminated the news about the disappearance of the ultra-absorbent o.b. tampon line. Women were upset because this product represents a unique niche in the feminine hygiene market. The o.b. tampon brands do not include applicators, making them smaller than most of the products on the market and friendlier to the environment. Additionally, the product, itself, is marketed as a unique design to mold to the body, so many women feel that o.b. tampons fit better than other brands and work better for women with heavy menstrual flows (Singer, 2010). One loyal consumer posted to the ipetitions site:

> I have tried using other tampon brands & none have ever fit my needs as well as o.b. Recently, I (and all other period-having ladies in my family and among my friends) have been on a wild goose chase trying to track down even one pack of O.B. Ultra Tampons. There are so many of us who rely on and trust this brand for that specific product and we are really being let down right now. (Rebecca, n. d., para 1, lines five through 7)

The ipetitions "O.B.: Bring back the ultra tampons" site garnered 754 co-signers.

In November of 2010, Bonnie Jacobs of McNeil-PPC, a unit of Johnson & Johnson, shared that there was a "temporary supply disruption that has resulted in some stores being out of stock" (Singer, 2010, para 2). Jacobs added that the company was working to "bring supply back in line with demand" and that they apologized to inconvenienced customers, but she did not provide a specific reason for the lack of supply. McNeil-PPC's response to consumer concern was that the company promised that the product would be back to market as soon as possible and they encouraged women to try other McNeil-PPC products (Stewart, 2010). The company's responses lacked transparency and speculation of government recalls and rumors of J & J working to shift women to menstruation medication swirled on blogs. One blogger wrote, "Yes, for real—maybe this is all some marketing scheme to counter the bad press Johnson & Johnson has been having!" (Carlson, 2011, para 3). Additionally, the lack of o.b. tampon inventory on store shelves led to eBay auctions of the product escalating in price to $130 per box (Goldberg, 2010, para 4).

In its first definitive response to consumer and media speculation about the disappearance of o.b. brand tampons, McNeil-PPC released the "Triple Sorry" music video on the o.b. tampon Canadian website in December of 2011. Video users were able to enter their names at the beginning of the video and computing power personalized several frames of the video with the name, thus making the entire apology personalized. Specifically, the name was featured in the one minute, 49 second video on four occasions: as the title to the song, written in rose petals, featured as a tattoo on the singer's arm, and on a hot-air balloon rising in the sky. A coupon was offered to customers at the end of the video (see Table 1).

On December 8, 2011, the *L.A. Times* featured the story with a link to the video, calling the effort "brilliant marketing" (Stein, 2011, para 8). Other media outlets, such as *CBS News* and *New York Daily News*, also ran the story, with similar accolades for its originality.

In January of 2011, the official o.b. tampon website posted a message to American customers that the brand was in the shipping process to retailers across the United States and to expect minor delays (Stewart, 2011). At this point, consumers were told that the o.b. ultra-absorbent tampons were permanently discontinued. While a product called "ultra" did return to store shelves, bloggers were quick to note that the new product had an absorbency of 15–18 mg: a difference from the 18–23 mg absorbency previously manufactured.

In an effort to address social media commentary, Johnson & Johnson sent 65,010 emails to registered women who used the product, encouraging them to view the personalized apology in December of 2011 (Lowe & Partners, 2012). Upon entering the site, the user is asked to input a name, after which there is a brief pause before a large blue card, stating "We're Really Really Really Sorry," appears and opens to an attractive young man playing a white baby grand piano from a cliff overlooking the ocean. He is singing a song of apology to consumers, stating "I know we went away and let you down." The apology could be personalized with a name and the viewer could download a coupon for o.b. tampons at the end of the video. The email garnered a 61% click-through rate and, from there, the dissemination skyrocketed (Lowe and Partner, 2012). According to the advertising agency's public relations case study, within three months, the video harvested more than one million Facebook shares, 1.8 million Twitter impressions, and over 900,000 coupon downloads (Lowe & Partners, 2012). Tracking the total unique views of the video on the o. b. tampon website indicated that more than 27 million users viewed the personalized apology.

The o.b. tampons *Triple Sorry* video is an example of crisis response using social media as a channel to deliver an apology for an organizational failure. This single case study represents a social media intervention to an organizational crisis that subsequently went viral and offers insights to public relations professionals and crisis communicators for addressing web-borne outrage with web-borne crisis response. To provide context for this study, the next sections review literature addressing social media and viral marketing and crisis communication efforts using social media.

CONCLUSION

There are theoretical implications and practical implications from this analysis about using social media as a viral marketing approach to crisis communication. Specifically, the results suggest that ingratiation (bolstering) could be added as a subcategory to Benoit's (1995) strategy of mortification. Consistent with much of the current scholarship dealing with crisis response, mortification can be an effective strategy for mitigating negative organizational personae during crisis events (see Blaney, Benoit & Brazeal, 2002; Compton, 2014). When the lyrics are attached to the video representation, the meaning of the situation, as a whole, translates into organizational self-deprecation. The grand gestures of "calling out your name," and of hiring a sky-writing pilot to write the user's name across the sky ("cue the airplane guy"), bolsters the mortification strategy into ingratiation as an expression of humor. Ingratiation, in this sense, is not as Coombs (2007) defines it: as the process by which those who manage a crisis ultimately provide stakeholder praise. Rather, ingratiation, in this context, emerges from the social psychological sense of seeking affinity (see Gordon, 1996). This approach expands our understanding of image repair strategies, the role of ingratiation in crisis communication, and the use of humor to restore organizational personae.

While many organizations avoid using a mortification strategy because of implied guilt, J&J boldly repeated the phrases. Haigh and Dardis (2012) argue that the mortification strategy has both micro and macro implications with key publics, stating that "When an organization chooses to apologize (mortification strategy), it should lead to positive perceptions of organization public relationship and corporate social responsibility because the company says 'I'm sorry.' These words mean everything in interpersonal relationships, so they may have the same effect on organization public relationships" (p. 5). In this case, the use of ingratiation as mortification bolstered the organization's apology.

This case study demonstrates that viral marketing can be a viable avenue for crisis communication; however, there are confounding variables. First, one cannot guarantee that a video or social-media-seeded response will go viral. Despite the literature on effective seeding strategies, peer-to-peer network influences, and creative design, the reality is that no one can really guarantee that an apology will go viral and that it will permeate the marketplace in the manner consistent with that of the o.b. tampons apology. This is aligned with Scott (2012), who posits that "it is virtually impossible to create a Web marketing program that is *guaranteed* to go viral. A huge amount of luck and timing are necessary" (p. 94).

Second, the personalized and humorous approach of the o.b. tampons apology video is largely what endeared it to social media constituents. This approach, however, would not be appropriate in crisis situations that included loss of life or severe injury. Indeed, based on current studies, this approach could severely damage the reputation of the organization that addressed mortality and morbidity with humor and sarcasm.

Finally, this study adds to the growing body of literature that advocates responding to social media crisis events via the same medium. Consistent with Domino's Pizza's response to its crisis with its food handlers, the online commotion from consumers via blogs, Facebook, and Twitter was met by J&J with a humorous song of mortification. Organizations would do well to follow the lead of Domino's and Johnson & Johnson and meet social media crises with social media crisis responses.

The o.b. tampon case study represents an opportunity to examine crisis communication as viral marketing. From the initial seeding of the video, the *Triple Sorry* video was viewed more than two million times (Lowe & Partners, 2012). Although viral marketing cannot be guaranteed to hit the mark, and may come with some confounding variables, organizations can use such creative approaches in communicating crisis.

In the o.b. tampon case, Johnson & Johnson used the crisis as an opportunity to bolster its image by releasing the apology video that went viral. Part of the appeal of the video was the lyrics that ingratiated the organization through the triple sorry apology, thus suggesting that there are opportunities to build on the strategy of mortification. Identifying issues and communicating about crises with stakeholders is as important as organizational action during crises. Organizations that act in a manner consistent with stakeholder expectations pre-crisis and during crisis recover more quickly from events (Coombs, 1998; Hearit, 1987; Heath, 1996). Indeed, some of the most current work in the field of crisis communication advocates organizational crisis as an opportunity, not just a threat (Ulmer, Sellnow & Seeger, 2007). This case study is unique because the crisis of lack of ultra o. b. tampon inventory became an opportunity for J&J to woo women with a love song, turning a bloody mess into a beautiful day.

DISCUSSION QUESTIONS

1. What can we learn from this case study about crisis communication as viral marketing?
2. As we grow in our use of digital technology, how does social media affect crisis communication?
3. What public relations or crisis communication theories best explain this case study?
4. In what ways can this case study influence future crisis communication cases?

REFERENCES

Ads of the World (2012) retrieved March 12, 2012 from http://adsoftheworld.com/media/online/ob_tampons_apology

Benoit, W. L. (1995). *Accounts, excuses, and apologies: A theory of image restoration strategies.* Albany, NY: State University Press.

Carlson, J. (2011, January 20). Code red: o.b. tampon shortage continues (allegedly!). *The Gothamist.* Retrieved June 5, 2014 from http://gothamist.com/2011/01/20/the_ob_tampon_shortage.php

Clifford, S. (2009, April 15). Video prank at Domino's taints brand. *New York Times,* B1.

Coombs, W. T. (2007) *Ongoing crisis communication: Planning, managing and responding.* Thousand Oaks, CA: Sage.

Coombs, W. T. (2007b). Crisis management and communication. *Crisis Communication.* The Institute for Public Relations. Retrieved at http://www.instituteforpr.org/topics/crisis-management-and-communications/

Ellison, C. (2006, September). Marketing goes viral. *Consumer Relationship Management,* pp. 26–32.

Fink, S. (1986). *Crisis management: Planning for the inevitable.* New York: American Management Association.

Ferguson, D. P., Wallace, J. D., & Chandler, R. C. (2012). Rehabilitating your organization's image: Public relations professionals' perceptions of the effectiveness and ethicality of image repair strategies in crisis situations. *Public Relations Journal, 6* (1), 1–19.

Goldberg, C. (2010, December 20). The great tampon mystery: Where have all the o.b.'s gone? *WBUR Commonhealth: Reform and Reality.* Retrieved January 5, 2012 from http://commonhealth.wbur.org/2010/12/ob-tampons-mystery.

Grunig, L. A., Grunig, J. E., & Dozier, D. M. (2002). The value of the public relations function. In J. E. Gruning and D. M. Dozier's (Eds.), *Excellent public relations and effective organizations.* Mahwah, NJ: Lawrence Erlbaum Associates.

Haigh, M. M. & Dardis, F. (2012). The impact of apology on organizations: Public relationships and perceptions of social responsibility, *Public Relations Journal, 6* (1), 1–16.

Hearit, K. M. (1995). From "we didn't do it" to "it's not our fault": The use of apologia in public relations crises. In W. N. Elwood (Ed.), *Public relations inquiry as rhetorical criticism: Case studies of corporate discourse and social influence* (pp. 117–131). Westport, CT: Praeger.

Heath, R. L. (1997). *Strategic issues management: Organizations and public policy challenges.* Thousand Oaks, CA: Sage.

Lindlof, T. R. & Taylor, B. C. (2002). *Qualitative communication research methods.* Thousand Oaks, CA: Sage.

Johnson & Johnson. (2012). *Johnson & Johnson History.* Retrieved January 10, 2012 from Johnson & Johnson: http://www.jnj.com/connect/about-jnj/company-history/

LYSTEDA - Prescription Medicine for heavy monthly bleeding. (2012). Retrieved 2012, 2-February from Lysteda: http://www.lysteda.com/about_lysteda.aspx

Mitchell, M. L. (1989). The impact of external parties on brand-name capital: The 1982 Tylenol poisonings and subsequent cases. *Economic Inquiry, 27*(4), 601–618.

o.b. Super Absorbency Tampons Reviews. (2010, 5 September). Retrieved February 25, 2012 from Viewpoints: http://www.viewpoints.com/O-B-Tampons-Ultra-Absorbency-reviews?featured=025f7

o.b. Ultra Absorbency Tampons Discontinued Without Reason or Warning. (2011, 26 February). Retrieved February 2, 2012 from Wikinut: http://health.wikinut.com/O.b.-Ultra-Absorbency-Tampons-Discontinued-Without-Reason-or-Warning/1jo_7isz/

o.b. ultra tampons. (2012, 4-March). Retrieved March 4, 2012 from eBay: http://www.ebay.com/sch/i.html?_nkw=o.b.+ultra+tampons&_sacat=0&_odkw=o o.b.+tampons&_osacat=0&_from=R40

Phelps, J. E., Lewis, R., Mobilio, L., Perry, D., Raman, N. (2004, December). Viral marketing or electronic word-of-mouth advertising: Examining consumer responses and motivations to pass along email. *Journal of Advertising Research, 44*(4), 333–348.

Rebecca, S. (2010, 28-October). *O.B.: Bring back the Ultra Tampons!* Retrieved 2012, 2-February from iPetitions: http://www.ipetitions.com/petition/ob_ultra_tampons/

Scott, D. M. (2010). *The new rules of marketing and PR.* Hoboken, NJ: Wiley.

Seeger, M. W. (2006). Best practices in crisis communication: An expert panel process. *Journal of Applied Communication Research, 34*(3), 232–244.

Seeger, M. W., Sellnow, T. L., & Ulmer, R. R. (1998). Communication, organization, and crisis. *Communication Yearbook 21*, 231–275.

Singer, N. (2010, December 22). *The case of the missing o.b. tampons.* Retrieved January 10, 2012 from *The New York Times - The Business of Health Care:* http://prescriptions.blogs.nytimes.com/2010/12/22/the-case-of-the-missing-o-b-tampons/

Stein, J. (2011, December 8). o.b. Ultra tampons are coming back, and the company apologizes with a song. *Los Angeles Times* website.

Stewart, D. (2010, November 4). *Bloody hell: My favorite tampon has been discontinued.* Retrieved 10 January, 2012 from Jezebel: http://jezebel.com/5681837/bloody-hell-my-favorite-tampon-has-been-discontinued

Stewart, D. (2011, 17-January). *o.b. tampons return to shelves.* Retrieved February 2010, from Jezebel: http://jezebel.com/5735675/ob-tampons-return-to-shelves

Subramani, M. R. & Rajagopalan, B. (2003). Knowledge-sharing and influence in online social networks via viral marketing. *Communications of the ACM, 46*(12), 300–307.

Ulmer, R. R., Sellnow, T. L., & Seeger, M. W. (2007). *Effective crisis communication: Moving from crisis to opportunity.* Thousand Oaks, CA: Sage.

Veil, S. R., Buchner, T., & Palenchar, M. J. (2011, June). A work-in-progress literature review: Incorporating social media in risk and crisis communication. *Journal of Contingencies and Crisis Management, 16*(3), 110–122.

Weissfeld, A. S. (2010, May 15). The history of tampons: From ancient times to an FDA-regulated medical device. *Clinical Microbiology Newsletter, 32*(10), 73–76.

Write the Company. (2010, March 31). *Write The Company.* Retrieved January 10, 2012 from Sizing Up o.b. Tampons: http://writethecompany.com/sizing-up-o-b-tampons

Yin, R. K. (2009). *Case study research: Design and methods. Applied Social Research Methods.* Thousand Oaks, CA: Sage.

Appendix A

Table 15.1 Information about the Triple Sorry music video that appeared on the o.b. tampon Canadian website in December of 2011

Video:	Triple Sorry - Total Running Time 1:49
Open on wide shot of white grand piano on a cliff with younger man at the keys, cut to hands playing piano; cut to sheet music on top of piano with the title of the song A Tender Song for (personalized name, ex. Emily), then back to hands and keys, before a medium shot of the young male singer who emphasizes "and let you down" by lower his head in a manner that represents shame.	Audio: Piano plays chords; singer whispers (personalized name, ex. Emily) I know we went away, and let you down.
Camera pans around a medium tight shot of singer who is looking directly into camera.	
Male singer is crouched in a tree and stands as he sings, grabbing an overhead branch. Camera pans and singer fist pumps the air for emphasis. medium tight of singer who blowd rose petals at camera	(Personalized name) believe me when I say, we want to turn this thing around. Calling out your name, and calling out your name Again
Cut to rose petals spelling out personalized name	
Male sings walks down beach and sits on a log where he skips a stone into the water	In case you didn't hear it the first time.
Zoom into to male singer with "Really Sorry" card and quill pen thinking about what to write in the card	(Personalized name) didn't mean to make you cry, didn't want to say goodbye. We're so sorry.
Dissolve to male singer who reveals a megaphone and uses it to "cue the airplane guys"	
Cut to blues sky with personalized name presented as skywriting	
Male singer jumps down from free limb, rips right shirt sleeve exposing a heart tattoo with I'm sorry written on it. Male singer rips opposite shirt sleeve to reveal heart tattoo with personalized name. Dissolve to male singer holding then releasing a dove.	We'll write your name across the sky, cue the air-plane guy. We're double sorry.
Shot of sky and ocean with birds spelling out "sorry." A hot-air balloon on the left of the screen features personalized name. Dissolve back to male singer at piano.	Triple sorry (chorus sings: didn't mean to make you cry) Didn't want to say goodbye. We're so sorry.
Dissolve to male singer on the beach. Tight shot of male singer's face. Camera pans up to a cliff with a rainbow in the background. An electronic banner comes in to encourage the viewer to click to download a coupon.	We were really super wrong so here's a tender song. (music slows) You deserve the best and more. (mmmmm) So take this coupon to the store.

Chapter 16

Risk Communication: Community Relations Efficacy or Calamity?

ROBERT L. HEATH, PH.D.
University of Houston

Introduction

Risk communication is as old as human society. It, along with its partner, risk management, is qualitatively fundamental to the human condition. By that reasoning, society can be defined as the collective management of risk. Societies, communities, small groups, and even individuals that manage and communicate best about risks seem to be safer, healthier, and have a better quality of life. The successful ones are more efficacious, and more effective in assessing and responding to risks, than those who are less adept.

With that premise in mind, this chapter focuses on the quality of infrastructures that are contextually relevant to various risks. Sometimes the context calls for one-way communication from elites/advisors to users/advisees, conforming to a power/knowledge interpretation, and becomes effective because the nature of risk communication is fairly linear. In the human condition, this paradigm is timeless, where parents inform children about risks and elders inform younger members of the community and sages offer advice and prescriptions. The latter, for instance, might have to do with matters of diet, health, and procreation. As "ancient" as this sounds, it continues in modern, and even post-modern, society. As was the case with sages long ago, who advised farmers when to plant, how to plant, and what measures increase yield, county extension agents ply their trades across a nation such as the United States. So, too, there is emergency response information and public health advice.

But there are other forms and contexts of community risk communication: ones that variously call for public engagement and even what is currently championed as deliberative democracy. The paradigm presumes, as does infrastructural risk communication theory, that the quality of the dialogue within the power/knowledge structures of the community predict how well people engage with one another in risk communication and how well the "elite" risk communicators acknowledge the community members as partners in risk management and communication. Experts such as Roger Kasperson (2014) worry that the commitment to risk dialogue that occurred in the 1980's has failed to sustain itself.

This chapter explains, first, the infrastructural theory of risk management and communication, which opens the discussion to consider how risk elites can create dialogue, ethically use monologue, and ethically combine the two processes to increase public safety and community risk response efficacy. To do so, the chapter next proposes cases that illuminate how and why "dialogue" fails or succeeds and explains why one-way communication can be ethical and useful, but in a dialogic context. Finally, practical implications are presented to serve as guidelines for those who want to make risk communication and management infrastructures effective tools by which communities can collectively manage risks.

Infrastructural Theory of Risk

I first began to think about risk communication and management infrastructures by observing, for instance, efforts by advocates supporting the use of nuclear energy to generate power. This interest began in the 1970's as utility companies which wanted approval to locate, build, and operate such facilities began to hold community meetings and commit to community safety/emergency response programs. This process required public hearings. It matured into public meetings and personal contact between companies and citizens to explain, for instance, emergency measures that should be taken in the event that a release of nuclear material occurred. In the United States, the paradigm case of nuclear crisis occurred at Three Mile Island in Pennsylvania. Internationally, a cataclysmic release occurred at the generating facility in Chernobyl, Ukraine (USSR), which affected much of Europe and Russia/Soviet Bloc. More recently, a similar event occurred in Fukushima, Japan, when a wave caused by a tsunami breached the protective walls around the generating facility. How well are workers, emergency responders, and near neighbors prepared to respond to a serious industrial event? That is the key question of emergency management, risk communication response.

At the same time, this risk/crisis challenge came into play as part of a research and communication design effort in high-risk communities, near Houston, Texas, where massive industrial facilities produce chemicals. How such facilities, and the communities where they operate, communicated and managed risks was dramatically affected by the MIC release in Bhopal, India, in 1984. Thousands of people were injured or killed by a release of a toxic gas (methyl isocyanate) from a manufacturing plant operated by Union Carbide (Broughton, 2005). That event brought about a new era of risk management planning and community outreach that is now state-of-the-art practice in high-risk communities. This event motivated commitment to the principle of community right-to-know, to a better understanding of, and commitment to, risk democracy. This principle assumed that people at risk have a right to know about the risk and participate, democratically and deliberatively, in reducing the likelihood that the risk will occur, that its effect will be cataclysmic, and how people should best protect themselves in the event of an incident.

Development of the principles of risk democracy, as it was originally explained (National Research Council, 1989), led to theories of risk assessment, perception, and mitigation. One of these theories has been termed risk infrastructure. As one of the pioneers of this successful community-based program on health and environmental hazards, Renn (2009) pointed to three challenges, or what he called levels of risk debates:

- factual evidence and probabilities;
- institutional performance, expertise, and experience;
- conflicts about worldviews and value systems. (p. 81)

These issues of conflict called for various communication needs, including information transfer, dialogue, mediation, and collaboration. To achieve these communication needs, even the elitist elements of each infrastructure should have a public/stakeholder engagement focus.

Renn's (2009) advice focused on each of these challenges. Technical expertise, for instance, presumes that its effectiveness results from transparent access to audiences, comprehensible presentations, empathic attention to public concerns, and realization: even acknowledgement that differences of how risks are framed are likely to be at play and affect the communication process. Experience can raise trustworthiness and willingness to dialogue, depending on the goodness of fit between the stakeholders, the public expectations, and the performance of organizations (spokespersons). It presumes openness to public concerns, regular engagements that are consultative, and commonly "agreed-to" procedures for responding to crisis events. The values dimension required fair representations by, and concerns of, all parties, involvement of stakeholders, and commitment to transparent and inclusive forms of decision-making.

As a means to draw together emerging theory and best practices, Heath, Palenchar, and O'Hair (2009) set out the rationale for the infrastructural theory of risk management and communication as being, or requiring, a collective process. It presumes that the foundational quality of any infrastructure, some structural components of a community, is its ability to perceive a risk. In addition to recognizing a risk for what it is, the quality of an infrastructure depends on the kinds and degrees of participation in discussion and decision-making. The environmental movement of the 1960's arose because people believed they were cut out of the process of understanding, evaluating, and morally judging risks, as well as determining which solutions and responses lead to the greatest safety. Such concerns led, necessarily, to specific government agency plans and policies, corporate devised meetings, and formal agencies at the local, state, and federal levels. Industry has tended, at some times more than others, to prevent, frustrate, and derail community engagement. But, research abounds (including failed attempts to mount liability litigation) to prove that community engagement creates better and more accepted interpretations of risk—and more effective emergency responses (Heath & McComas, 2015; Heath & Lee, 2016). Such risks, in the case of petrochemical facilities, can range from health effects of long-term exposure to cataclysmic moments requiring effective emergency response.

Community relations (CR) is an anchor of the infrastructural approach to risk communication. Community relations developed over the years on the assumption that in various ways industrial complexes had to earn their right to operate and reward (Heath and Ni, 2010). Structurally, community relations presumes a multi-dimensional, layered, and multi-textual commitment that results from organizations' sense of, and commitment to, doing what is necessary to protect near neighbors' health and safety.

Connecting corporate social responsibility (CSR) and its companion concept, legitimacy, Heath and Ni (2010) reasoned that community relationships could be defined and implemented by the layers of "neighborliness," defined as nice neighbor, good (generous) neighbor, and reflective/responsible neighbor. The first, *nice*, presumes that businesses, often in cooperation with non-profit organizations, visibly sponsor feel-good programs and projects, such as youth sports activities and school programs. The good, *generous* neighbor could include sponsored environmental reclamation and restoration programs, for instance. Corporate dollars and employee volunteer hours can support projects that raise local standards of living and quality of life in significant ways. The *reflective/responsible* neighbor presumes that an industry should not work to bend the community to serve its will, but, rather, to bend itself to earn the support of the communities where it operates. This third layer of community relations becomes vitalized when high-risk industries work to create a robust dialogic and community-based planning program designed to achieve the highest standards of public health and safety in the community. This layer presumes that control, as well as power/knowledge, is shared within the community. Thus, it becomes the rationale for communication outreach.

Such strategic risk communication considerations are central to the thinking, planning, and implementation of programs by industries, in conjunction with communities where they operate. Such strategies certainly are vital to, and defining of, the quality of decision-making institutions that operate in communities where industrial activities pose substantial, real, and manageable risks.

Given this overview, the next section highlights the kinds of infrastructures, the industry-local government alliance risk communication programs that operate in high-risk communities. The section offers details on specific kinds of risk management and communication infrastructures: hearings, LEPS's, CAC's/CAP's, and emergency planning.

Infrastructures: Hearings, LEPC's, CAC's/CAP's, Emergency Planning

Communities with huge industrial complexes have a history of community engagement. Many tools, credibility challenges, issues of transparency, and perils of elitist corporate-centrism have received substantial attention. Such matters are discussed in comprehensive works, such as the *Handbook of Risk and Crisis Communication* (Heath & O'Hair, 2009). Also, for more focused attention on tools and tactics of community engagement, see Heath (1995). Such programs provide structured moments and places when companies, governmental agencies, activists, experts, and concerned citizens come together to share information and collaborate on best-practices programs for public safety.

Among these meetings are *public hearings* (often mandated by government regulatory agencies), especially on special occasions such as licensing petitions and review of incidents, such as an explosion or major toxic chemical release. License petitions are filed by companies, but can be filed by community governments, relevant to some change of operation. For instance, any company planning a new chemical manufacturing facility or major update typically is required to hold and conduct at least one, and often more, public hearing, as a first step to acquiring the government's approval for the construction and operation. In a licensing sequence, each step is likely to require one or more environmental impact and safety standards review. In Texas, for instance, there can be as many as 30 specific types of license that become packaged into the total authorization for siting, construction, and operation—and restoration, as in the case of nuclear power waste storage and remediation.

These can be conducted with a government, "nonpartisan/neutral," or industry moderator. They can begin, and even continue, with a limited number of representatives on stage or they can have a large panel that represents "all" interests. They also almost invariably have a hearing segment open to any interested member of the public who agrees to speak for a limited amount of time. But limitations should not prevent reasonable comments from being fully aired.

Hearings can occur in the community or another venue, such as a governmental hearing room. They occur after public notification of the meeting date, time, topic, and place. They may follow an agenda, even a pre-scheduled sequence of presenters. Such presenters, at least the official list, presume to represent all of the relevant interests in some matter and assure them time at the microphone.

In such hearings, sound science can get lost in the midst of many other issues, but such difficulties are more of a symptom of the quality of relationships in the community than something inherent to the hearing process. Hearings can become shouting matches and even promote protests. Thus, in addition to scientific discussions, they can be highly value-laden and sociopolitical. They can destroy, as well as build, community efforts at joint decision-making. And, some skeptics say that "hearings" is a misnomer because there is lot of "speaking" and little "listening." For example, I once sat in on a licensing hearing relevant to upper limits of air pollution in regard to the licensing of electric generating facilities in the Four Corners area of New Mexico/Arizona. The presentations were so routine and scripted that the various advocates chided each other for "changing the scripts."

McComas, Arvai, and Besley (2009) (see also, McComas, 2010) detailed the kinds of community engagement typical of public hearings: Community surveys, focus groups/other controlled discussion group formats, written comments (even web postings), availability sessions/open houses, public meetings, traditional advisory boards/committees, workshops/working dinners, and deliberative conferences and workshops that often have a decision-aiding scope/purpose/initiative. Each of these formats of public engagement can offer substantial gain at assessing resistance to an industry and support for various management policy options. Often, at least in the perception of participants (or those who refuse to participate but, nevertheless, endorse or oppose outcomes), these kinds of formats can be more symbolic than substantive. They may be used to defend an unresponsive industry which can say that the public has no right to complain after a decision is made because they had the opportunity to voice their concerns. The quality of participation reflects the amount of anger and the extent to which the public, in particular, believes it will be, is, or was taken seriously. For instance, if a report is made with recommendations as a result of such hearings, will "minority" reports and statements of agreement and disagreement be included?

Studies, nicely summarized by McComas and others (2009, 2010), suggest that the quality of community participation is never a given, but a critical standard of the quality of community relations. Such meetings must address issues that account for the specifics of public concern. Meetings should not dismiss concerns or denigrate the motives of critics. Because technical discussions and decisions often require technical language, such terms should not be used to baffle, confuse, or marginalize concerned citizens. Jobs, and the strength of the local economy, may be key factors in hearing-based decision-making, but not all citizens are willing to assume risks for those outcomes. The most severe critics are likely to demand zero risk, which is unlikely, but what level is reasonable, and understandable, in terms of critics' perceptions? Trust and respect are earned. The baseline requirement is to demonstrate, to citizens, that public participation is not a waste of time: that industry and regulators hear concerns and care about near residents and employees. Corporations that fail to heed the concerns of the community may achieve a favorable decision from the government agencies that require the hearing, but citizens can sue for redress. So, the prospects of deliberative democracy and stakeholder participation can become derailed (Heath, 1985).

Another of the sorts of community relations tools worth considering are *local emergency planning committees (LEPC's)*. They are an artifact of the 1980's: the result of the Emergency Planning and Community-Right-to-Know Act (see, for instance, http://www.epa.gov/epcra/local-emergency-planning-committees). The primary mandate is for key members of each community to plan for, and communicate to, the public what is needed to know to understand risk and prepare for emergency response in the event of a crisis. LEPC membership is to consist of elected state and local officials, including members from the following departments: police, fire, civil defense, public health, environment, and transportation (along with hospital officials, facility representatives, and representatives from community groups and the media).

LEPC's are designed to identify which facilities and transportation routes pose substantial risks to communities and prepare plans designed for emergency response in the event that an industrial event should occur at the plant or along the route. The assumption is that the plans will be realistic, responsive to local concerns, and funded to be operable. LEPC's have been found to be variously effective. The creation of plans can be nothing more than a formality paying lip service to local response capabilities. Many end up on shelves, but are never, or only badly, implemented. To be successful, they need continued commitment by industry and local government to help increase community and individual response efficacy. They require that members meet with purpose, a planned agenda, and commitment to community safety.

Understanding the limits often associated with LEPC's, industries have created more tailored communication, planning, and implementation tools. These are variously called *community advisory committees/panels (CAC's/CAP's)*. In responsive communities, they meet regularly, at times convenient to the public, and under the guidance of a paid facilitator who avoids taking sides. The responsibility is to "facilitate" communication and engagement, not to direct it in any particular way or to particular, pre-determined outcomes. Typically, CAC's in cities with large petrochemical facilities follow a prepared agenda, which requires comments by plant managers on safety and environmental impact. If one of the plants has had a "reportable event" since the previous meeting that company is scheduled for a report. Such reports include details of the event, causes of the event, and precautions/changes in procedures to reduce the likelihood of recurrence. It is important that plant managers appear and speak even if supported by technical and communication personnel. The buck stops on the plant manager's desk.

For instance, one evening a plant manager (the person responsible for operating facilities profitably and safely) reported that two employees had died because their air supply systems had failed while working inside of a "vessel" (a huge cylinder that may contain toxic fumes). The workers were being monitored by a third party, who became aware that the workers "seemed to have slowed or stopped," but who was fooled by slow asphyxiation, leading the person protecting the workers to falsely interpret that reduced sound from inside the vessel was the workers taking a break. Analysis discovered that the bottles of oxygen had not been fully charged by the vendor and had not been checked by the company prior to the activity.

In the standard lore of "crisis" communication, some scholars and communication practitioners might interpret this industrial "accident" as a crisis. But industry does not. They employ a lesson-learned approach to such events and would never presume that explanation or apology is ample. And such candor regarding events inside and outside of plants is what can make CAC's so effective as risk communication tools. Blame is assigned only as far as it provides a lesson learned and serves as a rationale for change. CAC's can be substantially transparent and self-policing. They have the ability, when implemented correctly, to instill confidence, build trust, and demonstrate how industry is committed to responsive/reflective community relations (and employee relations).

Part of the mandate of LEPC's is the creation and implementation of emergency warning and response plans. As noted above, such plans can be, and perhaps often are, more symbolic than useful. But, as part of their community relations, certain high-risk facilities and communities have taken responsible care seriously.

The cornerstones to community emergency management are plans that include strategic communication to help the community know the plan, know how to implement it, and be confident that it will work. Such plans are sensitive to citizen concerns, risk awareness, and the response efficacy that can be achieved through expert efficacy (good planning), individual efficacy (knowing what they need to do), and community efficacy (effective community responses) (Heath & Lee, 2016).

Warning systems can include sirens, alerts placed online and sent to computers/handheld devices, telephone alerts, emergency radio broadcasts, smart phones, and social media. Such alerts are designed to initiate public actions, typically to shelter-in-place, in the event of an emergency. That means that citizens who become aware of the plan, trust the plan, and know how to implement the plan do so by getting inside of a building (or an automobile) where exposure to toxic fumes is reduced. "Go inside, shut the doors and windows, turn off heat/AC systems, and monitor the alert through available communication tools." Such programs are especially designed to reach children who need to know when to go inside or stay inside whether at play (such as in a park), at home, at a business, or at school. Studies even reveal that children become a useful part of the system to help other members, especially siblings and moms, learn about and know shelter-in-place protocols.

One of the key communication tools in communities' shelter-in-place campaigns is *Wally Wise Guy*, which was created in, and is copyrighted by, the LEPC in Deer Park, Texas: one of the largest concentrations of chemical manufacturing in the USA. Wally is a turtle. What does a turtle do when it senses danger? It tucks inside its protective shell. For analysis of how this program helps create legitimacy, trust, support, and citizens' response efficacy, see Heath and Lee (2016).

Wally is part of a multi-dimensional campaign. He has his own website (http://www.wally.org/). He is a costumed character that meets and greets at community events, especially those where children are likely to attend. He is a key to school-oriented campaigns. The purpose of the campaign is to have his image everywhere, with the list of steps to take in the event of an emergency. Thus, he is on refrigerator magnets, calendars, and coloring sheets. And where do coloring sheets end up? On the refrigerator.

Wally's message is simple and doable. It does not deny the reality that some cataclysmic event could happen. In fact, its origins were the 1990's-era emphasis on government-mandated Risk Management Planning. The EPA, motivated by environmental activists, mandated that high-risk communities create an analysis to define the worst case scenario: what would happen if a massive release of some deadly chemical (such as MIC) occurred with the wind blowing in a direction that would result in maximum damage to humans and animals? The Houston Ship Channel industries (perhaps the largest petrochemical complex in the world) are downwind of a population of about six million people (with Houston as the centerpiece).

Fighting the mandate as stupidly improbable would likely have generated greater activist and community concern. So, the industry engaged in a massive planning and communication project, with Wally and shelter-in-place as the centerpiece. "Know Wally, and do what he would do in the event of an emergency." This campaign, and Wally, are now prominent, well beyond Deer Park, Texas, as an online computer search will reveal. This campaign is multi-dimensioned, layered, and textual. But, most importantly, it is simple, appealing, and practical.

One last glimpse into the problems and perplexities of risk communication is warranted, at least as speculation. Each plant operating in communities such as those noted above has at least one, and often more than one, company spokesperson. Among their duties, these persons answer "complaint" phone calls. For instance, if a company flare ignites, some near neighbors are likely to phone the company expressing concern. A flare often ignites with an "explosion" similar, but louder, to the ignition of a gas-filled lighter of the kind used to start a barbeque. These are located on towers (some plants have several) and the burn gives off a yellow light. The flares are used to burn off gases that otherwise could cause a greater industrial hazard, but even though they are for safety, they cause concerns—almost invariably.

What communication style should be used by the person answering the phone? Are women likely to be better communicators under these circumstances? Reluctantly, male members of such staffs agree that their female counterparts are less likely to dismiss concern and more likely to engage in conversation. One standard line is to tell the caller that "the flares are not something that should concern them. They are merely a tool that increases safety of operations. Don't worry."

Prior to such responses, women (and empathetic men) tend to "visit" with the caller, especially if the motive for the call becomes apparent. "Do you realize that my grandchildren are here with me this evening and that flare terrifies them?" Should the company representative ask about the children and engage the caller as a grandmother or merely an annoying caller who has no earthly reason to fear the flare?

In this context, a senior community relations spokesperson for an international petrochemical facility located in Deer Park designed a community outreach program to discuss flares. He placed notices in the paper and on television and radio telling concerned citizens what evening the meeting would occur, where, and at what time. It was an open forum. It included "refreshments." He planned the event to include comments by the heads of the plant's safety and environmental impact departments. He prepared posters and PowerPoint presentations. No one showed up. Should he have been upset and give up? Or should he have scheduled the event again for the coming year?

CONCLUSIONS

Risk communication (planning and management) is many things to many people. Well done, effective risk management, planning, and communication are keys to companies' right to operate. Effective risk communication is not only vital to community interests, but also to that of industry legitimacy and support by community residents (Heath & Lee, 2016). The communication tools discussed above must be recurring and enduring. They can bring technical discussions down to an understandable level and can acknowledge, rather than dismiss, citizen concerns.

Thus, risk management communication infrastructures need to be in place. People need to know when, where, and why meetings occur. They should feel welcome. Officials must listen to them and provide information that can be understood and used to make individual and group decisions. Persons who are risk communication professionals, often under the title of community relations, must be committed to getting information to people who also want to know how to use it. Professional communicators must be tolerant, empathic, and clear. They are communication facilitators who bring people together to make communities safer.

DISCUSSION QUESTIONS

1. What is the ethical and pragmatic value of expert communicators and risk managers in the process of helping citizens to live healthier and safer lives?

2. What three challenges are important to keep in mind when designing a community risk communication/management program and assuring that infrastructures are in place to implement it?

3. Can public meetings and standing committees in high-risk communities be designed and operated to serve the citizens as well as the companies and governmental agencies that are responsible for ethical and pragmatic risk communication and management?

4. Explain the pros and cons of using a spokes character, such as Wally Wise Guy, as a campaign spokes-entity for shelter-in-place.

5. The last paragraphs of the paper describes a community outreach program that seemed to fail because citizens concerned about the use of flairs in their community failed to show up at an event designed to discuss this safety process. As the chapter asks, should the person in change of the outreach give up and never offer to hold such a public meeting again?

REFERENCES

Broughton, E. (2005). The Bhopal disaster and its aftermath: A review. *Environmental Health: A Global Access Science Source, 4*, 1–6. http://www.ehjournal.net/content/4/1/6, downloaded 12, 14, 2015.

Heath, R. L. (1995). Corporate environmental risk communication: Cases and practices along the Texas Gulf Coast. In B. R. Burleson (Ed.), *Communication yearbook 18* (pp. 255–277). Thousand Oaks, CA: Sage.

Heath, R. L., & Lee, J. (2016). Chemical manufacturing and refining industry legitimacy: Reflective management, trust, pre-crisis communication to achieve community efficacy. *Risk Analysis 36*(6), 1108–1124. doi: 10.1111/risa.12504. Epub 2015 Oct 27.

Heath, R. L., & McComas, K. (2015). Interest, interest, whose interest is at risk? Risk governance, issues management, and the fully functioning society. In Urbano Fra Paleo (Ed.), *Risk governance: The articulation of hazard, politics, and ecology* (pp. 117–133). New York: Springer.

Heath, R. L., & Ni, L. (2010). Community relations and corporate social responsibility. In R. L. Heath (Ed.), *Sage handbook of public relations* (pp. 557–568). Thousand Oaks, CA: Sage.

Heath, R. L., & O'Hair, H. D. (Eds.) (2009). *Handbook of risk and crisis communication*. New York: Routledge.

Heath, R. L., Palenchar, M. J., & O'Hair, H. D. (2009). Community building through risk communication infrastructures. In R. L. Heath & H. D. O'Hair (Eds.). *Handbook of risk and crisis communication* (pp. 471–487). New York: Routledge.

Kasperson, R. (2014). Four questions for risk communication. *Journal of Risk Research, 17*(10), 1233–1239.

McComas, K. A. (2010). Community engagement and risk management. In R. L. Heath (Ed.), *Sage handbook of public relations* (pp. 461–476). Thousand Oaks, CA: Sage.

McComas, K. A., Arvai, J., & Besley, J. C. (2009). Linking public participation and decision making through risk communication. In R. L. Heath & H. D. O'Hair (Eds.). *Handbook of risk and crisis communication* (pp. 364–385). New York: Routledge.

National Research Council (1989). *Improving risk communication*. Washington, DC: National Academy Press.

Renn, O. (2009). Risk communication: Insights and requirements for designing successful communication programs on health and environmental hazards. In R. L. Heath & H. D. O'Hair (Eds.). *Handbook of risk and crisis communication* (pp. 80–98). New York: Routledge.

Chapter 17

Don't Drink the Water: Warning Communication in a Northern Ohio Water Emergency

MATTHEW W. SEEGER, PH.D.
Wayne State University

HENRY S. SEEGER, B.A.
Illinois State University

Introduction

During many natural disasters and industrial accidents, there is an acute need for an effective warning message. In a wide range of emergency situations, warning messages are used as a persuasive effort to convince those at risk to take action to reduce or avoid possible harm. Analytical frameworks, such as Mileti and Sorensen's (1990) *Hear-Confirm-Understand-Decide-Respond Model*, examine the efficacy of these warning messages in order to better prepare for future crises (Mileti & Peek, 2000; Sorensen, 2000). Public warning systems for crises consist of three interrelated subsystems: detection subsystem, management, and response. The process of *Hear-Confirm-Understand-Decide-Respond* relates to this last stage in the warning system, where the public receives the messages about a risk and recommended response, confirms the response (usually through a second channel), understands what is being communicated, makes a decision about the information, and responds.

Many crises concern the safety of public water supplies or have implications for the safety of water. According to the U.S. Centers for Disease Control and Prevention:

> Water-related emergency preparedness and outbreak response has become one of the most significant and crucial issues in recent history. Individuals, families, and businesses have been advised to be prepared for emergencies by creating disaster supply kits that include appropriate amounts of safe drinking water. Emergencies can include natural disasters (for example, hurricanes, floods, and droughts), man-made disasters (for example, intentional contamination), and outbreaks (for example, infections linked to water exposure) (CDC, 2014).

Several recent cases of water-related emergencies have surfaced. For example, the 1993 *Cryptosporidium* contamination of the Milwaukee, Wisconsin water supply resulted in more than 400,000 people becoming ill with diarrhea from a water-borne parasite. The contamination was linked to a runoff from agricultural operations, which contaminated the city's drinking water supply. Another incident occurred when Walkerton, Ontario suffered a contamination of its municipal water supply in 2000 with *E. coli* bacteria (Kondro, 2000). Several thousand residents began suffering from bloody diarrhea and seven eventually died. For several days after the initial report, the operators of the municipal water supply continued to claim that the water was safe, thus exposing more residents to the contamination. As discussed by Getchell and Sellnow (2015), in 2014, 7,500 gallons of crude 4-methylcyclohexanemethanol (MCHM), a chemical used in coal cleaning, contaminated West Virginia American Water's drinking water intake, treatment, and distribution center (Getchell & Sellnow, 2015). Residents of the nine affected counties were advised not to drink, cook with, bathe in, or wash with the water. A total of 300,000 people were affected by the spill, with 14 people hospitalized after showing symptoms such as nausea, vomiting, and rashes (Getchell & Sellnow, 2015).

Methods for responding to water contamination depend on the specific agents involved, their concentration, the location of the contamination, and the communities affected. All, however, require effective communication with the public. Water contaminated with some organisms can be boiled to sterilize the water or treated with chemicals such as chlorine. However, water contaminated with chemicals generally cannot be made safe to drink by boiling. In some cases, the contamination may be such that it should not even be used for bathing or washing. Water advisories often mean that all restaurants and, in some cases, schools, will be closed. The warning messages (boil water, don't drink the water, avoid all contact with the water) can be complex and not easily understood. Because water is a necessary commodity and the access to potable water is a basic human need, methods of response become more difficult.

Theories of Warning

As noted, warnings are among the most common communication strategies used to mitigate harm immediately before or after a crisis (Sellnow & Seeger, 2013). They are used in weather events, such as hurricanes or tornadoes, wildfires, floods, industrial accidents, chemical discharges, radiological events, infectious disease outbreaks, and many other kinds of crises. Warning communication, therefore, has been extensively studied, primarily from the standpoint of disaster sociology. A warning system is composed of three subsystems: a detection system, an emergency management system, and a public response system (Mileti & Peek, 2000). The detection system identifies a potential or emerging risk. In many cases, the speed of detection is closely associated with the level of harm. For example, early detection of an impending earthquake can enhance the effectiveness of warnings. The second subsystem employs an emergency management process to interpret the risk and determine when a disaster took place, how it took place, and what form a response should take. Typically, the emergency management system involves decision makers who determine if a public alert should be issued. The integration of these subsystems is both dynamic and interactive and requires effective communication among decision makers, subject-matter experts, and emergency management personnel (Mileti & Peek, 2000).

The last subsystem involves a public communication system that alerts the public to a risk and recommends some action designed to limit or mitigate the harm. Some communities, for example, have elaborate siren systems in order to warn of tornados. Warning systems increasingly include the use of digital technology, such as text alerts and social media posts. In this chapter's analysis, Mileti and Sorensen's (1990) Hear-Confirm-Understand-Decide-Respond Model is employed to examine this public warning process. Like all forms of communication, warnings consist of a message framed by a sender and communicated to a receiver, who then interprets and responds to the message. Mileti and Sorensen's

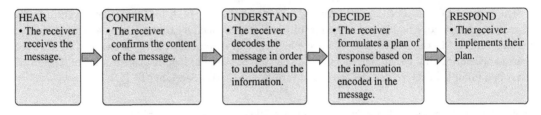

Figure 17.1 Mileti and Sorensen's Warning Model

model illustrates this process within the context of risk communication. The model in Figure 17.1 details the process by which a receiver interprets and responds to a warning.

A properly constructed warning message should facilitate the receiver's movement from the first step (hearing the message) to the last (responding to the risk). Intermediate steps, including confirming the message, understanding the message, and deciding what to do, intervene between the hearing and responding stages.

The Hear-Confirm-Understand-Decide-Respond Model is proven effective at framing warning messages and facilitating an effective public response. It should be noted, however, that no system of warning communication is 100% effective, either in reaching the entire audience or in generating 100% compliance with the recommendations. Technologies, such as text alerts, early detection systems for threats, and rapid distribution systems, have been employed to enhance the speed and reach of warning messages. In large-scale warnings, however, some people do not receive the message, some do not interpret it correctly, and some do not respond appropriately.

The Toledo Water Case

Toledo, Ohio is a city of approximately 400,000 residents, and is located on the western shore of Lake Erie. The city draws its municipal water supply from the lake and processes some 80 million gallons of water each day through a continual process. Water is regularly tested for quality assurance (Division of Water Treatment, 2014). On August 3, 2014, testing showed heightened levels of the toxin microcystin, produced by cyanobacteria, which had multiplied at a high level in Lake Erie due to fertilizer runoff. Cyanobacteria, sometimes called "blue-green algae," is a naturally occurring organism that can reach dangerous levels when agricultural runoff promotes a "bloom." Such blooms, called harmful algae blooms (HAB), are not uncommon and often follow periods of high rain and warm temperatures.

Microcystins are hepatoxic, causing severe damage to the liver (Falconer, 1998). Microcystin-producing cyanobacteria thrive under warmer water conditions and, in particular, eutrophication of a freshwater environment can lead to large microcystis growth (Oregon State University, 2013). In August of 2014, the influx of phosphorus into Lake Erie from surrounding farmland and residential sewage systems, coupled with the warmest summer on record, produced ideal conditions for the growth of cyanobacteria in western Lake Erie.

The risk posed to Toledo's city water was detected by routine testing. The testing was complicated, however, due to both the lack of an established national standard for safe levels of microcystin and by inconsistent results. In addition, some samples showed high levels, while others did not, leading to confusion and enhancing uncertainty. Nonetheless, the decision was made by Toledo's leaders to issue a water ban.

The Mayor of Toledo, D. Michael Collins, was elected in January of 2014. Prior to his election, he had served on the city council. He had retired from the Toledo Police Department, after serving 27 years as a police officer. Mayor Collins had extensive experience in emergency management, as well as a long-term association with the community. Thus, he was well prepared to help manage this event. The Toledo water ban unfolded over a three-day period in early August 2014 (See Table 17.1).

Table 17.1 The Toledo Water Crisis Timeline (Based on *Toledo News Now*, August 5, 2014)

August 2, 2014

2:00 am on Saturday - The City of Toledo issues a "Do Not Drink" notice, warning residents to not drink the water, boil it, or bathe in it, because of an algae bloom in Lake Erie contaminating city water.

6:00 am Saturday - Representatives from Lucas County confirm that they are also affected by the contamination.

7:00 am Saturday - The City of Oregon, Ohio issues a statement saying they're unaffected by the contamination.

7:00 am–9:00 am Saturday - Dozens of other areas confirm that they, too, are affected and they also put in place "Do Not Drink" advisories.

10:00 am Saturday - Oregon fire departments begin offering free water to people who bring containers.

10:45 am Saturday - Lucas County Health Department says it's safe to bathe, but maintains its "Do Not Drink or Boil" advisory

11:00 am Saturday - Parts of Fulton County are added to list of places affected.

11:45 am Saturday - Toledo Mayor Collins addresses the media and announces water distribution centers at Waite and Central Catholic High Schools. He says samples of the contaminated water have been sent to Columbus, Cincinnati, Lake Superior State for testing and results are expected Saturday night around 5:00–7:00 pm.

12:00 pm Saturday - Ohio Governor Kasich declares a state of emergency.

12:15 pm Saturday - Lucas County Health Department urges restaurants to close.

2:00 pm Saturday - Health Commissioner Dave Grossman says "this is the beginning, not the end."

3:00 pm Saturday - Water distribution is scheduled at Waite and Central Catholic High Schools at 5:00 pm and 6:00 pm.

3:30 pm Saturday - Local hospital Promedica spokesperson says 60 people at Toledo hospital with "gastroenterological problems."

8:00 pm Saturday - Mayor Collins says water test results delayed to 9:00 pm.

8:00 pm Saturday - National Guard arrives with water at Woodward High School.

8:00 pm Saturday - Mayor Collins says testing showed two different results. The ban is kept in place.

9:00 pm Saturday - City Spokesperson Lisa Ward says no test results from EPA will be given Saturday due to lack of sampling material.

10:00 pm Saturday - Mayor Collins says he expects to receive all results at 7:00 am Sunday.

10:00 pm Saturday - Health Commissioner says people with sensitive skin and liver problems should not bathe in contaminated water.

August 3, 2014

10:00 am Sunday - Mayor Collins says Ohio Governor Kasich will arrive in Ohio around 1:00 pm.

11:00 am Sunday - Mayor Collins says "everything is trending in a positive direction," still waiting on confirmed results.

11:00 am Sunday - Cherry Street Mission distribution center runs out of water.

1:00 pm Sunday - Health Department says people will need to flush their water system once water is cleared.

1:45 pm Sunday - Ohio Congresswoman Marcy Kaptur says no results have been received yet, but they should arrive around 4:00 pm.

2:00 pm Sunday - State Emergency Center says it is still waiting on test results.

3:00 pm Sunday - Head of Toledo Utilities says city will not shut off water.

3:30 pm Sunday - Ohio Gov. Kasich says improvement in the water quality has been seen, but more confirmation needed.

4:00 pm Sunday - Toledo Waite High School distribution center runs out of water, expects shipment around 4:45 pm.

4:00 pm Sunday - Air National Guard arrives at University of Toledo Scott Park campus with 10,000 gallons of water.

5:00 pm Sunday - No results yet reported from water testing.

August 4, 2014

9:29 am Monday - Water advisory is lifted. The city reports that municipal water is now safe for drinking and all other uses.

10:00 am Monday - Mayor Collins holds press conference announcing water is safe and toasts Toledo with a glass of tap water.

The initial water warning was posted at approximately 2:00 am, on the City of Toledo website, as a public notice and on the City's Facebook page. Additional notices were sent out through social media and to print, television, and radio outlets. The initial announcement posted on the city website, by Lisa Ward, on Saturday, August 2, 2014, and filed under Public Notices, was titled *Urgent Water Notice.* It proclaimed in all capital letters that the residents of Toledo and Lucas County who receive water from the city of Toledo DO NOT DRINK THE WATER. DO NOT BOIL THE WATER. It went on to explain about the testing that had been done on the water and how they came to the conclusion that it could not be used for drinking. Also, the notice explained that the water should not be boiled and that, in fact, boiling the water would increase the toxins. If the water was consumed, it may cause abnormal liver function, diarrhea, vomiting, nausea, numbness, and dizziness. The water should not be used for drinking, making infant formula, making ice, brushing teeth, preparing food, and should not be given to pets. The notice recommended seeking medical attention if a person felt they had been exposed and were suffering ill effects. Also, the notice explained that the source of the problem was a harmful algal bloom (HAB) in Lake Erie, caused by runoff of over-fertilized lawns and fields. It explained that further testing was being run to verify the severity of the toxic levels and that water distribution points were being set up for the community. The notice ended with a phone number to call for further information.

The notice created an immediate run on supplies of bottled water. Residents began buying up existing stocks and many drove to surrounding communities in order to buy bottled water. Relief agencies, including the American Red Cross, shipped water to Toledo and companies, such as Kroger, diverted shipments of bottled water to the city. The initial public notice banning the use of city water was soon followed by information about the availability of water through distribution centers.

The logistics of providing bottled, or safe, potable water for the community was initially complicated by the sudden demand. A system of distribution centers, and additional supplies from relief agencies, soon helped ease the demand. Nonetheless, bottled water was a scare commodity throughout the area and several of the distribution centers ran out of supplies.

By August 4, testing began to show positive results, although not all tests were showing safe levels. Later in the day, tests showed that the water was, again, safe, and Toledo lifted the ban on drinking water. The city did ask that residents conserve water until such time as treatment facilities could meet the demand. At a press conference, held to announce that the ban had been lifted, the mayor proposed a toast with city water, saying "Here's to you, Toledo. You did a great job."

Discussion and Implications

Sudden and unexpected loss of access to safe and clean water is startling and threatening. The residents of Toledo, Ohio, as with most residents in the United States, take access to safe water for granted and readily available water is a routine of modern life. Because water is a necessity, the loss of access constitutes a significant threat and merits an immediate response. An effective response requires that warning messages be communicated to the public so that they may take appropriate action.

The warning process for Toledo water largely followed the Hear-Confirm-Understand-Decide-Respond Model. In order to insure the widest possible dissemination of the warnings, the message was released through multiple channels. The timing of the release, in the early morning, likely facilitated greater message diffusion, as most residents probably woke to the news of the water ban. Use of social media also likely sped dissemination of the message and, importantly, the messages were stated in as simple terms as possible to promote understanding.

The process of communication created several confirmatory steps. Local communities confirmed the message and ban. The redundancy of the message, particularly as it was covered by local, regional, and national news outlets, also confirmed the warning. Another opportunity to confirm the message was created by including a telephone number in the initial press release. In many cases of warnings, confirmation occurs by word-of-mouth with friends, neighbors, and acquaintances and it is likely that many residents discussed the warning with others to confirm what they had heard.

Understanding was complicated in this case by the complexity of the risk. The ban was on drinking water and parents were warned not to allow their children to bathe in the water because they might inadvertently drink it. Boiling, which is recommended for some types of contamination, is ineffective for microcystin-produced toxins and, in this case, residents were warned that boiling might increase the level of contamination. In addition, initial questions emerged about conflicting test results and about which communities were included in the ban. Complicating matters further were details of the contamination. The harmful agents, microcystins, are a by-product of freshwater cyanobacteria, which are sometime referred to as "blue-green algae." Different use of the common term "blue-green algae," and the technical term, cyanobacteria, added to the confusion.

While Toledo residents likely received the message quickly and understood that their tap water was not safe to drink, the last two stages in the model, decide and respond, were complicated by inadequate supplies of safe water. Simply stated, deciding and responding requires the capacity to respond. Because at some point not drinking is not an option, responding appropriately to the water warning requires replacement supplies. In this case, the initial supply of bottled water was not adequate, but efforts were quickly made to coordinate with other agencies and groups to insure that adequate supplies were available.

CONCLUSION

The response to the Toledo water crisis was both fast and effective and, as a result, the negative effects of the contamination were likely minimized. However, warning systems are not perfect and some residents likely drank contaminated water before learning about the risk. In addition, crises of this sort will become more common in the future. Models, such as Mileti and Sorensen's (1990) Hear-Confirm-Understand-Decide-Respond Model, provide useful explanations for how warning messages function. They can also help identify ways to improve warning systems.

DISCUSSION QUESTIONS

1. What role did social media play in communicating warning messages in this case and how might it function in others?
2. How did the timing of the water crisis impact the communication?
3. How might the processes of hear, confirm, understand, decide, respond occur in other crises such as tornadoes or floods?
4. How do the various levels of water warnings (do not drink, do not boil, no contact) complicate warning messages?

REFERENCES

The Associated Press. (2014). Ohio Attorney General to monitor bottled water prices in Toledo. *WOSU Public Media*. Retrieved from http://wosu.org/2012/news/2014/08/04/ohio-attorney-general-monitor-bottled-water-prices-toledo/

Dolan, M. (2014). In Toldeo, Ohio, residents warned water unsafe to drink. *The Wall Street Journal*. Retrieved from http://online.wsj.com/articles/in-toledo-ohio-residents-warned-water-unsafe-to-drink-1406992024

City of Toledo, Ohio. (2014). Urgent Water Notice. Public Notices. Retrieved from http://toledo.oh.gov/news/2014/08/urgent-water-notice/

City of Toledo, Ohio. (2014). Water Distribution Centers Open. Public Notices. Retrieved from http://toledo.oh.gov/news/2014/08/update-on-water/

City of Toledo, Ohio. (2014). Division of Water Treatment. Retrieved from http://toledo.oh.gov/services/public-utilities/water-treatment/

City of Toledo, Ohio. (2014). Water in Toledo Declared Safe. Public Notices Retrieved from http://toledo.oh.gov/news/2014/08/water-in-toledo-declared-safe/

Falconer, I. R. (1998). Algal toxins and human health. In Hrubec, Jiři (Ed.). *Quality and treatment of drinking water II. (The handbook of environmental chemistry)* (pp. 53–82). New York: Springer.

Getchell, M. C., & Sellnow, T. L. (2015). A network analysis of official Twitter accounts during the West Virginia water crisis. *Computers in Human Behavior 54*, 597–606.

Kondro, W. (2000). *E coli* outbreak deaths spark judicial inquiry in Canada. *The Lancet, 355*(9220), 2058.

Henry, T. (2014). Area U.S. lawmakers seek national standard for microcystin levels. *Toledo Blade*. Retrieved from http://www.toledoblade.com/State/2014/09/10/Area-U-S-lawmakers-seek-national-standard-for-microcystin-levels.html

Jarman, J. (2014). Bottled-water shipments diverted to Toledo. *The Columbus Dispatch*. Retrieved from http://www.dispatch.com/content/stories/local/2014/08/03/bottled-water-shipments-diverted-to-toledo.html

Lucas County Health Department. (2014). Welcome. *Lucas County Health Department*. Retrieved from http://www.lucascountyhealth.com/#/welcome

Mileti, D. S., & Peek, L. (2000). The social psychology of public response to warnings of a nuclear power plant accident. *Journal of Hazardous Materials, 75*(2), 181–194.

Mileti, D. S., & Sorensen, J. H. (1990). *Communication of emergency public warnings: A social science perspective and state-of-the-art assessment* (No. ORNL-6609). Oak Ridge National Lab., TN (USA).

Mileti, D. S., & Sorensen, J. H. (1990). *Communication and emergency public warning.* ORLN-6609. Washington, D.C.: Federal Emergency Management Administration.

Niquette, M. (2014). Not a Drop to Drink in Toledo as Algae Toxin Fouls Water. *Bloomberg News*. Retrieved from http://www.bloomberg.com/news/2014-08-03/not-a-drop-to-drink-in-toledo-as-algae-toxin-fouls-water.html

Oregon State University. (2013). Increasing toxicity of algal blooms tied to nutrient enrichment and climate change. Oregon State University. Retrieved from http://oregonstate.edu/ua/ncs/archives/2013/oct/increasing-toxicity-algal-blooms-tied-nutrient-enrichment-and-climate-change

Sellnow, T. L., & Seeger, M. W. (2013). *Theorizing crisis communication* (Vol. 4). John Wiley & Sons.

Sorensen, J. H. (2000). Hazard warning systems: Review of 20 years of progress. *Natural Hazards Review, 1*, 119–125.

Water-Related Emergencies & Outbreaks (2014). Centers for Disease Control and Prevention. Retrieved from http://www.cdc.gov/healthywater/emergency/index.html

WTOL Staff. 2014. Toledo Water Crisis: A timeline of What's happened so far. *19 Action News*. Retrieved from http://www.19actionnews.com/story/26185546/toledo-water-crisis-a-timeline-of-whats-happened-so-far

United States Environmental Protection Agency. (2014). National Drinking Water Advisory Council. *National Drinking Water Advisory Council*. Retrieved from http://water.epa.gov/drink/ndwac/

Chapter 18

Hawksbill Turtle Conservation in the Eastern Pacific: Weighing Biodiversity and Livelihood Risks

TARLA RAI PETERSON, PH.D.
Texas A&M University

MICHAEL LILES, PH.D.
Texas A&M University

Communicating Risks

In this chapter we explore the rhetorical strategies that community members use to (a) define risk, (b) prioritize various aspects of risk, and then (c) motivate responses to risk that seem appropriate. This case illustrates the usefulness of Tansey and Rayner's (2010) cultural approach to risk, which "assumes an active, rather than passive, perceiver . . . driven by organizational imperatives. [The focus on shared meaning emphasizes the centrality of] dynamic relationships among human beings" (p. 60). This statement should not be taken to mean that individuals do not have agency. Rather, we take it to mean that individual agency always exists, but never in a state of absolute freedom. Individual subjects can and do make a difference, but they operate within a cultural context, one that includes history and institutions, rather than in isolation.

Our approach to risk communication focuses on how people imagine and respond to risk and the strategies they use to support one response rather than another. It builds from Fischhoff's (1995) exhaustive review and then focuses on how strategies for defining and coping with risk emerge within pre-existing cultural contexts. The work of Mary Douglas (1992) and others encourages recognition that all people have beliefs and values, which means that their interpretation of any event includes perspectives that emerge from those beliefs and values. This does not mean that facts are irrelevant. It simply means that any claim is both factual and value-laden. Douglas (1992) argued further that culture directly influences what people define as a risk and any supposedly objective account of risk obscures much of the ideological dimensions of the account. This suggests that any definition of risk is culturally mediated and is influenced by both psychological and sociological processes. This way of framing risk draws attention to rhetoric as a communication phenomenon of central concern. The people who are involved use various rhetorical strategies to craft both their definitions of the risks and their descriptions of appropriate ways to mitigate the risks. The existence of values and beliefs is part of the reason for introducing rhetorical strategy, but does not remain the focus. Rather, the focus of a rhetorical exploration is on how those beliefs and values motivate action. Thus, the dialogue that emerges between various parties involved in a risky situation is fundamentally important. From this perspective, risk communication refers to a process of argumentation among interested parties, for the purpose of choosing how to act. These decisions should be made as transparently as possible, to enable participants to accept the responsibility for the eventualities that emerge from those decisions, while at the same time recognizing that it is not possible to predict all eventualities.

This approach to risk communication recognizes that social struggles over power relations make a difference in both the perception of risks and the social actions that are encouraged and discouraged by that perception. Social institutions can both amplify and attenuate risk perceptions. The arguments that matter are rarely over whether risks exist, but over "the magnitude of the risks and over who is responsible for them" (Tansey & Rayner, 2010, p. 58). This idea grows out of the expectation that contention or argumentation is fundamental to human society and people are conscious agents who recognize demands made on them by other members of their society (Douglas 1966, 1982, 1994; Peterson, Peterson, & Peterson, 2005).

Although most risk communication research is grounded in some variant of positivist social science, a small number of researchers have explored risk communication from a cultural, critical, or rhetorical perspective (i.e., Farrell & Goodnight, 1998; Grabill & Simmons, 1998; Hamilton, 2003; Katz & Miller, 1996; Peterson, 2003; Sauer, 2002). Although this research is diverse, it is unified by a humanistic curiosity about the epistemology of risk and an insistence that risk assessment and risk communication are intertwined aspects of the same endeavor. They explore questions such as how individual beliefs about appropriate power relationships in society may contribute to some social control preferences over others (Peterson, 2003); how risk communicators might employ a rhetorical framework to discover what arguments might be most effective when explaining risks (Sauer, 2002); and how collective memory of specific controversies may set the stage for risk perception, thus animating future argumentation pertaining to that risk. Although scientists, and others with related formal expertise, may develop technically appropriate responses to risks, these responses remain unpalatable unless they integrate experiences and perceptions drawn from cultural knowledge. Concepts and strategies drawn from a critical or rhetorical perspective may enable the appreciation for both formal and informal expertise that is required to achieve a robust policy response to risk.

Rhetorical strategies for responding to risk are not limited to formal public situations, but emerge from both interpersonal exchanges and in electronically mediated accounts. Research has demonstrated that interpersonal communication directly contributes to the amount of information people have regarding potential risks (Coleman, 1993; Robinson & Levy, 1986; Dunwoody & Neuwirth, 1991; Peterson & Thompson, 2010). The influence of that information, however, depends on how trustworthy the receiver perceives the source to be. Generally speaking, information from credible, interpersonal sources is more likely than information from electronic media to influence behavioral change regarding risks. This research should not, however, be interpreted as demonstrating that either face-to-face communication or mediated communication is more central to risk communication. What it suggests is that both are important and that it is difficult to de-tangle their influence (Singer & Endreny, 1993). For example, Robinson and Levy (1986) argued that not only does news reporting communicate risk information to media audiences, but it also communicates indirectly to acquaintances that may participate in discussions of whatever was seen, heard, or read. Despite the evidence that interpersonal communication is more likely to motivate people to change behaviors, many of the participants in those interpersonal conversations likely obtained their information from the media (Peterson & Thompson, 2010).

Numerous studies have demonstrated strong correlations among media coverage, public awareness, and political agendas regarding risks (O'Hair & Heath, 2010). This should not be taken as a simple claim that media set the political agenda, however, for considerable debate remains regarding the circumstances that enable media to drive the political agenda (Feldpausch-Parket et al., 2013). Many communication researchers (see O'Hair & Heath, 2010) have found that rather than setting the political agenda, the media stabilize the status quo, and argue that media establish the context within which future information is judged. Pidgeon, Kasperson, and Slovic (2003) suggested that with the huge expansion of non-traditional media, electronic communication and cultural fragmentation were changing the way risks would be communicated.

Culturally Focused Study of Risk Communication

Pidgeon and Fischhoff (2011) note that contemporary risks are highly politicized, which heightens the challenge of communicating them appropriately. The *Handbook of Risk and Crisis Communication* (O'Hair & Heath 2010) explores the scope and purpose of risk and its counterpart, crisis, to facilitate the understanding of these issues from conceptual and strategic perspectives. Recognizing that risk is a central feature of everyone's life, they explore how various people have attempted to manage the risks they face.

Values shape how people perceive different situations, risks, and benefits because values provide a lens through which they see the world (Douglas 1966, 1982; Douglas & Wildavsky, 1982). It has become increasingly clear that divergence in risk perceptions cannot be overcome solely by providing more information. One alternative is to focus on how communication operates, rather than on what information is communicated. Examples include experiential learning environments, such as interactive simulations (Thompson et al., 2010). Risk communicators also can be more effective if they understand, and work within, the mental models of the audiences that they seek to reach (Morgan et al., 2002).

Psychological Influences

As noted above, both psychological and sociological influences are important to a cultural approach to risk. Psychological research suggests that when people have to deal with risk, they tend to focus on day-to-day hazards they believe they can control (Morgan et al., 2002; Fischer et al., 1991). This suggests that the belief that it is possible to control what happens in a situation exerts an important influence on individual decisions about risk. These studies suggest that when an individual does not have direct, voluntary control over a risk, that risk becomes less tolerable. Being intolerable, however, does not necessarily translate into attention or action. Individuals often focus on hazards they believe they can protect themselves from, rather than attending to more frightening risks over which they believe they have no control.

Slovic, Fischhoff, and Lichtenstein (1985) argued that the two most important elements to shape risk perceptions are "dread" risk and "unknown" risk. These two categories are not mutually exclusive, but may emphasize different elements of risk. "Dread" risk, for example, refers to dimensions such as catastrophic disaster, where "unknown" risk refers to lack of direct knowledge, observation, or other experience regarding a risk. Slovic (1987) also produced cognitive maps of risk attitudes and perceptions, finding that technical experts and laypersons often disagree about the significance of risk. Fischer, Morgan, Fischhoff, Nair, and Lave (1991) found that people were most concerned about threats to life and limb, accidents, disease, and crime, and some mentioned economic risks.

Social Influences

Although important, psychological explanations of risk perception provide only part of the picture. Human beings are social animals and attitudes, understandings, and behaviors are influenced by society. Current research in the area of social influences on risk perception is rooted in cultural and anthropological studies. Cultural anthropologists, social anthropologists, and political scientists have tended to define the evaluation of risk and the willingness to accept risk as social problems. Rosa, Mazur, and Dietz (1987) found that people perceived risks through perceptual lenses shaped by social and cultural meanings that have been transmitted via primary influences such as family, friends, and fellow workers. They also found that public figures and the media served as secondary influences on risk perceptions. As Luhmann (1993) argued, people conform to social norms, usually behaving as they believe their primary reference groups expect them to behave. This does not mean that individuals do not matter, but that they operate within a complicated cultural context.

Douglas and Wildavsky (1982) specifically examined how culture impacts perceptions of environmental risk. Their research emerged from Douglas' (1966, 1982, 1994, 1999) anthropological synthesis of Western philosophy and social scientific theory that provides an explanatory framework for how people organize their world, including what they believe to be dangerous. Horlick-Jones, Sime, and Pidgeon (2003) pointed out that environmental risk communication has evolved to incorporate a social dynamic that intertwines risk perception with policy development. Their research expanded on the social amplification of risk framework (SARF) (e.g. Kasperso et al., 1988; Kasperson, 1992; Pidgeon, 1999; Pidgeon, Kasperson, & Slovic, 2003; Renn, 1992). Basically SARF launched from the assumption that risk events will remain largely irrelevant or localized in their impact unless people observe and communicate them to others (Pidgeon et al., 2003). Ultimately, scholars advocating the SARF approach argued that the experience of risk is not so much an experience of physical harm as it is an outgrowth of systemic social processes that guide how people learn to frame interpretations of risk. These interpretations provide rules used to select, organize, and explain signals emanating from the material world (Pidgeon et al., 2003). The centrality of communication to SARF indicates how important it is to understand communicative acts when taking a cultural approach to risk.

Conserving Hawksbill Sea Turtles in the Eastern Pacific

To highlight the cultural element of risk interpretation by diverse individuals and human populations at multiple scales, we examine the case of the endangered hawksbill sea turtle and its conservation in low-income regions of the Eastern Pacific Ocean. Hawksbill turtles were once common from Mexico to Ecuador (Cliffton et al., 1982), but now are among the world's most critically endangered sea turtle populations (Wallace et al., 2011), with only 200–300 females nesting annually (Gaos et al., 2010). Not surprisingly, the conservation community, including the Marine Turtle Specialist Group of the International Union for Conservation of Nature (IUCN), seeks to establish conservation measures to preserve the species. At the same time, sea turtles are a subsistence resource that is part of the cultural heritage in low-income regions (Thorbjarnarson et al., 2000; Nietschmann, 1973; Morgan, 2007). This divergence indicates that for some participants, the most serious risk is the extinction of hawksbills, while for other participants, the most serious risk is the erasure of the human communities in the region. How culturally diverse participants view the risks associated with hawksbills and human well-being dictates their priorities for action, with the priorities of the international conservation community centering on the needs of hawksbills and the priorities of coastal residents focusing on the needs of human communities.

Because roughly 45% of all known nesting for the species now occurs along the 300 km coast of El Salvador, conservation efforts targeting hawksbills along the Salvadoran coast are a top priority (Liles et al., 2011). Turtle egg consumption, incidental capture in fisheries, and coastal development threaten hawksbill survival in the region, however (Gaos et al., 2010). With reduction of hawksbill turtle populations by more than 80% worldwide, the IUCN has classified them as critically endangered (Mortimer & Donnelly, 2008). Despite evidence that the listing was based on rigorous scientific investigation, the decision sparked harsh criticism that highlights the cultural controversy of the issue (Campbell, 2012).

Direct use of natural resources remains a central livelihood strategy for many residents in low-income regions, such as the Salvadoran beaches and estuaries where hawksbills nest (Liles et al., 2014). Because satisfying immediate needs takes precedence over concern for dwindling natural resources, unregulated extraction has led to the collapse of many ecosystems nationwide (JICA and MAG, 2002; Catterson et al., 2004; FAO, 2009), including sea turtles. International concerns regarding the potential extinction of previously healthy sea turtle populations led to pressures for the Salvadoran government to establish a legal framework to provide sea turtle protection through national legislation and the ratification of international agreements (República de El Salvador, 1994b, 1997, 1998).

Despite these steps, however, high human density and acute poverty have made the protection of sea turtle nests at their original site of deposition unfeasible. *Tortugueros* (sea turtle egg collectors from impoverished communities) collect and sell nearly 100% of eggs deposited by hawksbills. Local informants unequivocally stated that hawksbill eggs not purchased for protection by hatcheries would continue to be sold on the black market (Liles, 2014). Within this context, hatcheries are the primary method of nest protection. By purchasing eggs from *tortugueros*, hatcheries provide an alternate economic incentive to sell for human consumption and, thus, have gained acceptance among coastal communities. For *tortugueros*, the primary value of hawksbills is the economic value of egg sales. At the same time, *tortugueros* express deep connections to turtles that are rooted in cultural tradition. From their perspective, egg purchases by hatcheries provide a conservation strategy that mitigates risks to both hawksbill survival and their livelihoods (Liles et al., 2014).

The ubiquitous use of hatcheries for sea turtle eggs, worldwide, underscores their importance as a tool for sea turtle conservation (e.g. Mortimer et al., 1993; Marcovaldi & Marcovaldi, 1999; Formia et al., 2003; García et al., 2003; Chacón-Chaverri & Eckert, 2007; Patino-Martinez et al., 2012a). This approach to nest protection, however, is discouraged by the Marine Turtle Specialist Group. Instead, it pressures for the protection of hawksbill eggs at the original site of deposition and disapproves of the use of international conservation funds to pay for hatchery operations, including purchase of hawksbill eggs. Conservationists often criticize hatcheries for operating under poor management practices that produce inadequate biological processes and outcomes (Pritchard 1980), such as low hatching success (Boulon et al., 1996), biased sex ratios of hatchlings (Morreale et al., 1982), and increased hatchling mortality (Pilcher & Enderby, 2001). Indeed, the Marine Turtle Specialist Group has made its position regarding hatchery use unequivocal: "relocation of eggs to a protected hatchery site should be undertaken only as a last resort and only in cases where *in situ* [original site of deposition] protection is impossible" (Mortimer, 1999, p. 175). Additionally, it disapproves of the use of international conservation funds to pay for hatchery operations, including purchase of hawksbill eggs. Utilizing proper methodologies throughout the hatchery implementation process, however, many of the undesired biological outcomes can be avoided or successfully mitigated (e.g., Marcovaldi & Marcovaldi, 1999; Kornaraki et al., 2006; Patino-Martinez et al., 2012b).

The divergence of the priorities of experts within the international conservation community from those of coastal residents in low-income regions can have serious implications for both hawksbill conservation and local community survival. The approval or disapproval of a given practice by the international conservation community can essentially grant or deny its legitimacy in the eyes of international policymakers and funding organizations (Rodriguez et al., 2007).

For local communities, the value of hatcheries extends beyond their biological output of turtles. The widespread implementation of hatcheries in low-income regions speaks to their persuasive ability to garner local support for sea turtle conservation. Hatchery operations can be linked to human well-being via egg purchases from *tortugueros*, where coastal residents are rewarded for active participation in nest protection and, thus, become joint owners of conservation successes. Direct payments for conservation outcomes have been shown to be an effective motivator for initiatives to protect sea turtle nests (Ferraro & Gjertsen, 2009). For example, if the desired outcome is to protect a hawksbill nest, the hawksbill nest is purchased directly from the *tortuguero* who found the nest: for protection. Direct payments for conservation often are more cost-effective than regulatory-based initiatives in dispersed nesting environments (Gjertsen & Stevenson, 2011), such as hawksbill nesting beaches, and offer a socially just strategy for nest protection that recognizes human need. Moreover, direct payment schemes are considered ethical by members of communities where human population density and poverty are high.

Although *tortugueros* prefer direct payment for turtle eggs, we are not suggesting that market forces somehow will guarantee the well-being of both hawksbill turtles and the *tortugueros* in El Salvador. The *tortugueros* sell sea turtles eggs at market value, just as commercial fishers sell fish at market value. The fact that some eggs are purchased by conservation organizations, as opposed to those wanting turtle eggs for consumption, does not guarantee that the *tortugueros* are any more likely to employ sound conservation practices than commercial fishers whose livelihood also relies on the natural resource. What it does accomplish, however, is to alter the *tortugueros'* position in the hawksbill conservation milieu. By selling turtle eggs to hatcheries for conservation, these local residents become part of the conservation effort, which allows local communities to move beyond the crisis mode.

Some experts within the international conservation community recommend nest protection tactics that appear to ignore the need for coexistence between humans and sea turtles. One recommendation, for example, directs conservationists to conduct beach patrols to deter poachers and disguise nests by erasing tracks and smoothing out the area to match its surroundings (Boulon, 1999). To emphasize this point, an influential Marine Turtle Specialist Group member stated: "To address poaching—I argue that to move the eggs to a new nest cavity 20 feet from its current location works just fine to shut down poachers, they'll never know where to look." This recommendation attempts to exclude *tortugueros*, who are likely the most knowledgeable members of local communities regarding sea turtles, from turtle conservation, and they rely on the unsubstantiated belief that the *tortugueros* will easily be fooled. Conceiving of *tortugueros* as almost inanimate objects to be "shut down," like an unwanted machine, negates the cultural ties they have to sea turtles and invalidates the context within which they live. Such recommended approaches foster a false conservationist versus *tortuguero* dualism that promotes direct competition for resources between the two groups. Situating *tortugueros* as enemies to sea turtles is both a simplistic and an inaccurate construction of local reality that fails to acknowledge the underlying cultural context for egg collection.

Advocating that conservationists compete with impoverished *tortugueros* for resources that support local livelihoods is not only ethically questionable, but also can elevate tensions and provoke continued crisis between international conservation organizations and local *tortugueros*. Alternatively, a cultural approach to risk communication may promote integration of coastal communities into conservation initiatives, thus contributing to more effective sea turtle conservation (Nichols et al., 2000b). Experts within the international conservation community, however, often limit the role of coastal communities to superficial levels, citing limited decision-making capabilities among local residents as justification (Campbell, 2000, 2012). Liles et al. (2014) suggest the benefits of a fundamentally different approach, where local culture becomes central to hawksbill research and conservation, and direct participation of *tortugueros* in the development and implementation of project activities is encouraged.

Marginalized members of low-income regions collect millions of sea turtle eggs each year throughout the world: a number that can only be expected to rise as human numbers continue to increase in these regions. A myopic focus on the biological risks that dismisses the social and political risks fails to address the livelihood needs of local residents. The international conservation community has the power and prestige to shape international policy and to determine funding priorities for sea turtle conservation activities. The actions they choose to support can have seriously negative consequences for local conservation efforts, particularly in low-income regions that require context-specific approaches to conservation that are informed by local realities. The divergence of international policy and funding priorities from local realities can dissuade local participation in conservation activities and construct a false dualism that fosters a perception of local egg collectors as the enemy of conservation and escalate latent conflict via direct competition for livelihood resources. In contrast, by connecting international policy and funding priorities to local realities, such as providing support for hatcheries for hawksbill conservation in El Salvador, all participants are enabled to build on existing synergies to garner local support for conservation that promotes joint ownership in decision-making and active participation in all aspects of research and conservation, ultimately leading to success in achieving and sustaining socially just conservation outcomes.

DISCUSSION QUESTIONS

1. What are some cultural constraints that may restrict individual choices in efforts to cope with livelihood risks in low-income regions and specifically relating to hawksbill conservation in the eastern Pacific Ocean?

2. How might biodiversity risks perceived by sea turtle biologists differ from livelihood risks perceived by *tortugueros* who rely on hawksbill egg sales?

3. Can you identify and describe rhetorical strategies *tortugueros* use to frame their definitions of risks and ways to mitigate those risks?

4. How do primary reference groups (e.g., family, friends, and fellow resource users) influence *tortugueros*' perceptions of risks and crisis associated with their livelihoods?

5. What risk management strategies could effectively deconstruct the biodiversity versus livelihood dualism that the international conservation community has fostered? How might the concept of 'crisis' contribute to these strategies?

REFERENCES

Boulon Jr., R.H. (1999). Reducing threats to eggs and hatchlings: *In situ* protection. In: K.L. Eckert, K.A. Bjorndal, and F.A. Abreu-Grobois, eds. *Research and management techniques for the conservation of sea turtles*. Publication no. 4. Washington, DC: IUCN/SSC Marine Turtle Specialist Group, 169–174.

Boulon Jr., R.H., Dutton, P.H., & McDonald, D.L. (1996). Leatherback turtles (*Dermochelys coriacea*) on St. Croix, U.S. Virgin Islands: Fifteen years of conservation. *Chelonian Conservation and Biology 2*, 141–147.

Campbell, L.M. (2000). Human need in rural developing areas: perceptions of wildlife conservation experts. *The Canadian Geographer*, 44 (2), 167–181.

Campbell, L. M. (2012). Seeing red: Inside the science and politics of the IUCN Red List. *Conservation & Society*, 10 (4), 367–380.

Catterson, T.M., Hasbún, C.R., & Dreikorn, C. (2004). *El Salvador: biodiversity, tropical forestry and water resources assessment*. Technical report. USAID, San Salvador.

Chacón-Chaverri, D., & Eckert, K.L. (2007). Leatherback sea turtle nesting at Gandoca Beach in Caribbean Costa Rica: Management recommendations from fifteen years of conservation. *Chelonian Conservation and Biology*, 6(1), 101–110.

Cliffton, K., Cornejo, D.O., & Felger, R.S. (1982). Sea turtles of the Pacific coast of Mexico. In: K.A. Bjorndal, ed. *Biology and conservation of sea turtles*. Washington, DC: Smithsonian Institution Press, 199–209.

Coleman, C.L. (1993). The influence of mass media and interpersonal communication on societal and personal risk judgments. *Communication Research 20*, 611–628.

Douglas, M. (1966). *Purity and danger: An analysis of the concepts of pollution and taboo*. London: Routledge & Kegan Paul.

Douglas, M. (1982). *Essays in the sociology of perception*. London: Routledge and Kegan Paul.

Douglas, M. (1994). *Risk and blame: Essays in cultural theory*. London: Routledge.

Douglas, M. (1999). Environments at risk. In M. Douglas (Ed.), *Implicit meanings: Selected essays in anthropology* (2nd ed, pp. 204-217). London: Routledge.

Douglas, M., & Wildavsky., A. (1982). *Risk and culture: An essay on the selection of technological and environmental dangers*. Berkeley: University of California Press.

Dunwoody, S., & Neuwirth, K. (1991). Coming to terms with the impact of communication on scientific and technological risk judgments. In L. Wilkins & P. Patterson (Eds.), *Risky business: Communicating issues of science, risk and public policy* (pp. 11–30) Westport, CT: Greenwood Press.

FAO (Food and Agriculture Organization), 2009. *El Salvador: estado del recurso "camarón"*. Reporte técnico. FAO, San Salvador.

Farrell, T. B., & Goodnight, G. T. (1998). Accidental rhetoric: The root metaphors of Three Mile Island. In C. Waddell (Ed.), *Landmark essays on rhetoric and the environment* (pp. 75–105). Mahwah, NJ: Erlbaum.

Feldpausch-Parker, A. M., Ragland, C., Chuadhry, R., Melnick, L. L., Hall, D. M., Stephens, J. C., Wilson, E. J., & Peterson, T. R. (2013). Spreading the news on carbon capture and storage: A state-level comparison of US media. *Environmental Communication: A Journal of Nature and Culture*, 7, 336–354.

Ferraro, P.J., & Gjertsen, H., 2009. A global review of incentive payments for sea turtle conservation. *Chelonian Conservation and Biology*, 8(1), 48–56.

Fischer, G. W., Morgan, M. G., Fischhoff, B., Nair, I., & Lave, L. B. (1991). What risks are people concerned about? *Risk Analysis, 11*, 303–314.

Fischhoff, B. (1995). Risk perception and communication unplugged: Twenty years of process. *Risk Analysis 15*, 137–145.

Formia, A., *et al.* (2003). Sea turtle conservation along the Atlantic coast of Africa. *Marine Turtle Newsletter, 100* (1), 33–37.

Gaos, A.R., *et al.* (2010). Signs of hope in the eastern Pacific: International collaboration reveals encouraging status for a severely depleted population of hawksbill turtles *Eretmochelys imbricata*. *Oryx 44* (4), 595–601.

García, A., Caballos, G., & Adaya, R. (2003). Intensive beach management as an improved turtle conservation strategy in Mexico. *Biological Conservation, 111* (2), 253–261.

Gjertsen, H., & Stevenson, T.H. (2011). Direct incentive approaches for leatherback turtle conservation. In: P.H. Dutton, D. Squires, and M. Ahmed, eds. *Conservation of Pacific sea turtles*. Honolulu, HI: University of Hawaii Press, 164–182.

Grabill, J.T., & Simmons, W. M. (1998). Toward a critical rhetoric of risk communication: Producing citizens and the role of risk communicators. *Technical Communication Quarterly*, 7, 415–441.

Hamilton, J.D. (2003). Exploring technical and cultural appeals in strategic risk communication: The Fernald radium case. *Risk Analysis, 23*, 291–302.

Heath, R. L., & O'Hair, H. D. (Eds.) (2010). *Handbook of risk and crisis communication*. Mahway, NJ: Lawrence Erlbaum.

Horlick-Jones, T., Sime, J., & Pidgeon, N. (2003). The social dynamics of environmental risk perception: Implications for risk communication research and practice In N. Pidgeon, R.E. Kasperson, & P. Slovic (Eds.). *Social amplification of risk* (pp. 262–285). Cambridge, UK: Cambridge University Press.

JICA (Asociación de Cooperación Internacional de Japón) and MAG (Ministerio de Agricultura y Ganadería) (2002). *El estudio sobre el desarrollo de la pesca artesanal en El Salvador*. Reporte técnico. JICA-MAG, San Salvador.

Kasperson, R. E. (1992). The social amplification of risk: Progress in developing an integrative framework. In S. Krimsky & D. Golding (Eds.). *Social theories of risk* (pp. 153–178). London: Praeger.

Kasperson, R. E., Renn, O., Slovic, P., Brown, H.S., Emel, J., Goble, R., Kasperson, J.X., & Ratick, S. (1988). The social amplification of risk: A conceptual framework. *Risk Analysis 8*, 177–187.

Katz, S., & Miller, C. (1996). The low-level radioactive waste siting controversy in North Carolina: Toward a rhetorical model of risk communication. In C. Herndl & S. Brown (Eds.), *Green culture: Environmental rhetoric in contemporary America* (pp. 111–140). Madison: University of Wisconsin Press.

Kornaraki, E., *et al.* (2006). Effectiveness of different conservation measures for loggerhead sea turtle (*Caretta caretta*) nests at Zakynthos Island, Greece. *Biological Conservation, 130* (3), 324–330.

Liles, M.J., *et al.* (2011). Hawksbill turtles *Eretmochelys imbricata* in El Salvador: nesting distribution and mortality at the largest remaining nesting aggregation in the eastern Pacific Ocean. *Endangered Species Research, 14* (1), 23–30.

Liles, M., Peterson, M. J., Lincoln, Y. Seminoff, J. A., Gaos, A. R., & Peterson, T. R. (2014). Connecting international priorities with human wellbeing in low-income regions: Lessons from hawksbill turtle conservation in El Salvador. *Local Environment,* DOI:10.1080/13549839.2014.905516.

Luhmann, N. (1993). *Risk: A sociological theory* (R. Barrett, Trans). Hawthorne, NY: Aldine de Gruyter.

Marcovaldi, M.Â., & Marcovaldi, G.G. (1999). Marine turtles of Brazil: The history and structure of Projeto TAMAR-IBAMA. *Biological Conservation, 91* (1), 35–41.

Morgan, M. G., Fischhoff, B., Bostrom, A., & Altman, C.J. (2002). *Risk communication: A mental models* approach. New York: Cambridge University Press.

Morgan, R.C. (2007). Property of spirits: Hereditary and global value of sea turtles in Fiji. *Human Organization, 66* (1), 60–68.

Morreale, S.J., *et al.* (1982). Temperature-dependent sex determination: current practices threaten conservation of sea turtles. *Science, 216* (4551), 1245–1247.

Mortimer, J.A. (1999). Reducing threats to eggs and hatchlings: Hatcheries. In: K.L. Eckert, K.A. Bjorndal, & F.A. Abreu-Grobois, eds. *Research and management techniques for the conservation of sea turtles.* Publication no. 4. Washington, DC: IUCN/SSC Marine Turtle Specialist Group, 175–178.

Mortimer, J.A., Ahmad, Z., & Kaslan, S. (1993). The status of the hawksbill *Eretmochelys imbricata* and green turtle *Chelonia mydas* of Melaka and Negeri Sembilan. *Malayan Nature Journal, 46* (1), 243–253.

Mortimer, J.A., & Donnelly, M. (IUCN SSC Marine Turtle Specialist Group) (2008). *Eretmochelys imbricata.* In: *IUCN 2012. IUCN red list of threatened species.* Version 2012.2. <www.iucnredlist.org>. Downloaded on 17 February 2013.

Nichols, W.J., Bird, K.E., & Garcia, S. (2000b). Community-based research and its application to sea turtle conservation in Bahía Magdalena, BCS, Mexico. *Marine Turtle Newsletter, 89* (1), 4–7.

Nietschmann, B. (1973). *Between land and water: The subsistence ecology of the Miskito Indians, Eastern Nicaragua.* New York, Seminar Press.

Patino-Martinez, J., *et al.* (2012a). How do hatcheries influence embryonic development of sea turtle eggs? Experimental analysis and isolation of microorganisms in leatherback turtle eggs. *Journal of Experimental Zoology, 317A* (1), 47–54.

Patino-Martinez, J., *et al.* (2012b). A potential tool to mitigate the impacts of climate change to the Caribbean leatherback sea turtle. *Global Change Biology, 18* (2), 401–411.

Peterson, M.N., M.J. Peterson, M.J., & Peterson, T. R. (2005). Conservation and the myth of consensus. *Conservation Biology 19,* 762–767.

Peterson, T. R. (2003). Social control frames: Opportunities or constraints? *Environmental Practice 5,* 232–238.

Peterson, T. R., & Thompson, J. L. (2010). Environmental risk communication: Responding to challenges of complexity and uncertainty, In R. L. Heath & H. D. O'Hair (Eds.). *Handbook of risk and crisis communication* (pp. 591–606). Mahway, NJ: Lawrence Erlbaum.

Pidgeon, N.F. (1999). Social amplification of risk: models, mechanisms and tools for policy. *Risk, decision and policy 4,* 145–159.

Pidgeon, N., & Fischhoff, B. (2011). The role of social and decision sciences in communicating uncertain climate risks. *Nature Climate Change 1,* 35–41.

Pidgeon, N., Kasperson, R. E., & Slovic, P. (2003). *The social amplification of risk.* Cambridge, UK: Cambridge University Press.

Pilcher, N.J., & Enderby, S. (2001). Effects of prolonged retention in hatcheries on green turtle (*Chelonia mydas*) hatchling swimming speed and survival. *Journal of Herpetology, 35* (4), 633–638.

Pritchard, P.C. (1980). The conservation of sea turtles: Practices and problems. *American Zoologist, 20* (3), 609–617.

Renn, O. (1992). Risk communication: Toward a rational discourse with the public. *Journal of Hazardous Materials*, 29, 465–519.

República de El Salvador. (1994a). *Convenio sobre la diversidad biológica*. Diario Oficial No. 92. Tomo No. 323, 19 Mayo.

República de El Salvador. (1994b). *Ley de conservación de vida silvestre*. Diario Oficial No. 133. Tomo No. 352, 16 Julio.

República de El Salvador. (1997). *Código penal*. Diario Oficial No. 105. Tomo No. 335, 10 Junio.

Robinson, J.P., & Levy, M.R. (1986). Interpersonal communication and news comprehension. *The Public Opinion Quarterly, 50*, 160–175.

Rodríguez, J.P., et al. (2007). Globalization of conservation: A view from the South. *Science, 317* (5839), 755–756.

Rosa, E., Mazur, A., & Dietz, T. (1987). Sociological analysis of risk impacts associated with a high level of nuclear waste repository: The case of Hanford. *Proceedings of the workshop on Assessing Social and Economic Effects of Perceived Risk*. Seattle: Battelle Human Affairs Research Centers.

Sauer, B. J. (2002). *The rhetoric of risk: Technical documentation in hazardous environments*. Mahwah, NJ: Erlbaum.

Singer, E.T., & Endreny, P.M. (1993). Reporting hazards: Their benefits and costs. *Journal of Communication, 37*, 10–26.

Slovic, P. (1987). Perceptions of risk. *Science, 236*, 280–285.

Slovic, P., Fischhoff, B., & Lichtenstein, S. (1985). Facts and fears: Understanding perceived risk. In R. C. Schwing & W.A. Albers (Eds.), *Societal risk assessment: How safe is safe enough* (pp. 181–214). New York: Plenum Press.

Tansey, J., & Rayner, S. (2010). Cultural theory and risk. In R. L. Heath & H. D. O'Hair (Eds.). *Handbook of risk and crisis communication* (pp. 53–79). Mahway, NJ: Lawrence Erlbaum.

Thompson, J. L., Forster, C. B., Werner, C., & Peterson, T. R. (2010). Mediated modeling: Using collaborative processes to integrate scientist and stakeholder knowledge about greenhouse gas emissions in an urban ecosystem. *Society and Natural Resources 23*, 742–757.

Thorbjarnarson, J., et al. (2000). Human use of turtles: A worldwide perspective. In: M.W. Klemens, ed. *Turtle conservation*. Washington, DC: Smithsonian Institution Press, 33–84.

Wallace, B.P., et al. (2011). Global conservation priorities for marine turtles. *PLoS One 6* (9), e24510.

Chapter 19

Communicating a Surge of Information: How do Individuals Understand, React, and Respond to Storm Surge Media Messages?

Gina Eosco, Ph.D.
Eastern Research Group

Laura Rickard, Ph.D.
The University of Maine

Cliff Scherer, Ph.D.
Cornell University

Background and Case Study

For those living directly on the coast, storm surge is the most dangerous, and potentially deadly, hurricane-related risk. During Hurricane Sandy in 2013, 40 deaths were directly attributed to flooding that occurred due to a dramatic slow rise of ocean surge. Beyond Sandy, storm surge has easily been one of the most challenging risks to communicate over the last decade. Hurricanes Katrina (Knabb, Rhome, & Brown, 2005), Ike (Berg, 2009) and Isaac (Berg, 2013) all brought high surge levels that differed from their categorical wind strength. At landfall, Katrina was a category-3 storm, Ike a category-2 storm, and Isaac a category-1 storm. However, *all* boasted dramatic storm surges. In response to this disparity, after Hurricane Ike in 2008, the National Hurricane Center (NHC) started separating storm surge from hurricane wind category (NOAA, 2010) in its classification system because biophysical scientists realized that wind strength was not the sole cause of an intense storm surge. Rather, many contributing factors, such as wind, wave action, astronomical tide, and bathymetry of the coastline contribute to the height of the surge. NHC determined that hurricane category, which is used to describe wind strength, was confusing public audiences' understanding of storm surge, as the surge amount is not associated solely with category (NHC, 2012; NOAA, 2010). Based on this re-categorization, two challenges face those tasked with communicating hurricane-related risk.[1] First, communicators must ensure that public audiences consider

---

[1] Those who communicate about hurricane-related risk include (but are not limited to) National Hurricane Center forecasters, National Weather Service forecasters, broadcast meteorologists, and private sector meteorologists, who all work tirelessly to communicate risks to public audiences during a hurricane.

storm surge as a risk *distinct from*, and not explicitly communicated by, hurricane category. Second, communicators must determine *how* to convey storm surge risk so that the impacted populations will understand the nature of their personal risk.

Within the meteorological and forecasting realms, conveying storm surge risk remains an ongoing challenge. However, the NHC has made great strides in designing a new storm surge inundation map that was employed, on an experimental basis, during the 2014 hurricane season: specifically during Hurricane Arthur. This new map visually displays the predicted level of storm surge above ground at each specific location included in the hurricane track (see http://www.nhc.noaa.gov/experimental/inundation/#examples for examples of the map). Social scientists worked closely with NHC to conduct research, using both surveys and focus groups with specialized stakeholders, to determine how best to visualize storm surge. For instance, researchers documented participants' reactions to three variations of a storm surge map. From an applied perspective, the research focused primarily on gauging how National Weather Service (NWS) forecasters, emergency managers, and broadcast meteorologists would interpret and use the newly designed storm surge inundation map in their daily work (ERG, 2013). In short, although the storm surge graphic was studied by social scientists, the emphasis of this research was on the development of the graphic design alone, not on testing its effects in-situ (in the context of the mass communication environment in which the graphic will be viewed by public audiences).

Surveys of public audiences' information-seeking during weather events provide a clearer picture of the complex media environment in which a weather graphic, such as the storm surge inundation map, circulates. Although Internet use during hurricane events is high, television weather reporting—particularly on local channels—remains the primary source of storm-related information during a severe weather event (Lazo & Morrow, 2013). Further, although NHC's website includes storm-specific information, the majority of respondents in a recent study (61%) reported never using the website to obtain information about storm events (Lazo & Morrow, 2013). In the span of a limited television forecast, broadcast meteorologists present many visuals to convey the numerous and varied risks associated with hurricane events (the storm surge inundation graphic may represent only 30 seconds out of a three-minute forecast).[2] As such, individuals are exposed to an array of weather information in a short time. Specifically, during Hurricane Sandy, news stations from New Jersey to Connecticut covered the multitude of potential impacts, including high precipitation amounts, snowfall in high altitude areas, wind impacts, and storm surge. In addition to covering multiple risk issues and displaying various images, television weather broadcasts also feature accompanying verbal messaging, which may strengthen (or, in other cases, contradict) the visual images displayed.

Given the (potentially) competing visual and auditory information provided in one forecast, how do individuals perceive the risk that is most relevant to them for making behavioral decisions, such as to evacuate an area? Moreover, given the brevity of most forecasts, will audiences have sufficient time to process the information to assess their storm surge risk and make related behavioral decisions? If these new graphics are to impact hurricane-related behaviors, it is important to understand how public audiences understand, react to, and use this new information during their decision-making processes.

Theory and Its Applications

Risk communication is multi-dimensional, both in terms of the many disciplines that contribute to its theoretical foundations, as well as the components that can be considered in any given application. Given the complexity of hurricane storm surge media messages, there are many variables that researchers could

---

[2] Broadcast times may change during live, wall-to-wall coverage.

study. Of particular interest, for example, is the role that visual information plays in conveying risk. Outside of one's exposure to weather graphics, other considerations may also influence perceptions of storm surge risk and subsequent decision-making, such as trust in authorities, past experience in hurricanes, and knowledge of the effects of storm surge. In this section, an overview of relevant communication theory will be provided, which may be applied to understanding individuals' perceptions of storm surge risk and related decision-making.

An iconic visual representation, like the storm surge flooding map, "characterize[s] some form of similarity or analogy between the sign and its object" (Messaris, 1997, p. viii). The storm surge map is an interpretation, or sign, of the magnitude of surge. On the ground, of course, storm surge will not appear in rainbow-colored gradations. Rather, the color becomes a representation of, or an analogy for, the amount of water to expect in a particular location. In comparison, a photograph or video of storm surge can be considered indexical, meaning that the visual features are "caused by its object and [serve] as a physical trace pointing to its existence" (Messaris, 1997, p. viii). Photographs and live video act as "proof" that an object exists (Eosco, Steinhardt, Scherer & Chock, 2012; Messaris, 1994; Sontag, 1977): an important distinction from iconic visual representations.

The challenge for those tasked with communicating about hurricane risk is that providing indexical proof is not possible for events that have yet to occur, which encompasses much of the subject matter of risk communication, broadly, and meteorology, specifically (Ulmer, Seeger & Littlefield, 2009). Thus, iconic images, such as hurricane track maps, hurricane watch and warning maps, and the new storm surge flooding map, are the norm for presenting representations of hurricane risk. Importantly, the act of showing an iconic visual, such as the storm surge inundation map, implicitly conveys several forms of uncertainty (Eosco, 2015), including, in relation to the timing of the event, the level of risk to a particular location, or if the event will even occur. Eosco (2015) conducted a real-time response (RTR) study examining individuals' perceptions of uncertainty related to watching live coverage broadcasts of tornadoes. Results indicated that indexical images (in this case, photographs of tornadoes) inspired higher judgments of certainty about the impacts of the storm and perceived risk of tornado threat than iconic visuals, such as radar and velocity images. These iconic visuals, in comparison, prompted more information *uncertainty* and *lower* perceived risk.

Unlike broadcast coverage of tornados, hurricane coverage cannot include indexical, photographic "proof" until much later in the progression of the storm, at which point evacuation is often unsafe, if not impossible. Therefore, almost all of the visuals presented during hurricane coverage can be classified as non-indexical. Within the context of visual persuasion, Messaris (1997) emphasizes the effectiveness of iconicity in evoking an emotional response, such as the use of the color red to indicate warnings and conjure heightened awareness. Storm surge maps may also elicit emotion for some individuals, but, due to their iconic visual quality, cannot "prove" that storm surge exists or is likely to happen at a particular moment in time.[3] Using this (possibly contradictory) set of conditions as a starting point, the obvious question becomes *how do individuals react to, and understand, iconic storm surge representations?*

How these visual types relate to the accompanying verbal message is equally important. Redundancy, the semantic overlap between a visual and its verbal message (written or audio), influences whether a person will understand the overall message (Drew & Grimes, 1987). For example, if a newscaster provides a list of evacuation orders, but shows video of "business as usual" (e.g., people walking down a city street), then the image and message cannot be considered related, semantically. Providing an image of people

---

[3] Experts, such as hurricane forecasters, may disagree with this statement, as the storm surge inundation map is not implemented unless there is certain proof that the risk of surge exists. But from the perspective of visual communication theory, an iconic representation *cannot* prove that storm surge exists.

boarding up their homes or driving out of town, on the other hand, would be considered more semantically related to the novel "evacuation order" message. Semantic overlap, or redundancy, is critical to message comprehension, as individuals combine visual and verbal content when both the auditory and visual channels are semantically complementary (Grimes, 1990). Increased message comprehension, in turn, leads individuals to prioritize processing on the verbal channel of the message. Thus, while the design of the storm surge inundation map is important, so, too, is the verbal message that provides the "context, content, and format" (Lazo & Morrow, 2013, p. 32).

As past research suggests (Griffin, Neuwirth, & Dunwoody, 1999; Eagly & Chaiken, 1993), multiple factors influence individuals' perceptions of risk, including what information they seek and why (Griffin et al., 1999), how they process it (i.e., heuristically or systematically) (Eagley & Chaiken, 1993), and the affect and emotions generated (Slovic, 2004; Zajonc, 1980), which may include anxiety, dread, fear, or worry (Loewenstein, Weber, Hsee, & Welch, 2001; Sandman, 1989).

Several models may be applicable to measuring risk perception in the context of storm surge communication. One well-known model is the Risk Information Seeking and Processing Model (Griffin, Dunwoody, & Yang, 2012; Griffin, Dunwoody, & Neuwirth, 1999), which includes variables such as trust, affect, and channel beliefs (see below). A newer model is the *Protective Action Decision Model* (Lindell & Perry, 2012; Terpstra & Lindell, 2012), which considers individuals' social, economic, and time constraints on taking protective action. For example, although an individual may want to evacuate from an impending storm surge, the person may not have a location to evacuate to or may not be able to miss work and the related lost income. These time and cost constraints may impede an individual's desire and ability to evacuate from the risk. Whether broadcasters' and journalists' acknowledgement of these multifaceted concerns in their reporting influences audiences' decision to heed an evacuation warning remains an empirical question.

Prior research provides strong evidence that trust is a critical component to garnering cooperative action: the type necessary for large, coordinated hurricane evacuations (Cvetkovich & Lofsted, 1999; Dash & Gladwin, 2005; Renn & Levine, 1991; Slovic, 1993; Siegrist, Earle, & Gutscher, 2003). Compliance rates for evacuation have ranged from 32% to 98%, depending upon individual risk perceptions and issued warning levels (Sorensen & Mileti, 1988). During Hurricane Katrina, for example, evacuation rates for highly damaged areas were estimated at 94% (Groen, Polivka, Ja, & Ae, 2010), despite an estimated 100,000 people who stayed behind (Brinkley, 2006). As Dow and Cutter (2002) found with respect to Hurricane Floyd, many individuals waited to evacuate until an official order was issued (61% percent of their sample evacuated the day the evacuation order was given). Since individuals rarely leave prior to an evacuation order (Baker, 2000), emergency managers' evacuation decision-making, and subsequent communication to the public, are critical. Determining whom individuals trust to provide their risk[4] and evacuation information is a major communication challenge.

Along with trusted communication sources, individuals also maintain distinct beliefs about various communication channels. With the current media landscape and available technology, individuals not only have many possible information sources to choose from, but also have various communication channels through which they can access these sources. Although an individual may receive his or her hurricane information from a broadcast meteorologist's TV forecast, this information may be accessed via a TV spot, a Facebook newsfeed, or a news website. Little is known about how individuals' channel beliefs influence their hurricane-related information-seeking. Two factors that may influence channel beliefs include the amount of perceived media bias and the perceived utility of the channel (Griffin et al., 1999;

---

[4] Risk in this context refers broadly to hurricane impacts, including storm surge.

Griffin et al., 2008). On the one hand, perceived utility of the channel leads to more systematic processing, allowing an individual to process more of the information presented and in a deeper, more thoughtful manner. Perceived media bias, on the other hand, leads to more heuristic processing, prompting more limited processing of information and more superficial judgments (Eagly & Chaiken, 1993; Griffin et al., 2008). In the context of a hurricane event, more research is needed to determine how individuals may rely on the Internet (and, more specifically, social networking sites), radio, television, and print media (i.e., newspapers) for information and which information sources and channels they may prefer (and why).

In addition to trust in sources and channels of communication, past experience with hurricanes, as well as various social factors, may help explain why some individuals choose to evacuate, while others do not. Among U.S. Gulf Coast residents, having experienced evacuation or property damage in a past hurricane predicted stronger beliefs that one would experience future hurricane impacts (Trumbo, Lueck, Marlatt, & Peek, 2011; see also Dash & Morrow, 2001; Dow & Cutter, 1998). The severity, and impact, of a past experience can also determine the valence of risk perception: experiencing a "near-miss," for instance, might motivate a false sense of security and lowered risk perception for future events (Wachinger, Renn, Begg, & Kuhlicke, 2013). These, and similar, studies suggest that understanding the nature of one's prior risk experience (negative or neutral; severe or slight) is critical. Other considerations that may impact an individual's evacuation compliance include prior evacuations (Dow & Cutter, 1998; Dash and Morrow, 2001), trust in one's home structure (Morss & Hayden, 2010), dispositional optimism (Trumbo et al., 2011), and living in a predetermined evacuation zone (Dash & Gladwin, 2005).

Past research suggests that the ability to accurately identify one's risk area is correlated with evacuation behavior (Zhang, Prater, & Lindell, 2004). Focusing solely on individuals' storm-specific knowledge, however, ignores the manner in which risk perceptions (e.g., individuals perceiving their risk of harm from storm impacts as minimal to none), feelings, and non-storm-specific information may influence behavior of the intended audience (Rowan, 1996; Slovic, 1999; Griffin et al., 1999). Similarly, Tierney (1994) suggests that people often do not make "objective" risk assessments of hazard events, such as with respect to the elevation level of their home or its distance from the coast, but, rather, use social lenses, such as context and culture, to judge hazard-related risks. In the case of Hurricane Ike, Morss and Hayden (2010) found that not just knowledge, but rather "experience, evacuation orders, forecasts, environmental cues, household interactions, and resources and constraints," all contributed to evacuation decisions (p. 180). These, and other, studies suggest that formal knowledge, such as what emerges from watching and understanding forecasts, and also social knowledge, such as what comes from household interactions and resources, all contribute to perceptions of risk and likelihood of evacuating.

Also important to behavioral decision-making is how individuals attribute responsibility for causing or responding to an event. An individual's choice to avoid evacuation when high storm surge is predicted, for instance, may place first responders in great danger and, thus, understanding how individuals perceive this responsibility may be critical for creating appropriate risk messaging. Social psychologists and sociologists have long shown that the manner in which individuals determine responsibility for the cause or treatment of phenomena (whether a failed test or a storm surge) can, in turn, influence attitudes and eventual behaviors (Brickman et al., 1982; Heider, 1958; Iyengar, 1989; Weiner, 2006). Whereas an *internal* attribution denotes personal responsibility to respond to a particular problem, an *external* attribution holds an external source, such as an institution, accountable for solving the problem.

To date, limited research has focused on how attribution of responsibility—either for causing or for treating/responding to—for a catastrophic, natural-resource-related event may influence individuals' risk perceptions, as well as behavioral decision-making. Some studies have focused on demarcating individuals' perceptions of government (i.e. external), as opposed to individual (i.e. internal) responsibility for natural-hazard-related response and/or prevention, and how this may impact behavioral intentions or actual behavior (Arlikatti, Lindell, & Prater, 2007; Arceneaux & Stein, 2006; Ben-Porath & Shaker, 2010; Duval & Mullis, 1999; Kumagai, Daniels, Carroll, Bliss, & Edwards, 2004; Lalwani & Duval, 2000; Terpstra & Gutteling, 2008). A handful of studies link media coverage of "risky" natural hazard events to the general public's perceptions of the preventability of such events (McClure, Allen, & Walkey, 2001; McClure, Walkey, & Allen, 1999; McClure, Sutton, & Wilson, 2007). For instance, McClure et al. (1999) suggested that media coverage of earthquakes in New Zealand tended to overemphasize the sheer *magnitude* of the event (e.g., an entire neighborhood destroyed), rather than the *distinctiveness* of the damage (e.g., a particular house damaged), leading the public to perceive the damage as uncontrollable and, thus, to downplay its preventability.

Outside of the natural hazards context, past research (Weiner, 2006) has suggested a causal pathway by which an individual's attribution of responsibility about a societal problem influences beliefs about who is responsible for solving the problem that, in turn, shapes the individual's emotional response, behavioral response, and support for relevant public policy. The findings of the studies reviewed above, however, indicate that a similar pathway may function in the context of natural hazards and, perhaps, hurricanes and storm surge. That is, attribution of responsibility may play a mediating role between the past experience of the individual and his or her perception of risk related to the weather event. These risk perceptions (and/or related feelings of fatalism or control), in turn, may influence behavioral decisions, such as whether to take preventive action or whether to follow prescribed orders from broadcasters or emergency managers.

CONCLUSION

Just as storm surge includes many physical parameters, risk communicators have many design parameters to consider in crafting risk messages for public audiences. From the type of message, verbal or visual, to factors including trust, affect, past experience, knowledge, and attribution of responsibility, risk communicators must balance various considerations that may influence perceptions and eventual behaviors. Storm surge communication requires synthesizing what scientists know about the science of hurricanes with what social scientists know about the science of risk perception and behavior.

DISCUSSION QUESTIONS

1. What challenges may be associated with informing public audiences about the risk of storm surge?
2. What is the difference between an "iconic" and an "indexical" visual representation? What should communicators consider when pairing visual and verbal (or textual) information about storm surge risk in a given message? Should these messages look different depending on the visual representation?
3. How people perceive (and, in some cases, act on) the risk of storm surge often depends on more than just the content of the communication they receive. What are some other potential factors that might help explain storm surge risk perceptions and behaviors?
4. Imagine that the National Weather Service has asked you to help them evaluate their new potential storm surge flooding map graphics. (Visit http://www.nhc.noaa.gov/surge/inundation/ to view examples of the graphic.) How might you measure the effectiveness of this graphic? In your answer, be sure to consider:
   a. What is the desired outcome of the graphic? (In other words, what does the National Weather Service intend that at-risk individuals will see, do, know, etc. after they view the graphic?)

b. What research method(s) might you use, and why? What population(s) might you sample from, and why?

c. How might you design your study to test the effect of visual and/or the textual information?

REFERENCES

Arlikatti, S., Lindell, M. K., & Prater, C. S. (2007). Perceived stakeholder role relationships and adoption of seismic hazard adjustments. *International Journal of Mass Emergencies and Disasters, 25*(3), 218–256.

Arceneaux, K., & Stein, R. M. (2006). Who is held responsible when disaster strikes? The attribution of responsibility for a natural disaster in an urban election. *Journal of Urban Affairs, 28*(1), 43–53.

Baker, E. J. (2000). Hurricane evacuation in the United States. *Storms, 1,* 306–319.

Ben-Porath, E. N., & Shaker, L. K. (2010). News images, race, and attribution in the wake of Hurricane Katrina. *Journal of Communication, 60,* 466–490.

Berg, R. (2009). Tropical cyclone report Hurricane Ike. Retrieved from: http://www.nhc.noaa.gov/pdf/TCR-AL092008_Ike_3May10.pdf

Berg, R. (2013). Tropical cyclone report Hurricane Isaac. Retrieved from: http://www.nhc.noaa.gov/data/tcr/AL092012_Isaac.pdf

Brickman, P., Rabinowitz, V. C., Karuza, J., Coates, D., Cohn, E., & Kidder, L. (1982). Models of helping and coping. *American Psychologist, 37*(4), 368–384.

Brinkley, D. (2006). *The great deluge: Hurricane Katrina, New Orleans, and the Mississippi Gulf Coast.* New York: William Morrow.

Cvetkovich, G., & Löfstedt, R. (Eds.). (1999). *Social trust and the management of risk.* London: Earthscan.

Dash, N., & Gladwin, H. (2005). *Evacuation decision making and behavioral responses: Individual and household.* Prepared for the Hurricane Forecast Socioeconomic Workshop, February 16–18, 2005, Pomona, CA.

Dash, N., & Morrow, B. (2001). Return delays and evacuation order compliance: The case of Hurricane Georges and the Florida Keys. *Environmental Hazards, 2,* 119–128.

Dow, K., & Cutter, S. (1998). Crying wolf: Repeat responses to hurricane evacuation orders. *Coastal Management, 26,* 237–252.

Dow, K., & Cutter, S. L. (2002). Emerging hurricane evacuation issues: Hurricane Floyd and South Carolina. *Natural Hazards Review, 3,* 12–18.

Drew, D. G., & Grimes, T. (1987). Audio-visual redundancy and TV news recall. *Communication Research, 14*(4), 452–461. doi:10.1177/009365087014004005.

Duval, T. S., & Mullis, J. (1999). A person-relative-to-event (PrE) approach to negative threat appeals and earthquake preparedness: A field study. *Journal of Applied Social Psychology, 29*(3), 495–51.

Eagly, A., & Chaiken, S. (1993). *The psychology of attitudes.* Fort Worth, TX: Harcourt Brace Jovanovich.

Eastern Research Group (ERG). (2013). Storm surge marketing: Audience analysis final report. Retrieved from: http://www.csc.noaa.gov/digitalcoast/sites/default/files/files/1377204582/storm-surge-marketing.pdf

Eosco, G. M. (2015). *Exploring risk and uncertainty perceptions in weather broadcasts using real-time response to measure visual effects* (Unpublished doctoral dissertation). Cornell University, Ithaca, NY.

Eosco, G. M., Steinhardt, J., Scherer, C. W., Chock, M. (2012). Visual typologies: Expanding how we think about visualizing risk uncertainty. Paper presented at the Society for Risk Analysis Annual Meeting. San Francisco, CA.

Griffin, R. J., Dunwoody, S., & Neuwirth, K. (1999). Proposed model of the relationship of risk information seeking and processing to the development of preventive behaviors. *Environmental Research, 80*(2), 230–245.

Griffin, R. J., Dunwoody, S., & Yang, Z. Y. (2012). Linking risk messages to information seeking and processing. *Communication Yearbook, 36,* 323–362.

Griffin, R. J., Yang, Z., ter Huurne, E., Boerner, F., Ortiz, S., & Dunwoody, S. (2008). After the flood: Anger, attribution, and the seeking of information. *Science Communication, 29*(3), 285–315.

Grimes, T. (1990). Audio-video correspondence and its role in attention and memory. *Educational Technology Research & Development, 38*(3), 15–25.

Groen, J. A., Polivka, A. E., Ja, G., & Ae, P. (2010). Going home after Hurricane Katrina: Determinants of return migration and changes in affected areas. *Demography, 47*(4), 821.

Heider, F. (1958). *The psychology of interpersonal relations.* New York: Wiley.

Iyengar, S. (1989). How citizens think about national issues: A matter of responsibility. *American Journal of Political Science, 33*(4), 878–900.

Knabb, R. D., Rhome, J. R., & Brown, D. P. (2005). Tropical cyclone report Hurricane Katrina. Retrieved from: http://www.nhc.noaa.gov/pdf/TCR-AL122005_Katrina.pdf

Kumagai, Y., Daniels, S. E., Carroll, M. S., Bliss, J. C., & Edwards, J. A. (2004). Causal reasoning processes of people affected by wildfire: Implications for agency-community interactions and communication strategies. *Western Journal of Applied Forestry, 19*(3), 184–194.

Lalwani, N., & Duval, T. S. (2000). The moderating effects of cognitive appraisal processes on self-attribution of responsibility. *Journal of Applied Social Psychology, 30*(11), 2233–2245.

Lazo, J., & Morrow, B. (2013). Survey of coastal U.S. public's perspective on extra tropical – tropical cyclone storm surge information. Retrieved from: http://www.sip.ucar.edu/projects/stormsurge/2013_01_07_ETTC_Storm_Surge_Public_Survey_Report.pdf

Lindell, M. K., & Perry, R. W. (2012). The protective action decision model: Theoretical modifications and additional evidence. *Risk Analysis, 32*(4), 616–632.

Loewenstein, G. F., Weber, E. U., Hsee, C. K., & Welch, N. (2001). Risk as feelings. *Psychological bulletin, 127*(2), 267.

McClure, J., Allen, M. W., & Walkey, F. (2001). Countering fatalism: Causal information in news reports affects judgments about earthquake damage. *Basic and Applied Social Psychology, 23*(2), 109–121.

McClure, J., Sutton, R. M., & Wilson, M. (2007). How information about building design influences causal attributions for earthquake damage. *Asian Journal of Social Psychology, 10*, 233–242.

McClure, J., Walkey, F., & Allen, M. (1999). When earthquake damage is seen as preventable: Attributions, locus of control and attitudes to risk. *Applied Psychology: An International Review, 48*(2), 239–256.

Messaris, P. (1997). *Visual persuasion: The role of images in advertising.* Thousand Oaks, CA: Sage.

Messaris, P. (1994). *Visual "literacy": Image, mind, and reality.* Boulder, CO: Westview Press.

Morss, R., & Hayden, M. (2010). Storm surge and "certain death": Interviews with Texas coastal residents following Hurricane Ike. *Weather, Climate, and Society, 2*, 174–189.

National Hurricane Center (NHC). (2012). National Hurricane Center's reviews on the use of scales to communicate the storm surge hazard (Press Release). Retrieved from: http://www.nhc.noaa.gov/news/20120910_pa_surgeScale.pdf

National Oceanic and Atmospheric Administration (NOAA). (2010). NOAA National Weather Service to use new hurricane wind scale: Storm surge and flooding prediction dropped in new scale. Retrieved from: http://www.noaanews.noaa.gov/stories2010/20100217_hurricane.html

Renn, O., & Levine, D. (1991). Credibility and trust in risk communication. In R. Kasperson & P.J. Stallen (Eds.), *Communicating risk to the public* (pp. 175–218). Dordrecht: Kluwer Academic Publishers.

Rowan, F. (1996). The high stakes of risk communication. *Preventive Medicine, 25*, 26–29.

Sandman, P. (1989). Hazard versus outrage in public perception of risk. In V.T. Covello, D.B. McCallum, & M.T. Pavlova (Eds), *Effective risk communication: The role and responsibility of government and nongovernment organizations* (pp. 45–49). New York: Plenum Press.

Siegrist, M., Earle, T. C., & Gutscher, H. (2003). Test of a trust and confidence model in the applied context of electromagnetic field (EMF) risks. *Risk Analysis, 23*(4), 705–716.

Slovic, P. (1993). Perceived risk, trust, and democracy. *Risk Analysis, 13*(6), 675–682.

Slovic, P. (1999). Trust, emotion, sex, politics, and science: Surveying the risk assessment battlefield. *Risk Analysis, 19*(4), 689–701.

Slovic, P., Finucane, M. L., Peters, E., & MacGregor, D. G. (2004). Risk as analysis and risk as feelings: Some thoughts about affect, reason, risk, and rationality. *Risk analysis, 24*(2), 311–322.

Sontag, S. (1977). *On photography.* New York: Farrar, Strauss, Giroux.

Sorensen, J. H., & Mileti, D. S. (1988). Warning and evacuation: Answering some basic questions. *Industrial Crisis Quarterly, 2*, 195–209.

Terpstra, T., & Gutteling, J. M. (2008). Households' perceived responsibilities in flood risk management in the Netherlands. *Water Resources Development, 24*(4), 555–565.

Terpstra, T., & Lindell, M. K. (2012). Citizens' perceptions of flood hazard adjustments: An application of the protective action decision model. *Environment and Behavior, 45*(8), 993–1018. doi:10.1177/0013916512452427

Tierney, K. J. (1994). Sociology's unique contributions to the study of risk. Paper presented at the 13th World Congress of Sociology, Bielefeld, Germany.

Trumbo, C., Lueck, M., Marlatt, H., & Peek, L. (2011). The effect of proximity to hurricanes Katrina and Rita on subsequent hurricane outlook and optimistic bias. *Risk Analysis, 31*(12), 1907–1918.

Ulmer, R. R., Seeger, M. W., & Littlefield, R. S. (2008). *Effective risk communication: A message-centered approach.* New York: Springer.

Wachinger, G., Renn, O., Begg, C., & Kuhlicke, C. (2013). The risk perception paradox—implications for governance and communication of natural hazards. *Risk Analysis, 33*(6),1049–1065.

Weiner, B. (2006). *Social motivation, justice and the moral emotions: An attributional approach.* Mahwah, NJ: Lawrence Erlbaum.

Zajonc, B. R. (1984). On the primacy of affect. *American Psychologist, 39*(2), 117–123. doi:10.1037/0003-066X.39.2.117

Zhang, Y., Prater, C. S., & Lindell, M. K. (2004). Risk area accuracy and evacuation from Hurricane Bret. *Natural Hazards Review, 5*(3), 115–120.

Chapter 20

Risk Communication at the Neighborhood Level Following Superstorm Sandy

Thomas D. Phelan, Ed.D.
Cazenovia College

Introduction

The decades-old discussion continues as to why practitioners and researchers cannot seem to connect so that research findings might have a greater influence on risk communication practice. An even greater gap exists between practitioners of risk communication and the public audiences with whom they are attempting to communicate. "Good risk communication can rally support, calm a nervous public, provide needed information, encourage cooperative behaviors, and help save lives" (Covello, 2006, p. 25). One way to improve risk communication, especially in vulnerable communities, is to train community volunteers to create and implement their own risk and crisis communication structure. Training on risk communication was initiated, and continues, in New York and New Jersey in neighborhoods impacted by Superstorm Sandy in 2012. This case study reports the training provided to several neighborhood volunteer organizations to improve risk communication and immediate disaster response going forward.

There are many forms of risk communication issued by government agencies, corporate communicators, educational institutions, and product safety guardians. Most are intended to reach vulnerable audiences who might want to take actions to prevent or mitigate harm. The 2016 version of *NFPA 1600, Annex J: Access and Functional Needs* lists four categories of people with either disabilities or other access and functional needs: health, economic, social, and language (NFPA, 2016, pp. 65–66). Risk communicators should be aware of the special circumstances in which urgent messages require attention to reach all people, including those in any one of the four categories identified.

Fischhoff (1995) worked in this area starting in the late 1970's, culminating in the identification of seven evolutionary stages of risk communication and best practices: get the numbers right, tell key publics what the numbers mean; explain what the numbers mean, show publics they have accepted similar risks before, explain how risk benefits outweigh the costs, treat publics with respect, make publics partners with risk communicators, and do all of the above. Since Fischhoff's (1995) seminal work, additional factors have been identified that contribute to effective public warnings, including information on how special needs publics respond differently than the general public to risks and the role of media in educating the public about risks (Sheppard, B., Janoske, M. & Liu, B., 2012, pp. 4–5).

Reaching everyone in time to save lives, property, and the environment is very difficult. One-way risk communication may not reach everyone, even if risk communicators have excellent connectivity to the system on which the messages are sent. For example, in New York City, the text on the Office of Emergency Management website is at a reading grade level of 15.9. The number of adults in New York City with reading grade levels below the 5th grade is 940,253[1] people (Phelan, 2015, June). The situation is similar in the larger cities across the United States. Additional barriers to effective risk communication are found in people's ability to use adequate numeracy and computer-based problem-solving skills (PIAAC, 2013).

Communities that have suffered serious losses from natural and man-made disasters tend to be the best prepared for the next serious incident. Following Superstorm Sandy, several neighborhoods along the Atlantic Coast of Brooklyn, Long Island, Manhattan, and New Jersey sought assistance to be better prepared by engaging in risk and crisis communication training provided by specialists in emergency management, risk communication, and advocacy. From 2013–2015, I was directly involved in designing and delivering training to neighborhood groups in Carnarsie, Brighton Beach, Gerritsen Beach, Long Beach, Centereach, Manhattan, and Flatbush in New York, and the Ironbound neighborhood of Newark, New Jersey. Neighborhood organizations banded together to obtain training through NeighborWorks® America, for whom I was both an instructional designer and instructor.

It was clear from the start that residents of these neighborhoods wanted to learn about ways to reduce risk, protect their property, and survive serious disasters. They wanted, in many cases, to become their own risk communicators, independent of government agencies, whose on-scene assistance seemed to take too long to be effective. I sensed that they believed that they could do a better job of communicating and taking care of themselves in the early hours or days following a disaster if they only had the knowledge and tools to help themselves survive.

One aspect of risk communication by government agencies is the way they structure emergency management. The Incident Command System (ICS) is not only widely used in the United States, but is a requirement for jurisdictions for compliance with the National Incident Management System (NIMS). Making a connection between neighborhood organizations and government emergency responders is facilitated when both entities adhere to the structure of ICS. In order for such a connection to be effective, neighborhood groups would need training in ICS and implementation plans to create local structures, similar in design to the systems in place in fire, police, emergency medical, and social services organizations. With awareness training provided face-to-face, diverse neighborhood groups could organize their risk communication efforts to be compatible with those emergency responders with whom they would need to communicate, coordinate, and collaborate when faced with a disaster.

Risk Communication for Neighborhood Volunteers

Engaging community leaders and volunteers in appropriate risk communication training requires an enormous amount of effort. Community advocates and organizers first have to determine the interest level of local residents. According to Turner's "Six-stage Sequence of Failure in Foresight," "... crises often create information and communication needs that fall outside the established channels of communication" (Turner, 1976, as cited in Sellnow & Seeger, 2013, p. 38). With risk communication

---

[1] Population figures from the original document were revised to exclude people under the normal age of fifth grade students (ages 0–10), who are therefore not expected to read at the fifth grade level.

needs impacting neighborhoods, and organizing neighbors for training, social structures might have great bearing on the success of such efforts. "These new understandings can lead to the radical restructuring of a social system in ways that constitute a full cultural adjustment" (Sellnow & Seeger, 2013, p. 39).

Sponsoring organizations agreed to fund the on-site training if members of the communities affected by Superstorm Sandy agreed to attend and use what they learned to advocate for risk management teams within their neighborhoods. Once the support and interest of community/neighborhood members was gained, the sponsoring organizations publicized the purpose, date, times, locations, and registration procedures for each day of training. Training sessions were scheduled for community centers, shopping mall community rooms, public libraries, host organization facilities, and Superstorm Sandy temporary feeding centers. Each of the neighborhoods involved had several different issues. Some had multiple high-rise housing complexes; others were single and two-family homes; one was a beach resort community. All had complex ethnic and nationality populations – Haitian Creole, African American, Irish, Italian, German, and Jewish community constituencies. In the interest of creating safer, better-prepared communities, they worked very well together in the training sessions.

Risk Communication Curriculum: The Case Study of Superstorm Sandy

Several modules were included in each one-day training session. Six competencies were identified for inclusion (NeighborWorks®, 2013). The first competency was entitled "The Emergency Management Structure: How to Organize Volunteers To Participate." Units in this module included the structuring of a "Block Captain" system for communication. Each Block Captain was to be assisted by eight positions staffed by volunteers. The positions mirrored the "Command and General Staff" of the Incident Command System. Position titles were the same as used in ICS, with the exception of the Block Captain, called the Incident Commander in ICS. Family risk communication procedures were listed, discussed, and included in a brief training exercise. Volunteers were asked to assume a role and explain that role to the other members of the Block Captain's team. Volunteers adopted roles for which they felt some affinity or for which they may have had prior training or experience. For example, a retired television reporter accepted the position of Public Information Officer, the main communicator to the neighborhood and the media. It was true, in most neighborhood training sessions, that community members had useful experience from their careers, the military, or participation in volunteer community or faith-based organizations. This is one asset often overlooked by public emergency responders and managers. There are valuable strengths among the citizenry.

The second competency was entitled "Engaging the Community." According to the literature, risk communication is best when there is strong, local leadership, often from volunteers:

> There are many opportunities to acquire transferable skills from volunteer and professional organizations. Faith-based organizations involved in humanitarian relief, corporate disaster relief programs, non-governmental organizations focused on disaster assistance . . . and student chapters of such organization[s] are among the many opportunities. Volunteering provides a chance to test one's interest in emergency management while providing a valuable service to the community. There are countless transferable skills to be acquired. (Phelan, 2008, p. 98)

During this section of the training, participants were asked to develop a resident/volunteer risk management plan. The ingredients of such a plan were listed, discussed, and reduced to easy-to-follow checklists. Forms were presented for registering community volunteers. In addition to contact information, the forms included availability, skills, languages, preferred methods of communicating, pertinent prior training, task preferences, and geographic area preferences (street level, high-rise buildings, single homes, transportation entrances, faith-based facilities). Discussion focused on volunteering, affiliations, phases of a disaster, management systems, shared responsibility, building on existing capacity, information management, and consistent terminology. These are all ingredients of effective risk communication systems.

The third competency was entitled "Structure and Risk Communication Tools."

The structure began with the ICS positions. It quickly moved into defining the tools for risk communication. In neighborhoods, communication with the outside world can be interrupted when infrastructure is damaged and electric power is lost. Though notifications from public and news agencies often precede a dangerous storm, they are not often heeded by the intended audiences. Prior experience and trust factors have more influence on prevention activities than risk messages from outside sources. Many cannot read or comprehend the messages from public emergency agencies, meaning that while communication is reaching the necessary (and important) constituencies, their decoding inabilities inhibit the risk communication process.

For example, and as mentioned earlier, in New York City, I found that the grade levels at which public emergency management messages are written on webpages is 15.9, or the equivalent of junior year of college. In New York City, **940,253** adults read at the 5th grade level or lower. Nationally, in the United States, 14% of adults read at the 5th grade level or lower (ProLiteracy, 2015, para 1). This may be why neighbors want to learn the best way to inform each other of impending disasters.

In one session, in Centereach, Long Island, a very conscientious participant, who had survived Superstorm Sandy, asked why the "Flood Evacuation Route" signs did not lead her to a shelter. The answer is that risk communication involves signage in only some instances. The missing concept was that flood evacuation routes lead to higher ground, away from rising water, not to shelters. In the training, mapping techniques, "Go Kit" contents for volunteers, and use of social media, landline telephones (POTS phones – Plain Old Telephone Sets), and youthful runners are all discussed as possible means of transmitting risk communication messages. Color-coded door hangers are presented as visual signs of those apartments or other residences where occupants are either evacuated safely (green hangers) or in need of help (red hangers). In one session, a participant expressed a concern that "looters" might prey upon residents with Green Door Hangers, indicating that no one was home. The question was followed by the comment, "Are you trying to save your TV and family silverware or are you more concerned with saving your life?" One merchant commented that he would probably get a greater insurance payment for goods stolen by "looters" than he would for goods damaged by flooding. Risk communication differs from normal expectations when you ask the neighborhood residents to assume the responsibilities for communicating risk.

The fourth competency was entitled "Partnerships for Risk Communication." As research has shown, risk communication can be greatly enhanced with an extended network of community leaders with their own stakeholders. Partnering with leaders of community organizations can create a collection of trusted sources to which many people turn in a crisis, which is what emerged here. Faith-based organizations and community centers top the list. Risk communication needs to come from a trusted source. In neighborhoods, communication had many channels for delivery. Certainly, it may be digital (social media, Internet websites, online newsletters, and so forth), but, when electric power is disrupted, other means must be used. Neighborhood organizations, by nature, are local – close to their stakeholders, making it possible to communicate face-to-face. Youthful runners may be able to go door-to-door to reach senior citizens or shut-ins. In some cases, stakeholders gather at a neighborhood house of worship or a community center. Such havens from the impending threat may have generators, cooking facilities, and a supply of food. In the risk communication phase, prior to the acute crisis stage, equipping such gathering places with risk communication tools, such as contact lists and organizational structures, such as ICS, may save time and lives.

The fifth competency was entitled "Day-to-Day Communication." If a risk communication plan is only activated when a crisis is eminent, those who need to use it may not be as familiar with it as is necessary to deliver urgent messages. Practice on a regular basis is highly recommended. This is true even at the corporate communication level. I recall an exercise at a major aircraft corporation where their crisis response team rehearsed activating their rapid notification system. The executive on the team prepared a recorded message to send regarding the corporation's pandemic plan, but was using the proprietary system for the first time. The situation was awkward and revealed a lack of training and practice that seriously delayed the urgent message.

Systems in place for delivering urgent messages rapidly need to be familiar to those using them and drilled or rehearsed frequently. Relying on a single method of communication during an emergency is no longer an option for today's emergency managers. Consider the diverse factors that make up United States communities, including multiple spoken languages, people with disabilities, a spectrum of ages and technical abilities, and much more. To communicate effectively with the varyious communication preferences and needs of all individuals and to improve overall public safety alertness and response, emergency managers must maintain flexibility and address complacency factors (http://www.9-1-1magazine.com/ Wilson-FedSignal-Changing-Technology?TopicID=522, para. 3). Similar to the radio-based Emergency Alert System (EAS), "this is only a test," regular activation of the system is highly recommended, even in neighborhoods. *9-1-1 Magazine* lists dozens of proprietary and government systems for rapid notification (http://www.9-1-1magazine.com/search/522/). At one point Microsoft attempted to create such a system (JEPRS) which was based on tools used every day by those with Microsoft Word, Excel, and Access. Infusion development and crisis management consultancy Catalyst Capabilities International recognized that Microsoft Office, server, and mapping technologies would provide an exceptional foundation for the Joint Emergency Planning & Response System (JEPRS). Many agencies likely to deploy JEPRS are familiar with the Microsoft IT environment and even already utilize some of the required technologies, such as Windows Server 2003 and Microsoft Office SharePoint Server 2007 (http://www. hazmatmag.com/features/jeprs-creepers/, para 2).

Such rapid notification systems are commonly used by government agencies and corporations, but are too expensive and too complex for effective use in neighborhoods. Local groups must depend on less-formal means, often cellular telephone texts and social media messages. Both are effective, as long as power is on and messages are crafted at appropriate readability levels. Neighbors are often also the best translators when audiences speak languages other than English.

The sixth and final competency was entitled "Records Management." In risk communication, it is important to know how to assemble a leadership team promptly. According to Melissa Agnes, an international social media crisis communication consultant and blogger, you have to have a detailed flow chart that will show every possible way that team members can reach the Communicator(s) no matter the time or place. (Agnes, 2015, p. 14).

Keeping up-to-date records of team members' contact information is critical. There are complete emergency response plans that list essential personnel either in an appendix or online. For more rapid access to such a list, it should be the first page, or even on the cover, of a printed plan document. Storage of callout lists might be in the leader's (Block Captain's) cellular telephone. Wherever the list is kept, it must be the first resource consulted and accessed when risk communication is required. One personal risk communication caution: If the leader has cellular telephone numbers of important contacts stored only in his/her personal cellular telephone, he/she must keep a hard copy of all contacts external to the telephone itself. Cellular telephone numbers are not available from directory assistance or even online telephone directories. If the leader loses his/her telephone or the electric power is lost, there will be no way of reaching the contacts stored. Many people no longer have landlines backed up with directory assistance.

Keeping records at the family level is critical. Each individual has needs that are best met if careful risk planning is detailed and complete. For example, a copy of a deed for property may be needed to have a FEMA trailer placed on one's property. Copies of physician prescriptions for prescription drugs will be required if access to medicines is lost or if the medicines themselves are destroyed. Hearing aids, eyeglasses, and respiratory equipment should all be accounted for in a risk or vulnerability analysis. Risk communicators can craft messages to alert or inform people of such planning needs and neighborhood risk activists can canvas, door-to-door, with printed materials and conversations to assist residents in planning ahead for such situations.

SUMMARY/CONCLUSION

Picture yourself as one of 20–40 employees in a government or corporate communications center. This might be an Emergency Operations Center (EOC) or a Joint Information Center (JIC), where the main objective is to communicate urgent risk messages to the community at large or corporate stakeholders. Now step outside that center and look at it from the neighborhood perspective. Can you receive those urgent messages? You may be in two feet of water, your iPhone battery is dead, and the power has been off for days. The urgent risk message may pertain to unsafe drinking water or the location of shelters. Add another factor: you are blind or confined to a wheelchair or you read below the 5th grade level. Can you benefit from the urgent messages being crafted inside the center? One last item. Look to your left or to your right. You have a neighbor, in similar circumstances, but asking, "How can I help?" Where do you place your hope and trust? Is it in the communication from the official center or is it in your neighbor? What if that neighbor had attended training on risk communication or disaster recovery? Would that have mattered? Who can provide assistance sooner? Is your neighborhood prepared? These are all questions I hope have been answered as a result of this case study.

DISCUSSION QUESTIONS

1. One way to improve risk communication, especially in vulnerable communities is to train community volunteers to create and implement their own risk and crisis communication structure. Why are volunteer organizations seeking and funding such training, rather than relying on DHS/FEMA or local government emergency management agencies?

2. Most risk communication messages are intended to reach vulnerable audiences who might want to take actions to prevent or mitigate harm. Why is it that interest in preparedness is often highest in communities recently affected by a disaster? Why aren't others learning from their lessons?

3. According to Fischhoff, starting in the late 1970s, there are several examples of a risk communication best practice? Explain why these steps are often ignored today.
   a. Get the numbers right
   b. Tell key publics what the numbers mean
   c. Show publics they have accepted similar risks before
   d. Explain how risk benefits often outweigh the costs
   e. Treat publics with respect

4. According to Turner's "Six-stage Sequence of Failure in Foresight," "... crises often create information and communication needs that fall beyond the established channels of communication." Why is it that people are more apt to trust a message from a friend or relative rather than an official message from a government, emergency management agency? How can this be altered?

5. Risk communication is best when there is strong, local leadership, often from volunteers. What steps can be taken to strengthen and maintain local volunteer participation in risk communication?

REFERENCES

Agnes, M. (2015, June 14). The Crisis Intelligence Podcast [web blogpost]. Retrieved from http://melissaagnes.com/tcip-053-literacy-levels-matter-in-emergency-management-messages-with-dr-thomas-d-phelan/.

Agnes, M. (2015). *The social media crisis management toolkit: Your guide to social media crisis management.* Montreal, ON: Agnes+Dey.

Covello, V. T. (2006, May/June). Risk communication and message mapping: A new tool for communicating effectively in public health emergencies and disasters, *Journal of Emergency Management 4* (3) 25–40.

Hazmat Management. (2007, October 1). JEPRS Creepers! Technology uses Microsoft Office to enhance crisis management. *Hazmat Management.* Retrieved from http://www.hazmatmag.com/features/jeprs-creepers/

NeighborWorks®. (2013). *Block captain training: Organizing neighborhood volunteers for managing natural disasters.* Washington, DC: Neighborhood Reinvestment Corporation.

NFPA. (2016). *NFPA 1600 Standard on Disaster/Emergency Management and Business Continuity/Continuity of Operations Programs 2016 Edition.* Quincy, MA: National Fire Protection Association.

Organization for Economic Co-operation and Development (OECD). (2015). The changing face of strategic crisis management. Paris, France: OECD Publishing. Retrieved from http://www.keepeek.com/Digital-Asset-Management/oecd/governance/the-changing-face-of-strategic-crisis-management_9789264249127-en#page17. doi:10.1787/9789264249127-en

Phelan, T. (2008). *Emergency management and tactical response operations: Bridging the gap.* Burlington, MA: Burterworth-Heinemann.

Phelan, T. (2015). *Literacy matters: EM messages and readability levels.* Retrieved from http://melissaagnes.com/tcip-053-literacy-levels-matter-in-emergency-management-messages-with-dr-thomas-d-phelan/

Phelan, T. (2015, June). Literacy Matters: EM Messages & Readability Levels. Paper presentation, FEMA Higher Education Symposium. Emmitsburg, MD.

Program for the International Assessment of Adult Competencies (PIAAC). (2013). Retrieved from http://www.proliteracy.org/the-crisis/piaac--survey-of-adult-skills#sthash.eGDAwX0V.dpuf

ProLiteracy. (2015). The Numbers Don't Lie. Retrieved from http://www.proliteracy.org/the-crisis/adult-literacy-facts

Sellnow, T.L. & Seeger, M.W. Eds. (2013). *Theorizing crisis communication.* Chichester, West Sussex: John Wiley & Sons.

Sheppard, B., Janoske, M. & Liu, B. (2012). *Understanding risk communication theory: a guide for emergency managers and communicators* (Report to Human Factors/Behavioral Sciences Division, Science and Technology Directorate, U.S. Department of Homeland Security). College Park, MD: START. Retrieved from http://www.start.umd.edu/publication/understanding-risk-communication-best-practices-guide-emergency-managers-and

Wilson, J. (2013). Changing technology: How the evolving communication landscape is improving emergency notifications. *9-1-1 Magazine.* Retrieved March 10, 2016 from http://www.9-1-1magazine.com/Wilson-FedSignal-Changing-Technology?TopicID=522

Chapter 21

From Lujo with Love

Jason S. Wrench, Ph.D.
State University of New York at New Paltz

Julie L. Taylor, Ph.D.
California State University at San Bernardino

Introduction

Often, risk communicators have to negotiate an awareness of legitimized, and illegitimate, public panic. That is, the difference between what causes public panic and what actually leads to injury or death, which is not always congruent. For example, a study found that people were more likely to die from a sand-sinkhole at the beach than from a shark attack (Maron & Haas, 2007). According to Burgess (2014), the curator for the international shark attack file within the Florida Program for Shark Research sponsored by the Florida Museum of Natural History at the University of Florida, in 2013, only 2.1% of the shark attacks in the United States were fatal, as compared to a 36% fatality rate elsewhere in the world. However, every year the Discovery Channel sets out to reinvigorate public panic by using tales of shark attacks during its annual "Shark Week." As a result, risk communicators must navigate the treacherous waters of worry in order to mitigate panic and disseminate information.

Moreover, Sandman (1993) has called the negotiation of public terror a problem that risk communicators must attend to. Sandman suggests that the public views risk as a cognitively "simple" formula: *Risk = Hazard + Outrage*. From this perspective, the first portion of the formula is how the public views "risk" is a matter of the "hazard" itself (i.e., the probability of loss of a life or a limb). Additionally, what Sandman calls "outrage," is the emotional response (i.e., panic or dismissal) a person has when presented with a specific risk. In essence, some risks may cause a high hazard level (i.e., automobile accidents), but receive only a small emotional response from people within the general public. Other risks, like shark attacks, tend to be less hazardous, but cause higher levels of outrage.

To understand outrage, Sandman (1993) proposed a list of 12 factors that play into whether or not the public becomes outraged as a result of the risk. For each of the following pairs, the first term indicates a low likelihood of outrage and the second term indicates a high likelihood of outrage (see Table 21.1 below).

To follow is an example of how Sandman's definition of "risk" can be applied to a fictionalized case study on this subject.

The Case Study

"Hello this is Mark Timor with your breaking news. We are just wrapping up a press conference being held by Dr. Kathleen Johnson, an infectious disease control expert with the CDC. That went well, a little off the rails. To help us analyze what we just witnessed, we have a slate of specialists ready to explain what

Table 21.1 Twelve Factors that Help Determine the Public's Level of Outrage at a Potential Risk

Low Likelihood of Outrage	High Likelihood of Outrage
Voluntary	Coerced
Natural	Industrial
Familiar	Exotic
Not Memorable	Memorable
Not Dreaded	Dreaded
Chronic	Catastrophic
Knowable	Not Knowable
Controlled by Individual	By Others
Fair	Unfair
Morally Irrelevant	Morally Relevant
Can I Trust You?	Can I NOT Trust You?
Is the Process Responsive?	Is this Process Unresponsive?

Dr. Johnson told us. First, we turn to Senator Jaquelin Aiden, from Arkansas, reporting directly from the source of where the outbreak has occurred."

"Yes, thank you, Mark," Senator Aiden began. "Well, according to Dr. Johnson," stressing her distaste for the physician by forming quotation marks with her fingers as she overly stressed the word doctor, "diseases and viruses that were assumed to be dormant are being rejuvenated and are currently spreading around the world and we shouldn't be overly worried when someone catches one because many of them are difficult to catch. A woman from my state has the *Lujo* virus that has killed 80% of the people who have come in contact with it. Folks, this is deadly…perhaps this is Armageddon."

***

It was a lazy afternoon in her Little Rock travel agency when Susie Nuñez's phone first rang.

"Nuñez travel, how can I help you?"

"Hi, I'm wanting to speak to a travel agent."

"My name is Susie and I'd be happy to assist you," Susie cheerfully replied into the phone.

Over the next 10 minutes, Susie got to know all about Marybeth Ashford and Donald Greer's upcoming nuptials. The two had been born and raised in Arkansas and met while they were high school students in South Africa: on a youth group mission trip. They had simultaneously fallen in love with Africa and each other. Additionally, both Marybeth and Donald had gone to medical school and even worked in Africa a couple of times with the *Doctors Without Borders* program, right after they had graduated. As such, for their nuptials, they wanted to share the place where their love began and decided to take their friends and family members on a safari/wedding excursion.

"Oh, my God!" Susie squealed into the phone, "That sounds like such an amazing experience for everyone."

"We sure hope so, which is where we need your help."

Marybeth quickly explained that they were planning their wedding/safari for the following spring and wanted Susie's help to arrange all of the travel for the couple and their 18 guests. Furthermore, Marybeth wasn't quite sure where they wanted to go in South Africa that would be idyllic for a wedding and which safari company could be trusted.

"Well, as a matter of fact," Susie started, "I'm actually vacationing in Madagascar with a friend in two weeks, so I can easily build into the trip a quick flight over to Johannesburg and then on to Cape Town. I always love a new adventure."

"You are fabulous. I heard you were the best, Suzie. I'm so glad I called. I can't wait to call Donald."

The two talked for a few more minutes before getting off the phone. Susie rearranged her flights and then phoned a couple of travel agent friends who had contacts in South Africa. Before she knew it, she had a seven-day excursion set up with a highly reputable firm in Africa that would introduce her to various Safari companies and show her some great destination locations for weddings.

★★★

Susie walked down the gateway exiting her South African *Airlink* flight and throwing her backpack over her shoulder. She followed the flow of travelers through customs and toward the baggage claim area. She looked down at the new outfit she had purchased from a street vender near her hotel in Antananarivo and was already missing the place and her best friend. Her best friend, Darlene Buttlebee, had flown down from London and the two had stayed in a fancy hotel that sat right on Lake Anosy. For anyone interested in the French Madagascar history, Antananarivo was a must-see destination location.

After picking up her bag, Susie noticed a man in a driver's uniform holding a sign with her name on it. She approached the man holding out her hand. "Hello, I'm Susie Nuñez. You must be from the *Alu Travel Agency*."

"Welcome, Ms. Nuñez, I am Dzingai Kekana. Just call me Dzi. I will be the driver/tour guide for your stay in South Africa. So, let's get you over to the *Cape Royale* and we can drop off your luggage and then discuss your itinerary over dinner."

★★★

The next seven days flew by Susie like a major league pitcher's fastball. Thankfully, she had a travel journal and camera that she used to document the various places she'd visited. She'd seen many different possibilities out in wine country. Of those, she really liked the Bakenhof Winelands venue. She also looked at more traditional locations, like a wide range of resorts known for amazing wedding venues. She was still deciding between La Vista Lodge above Plettenberg Bay and the Lagoon Beach Hotel in Cape Town. At the same time, her clients did ask for an African wedding, so she looked at a number of very interesting wedding spots only available in Africa: Bushfellows Private Game Lodge, Savannah Game & River Retreat, and Knysna Elephant Park. "I'm just glad I'm not the one making the final decision. I think any of these locations would be amazing," Susie thought to herself as she reread her travel journal and looked at the photos she'd taken on her iPad during her flight home to the United States.

★★★

"Marybeth? Susie Nuñez here. I just got back from South Africa and have so much to talk to you about. Please give me a call when you get my message," Susie spoke into her phone the morning after finally landing in Little Rock again. Susie loved going overseas, but the time changes were always killer. "I've heard about those people who just pop right back after an international flight… I wish!" she thought to herself.

She set about answering emails she'd let slide over the past week and returned a few phone calls. As far as first days back go, this one was fairly uninteresting. In fact, no one showed up at her office. Although travel agents were more common than people realized, their business was typically conducted through telephone calls and email exchanges, rather than face-to-face interactions.

Around 4:00 pm, Susie decided to call it a day because the jet lag was really starting to hit her. *The older I get, the harder these turnarounds seem to be on my body.* The drive from her office to her home took less than 10 minutes. She thought about running into the grocery store, but decided she needed sleep more than a TV dinner. She kicked off her shoes as she walked into the house and was immediately pounced on by Mr. Whiskers: her white, furry, Himalayan cat. "Ahh baby, I know I was gone for two weeks and then went to the office. It's OK, we can have all kinds of snuggle time after I feed you." With that, Susie walked into the kitchen, opened her cat a can of food, and placed it in his dish, and then poured herself a glass of Malbec.

★★★

Susie woke up around 3:00 am. *When did I go to sleep?* she questioned, looking at the glowing numbers on the clock on her nightstand. *My head is killing me.* She sat up, feeling a little light-headed as she did so. As she stood up, all of her muscles groaned in opposition. She walked into her bathroom and shuffled through her cabinets looking for pain medication. As she did, she caught a glimpse of herself in the mirror. *Dear God, I look atrocious.* She had clearly been sweating and her hair was sticking to her forehead in places. She almost looked like she'd been exercising. *OK, something is clearly wrong with me. This isn't just jetlag.* She looked around her bathroom for a thermometer and then took her temperature. She located her electronic thermometer and ran it across her forehead. *102.5° That's not good.* She decided to take a lukewarm shower and see if that would help bring down her temperature. When she got out of the shower, her fever was at 103°, so she texted her next-door neighbor, who took care of Mr. Whiskers when she was gone, and drove herself to the emergency room.

★★★

"Hello, my name is Dr. Kathleen Johnson, an infectious disease control expert from the Centers for Disease Control and Prevention. There have been a number of concerns that have risen because of a 42-year-old female patient who admitted herself to this hospital three nights ago."

Dr. Johnson had received the phone call late in the afternoon on the day Susie was admitted to the hospital. The hospital ran its usual tests, learned she'd been in Africa, and immediately put Susie into quarantine: fearing that it was Ebola. However, the Ebola hemorrhagic fever test came back negative. But Susie's condition appeared to be worsening, which was when the hospital administration decided to report the patient to the CDC.

Dr. Johnson had flown to Little Rock later that night and was suited up to help the patient around 1:00 am the next morning. As Dr. Johnson read the chart, she realized that all of the symptoms Ms. Nunez had clearly pointed to a hemorrhagic fever, but if it wasn't Ebola, which one was it? Viral hemorrhagic fevers (VHFs) belong to one of five different RNA strains: *Arenaviridae*, *Bunyaviridae*, *Flaviviridae*, *Filoviridae*, and *Rhabdoviridae*. On top of these five, each one has a number of variations that have existed: Ebola being just one of them.

Dr. Johnson had been sent into a number of emerging disease hot zones around the world, so she was used to dealing with a variety of VHFs. No physician had experience with all of them, but, thankfully, the symptoms were all pretty similar. Start with a headache, muscle soreness, and temperature spike, which is usually followed by intense vomiting and diarrhea. Most people think the virus actually kills people, but, generally, it's the medical care, or lack thereof, that leads to death. In the Western world, patients stricken with VHFs generally have a fairly good shot of recovery.

As she looked over the file once more, she realized that the likely origin of the fever was either in Madagascar or in South Africa. There had been an outbreak of one strand called the Rift Valley fever virus in 2008 in Madagascar, but that one was thought to be eradicated when they got it under control. In that outbreak, there were only 59 cases and 17 deaths. The more likely culprit was South Africa, which had VHF infections annually. Everything from Crimean-Congo hemorrhagic fever to Rift Valley fever to Lassa fever to Lujo hemorrhagic fever have been found. With this information, Dr. Johnson immediately asked for a blood panel to be run against these known South African strains. She told the lab to start with the more likely suspects, Lassa fever and Rift Valley fever, and then go to Crimean-Congo and Lujo fevers.

By noon the next day, the lab had their result … Lujo.

★★★

"The isolated patient has tested positive for the Lujo hemorrhagic virus. Lujo, named after the locations of the outbreak (Luska, Zambia, and Johannesburg, Republic of South Africa), is one of the deadliest viruses to date. An 80% mortality rate, but only five cases ever reported, meaning that four out of five died. However, we should note that, until today, there had only been five people in the world who had ever tested positive for Lujo. This virus is a bi-segmented RNA virus and also a known cause of viral hemorrhagic fever, which is similar to Ebola, but not the same strain. We contacted Cape Town, South Africa today and the driver who had spent a great deal of time showing the patient South Africa is still asymptomatic, but has now been isolated just in case. As with all hemorrhagic fevers, the likelihood of contracting this disease from person-to-person is difficult unless you've had direct contact with the patient's bodily fluids. In reality, driving here was more deadly than this virus will be. On that note, I'm open to questions."

Immediately, reporters' hands shot up, so Dr. Johnson randomly picked one sitting in the front row.

"Darnell Smith, with the *Arkansas Democrat Gazette*, what is the likely cause of the patient's virus?"

"Lujo is a strand of hemorrhagic fever, commonly referred to as an Old World arenavirus, which is generally transmitted through some kind of contact with, or inhalation of, rodent excreta. Next." This time Dr. Johnson pointed to an older woman she recognized from one of the national news networks.

"Lois Attias, National News Network, having seen how many hospitals in this country are not prepared to handle a patient with a biosafety level four (BSL-4) pathogen, are there any plans to move this patient to the BioContainment Unit at the Nebraska Medical Center?"

"As of right now, the medical staff here, and the CDC, believes that the patient's best bet is staying in isolation here. All necessary precautions have been made here to ensure the likelihood of transmission to medical staff is as minimal as possible. However, no one is ruling out sending the patient to Nebraska at this time."

Immediately, reporters started vying for her attention, so she randomly picked one towards the back.

"Hector Jassy, Conservative News Network, you just said that this virus has an 80% kill rate, shouldn't we be taking more precautions right now to protect U.S. civilians from this outbreak? Has the CDC talked about quarantining all incoming travelers from South Africa if not banning flights from South Africa altogether until we know this outbreak is over?"

"First, this is not an outbreak. As of right now, we have only one person in the world who has contracted this virus."

"How do you know it's not an outbreak? Have you tested everyone in Africa to see if they're not carrying it too? Are we even sure the South Africans know how to test people for this virus?"

The crowd immediately started throwing a whole barrage of questions at Kathleen. After 30 seconds of not being able to get a word in edgewise, despite the fact that she held the microphone, she finally spoke.

"Listen up! I'm only going to say this once so all of you get out your pencils and notebooks. One, this is not an outbreak. Two, we have this situation under control. Three," she said turning to look at the reporter from Conservative News Network, "Your questions have no scientific merit at all. All you are doing is riling up this crowd with fear about absolutely nothing. I'm amazed that you even bother calling yourself a journalist at this point. You should probably go back to the fifth grade and learn a little something about science before you try reporting it in the future."

With that, she turned away from the podium and walked back into the hospital. Once inside, she leaned against a wall and let out a scream. A couple of nurses walking past turned to look at her, but kept on going when Kathleen indicated that she was fine. She took in a deep breath. *Well, that went well!* She suddenly felt a buzzing in her lab coat, so she pulled out her phone and looked at the caller ID. *Great, it's the head of the CDC.*

CASE ANALYSIS

Sandman's (1993) definition of risk, *Risk = Hazard + Outrage*, can easily be applied to this situation. From the very beginning, one knows that Lujo hemorrhagic fever has had a very high death rate (80%). At the same time, to date, there have been only five individuals in the world to ever catch this specific viral strain (Paweska, 2009). Lujo was specifically chosen for this case because of its complete novelty and high death rate. When the average person hears that a virus has an 80% death rate, the outrage factor is sure to skyrocket.

Although not all of the factors associated with outrage apply to this case, there are definitely a few that would clearly impact the public's perception of the risk: exotic, catastrophic, and dreaded. First, Lujo is a virus that most people in the general public have never heard of, which increases the likelihood that people will panic, as they have no background information on which to base their perspective. Even though the flu virus (and its accompanying pneumonia) can cause anywhere from 3,000 to 49,000 deaths per year, new and exotic forms of viruses and diseases generally cause considerably more public outrage.

Second, one of the real factors of outrage related to a case like the Lujo virus is that is perceived as catastrophic. When one hears that the virus has a mortality rate of 80%, which clearly makes the virus sound highly deadly, this screams catastrophe. In the case of the Lujo virus, the small sample of actual, infected patients in history really makes the known mortality rate of contraction highly inflated. However, when large statistics are thrown around, people are more likely to react negatively.

Finally, contracting a deadly hemorrhagic fever of any kind is considered awful. People naturally find some diseases dreadful (e.g., Ebola, cancer, HIV) and others not as scary (e.g., influenza, asthma, emphysema). In this case, the Lujo virus not only has a high mortality rate, but the symptoms and physical effects of any hemorrhagic fever are horrible. As such, people are more likely to dread something like the Lujo virus than they are the common cold.

Overall, Dr. Kathleen Johnson was viewing the virus from her standpoint as a medical practitioner. One of the problems commonly associated with scientists, and the communication of risks, is that they view the risk in terms of the probability of morbidity and mortality and forget to consider how the public views not only the hazard, but also the coupling outrage. Dr. John's clear frustration is one commonly exhibited by scientists when they are forced to explain risk to the public. Ultimately, an effective risk communicator must know how to manage not only the scientific perspectives of risk, but also how the general public will evaluate and respond to that risk as well.

DISCUSSION QUESTIONS

1. Why do you think there is such a discrepancy between those items that cause low outrage and those that cause high outrage?
2. Why do you think the public's tendency to experience high outrage at low-risks and low outrage at high-risks is so common?
3. When examining the current case, which of Sandman's components of outrage do you see playing a role in this case?
4. Do you agree with Sandman's (1993) definition of risk, Risk = Hazard + Outrage? Explain your reasoning.
5. If you had been Kathleen in the case, how would you have handled the reporters' scientifically unfounded accusations and questions?
6. Is it possible for Kathleen to effectively work with the media after the last press conference? If you were the director of the CDC, what advice would you give Kathleen going forward?

REFERENCES

Barss, P. (1984). Injuries due to falling coconuts. *Journal of Trauma-Injury Infection & Critical Care, 24*(11), 990–991.

Burgess, G. H. (2014). ISAF 2013 worldwide shark attack summary. [online] *Florida Museum of Natural History.* http://www.flmnh.ufl.edu/fish/Sharks/ISAF/2013Summary.html

Maron, B. A., & Haas, T. S. (2007). Sudden death from collapsing sand holes. *New England Journal of Medicine, 356,* 2655–2656. doi: 10.1056/NEJMc070913

Paweska, J. T. et al. (2009). Nosocomial outbreak of novel arenavirus infection, southern Africa. *Emerging Infectious Diseases, 15*(10), 1598–1602.

Pinker, S. (2002, March 19). The truth about falling coconuts. *Canadian Medical Association Journal, 166*(6), 801.

Sandman, P. M. (1993). *Responding to community outrage: Strategies for effective risk communication.* Fairfax, VA: American Industrial Hygiene Association.

Thompson, M. G. et al. (2010). Updated estimates of mortality associated with seasonal influenza through the 2006–2007 influenza season. *Morbidity and Mortality Weekly Report, 59*(33), 1057–1062.

Author Note

The example in this case study was a fictional, hypothetical account and was used to illustrate Peter Sandman's (1993) strategies for responding to risk communication and [potential] public outrage.

Printed in the USA
CPSIA information can be obtained
at www.ICGtesting.com
JSHW050221281223
54275JS00004B/14

9 781465 288059